CAUSE AND CONSIDERATION: EXPLORING THE FOUNDATIONS OF CONTRACT LAW

This book provides a comprehensive study of two parallel notions of civil and common law: cause and consideration.

It does this in three ways; with historical, comparative, and functional perspectives. Aspects of cause and consideration are hotly contested by contract lawyers and this book will bring clarity by looking at the English and Continental positions. Key areas of focus include: enforceability, questions of legality and morality, contractual justice, and the correction of unjustified property displacements.

Bringing together a team of experts, the book discusses (in some cases for the first time in English) complex questions of both academic and practical importance.

Volume 54 in the series Hart Studies in Private Law

Hart Studies in Private Law

This monograph series brings together in one place two types of book: works which examine in-depth the fundamental doctrines and principles of private law, and works which engage with the theoretical underpinnings of private law. The series thus aims to contribute to ever-evolving debates about the nature of private law such as problems of classification and taxonomy, remedies, the relationship with public law and the boundaries of private law generally.

The series includes, but is not confined to, works on contract, tort, unjust enrichment, equity, property and the conflict of laws, welcoming work which intersects with other fields of study to enable a deeper understanding of private law theory and practice.

Cause and Consideration

Exploring the Foundations of Contract Law

Edited by
Bruno Rodríguez-Rosado
Rocío Caro Gándara
and
Antonio Legerén-Molina

•HART•
OXFORD • LONDON • NEW YORK • NEW DELHI • SYDNEY

HART PUBLISHING

Bloomsbury Publishing Plc

Kemp House, Chawley Park, Cumnor Hill, Oxford, OX2 9PH, UK

1385 Broadway, New York, NY 10018, USA

Bloomsbury Publishing Ireland Limited, 29 Earlsfort Terrace, Dublin 2, D02 AY28, Ireland

HART PUBLISHING, the Hart/Stag logo, BLOOMSBURY and the Diana logo are trademarks of Bloomsbury Publishing Plc

First published in Great Britain 2025

A catalogue record for this book is available from the British Library.

A catalogue record for this book is available from the Library of Congress.

Library of Congress Control Number: 2025933508

ISBN: HB: 978-1-50997-139-8
ePDF: 978-1-50997-141-1
ePub: 978-1-50997-140-4

Typeset by Compuscript Ltd, Shannon

For product safety related questions contact productsafety@bloomsbury.com

To find out more about our authors and books visit www.hartpublishing.co.uk. Here you will find extracts, author information, details of forthcoming events and the option to sign up for our newsletters.

'Both *cause* and consideration performed the function of insisting that a person was not to be made liable under an obligation without some good reason'

PS Atiyah, *The Rise and Fall of Freedom of Contract* (Oxford, Oxford University Press, 1985) 452*

PREFACE

Cause and consideration are two of the most debated institutions of contract law in both the civil and common law systems. Practically everything about them is discussed: their significance, their applications, their effects and even the need for their very existence. This is so much the case that, if the most common distinction of legal systems is that between those of civil law and those of common law, a transversal distinction could also be made between the systems that consider cause or consideration as an essential requirement of the contract and those that have renounced its presence.

This book is a new attempt to clarify the issues involved in the concepts of cause and consideration, analysing them from a historical and comparative law perspective. Logically, there are many risks involved in this attempt, and the authors and editors are well aware of them. Although, as PS Atiyah said in the words that precede this preface, both institutions tend to justify the fact that a subject is bound by an obligation, cause and consideration do not have the same meaning; rather, each has its own origin and development in the civil law and common law systems – and also within the specific legal orders that embody those systems. For this reason, there is always a risk of over-generalisation in a common and general treatment of both institutions or of imposing a framework around elements that are too diverse. Despite this, we are convinced that this joint treatment could offer the advantages of a broader perspective, typical of comparative studies, and we have tried to reduce the risks by maintaining an approach linked to the different legal systems, so that the general concepts are not detached from the legal data.

The book is structured in three distinct parts. The first contains a historical analysis of the development of cause and consideration. With regard to the former, it starts from the origins of Roman law to narrate the emergence of the concept in medieval law, its development in modern times and the decline into which it seems to have fallen for more than 100 years. In parallel with this, a careful synthesis of the origin, rise and crisis of the institution of consideration in the English legal system is also provided.

The second part deals with the detailed study of five legal systems that we consider particularly representative for their different treatments of cause and consideration: England and Wales, France, Germany, Italy and Spain. We considered adding other systems, but it seemed better to focus on this small number and to offer a treatment of some depth rather than to make a quantitatively broader but less detailed analysis, in the manner of a superficial legal atlas.

The third and final part deals with a cross-sectional analysis, which looks at the various functions for which cause and consideration have been used. Despite the fact that the concept of consideration as counter-performance is clearly objective, while cause also presents a subjective profile that allows its use as an instrument of control of legality or morality – even at the cost of increasing the complexity of the figure – it is true that most of the functions fulfilled by both institutions are similar, and that it seemed possible to carry out a parallel treatment of the issues. The book closes with a concluding chapter that attempts a general assessment of and judgement on the possibilities still offered by cause and consideration as institutions designed to settle legal controversies in a logical and predictable way.

The whole book is, unsurprisingly, focused on a 'problematic' perspective. It is not so much, or only, about the functions of cause and consideration as it is about the advantages and disadvantages of the very existence of these institutions. In taking this approach, each author has clearly acted with complete freedom, even if he or she is largely aware of the position of the others. In this sense, it can be said that the book is not 'univocal', but perhaps 'harmonious', as the different opinions and points of view may offer a comprehensive picture of the functions that cause and consideration fulfil, and also of the different advantages and disadvantages that their maintenance or suppression would entail.

We would like to express our gratitude to the authors for their contributions to the book. This is the final result of a seminar that took place in Málaga on 20–21 April 2023. We have the best memories of that meeting: we invited a group of renowned international specialists in the field – some of whom we did not yet know personally – and they agreed to participate in the seminar and the subsequent book with a confidence that is a proof of their own personal worth. The two days spent in Málaga were intellectually stimulating, but also personally extremely gratifying. They gave us all the opportunity to discuss the issues in depth and to understand the different points of view. We hope that readers will enjoy the result, and that the book may contribute to a debate that goes to the very foundations of contract law.

Bruno Rodríguez-Rosado
Rocío Caro Gándara
Antonio Legerén-Molina

LIST OF CONTRIBUTORS

Gregor Albers, Professor of History of Private Law and Roman Foundations, Johannes Kepler University, Linz (Austria)

Francisco-Javier Andrés Santos, Professor of Roman Law, University of Valladolid (Spain)

Rocío Caro Gándara, Associate Professor of Private International Law, University of Málaga (Spain)

John Cartwright, Emeritus Professor of the Law of Contract, University of Oxford (UK)

Wojciech Dajczak, Professor of Law (Department of Roman Law, Legal Traditions and Cultural Heritage Law), Adam Mickiewicz University, Poznań (Poland)

David Deroussin, Professor of Legal History, University of Lyon 3 (France)

Olivier Deshayes, Professor of Private Law, Paris Nanterre University (France)

Birke Häcker, Schlegel Professor of Civil Law, Common Law and Comparative Law, University of Bonn (Germany)

David Ibbetson, Emeritus Regius Professor of Civil Law, University of Cambridge (UK)

Nils Jansen, Professor of Civil Law, University of Münster (Germany)

Antonio Legerén-Molina, Associate Professor of Civil Law, University of A Coruña (Spain)

Juan Pablo Murga, Associate Professor of Civil Law, University of Seville (Spain)

João de Oliveira Geraldes, Assistant Professor of Private Law, University of Lisbon (Portugal)

Francesco Patti, Associate Professor of Private Law, Bocconi University, Milan (Italy)

Bruno Rodríguez-Rosado, Professor of Civil Law, University of Málaga (Spain)

CONTENTS

CONCLUSIONS

ABBREVIATIONS AND NON-ENGLISH EXPRESSIONS*

ABGB	Austrian Civil Code
BGB	Bürgerliches Gesetzbuch, German Civil Code
BGH	German Supreme Court
C	Code of Justinian
CC	Code civil, French Civil Code
CESL	Common European Sales Law
Cour de cassation	French Supreme Court
D	Digest
DCFR	Draft Common Frame of Reference
ECLI	European Case Law Identifier
ICC	Codice Civile, Italian Civil Code
Inst	Institutes of Justinian
KC	Polish Civil Code
PECL	Principles of European Contract Law
PICC	Unidroit Principles of International Commercial Contracts
SCC	Código Civil, Spanish Civil Code
SCJ(J)	Spanish Supreme Court Judgment(s)
Tribunal Supremo	Spanish Supreme Court
UCC	Uniform Commercial Code (USA)
VC	Vienna Convention on Contracts for the International Sale of Goods

* For the abbreviation of the English Law Reports, we refer to the Cardiff Index to Legal Abbreviations.

PART I

Historical Development

1

Cause in Ancient Roman Law of Contract

FRANCISCO J ANDRÉS SANTOS*

I. Introduction

The concept of cause of the contract stems from a certain circle of problems in Roman law. Nevertheless, it must be said from the very beginning that the Romans never thought of 'the cause of the contract', and only belatedly did they think of the contract as a general concept.[1] The use of the term '*causa*' was extensive and it had a very broad meaning in Latin: the *Thesaurus Linguae Latinae* lists hundreds of occurrences in the transmitted sources (occupying up to 22 folio pages)[2] and the *Oxford Latin Dictionary* distinguishes as many as 20 different meanings of the term.[3] In Ernout and Meillet's etymological dictionary,[4] we are told that the first meaning of the term was possibly that of motive. *Causa* must have been understood initially in the sense of efficient cause. *Causa* also very soon came to be known as the subject of each of the parties in a trial, and from there it came to mean the trial itself and then subject in general, as *res*, 'thing'. It is often associated with *ratio*, but, although *ratio* is a cause, there is no *ratio* in every cause. This is well expressed by a Latin grammarian of the third century:

> Between cause and reason it turns out that in reason there is always a cause, but in cause there is not always reason, and that in reason there is a plan, but in cause not always. There is a cause for Juno's anger against Aeneas, but no reason. The learned man has reason for being learned and also cause.[5]

* I would like to thank Prof José Javier de los Mozos Touya (University of Valladolid) for his generous help in the preparation of this chapter.

[1] See generally, more recently, R Fiori, 'The Roman Conception of Contract' in TAJ McGinn (ed), *Obligations in Roman Law: Past, Present, and Future* (Ann Arbor, University of Michigan Press, 2017) 40–75.

[2] *Thesaurus Linguae Latinae*, vol 3 (Leipzig, Teubner, 1906–12) 659–701.

[3] *Oxford Latin Dictionary*, fasc 2 (Oxford, Clarendon Press, 1969) 289–90.

[4] A Ernout and A Meillet, *Dictionaire étimologique de la langue latine. Histoire des mots* (Paris, Klincksieck, 1985) 108.

[5] *Inter causam autem et rationem hoc est ut in ratione semper causa est, in causa vero non semper est ratio, et quod in ratione semper consilium continetur, in causa vero non semper. Causas habet Iuno ut irascatur Aeneae, non rationem; habet rationem doctus ut sit litteratus, habet et causam.* The text was written by Marius Plotius Sacerdos, a grammarian of the 3rd century, author of the work *Artium grammaticorum libri tres*, edited by H Keil, *Grammatici Latini*, vol 6, fasc 2 (Leipzig, Teubner, 1874) 446.

In classical Latin, our term covers all the uses that 'cause' has in English.[6] It is used profusely in legal language,[7] normally without a dogmatic meaning, as it has rather an argumentative or topical use[8] that can sometimes confuse us, when we read Roman texts 'prejudiced' by our training in civil law. For example, a text by Ulpianus speaks of cause in the sense of final cause and might make us think that the Romans used the term in question as a French, Italian or Spanish jurist would:

> Ulpianus/Labeo D. 17,1,8 pr. (31 *ad ed.*): If I appoint a procurator and he does not return the documents relating to the case to me, under which action may he be liable to me? Labeo takes the view that he is liable on mandate and that the opinion of those who hold that an action on deposit can be raised on these grounds is not sustainable; for one must look to the origins of each and every contract and the factors lying behind it.[9]

There is an apparent coincidence between one of the senses in which we use the concept of cause today, the socio-economic purpose of the contract, related to the type of contract, and the use made by the jurist Ulpianus of our term, which allows him to qualify the contract and consequently choose the appropriate action to claim the return of the documents. We might therefore think that the Romans used a dogmatic concept of cause similar to that found in Italian doctrine. However, Ulpianus' course of thought is simpler. He asks what is the relationship that binds the parties and examines what they have done. It turns out that the plaintiff had given some documents to the procurator to litigate on his behalf. The handing over of the documents alone would constitute a deposit, but the jurist recalls that the act makes sense if it serves the purpose of creating a procedural representation. He thus expresses a truth of the world of interpretation: that human actions are understood when their purpose is understood. Nothing more.

II. Just Cause for the Delivery of the Thing and Acquisition without Cause

There is an area in which the term *causa* is used with a technical meaning that survives in modern law, that of the *iusta causa traditionis*. It is sufficient to recall the text of Justinian's *Institutes*, 2,1,41: '[corporeal things] are undoubtedly transferred if they are delivered by reason of gift or dowry or by virtue of any other cause'.[10]

In this use of the term 'cause', the idea of purpose is present, eg the seller delivers because he wants to fulfil the obligation incumbent on him, in exchange for which he receives or will receive the price, but when delivering 'by way of sale', the idea of efficient

[6] See n 2 above.

[7] H Heumann and E Seckel, *Handlexikon zu den Quellen des römischen Rechts*, 10th edn (Graz, Akademische Druck, 1958) 59–61 distinguishes up to eight meanings for the term in the sources.

[8] About the use of *causa* in Roman legal language, see VA Georgesco, 'Le mot *causa* dans le latin juridique. Introduction à la théorie générale de la cause en droit romain' in *Études de philologie juridique et de droit romain, I, Les rapports de la philologie classique et du droit romain* (Bucharest, Revista Clasică, 1940) 129ff (*cf* the review by EH Kaden (1938) 58 *Zeitschrift für Rechtsgeschichte. Romaninitische Abteilung* 307).

[9] *Si procuratorem dedero nec instrumenta mihi causae reddat, qua actione mihi teneatur? Et Labeo putat mandati eum teneri nec esse probabilem sententiam existimantium ex hac causa agi posse depositi: uniuscuiusque enim contractus initium spectandum et causam.*

[10] *Sed si quidem ex causa donationis aut dotis aut qualibet alia ex causa tradantur, sine dubio transferentur.*

cause prevails, at least from the legal point of view, since the delivery is the effect of the sale and is also justified by it as an act of transfer of ownership. The *iusta causa traditionis* is the cause and *ratio iuris* of the acquisition of ownership by delivery of possession. The Spanish Civil Code follows the same rule in Article 609. I believe that this meaning is present in the other relevant usages for posterity that we find in Roman law. In this respect, it should be pointed out that the concept of cause is 'iridescent' in its application, like crystal prisms which give different reflections depending on how they are turned. If we look at the cause of action to deliver the thing sold, we can see, by turning it around, final causes, efficient causes and legal reason. In any case, this cause qualified as *iusta* is accompanied by a *ratio valorativa*; it is not mere *factum* and it is not mere will.

The transmission of tangible things and, in the last stage of Roman law, of all things transmissible *inter vivos* requires just cause, which justifies the transmission in law.[11] Now, in classical Roman law (until the end of the third century AD), there were two abstract transactions for the transmission of property, the *mancipatio* and the *in iure cessio*.[12] It could happen, therefore, that a thing was transferred by means of one of these transactions and that the transfer lacked just cause, for example, because of an essential error that vitiated the underlying purchase and sale. In such a case, the acquirer had become owner of the thing, but his acquisition was not justified. It could also happen that the delivery without just cause was of money or generic things, which when delivered could no longer be identified and therefore could not be claimed, as in the case of payment of a sum of money that is not owed, where something had been delivered for an unlawful reason or expecting to receive something that was not received. In all these cases, Roman law did not allow the acquirer, against whom no real action could be brought, to keep what he had obtained without justification, but granted a personal action of strict law[13] called *condictio*. The *condictio* was used to reclaim what had been transferred without a justifying cause. This action had different names depending on the type of claim, but the characteristic and common feature of these actions is that there was no reason for withholding something, which only one of them expresses with its name – the *condictio sine causa* [condictio without cause] – but it can be applied to all *condictiones*.[14] I will return to *condictio sine causa* later.

Thus, in Roman law, there is certainly a technical concept of *causa–ratio iuris* of acquiring ownership, and, in parallel, when the transfer has taken place despite not being justified, the absence of cause justifies the exercise of the *condictio*. In both cases, the principle of unjustified enrichment comes into play, which the jurist Pomponius

[11] See especially M Kaser, R Knütel and S Lohsse, *Derecho privado romano* (Madrid, BOE, 2022) 268–71.

[12] ibid 266–67.

[13] Personal actions could be due to either good faith (*bonae fidei*) or strict law (*stricti iuris*) actions. In the latter, the interpretation of the applicable rules was strict.

[14] D. 12,4 *De condictione causa data causa non secuta*: with this action, one could claim back what was given in the expectation of receiving something in return when one did not receive what was expected. D. 12,5 *De condictione ob turpem vel iniustam causam*: this allowed the recovery of what was given for an illicit or immoral cause, but if the illicitness or immorality also affected the transmitter, it could not be claimed, eg the payment made for committing an illicit act. D. 12,6 *De condictione indebiti*: this is the action with which one claims the payment of what is undue. D. 12,7 *De condictione sine causa*: with this action, one could generally claim what was obtained without cause; it is important here, because one can also claim the release of the obligation arising from a *stipulatio* without cause. I will deal with this later.

expresses in these words: 'D. 50,17,206 (*var lect* 9): According to natural law it is equitable that no one become richer by the loss and injury of another.'[15]

The meaning of cause that we find in this area of the transfer of property and of 'enrichment without cause' must have influenced the use of the term in two areas of problems that will be of great importance in the discussion of the cause of contract in medieval and modern jurists. I am referring to the *causa stipulationis* and the cause of unnamed contracts.

III. *Causa Stipulationis*

The *stipulatio* was a solemn, unilateral, strict and abstract contract. Its performance was very simple. The stipulator, the one who receives the promise, would ask the promisor if he promised to give him or do something to him, and the promisor would answer in the affirmative, using (in the first person of the present indicative) the same verb or expression meaning to promise that the stipulator had used in the question, eg:

- Do you promise that you will give me one hundred sesterces?
- I promise.

The form was oral and therefore required unity of act, which meant that the parties had to be present at the same time and place to conclude the business. A document was often drawn up, but in classical times, until the end of the third century AD, what was valid was the oral act, the document (*cautio*) having merely probative value. Later, the written form was also valid and even came to the fore.[16]

This form of contract was widely used, as it was used to make all types of performance binding. Moreover, its strict nature was well suited to the business world. Its initial abstract nature stemmed from the fact that it was a strict legal transaction. The promise was valid even if the reason for which it had been promised was missing or came to be missing. However, very early on, probably from the middle of the first century BC, which is when the *actio* and the *exceptio doli* (action and defence of fraud) were created, if the stipulating party claimed 'without cause', the praetor granted a defence of fraud to the defendant which prevented his conviction. In his *Institutes*, Gaius refers to a case of application of the *exceptio doli* corresponding to an action based on a stipulation where the cause should be lacking:

> Gai. 4,116: Exceptions have been introduced for the purpose of defending those against whom actions have been brought; for it often happens that a party is liable by the civil law, when it

[15] *Iure naturae aequum est neminem cum alterius detrimento et iniuria fieri locupletiorem.*

[16] The evolution possibly started in the 3rd century: *Pauli Sententiae* 5,7,2: *Verborum obligatio inter praesentes, non etiam inter absentes contrahitur. Quod si scriptum fuerit instrumento promisisse aliquem, perinde habetur, atque si interrogatione praecedente responsum sit* [The stipulation is made between those present, but not those absent. But if it has been written in a document that someone has promised, it will be considered as if the preceding question had been answered]. The law pretends that a stipulation has been made. It follows that there is an oral stipulation and a written stipulation. Finally, the Emperor Leo admitted as *stipulatio* any written binding contract (C. 8,37,10 [472 AD]; *Inst.* 3, 15, 1). Justinian's strange solution is that the stipulation is oral, but the document of stipulation is valid if it cannot be proved that one of the parties was not at the place where it was signed on the day of the date (C. 8,37,14; *Inst.* 3,19,12).

> would be unjust for a judgement to be rendered against him. For example, if I stipulate for a sum of money from you on account of my having advanced it to you, when I never did so; as it is certain that I can bring an action against you for the money and you would be obliged to pay it as you are liable under the stipulation, but because it would be unjust for judgement to be rendered against you on this account, it is settled that you can defend yourself by the exception on the ground of fraud.[17]

Gaius does not say that the cause was lacking, but the reason for the injustice of the case is clear: there is no justification for claiming what was promised. Ulpianus, a generation later, does speak of cause in relation to this problem in D. 44,4,2,3 (76 *ad ed.*):

> If someone without good cause stipulated something from another and then sues him in terms of that stipulation, the defense of fraud will surely bar him; for even though he has committed no fraud at the time that he stipulated, nevertheless, it must be said that he was acting fraudulently at the time of joinder of issue, if he perseveres in claiming in terms of that stipulation, and also if he had a good cause when the stipulation was made, but seems to have no proper cause now. Consequently, even if a person intending to give a loan stipulated for the money and then did not give the loan, then, although there was a definite cause for the stipulation but it has either not eventuated or been completed, it will have to be said that the defense will avail.[18]

Formally, the stipulation is not declared null and void if the cause is lacking, but it is useless as soon as an exception of fraud can be raised. And the cause of the stipulation is spoken of with a meaning clearly similar to that of the *iusta causa traditionis*.[19] The effects of the stipulation are produced in practice if there is cause, which is required in order for a practically enforceable obligation to arise, but also in order for it not to be

[17] *Conparatae sunt autem exceptiones defendendorum eorum gratia, cum quibus agitur. saepe enim accidit, ut quis iure ciuili teneatur, sed iniquum sit eum iudicio condemnari. uelut si stipulatus sim a te pecuniam tamquam credendi causa numeraturus nec numerauerim. nam eam pecuniam a te peti posse certum est. dare enim te oportet, cum ex stipulatu tenearis; sed quia iniquum est te eo nomine condemnari, placet per exceptionem doli mali te defendi debere ….*

[18] *Si quis sine causa ab aliquo fuerit stipulatus, deinde ex ea stipulatione experiatur, exceptio utique doli mali ei nocebit: licet eo tempore, quo stipulabatur, nihil dolo malo admiserit, tamen dicendum est eum, cum litem constestatur, dolo facere qui perseveret ex ea stipulatione petere: et si cum interponeretur, iustam causam habuit, tamen nunc nullam idoneam causam habere videtur. proinde et si crediturus pecuniam stipulatus est nec credidit et si certa fuit causa stipulationis, quae tamen aut non est secuta aut finita est, dicendum erit noceri exceptionem.*

[19] Heinrich Honsell, in his review of JG Wolf, *Causa Stipulationis* (Cologne, Böhlau, 1970) (1975) 92 *Zeitschrift für Rechtsgeschichte. Romanistische Abteilung* 38, says that the cause of the *stipulatio* is understood as the material reason for the conclusion. Wolf (ibid) argues that the cause of the stipulation is not the legal reason which would justify, so to speak, the effect of the promise, but the 'material purpose of the promisor', see, in particular, 2, 4, 25, 76ff. Wolf notes that the donation and the constitution of a dowry, which appear as possible causes of the stipulation, together with the sale and other transactions that are in themselves effective, cannot be regarded as legally binding relationships, but rather as purposes that are made legally relevant by the stipulation. However, this criticism of the traditional and dominant view is based on the misunderstanding that cause, understood as justification (*Rechtsgrund*), implies a legally effective relationship prior to the *stipulatio*. But the traditional view did not intend to say such a thing. *Causa* is rather, in this context, something akin to the *iusta causa traditionis*, which, when it is *causa emptionis*, for example, does presuppose a valid purchase and sale, which creates reciprocal obligations between the parties, but not, however, in the case of *causa donationis*, since prior to the *traditio*, the donation agreement does not produce any legal effect, even though, once the delivery has taken place, it is what justifies the transfer of ownership. In reality, the reason for or justification of the promise, in accordance with the traditional idea of *causa stipulationis*, is no different from the purpose of the promise of which Wolf speaks, which is relevant because it justifies the obligation arising from the *stipulatio*. There has, however, been an evolution in this area.

extinguished, since it can be lacking from the outset, but can also come to be lacking at a later point in time, when its justification disappears. This cause is related to the purposes of the obligor, of course, but it is also clearly the legal basis of the obligation, *ratio iuris* and efficient legal cause of the obligation. This is why an analogy is to be seen between the situation of the person who gives something without cause and cannot recover it by real action, for which he is granted a *condictio sine causa*, and the person who has bound himself by stipulation also *sine causa*, who remains formally bound. This similarity of situations gives rise to the fact that the law grants to the obligor without cause a *condictio liberationis*, an action to ask for release from the obligatory bond, which Ulpianus explains in D. 12,7,1 pr.-3 (43 *ad Sab.*):

> There is also this kind of *condictio* for the case in which someone makes a promise with no basis or pays what is not owed. But one who promises with no basis cannot bring a *condictio* for the amount promised but for the obligation itself.
>
> 1. Further, if he gives a promise on a basis which fails to materialize, the *condictio* must be said to lie.
> 2. Whether the basis of the promise is absent from start or is present but fails to endure or fails to materialize, the *condictio* must be said to lie.
> 3. It is agreed that the *condictio* can only go against someone for something which came to him other than on a legally sufficient basis or comes to be referable to a basis which is not legally sufficient.[20]

The text is placed at the beginning of the title of the *Digest*, which deals with the *condictio sine causa* and speaks for itself. With this action, it is possible to request the release from the obligation contracted without cause or which has lost its cause and to take the procedural initiative against the other party. Paragraph 3 expresses the analogy with the delivery of something without cause.

The validity of the stipulation in practice depends on the justification of the obligation. This cause of the stipulation will be relevant for many purposes, not only for defending against a claim or for claiming release. For example, with regard to the interpretation of the transaction, there is a text in which the cause determines the object owed:

> Iavolenus D. 24,3,66,4 (6 *ex posterioribus Labeonis*): A woman whose husband had one hundred gold pieces of hers as a dowry stipulated after a divorce for the return of two hundred due to her husband's error. According to Labeo, she will only be entitled to what was in her dowry, whether she knowingly stipulated for more or did this in innocence. I agree with Labeo's view.[21]

The text is very interesting, first, because it is very early: Labeo is a first-century jurist, from a time when one would expect a stricter interpretation of the *stipulatio*, binding

[20] Pr. *Est et haec species condictionis, si quis sine causa promiserit vel si solverit quis indebitum. qui autem promisit sine causa, condicere quantitatem non potest quam non dedit, sed ipsam obligationem.* 1. *Sed et si ob causam promisit, causa tamen secuta non est, dicendum est condictionem locum habere.* 2. *Sive ab initio sine causa promissum est, sive fuit causa promittendi quae finita est vel secuta non est, dicendum est condictioni locum fore.* 3. *Constat id demum posse condici alicui, quod vel non ex iusta causa ad eum pervenit vel redit ad non iustam causam.*

[21] *Mulier, quae centum dotis apud virum habebat, divortio facto ducenta a viro errante stipulata erat. Labeo putat, quanta dos fuisset, tantam deberi, sive prudens mulier plus esset stipulata sive imprudens: Labeonis sententiam probo.*

the husband to pay the promised 200. Zimmermann therefore thinks that the stipulation in this case must have mentioned the 'cause of restitution of the dowry'.[22] Knütel,[23] however, thinks that it could be an abstract stipulation, as the text does not say that it was concluded as a causal stipulation, mentioning the reason for the promise. If Knütel is right, this means that the cause of the stipulation is of such great importance that it takes precedence over the form, so that the possibility does not even arise that, alongside the cause of restitution of the dowry, a cause of donation could operate. Perhaps there is a *favor iuris* in benefit of the woman in this case. In any case, the text shows the importance of the cause in the stipulation.

Another curious text is Paulus D. 20,3,4 (5 *resp.*), since it shows how the stipulation alone, without its cause, although formally permitting a claim – albeit unsuccessfully, because of the effect of the *exceptio doli* – is not effective for other purposes:

> As Titius wanted to borrow money from Mevius, he promised to repay Maevius the amount, listing certain assets to be mortgaged. He sold some of the listed property and then received the loan. The question was whether the property sold before the loan was also bound to the creditor. Paul answered that since, even after he had promised to pay Maevius, the debtor was free not to take the loan, the mortgage must be taken as entered into at the time when the loan was made. Hence, one must inquire what property was part of the debtor's estate at that moment.[24]

In Roman law, the mortgage and the pledge have the same regime; they only differ in that in the mortgage the thing is not delivered. They are constituted by an informal agreement and are accessory to the obligation they guarantee, so that they only arise if the obligation they guarantee has already been formed, and are extinguished with the extinction of that obligation. Paulus asks in this case whether the pledge is constituted with the conclusion of the stipulation, when it is still without cause, since Titius has not yet received the loan; or, rather, when Titius receives the money. If he had answered that it was at the moment when the stipulation is concluded, he would be recognising that the stipulation without cause had the effect of creating an obligation, to which the mortgage would be accessory, so that all the things included in the agreement would have been subject to the mortgage from that moment and those that had been sold and were in the possession of third parties could be pursued with the *actio in rem*. However, Paulus considers that, in order to comply with the accessory nature of the mortgage, there is still no obligation when the promise has no cause (as the loan money has not been delivered), so that the debtor may not accept the money; therefore, the obligation only arises when the debtor receives the money – when there is cause – and as a consequence, at that moment the mortgage agreement is effective. Therefore, only the things specified in this agreement that were not alienated and are still in the debtor's assets are

[22] R Zimmermann, *The Law of Obligations. Roman Foundations of the Civilian Tradition* (Oxford, Clarendon Press, 1996) 92.

[23] R Knütel, 'Zur Auslegung und Entwicklung der Stipulation' in M Aveniarius, R Meyer-Pritzl and C Möller (eds), *Ars iuris: Festschrift für Okko Behrends zum 70. Geburtstag* (Göttingen, Wallstein, 2009) 223, 228.

[24] *Titius cum mutuam pecuniam accipere vellet a Maevio, cavit ei et quasdam res hypothecae nomine dare destinavit: deinde postquam quasdam ex his rebus vendidisset, accepit pecuniam: quaesitum est, an et prius res venditae creditori tenerentur. Respondit, cum in potestate fuerit debitoris post cautionem interpositam pecuniam non accipere, eo tempore pignoris obligationem contractam videri, quo pecunia numerata est, et ideo inspiciendum, quas res in bonis debitor numeratae pecuniae tempore habuerit.*

encumbered by the mortgage; those alienated before that moment were not encumbered, because there was no obligation.

All of this leads one to think that cause became a requirement for the validity of a stipulation. In the first stage, the stipulation was purely abstract, but once the application of the *exceptio doli* began, cause began to be taken into account in practice. There is yet a third stage in which the perspective changes, for it is not that its absence is something exceptional against which one reacts, but that the cause comes to the fore as a condition of validity. This can be seen clearly in the problem of the accessory nature of the mortgage, but even more strikingly in the matter of the burden of proof. From the outset, the burden of proving the defence of fraud was on the defendant, since it was understood that the stipulation itself produced the obligation, and the plaintiff's fraud was an exceptional circumstance, the *onus probandi* of which was on the defendant. Thus, in Quintilian's manual of rhetoric (*inst. orat.* 4,2,6), widely used in the tribunals, we can read:

> It is enough for [the plaintiff] to say, 'I ask for a certain sum of money by virtue of a stipulation', 'I ask for a legacy by virtue of a will'; it belongs to the allegation of the other party to invoke why it is not due.[25]

Quintilian wrote his work at the end of the first century AD. More than a century later, the jurist Paulus, taking into account the evolution of the stipulation, raised the problem of the burden of proof and dealt jointly with the question of the burden of proof of the lack of cause in respect of the payment of what is not due and in respect of the lack of cause of a stipulation:[26]

> D. 22,3,25 pr. (3 *quaest.*): When money not owed is in issue, who must prove that it is not owed? The distinction to be adopted is that the party who said to have received money or property which was not owing denies this and the payer by lawful proof shows that the payment was made, the party who denies receipt must, to be heard, in every case show that the money was owing. It is quite absurd for the party who initially denied receipt, which was later proved, to require his opponent to show that the money was not owing. But if he from the start admits that he received money but asserts that it was owing, no one doubts the presumption is for the recipient. No payer is ever so careless as to throw his money around and waste it on debts not owed, especially if the payer is a careful and diligent head of his household, who would not easily be credited with a mistake. Hence, the party who says he has paid money not owing must prove that he did so through fraud of the recipient or some just cause of ignorance. Unless he does this, he fails to recover.

The burden of proof is normally on the plaintiff, and the reason given by the jurist is that the one who has paid has done so because he is normally obliged; the exceptional case is that he is not obliged, and then he will have to prove it if he claims what was given was undue. Paulus points out an exception to this rule that was maintained in Article 1900

[25] *Satis est dixisse 'certam creditam pecuniam peto ex stipulatione', 'legatum peto ex testamento'; 'diversae partis expositio est cur ea non deveantur'.*

[26] In the latter case, the dispute can arise in two ways. Firstly, if the plaintiff claims with the action arising from the stipulation a debt contracted without cause, the defendant will raise the defence of fraud and the problem of the burden of proof of fraud will arise. The second possibility is that the plaintiff is the debtor by stipulation of an obligation contracted without cause, and claims, with the *condictio sine causa*, the release in respect of this obligation, and the problem of the burden of proof of the lack of cause also arises.

of the Spanish Civil Code. After dealing with other problems related to the subject, he deals in paragraph 4 with the problem of the burden of proof of the lack of cause in the stipulation:

> So much for payment of what is not due. If, however, a deed is said to be executed for what is not owing and the cause is not stated in the deed, the creditor must show that the debt in the deed is owing, unless the party who executed it specifically explains the cause for his doing so ….[27]

The expression is redundant, but it makes it clear that the document in which the stipulation is recorded, when it does not mention the cause, is not sufficient proof of the existence of the debt, and therefore it is up to the one who appears as the creditor in that document to prove the debt (ie prove the cause). This means that the cause of the stipulation becomes a requirement of the obligation, in accordance with the meaning of the general rule of distribution of the burden of proof, a rule that is in the nature of things and according to which 'the burden of proof of the obligation falls on the one who claims its performance', in the words of Article 1214 of the Spanish Civil Code of 1889, now replaced in Spanish law by Article 217 of the Civil Procedure Act.

The clear conclusion in this field of the stipulation is that its evolution until the end of the second century led to its being configured as a causal contract. The cause here is the legal reason for its efficacy, a reason which is found in relation to the purpose of the transaction for the debtor, but without it being understood as the pure purpose of the debtor. Rather, the cause expresses the just relationship between the birth of the obligation and the purpose of the debtor: Titius promises 100 to Gaius, who lends it to him, the cause lying in the justice of the restitution of what was lent; Titius promises 100 to Gaius in gratitude for the favour the latter did him – here, the cause is not simply that he wants in the abstract to give him 100, but the gratitude, the remuneratory liberality, etc.

In the civil law tradition, the cause of the stipulation is the predecessor of the cause of the contract in the French Civil Code (recently reformed). However, the medieval authors did not fully understand the role of the fraud exception in its function of asserting the lack of cause against the action of the stipulator. For the Romans of the Late Antiquity, but certainly already at the end of the classical period, the exception was not a remedy to introduce a corrective principle of praetorian law in the old civil law,

[27] Pr. *Cum de indebito quaeritur, quis probare debet non fuisse debitum? res ita temperanda est, ut, si quidem is, qui accepisse dicitur rem vel pecuniam indebitam, hoc negaverit et ipse qui dedit legitimis probationibus solutionem adprobaverit, sine ulla distinctione ipsum, qui negavit sese pecuniam accepisse, si vult audiri, compellendum esse ad probationes praestandas, quod pecuniam debitam accepit: per etenim absurdum est eum, qui ab initio negavit pecuniam suscepisse, postquam fuerit convictus eam accepisse, probationem non debiti ab adversario exigere. sin vero ab initio confiteatur quidem suscepisse pecunias, dicat autem non indebitas ei fuisse solutas, praesumptionem videlicet pro eo esse qui accepit nemo dubitat: qui enim solvit numquam ita resupinus est, ut facile suas pecunias iactet et indebitas effundat, et maxime si ipse qui indebitas dedisse dicit homo diligens est et studiosus pater familias, cuius personam incredibile est in aliquo facile errasse. et ideo eum, qui dicit indebitas solvisse, compelli ad probationes, quod per dolum accipientis vel aliquam iustam ignorantiae causam indebitum ab eo solutum, et nisi hoc ostenderit, nullam eum repetitionem habere.* [1 … 2 … 3 …] 4. *Sed haec, ubi de solutione indebiti quaestio est. sin autem cautio indebite exposita esse dicatur et indiscrete loquitur, tunc eum, in quem cautio exposita est, compelli debitum esse ostendere, quod in cautionem deduxit.* See JJ de los Mozos, 'La carga de la prueba de la *causa stipulationis* y el concepto de *causa*' (2007–08) 20–21 *Seminarios Complutenses de Derecho Romano* 303.

which was always in force, but the procedural expedient to assert a circumstance that extinguished or prevented the exercise of the action, as civil law and praetorian law had merged.[28]

IV. The Problem of the Cause of Unnamed Contracts

In Roman law there was a principle of contractual typicity; only a few contracts were recognised, which had appeared at different times. Simply put, the stipulation was the oldest contract type, being recognised at the time of the Twelve Tables (450 BC) and probably even earlier. Then came the transactions that would end up being understood as real contracts – *mutuum* (loan for consumption), *commodatum* (loan for use), *depositum* (deposit) and *pignus* (pledge) – and in the third century BC consensual contracts appear, which are perfected by mere consent and are based on good faith: sale and purchase, mandate, partnership and the three types of leasing – of goods, services and work (*locatio conductio rei*, *operarum* and *operis*). In the last stage of Roman law, Justinian exempted promises of dowry and donation from the form of stipulation (C. 4,21,17 pr.). The concept of contract itself was formed only later, at the end of the classical period, when jurists became aware of the importance of the element of the agreement of wills in the various recognised types of contract. This importance is clear in consensual contracts, and gradually comes to the fore in other contracts as well. The term *contractus* does not have a clear and generalised technical meaning until the post-classical period (from the fourth century, the period of the Dominate), although it is based on earlier doctrinal developments.[29]

It was mainly the jurists Gaius and Ulpianus who promoted the specialised and technical use of *contractus* with the modern meaning of obligatory contract. The former pointed out in his *Institutes*, an elementary and therefore simplifying work, that the sources of obligations are contract and crime (Gai. 3,88). In turn, four kinds of contracts can be distinguished (Gai. 3,89 and 3,182). In the *Institutes*, Gaius starts from a concept of contract as a bilateral act aimed at creating obligations (Gai. 3,91).[30] In another, more extensive, work attributed to the same Gaius, entitled *Res cottidianae* (Everyday Law), it is stated that alongside contract and crime there are various other sources (D. 44,7,1 pr.), noting that in these cases the obligation arises from a contract (*quasi ex contractu*) or from a crime (*quasi ex delicto*) (D. 44,7,5 pr.-6). From this, Justinian, in his *Institutions*, takes the fourfold division of the sources of obligations (*Inst.* 3,13,2).

[28] M Kaser, *Das römische Privatrecht. Zweiter Abschnitt: Die Nachklassischen Entwicklungen* (Munich, CH Beck, 1975) 69–70, 379.

[29] See n 1 above.

[30] JJ de los Mozos, 'La clasificación de las fuentes de las obligaciones en las Instituciones de Gayo y de Justiniano y su valor sistemático en el moderno derecho civil' (1994) 6 *Seminarios Complutenses de Derecho Romano* 103; JJ de los Mozos, 'La formación de un concepto de contrato en el derecho romano: de Labeón a Teófilo' (2015) 28 *Seminarios Complutenses de Derecho Romano* 727.

Ulpianus, on the other hand, focuses on the element of *conventio*, common to all acts involving an agreement, and on the concept of pact, which is broader than that of contract, for he distinguishes between those pacts which are recognised by law and those which are not. The former are contracts and produce action, whereas the latter only produce exception, since by simple agreement an obligation or the exercise of a right can be extinguished or limited. Agreements which do not have their own name in law and do not produce action are called *nuda pacta* (bare agreements) (Ulp. D. 2,14,1 (4 *ed.*); 2,14,7 pr.-1 (4 *ed.*)).

Atypical pacts of exchange of performance can produce civilly enforceable obligations under certain circumstances, as expressed in paragraphs 2 and 4 of D. 2,14,7:

> 2. But even if the matter does not fall under the head of another contract and yet a ground exists, Aristo in an apt reply to Celsus states that there is an obligation. Where, for example, I gave a thing to you so that you may give another to me, or I gave so that you may do something, this is [Aristo says] a *synallagma* and hence a civil obligation arises …
>
> 4. But, when no cause exists, it is settled that no obligation arises from the agreement. Therefore, a naked agreement gives rise not to an obligation but to a defense.[31]

Ulpianus states that atypical covenants, which he previously called bare covenants, produce a civil action when they rely on a specific cause. He immediately describes when such a thing occurs, with the aid of two examples: first, there has been an agreement to exchange performance, then one of the parties has fulfilled the performance incumbent on them. So the cause of action arises in these cases when one of the parties fulfils the agreement and can therefore claim the counter-performance with a civil action.

In these atypical contracts, the cause continues to have the meaning of an element that justifies the legal effects, but it is not the same as in the stipulation or in the *traditio*. The stipulation is a formal act, whereas the *traditio* is the handing over of possession; the acts are recognised by law as having the effect of creating an obligation and of transferring ownership respectively. But the law also requires in both cases a justification (cause), which is the relation of justice between the effect they produce and the purpose of the one who promises or transmits, but does not require that this purpose has been realised. With the terminology of consideration, this may have been an executed consideration, but it can also be an executory consideration.

The atypical contract is not recognised by Roman law for the purpose of creating an obligation, just as a simple agreement, even one accompanied by a cause, is not sufficient to transfer ownership. Therefore, an atypical agreement, by itself, with a simple executory consideration, does not produce an effect. On the other hand, if one of the parties performs – executed consideration – then the situation changes, because the one who has performed could recover what has been delivered, if the other party did not perform, with the *condictio causa data causa non secuta* (performance made and not reciprocated),[32] since it would be unjust for the one who has received to enrich himself

[31] *2. Sed et si in alium contractum res non transeat, subsit tamen causa, eleganter Aristo Celso respondit esse obligationem. Ut puta dedi tibi rem ut mihi aliam dares, dedi ut aliquid facias: hoc synallagma esse et hinc nasci civilem obligationem … 4. Sed cum nulla subest causa, propter conventionem hic constat non posse constitui obligationem: igitur nuda pactio obligationem non parit, sed parit exceptionem.*

[32] Here *causa* has a very broad meaning related to the agreement of exchange of performances: matter or transaction performed by one and not reciprocated by the other. See above on *condictiones*.

at the expense of the other. However, in such a situation, it is more the fact that the one who has performed is justified in demanding consideration, so that the jurist Aristo can rightly say *subest causa*. This cause is different from that of the stipulation, in that it is the performance of one of the parties. A new category of 'unnamed' contract is thus formed which is enforceable on the party who has performed. Paulus gives an example in D. 19,5,5 pr. (5 *quaest.*) and sets out the pattern of such contracts:

> My natural son is your slave and yours is mine. We agreed that you manumit my son and I yours; I manumitted, but you did not. Through what action are you liable to me? As regards this question, an overview may be presented concerning everything that is given for a purpose. They arise in these forms:
>
> Either I give you in order that you give
>
> - or I give that you do,
> - or I do that you give,
> - or I do that you do ....[33]

In civil law doctrine, a cause has been sought in this cause of unnamed contracts that can be understood as the purpose of the parties.[34] But it is clear that there is cause in this field when one of the parties has fulfilled the performance. This was the understanding of the Byzantine jurists:

> 12. Schol. to Bas. 11,1,7 [Heimbach I, 562; Scheltema BI, 192], corresponding to D. 2,14,7 pr.-2:
>
> 2. Cyrillus. Of the agreements which are of the law of nations, some produce actions and others exceptions. Those which produce actions are called contracts, as in purchase, lease and the like. But if there is an underlying cause, as when something is given in order that it may be given, or something is done in order that it may be done, then there is a contract and a civil action arises.[35]
>
> Accursius, without having read Cyril's scholium, says the same thing: glosse *Causa* to D 2,14,7,1, explains: *id est datio vel factum* (this is giving or fact).

It is interesting that in the glosse *Idoneam* to D. 44,4,2,3, which establishes the requirement of cause for the stipulation, Accursius realises that it is something different from the cause of the unnamed contracts and therefore says *re, vel spe* [with the thing or with

[33] *Naturalis meus filius servit tibi et tuus filius mihi: convenit inter nos, ut et tu meum manumitteres et ego tuum: ego manumisi, tu non manumisisti: qua actione mihi teneris, quaesitum est. In hac quaestione totius ob rem dati tractatus inspici potest, qui in his competit speciebus: aut enim do tibi ut des, aut do ut facias, aut facio ut des, aut facio ut facias ....*

[34] With admirable erudition, but without sticking to what the sources say, the otherwise remarkable work by Tomasso dalla Massara stands out: *Alle origini della causa del contratto. Elaborazione di un concetto nella giurisprudenza classica* (Padova, CEDAM, 2004); 'La *causa* del contratto nel pensiero di Aristone: della necessità di un concetto' (2009) 22 *Seminarios Complutenses de Derecho Romano* 251; 'Die *causa* des Vertrages im Denken des Aristo: zu den Ursprüngen einer Idee' in G Albers, FP Patti and D Perrouin-Verbe (eds), *Causa contractus* (Tübingen, Mohr Siebeck, 2022) 37–66.

[35] Κυρίλλου. Τῶν ἰουρισγεντίων τὰ μὲν τίκτουσι ἀγωγάς, τὰ δὲ παραγραφάς. Ὅσα δὲ τίκτουσι ἀγωγάς, εἰς ἰδικόν ὄνομα μεταπίπτουσι συναλλαγμάτων, οἷον εἰς ἀγορασίαν, εἰς μίσθωσιν καὶ τὰ ὅμοια. Εἰ δὲ καὶ ὕπεστιν αἰτία, οἷον δόσις ἐπὶ δόσει ἢ ποιήσει, συνάλλαγμα τὸ γεγονός τίκτεται πολιτικὴ ἀγωγή.

the expectation]. This means that either the stipulator makes or has made a performance or there is an expectation that he will do so: eg Titius is promised a sum of money to do a work.

In any case, it was a puzzle for medieval jurists to explain in a logically coherent way the whole problem of bare covenants, their relation to cause and the different meaning of cause in *stipulation*.[36]

[36] See ch 2 in this volume, by João de Oliveira Geraldes.

2

The Rise of Cause in the Medieval Period

JOÃO DE OLIVEIRA GERALDES

I. Cause and the Decline of Abstract Contracts: The Case of *Exceptio Non Numeratae Pecuniae*

In the scope of this chapter, it is crucial to underscore the significance of the formalised contractual framework known as *stipulatio*,[1] and its important relation with the concept of *causa* (cause).

It can be asserted that *stipulatio* was initially conceptualised as a unilateral, solemn, abstract and *stricti iuris* contract.[2] Through *stipulatio*, because of its abstract nature, it became conceivable to establish contractual obligations without a precise scrutiny of their underlying cause.[3] *Stipulatio* then emerged as an important contractual instrument in Roman law due to its ability to provide legal shelter to various types of agreements. It conferred binding force to situations lacking a recognised source of obligations, and its functional versatility made it a significant tool in the Roman legal landscape.[4]

A significant milestone in Roman law, introducing important *nuances* to the originally abstract nature of *stipulatio*, was the establishment of certain control over it. This control was mainly implemented through defensive procedural measures, offering protection in cases of abstract contracts that depended solely on the fulfilment of specific formalities or solemnities, such as *stipulatio*.

As Roman law evolved, *stipulatio* was subjected to greater control, balancing the strict formality of the law with the need for substantive justice. Thus, in the case of

[1] Regarding formalities, the process was originally conducted in person. The promise–creditor would pose an interrogative question detailing the terms of the commitment, which was the subject of the *stipulatio*. Concurrently, the promisor–debtor would respond affirmatively, thereby accepting the terms outlined by the creditor. According to Roman terminology, the promisor's response – *spondee* – constituted a promise in itself, and the entire arrangement defined by the *stipulatio* was regarded as a contract, although only the promisor was bound by it. See G Albers, 'Zum Versprechen als Verpflichtungsgrund in der Spätantike: Urkunden, Kirchenväter und der westgotische Gaius' (135) 2018 *Zeitschrift der Savigny-Stiftung für Rechtsgeschichte, Romanistische Abteilung* 341.

[2] For a comprehensive view, see G Sacconi, *Ricerche sulla stipulatio* (Naples, Jovene, 1989).

[3] See G Albers, 'Versprechen und Vertrag in Rechtsgeschichte und Rechtsvergleich' in G Albers, J Harst und K Kaesling, *Wortgebunden. Zur Verbindlichkeit von Versprechen in Recht und Literatur* (Frankfurt am Main, Klostermann, 2021) 39.

[4] W Dajczak, *Derecho romano de obligaciones* (Santiago de Compostela, Andavira, 2019) 176–80.

stipulatio, even when all its formal requirements were met, to ensure substantive justice, the debtor was recognised as having the right to invoke exceptions (D. 4,116; D. 44,4,2,3; D. 12,7,1,1). This represented a significant advancement in controlling abstract formal obligations.

Additionally, from the third century AD onwards, the debtor of the promise contained in the *stipulatio* was also granted the right to invoke the *exceptio non numeratae pecuniae*[5] (C. 4,30,13), including through *querela*.[6] This type of defence or procedural means, particularly due to its crucial role in (re)distributing the burden of proof within a context of obligational abstraction, proved decisive: it allowed the debtor to control potential abuse in abstract obligations through procedural mechanisms. Specifically, the procedural measure known as the *exceptio non numeratae pecuniae* resulted in a decisive shift in the burden of proof, deviating from the classical model of its standard distribution. This shift transferred the burden typically borne by the debtor to the creditor. Simply put, through this procedural measure, the creditors of the promised amount became obligated, upon the invocation of the *exceptio non numeratae pecuniae*, to prove that they had previously made the payment they were seeking to be reimbursed. This contrasted with the traditional approach, where the debtors had to prove they had not received the amount and were thus relieved of the obligation to reimburse it.

Moving forward, during the medieval period, it can be observed that glossators, *grosso modo*, embraced the contractual system of Roman law.[7] In this context, it is commonly noted that glossators promoted a nominal reordering of the sources of obligations, focusing their classification on the concept of *pactum*. Due to the Roman law legacy regarding pacts – *nuda pactio obligationem non parit* (D. 2,14,7,4) – glossators were also confronted with the problem of the legal value of naked pacts, or *pacta nuda*.[8] In this context, the *pactum cum vestimentum* emerged as a source of voluntary obligations, assuming a central role in the medieval contractual system.[9] However, *vestimentum* was a broad concept without terminological stability, leading to uncertainty about what could be considered a *pactum cum vestimentum*.[10]

[5] D Unterholzner, 'Ueber die exceptio non numeratae pecuniae' (1824) 7(1) *Archiv für die civilistische Praxis* 1; H Kreller, 'Zur Geschichte der exceptio non numeratae pecuniae' in *Studi in onore di Salvatore Riccobono nel XL anno del suo insegnamento* (Palermo, Giuseppe Castiglia, Palermo, 1936) 285ff; E Levy, 'Die querela non numeratae pecuniae' (1953) 70 *Zeitschrift der Savigny-Stiftung für Rechtsgeschichte* 214; C García Carrasco, *Supuestos de hecho de la exceptio non numeratae pecuniae en el Derecho romano* (Madrid, Dykinson, 2000).

[6] See JJ de los Mozos, 'La carga de la prueba de la *causa stipulationis* y el concepto de *causa*' (2007) 20–21 *Seminarios Complutenses de Derecho romano* 303.

[7] JJ de los Mozos, 'Aproximación a la *causa* del contrato en la doctrina del Ius Commune' (2014) 27 *Seminarios complutenses de derecho romano* 131.

[8] J Creutzig, *Das selbständige Schuldversprechen* (Basel, Helbing & Lichtenhan, 1969) 19, noting how, in the context of the Bologna school, glossators did not fail to stress the importance of the cause and its relation to the *exceptio doli* in the control of *stipulatio*.

[9] A Söllner, 'Die *causa* im Kondiktionen- und Vertragsrecht des Mittelalters bei den Glossatoren, Kommentatoren und Kanonisten' (1960) 77 *Zeitschrift der Savigny-Stiftung für Rechtsgeschichte – Romanistische Abteilung* 219; de los Mozos, 'Aproximación a la *causa* del contrato' (n 7) 131.

[10] For that reason, seeking to systematise the growing number of vestments, Azo enumerated various possible cases in which *vestimentum* could be considered to exist, namely the following: *re*, *verbis*, *litteris* and *consensu* (equivalent to Roman named contracts), *interventus rei* (a *datio vel factum aristoniana*, ie the fulfilment of one of the reciprocal obligations of a Roman innominate syntagmatic contract) and *cohaerentia contractus* (Accessory Pacts): Azo, *Summa in Codicem* 4, C 23 (*de pactis*); *cf* de los Mozos, 'Aproximación a la *causa* del contrato' (n 7) 131–32.

It is also particularly relevant to emphasise that, in the glosses of Accursius,[11] it is possible to observe that the invocation of *exceptio non numeratae pecuniae* continued to be recognised as a procedural means available to debtors – *sufficit dicere pecuniam non esse numeratum* – but with the relevant limit that it could only be invoked for a period of two years.

On the other hand, in the general context of the progressive rise of the cause, a very relevant medieval development is also worth noting. This development consists in the generalisation of the importance of identifying the cause of the obligation, which had a direct impact on cases where a promise to pay a sum of money was made without specifying its cause.[12] This specific development was based on the texts of Paulus (D. 22,3,25,4) and a decision by Justinian (C. 4,30,13). According to these texts, in the case of a promise to pay a sum formulated in an abstract mode,[13] or, in other words, without indicating the cause of the obligation, the creditor had to prove that the demanded amount resulted from a valid cause. This evidentiary requirement could only be waived when the written act explicitly stated the cause of the obligation, ie the basis for the amount owed. As the loan contracts – *mutuum* – were not explicitly mentioned in the aforementioned texts, and it could be theorised that their application extended to all written contracts in which a promise to pay a sum of money was made without specifying the cause, this circumstance raised doubts about the validity of such written acts when they omitted the mention of the cause.[14] Due to this widespread practice during the medieval period, it is not surprising that a debate arose regarding the validity of cases where the cause of the obligation was not declared or mentioned. Thus, the aforementioned development provided a sufficient ground for substantive doubts to be raised by medieval jurists regarding the validity of written agreements when the cause of the obligation was not expressly stated.[15]

In the realm of glosses, it can be observed that this theme received considerable attention, and the omission of the mention of the cause was equated with the lack of cause, the putative cause or the false cause – *Sine causa promittere is videtur quoties vel causa non exprimitur vel ex falsa seu putativa causa quis promittit*[16] – stemming from the fact that the cause had become a central element in medieval contractual doctrine.[17] Therefore, the Bolognese jurists disregarded the *stipulatio sine causa*, similarly depreciating the *cautio indiscreta*.[18]

Having stated this and considering the medieval context with its rising 'causalism trend', it is quite appropriate to quote Henri Capitant on the characterisation of the

[11] C. 4,30,3.

[12] H Capitant, *De la cause des obligations (Contrats, Engagements unilateraux, Légacies)* (París, Dalloz, 1927) 134.

[13] For further development, see P Spada, 'Cautio quae indiscrete loquitur: lineamenti funzionale e strutture della promessa di pagamento' [1978] *Rivista di diritto civile* 673.

[14] What had particular relevance in the realm of *stipulatio* was its gradual transformation into a written document. For a comprehensive overview, see G Ferrari, *La degenerazione della stipulatio nel diritto intermedio e la clausola cum stipulatioe subnixa* (Venezia, C Ferrari, 1910), specifically 766, where the author highlights the mutation of *stipulatio* and the emergence of the new medieval formal contracts.

[15] PF Girard, *Manuel élémentaire de droit romain* (Paris, Rousseau, 1918) 497ff.

[16] In Capitant (n 12) 135.

[17] de los Mozos, 'La carga de la prueba' (n 6) 139ff.

[18] ibid 144.

debate surrounding the possibility of abstraction and the theme of cause in general. According to Capitant, the discussion was *becoming more complex*,[19] particularly due to the advent of the concept of *causa finalis*. To account for its growing importance, some considerations regarding the concept of cause as *causa finalis* are now due.

II. Trend: The Rise of Cause as *Causa Finalis*

From an Aristotelian–Thomistic perspective, Bartolus and Baldus provided an innovative interpretation of the concept of cause, significantly contributing to the theoretical understanding of cause as *causa finalis*.[20] The antecedents of the *causa finalis* concept trace back to ancient Greek philosophy, specifically Aristotle, with discernible indications of its incorporation into medieval juridical discourse by Johannes Bassianus. Nevertheless, as said, the *causa finalis* concept underwent meticulous refinement by medieval scholars such as Bartolus and Baldus during the fourteenth century. Bartolus and Baldus shared the conviction that a profound understanding of the ultimate purpose of a phenomenon – a *thing* – is indispensable for comprehending its ontological essence, nature and attributes.

It was with this framework that Bartolus argued that all agreements contain or possess a *cause*, because the parties involved seek to achieve a specific purpose or goal.[21] The concept of *causa finalis* came to require differentiation from *causa impulsiva* (a mere motivating factor for action). Only the former seemed to be truly relevant. According to Bartolus, after identifying *animus donandi* with *causa finalis* in donations, only the absence of *causa finalis* would have given the donor the right to recover what was given through *condictio* (unjust enrichment), which would not have been the case in situations of *causa impulsiva*. Bartolus noted that *causa impulsiva* was particularly relevant in conditional donations when it was used by the donor as a *conditio* (condition). This distinction became crucial as it differentiated *causa finalis* from *causa impulsiva*, with only the former (*causa finalis*) having the potential to give rise to *condictio*.[22]

Under this new approach proposed by Bartolus and Baldus, the focus transitioned towards determining the true nature of the cause, and whether it exists or not, rejecting the binary dichotomies proposed by the medieval glossators that led to the division between *pacta vestita* and *pacta nuda*.[23]

In Baldus's work, the evolution of the concept of *causa* can be distinctly understood as follows: every human action is driven by a specific purpose, and no action can occur without a clear intention. According to Baldus, the final cause is thus the object of

[19] Capitant (n 12) 135.

[20] Recently, Martin Schermaier has traced the historical and legal development that connected the notion of cause to the idea of *causa finalis*, highlighting the influence of medieval finalism rooted in Aristotelian–Thomistic philosophy. Schermaier emphasises the crucial role of St Thomas Aquinas's finalism in establishing the cause as a *causa finalis*: M Schermaier, 'Die Rolle der *causa* bei der Überwindung des Typenzwangs durch die mittelalterlichen Juristen' in G Albers, F Patti und D Perrouin-Verbe (eds), *Causa contractus* (Tübingen, Mohr Siebeck, 2022) 97ff.

[21] de los Mozos, 'La carga de la prueba' (n 6) 147ff.

[22] See de los Mozos, 'Aproximación a la *causa* del contrato (n 7) 147ff.

[23] Söllner (n 9) 231.

intellect, and every action is determined by a purpose: *Causa finalis est objectum intellectus, sicut signum est objectum visus, et portus est objectum navigantium et quidquid agimus propter finem agimus.*[24]

Furthermore, Baldus contends that the true foundation of an obligation stems from the *causa finalis*, referring to it as the underlying element from which the obligation arises. For this reason, when the *causa finalis* ceases to exist, it will also determine the end of the agreement: *Causa finalis in contractibus dicitur ea de cujus radice emanat obligatio. Causa finalis dicitur ea, qua posita inesse ponitur voluntas disponentis, et ea cessante, cessat consensus.*[25]

From this conceptual refinement of *causa* as *causa finalis*, it became necessary to determine whether a contract should be classified as an act of generosity (*liberalitatis*) or as an exchange operation governed by equivalence (*commutative justice*), to prevent unjust enrichment. Accordingly, Baldus and Bartolus concluded that a contract was legally binding if it had a *causa finalis*, which could generally be categorised as either *liberalitatis* or a transactional exchange (commutative justice). Baldus went further, recognising additional types of *causa finalis*, such as the promotion of peace and harmony (*pacis et concordiae*).[26]

With this new perspective in mind, challenging the viewpoint of the glossators regarding *pacta nuda* and *pacta vestita*, the idea emerges that every *pactum* is rooted in a *causa finalis* – a purpose, an objective – thereby precluding the existence of a truly bare pact.[27] Baldus, therefore, argued against the distinction between *pacta nuda* and *pacta vestita*, asserting that neither God nor a good conscience made such distinctions. For this reason, due to the rise of the concept of *causa finalis*, omitting the reference to the cause became increasingly significant. This development has unsurprisingly led to the rejection of the idea of abstraction. The abstract contract – particularly the *stipulatio sine causa* – was thus marginalised, as it conflicted with the finalist approach. Within the medieval framework under Aristotelian–Thomistic influence, the final cause of an act is now seen an essential element (*essentialia*).

Consequently, the legal implications of failing to mention the cause have sparked considerable controversy. From the outset, the glossators had already considered that the *stipulatio sine causa* would have no value. In general, for glossators, in the case of *stipulatio sine causa*, the existence of error should be presumed; hence, a promise without cause could not be considered to be a valid promise.[28] In addressing this issue, Bartolus proposed the theory of presumption of donation – *praesumptio donationis* – in cases where the cause of the *stipulatio* was omitted.[29] Therefore, the omission of the cause could be equated with a *liberalitatis*. For his part, Baldus rejected this thesis

[24] *Commentaria Corpus Iuris Civilis*, Venetiis, 1547, IV, 44, I, 17.

[25] ibid 3ª col.

[26] Söllner (n 9) 231ff.

[27] ibid 231.

[28] de los Mozos, 'La carga de la prueba' (n 6) 147ff.

[29] Bartolus expressly stated the following: 'Quando nulla causa exprimatur, a videatur inesse tacita causa donationis? Dicant doctores quidquid velint, nos habemus huius quaestionis casum in l. loh iure supra de dona (D 39,5,19) quod satis est causa ipsa liberalitatis. Et pro hoc optime facit infra de verb. l. si divortio, ubi dictur quod stipulatio ex falsa causa valet, ergo ubi nulla causa st, valet' in de los Mozos, 'Aproximación a la *causa*' (n 7) 148–49.

proposed by Bartolus, arguing that the omission of the cause could not be seen as presumed *liberalitatis*.[30] Baldus thus refuted the notion that the intention of generosity could arise from the omission of the cause and stated that this omission would not result in a manifestation of *liberalitatis*, but in a frivolous action or foolishness (*stultitia*).[31]

III. Cause and the Principle *Ex Nudo Pacto Oritur Actio*

Due to the increasing significance of the concept of cause during this period, the principle *ex nudo pacto oritur actio* – a shortened form of *ex nudo pacto oritur actio nudum a solemnitate sed non nudum a causa* – emerged. This principle indicates a transition towards reduced formalism in contract law while emphasising the importance of the cause element.[32] For this reason, it is necessary to provide a brief note on the movement of canonical rupture with Roman law. Understanding Baldus's causalist perspective requires acknowledging that the development of the concept of *causa finalis* is intrinsically linked to the general concept of *aequitas canonica*. Consequently, the topic of *vestimentum* was reconfigured within the ambit of canon law.

Due to the principles of *aequitas canonica*, obligations were systematically theorised in close association with an individual's standing before the divine. In this context, it is important to remember that the ultimate goal of canon law was the salvation of souls – *salus animarum lex suprema est*. This principle gave rise to the prohibition of lying, the duty not to deceive one's neighbour, the duty to keep promises and the duty not to cause harm to others. Violating these duties, considered a symptom of ethical corruption, fell within the realm of both illegality and sin.

At the origin of this canonical perspective, we find St Thomas Aquinas, who, in the *Summa Theologiae*, postulates in favour of the principles of *honestas*, *fidelitas*, *ratio peccati* and *aequitas naturalis*.[33] The obligation to keep a promise thus emerged as a voluntary, rational act through which an individual commits to performing or refraining from a particular action for the benefit of a third party.[34] Thomism, therefore,

[30] In the context of the emergence of *causa finalis*, it is noteworthy how Martin Schermaier meticulously examines the omission of cause, specifically addressing the doctrinal debate between Bartolus and Baldus. Schermaier, focusing on Baldus's perspective, explores the sufficiency of the *causa impulsiva*, questioning whether it could serve as the basis for *causa finalis*. Amidst the well-known interpretative complexities – such as those identified by Söllner (n 9) 182ff and JL Barton, '*Causa* Promissionis Again' (1960) 34 *Legal History Review* 41 – Schermaier provides significant clarifications on the role of the *causa impulsiva* in Baldus's thought, recovering elements that help to contextualise its relevance primarily within the scope of *stipulatio*, thereby delineating its applicability. See Schermaier (n 20) 97ff.

[31] According to Baldus, knowing the exact *causa finalis* is essential to contractual validity. On this point, see de los Mozos, 'Aproximación a la *causa*' (n 7) 151ff.

[32] Schermaier (n 20) 97ff.

[33] St Thomas Aquinas, *Summa Theologiae, secunda pars secundae partis a quaestione* LXXXII ad XCI, [42762] IIª–IIae q 88 a 3 co.

[34] V Carro, *La promessa unilaterale: studio sulla formazione unilaterale del rapporto obbligatorio tra diritto romano, tradizione romanistica e prospettive future* (Napoles, Satura editrice, 2013) 98.

situates the fulfilment of a promise within the realm of virtue, maintaining continuity with Aristotelian philosophy. It incorporates a heteronomous theological dimension, providing an immutable and virtuous foundation for the duty to fulfil promises.[35]

The violation of these duties was so serious as to jeopardise the spiritual life of the promisor (*ratio peccati*) and, externally, it introduced instability, moral uncertainty and scandal into social relations (*ratio scandali*),[36] thereby endangering Christian social life. In this light, the duty of honesty (*secundum honestatem*) and the duty of fidelity (*fidelitatis*) mandated the fulfilment of promises.[37] Consequently, Roman formalism was substantively rejected in favour of a new ethical–religious framework and the concrete principles of *aequitas*.[38]

It must be emphasised that the historical influence of St Thomas Aquinas on the theory of promise and obligation cannot be underestimated. Aquinas's duty of honesty (*secundum honestatem*)[39] prescribed the fulfilment of promises:[40] *mendacium est si quis non impleat quod promisit*.[41] In Aquinas's view, the need to fulfil a promise transcended issues of solemnities and formalities, given the substantive prevalence of fidelity, the duty of truth and respect for one's word.[42] This theological view was taken up by the canonists, who began to hold that the promise, regardless of its form, must be binding.[43] Under this new axiological framework, Baldus sought to connect with the glossators' legacy concerning the *vestimentum* by developing the concept of *pactum cum causa*. Baldus asserted that cause possessed the strength (energy) of the *vestimentum* – *vestimentum roboris* – thereby enabling the *pactum* to be 'vested' by the *causa finalis*, independent of formalities. Thus, the determination of the validity of the *pactum* depended on its *causa finalis*, making its identification essential. The explicit mention of the cause became a

[35] M Hogg, *Promises and Contract Law* (Cambridge, Cambridge University Press, 2011) 75. According to Aquinas, only in exceptional circumstances could or should the promisor not act as promised. This would be the case if the *causa promissionis* was illicit (see G Chevrier, *Essai sur l'histoire de la cause dans les obligations* (Sirey, Paris, 1929) 142–55, who underlined the duty not to fulfil the promise with an unlawful cause) or in the case of a change in the circumstances which led to the fulfilment of the promise (Aquinas (n 33) [42759] IIª–IIae q 88 a 3 arg 2). Outside of these cases, the existence of a duty of fidelity is strongly affirmed: 'si vero non faciat quod promisit, tunc videtur infideliter agere per hoc quod animum mutat' (idem [42763] IIª–IIae q 88 a 3 ad 1); and also the duty of honesty: 'secundum honestatem ex qualibet promissione homo homini obligatur; et haec est obligatio iuris naturalis' (idem [42763] IIª–IIae q 88 a 3 ad 1). See G Albers, 'Zum Versprechen als Verpflichtungsgrund in der Spätantike: Urkundenpraxis, Kirchenlehrer und der westgotische Gaius' (2018) 135 *Zeitschrift der Savigny-Stiftung für Rechtsgeschichte: Romanistische Abteilung* 334, 336.

[36] P Fedele, 'Considerazioni sull'efficacia dei patti nudi nel diritto canonico' (1937) 11 *Annali dell'Università di Macerata* 149; P Bellini, *L' obbligazione da promessa con oggetto temporale nel sistema canonistico classico con particolare riferimento ai secoli XII e XIII* (Milan, Giuffrè, 1964) 58.

[37] St Thomas Aquinas also analysed the promise of Roman law, pondering the limited provision in the *Digest* of its relevance as a source of obligations: Aquinas (n 33) [42763] IIª–IIae q 88 a 3 ad 1.

[38] ibid [42758] IIª–IIae q 88 a 3 arg 1.

[39] ibid [42763] IIª–IIae q 88 a 3 ad 1.

[40] F Spies, *De l'observation des simples conventions en droit canonique* (Paris, Recuel Syrey, 1928) 2ff; M Roberti, *L'influenza cristiana nello svolgimento storico dei patti nudi, in Cristianismo e diritto romano* (Milan, Società Editrice Vita e Pensiero, 1935) 96; Albers, 'Zum Versprechen als Verpflichtungsgrund in der Spätantike: Urkundenpraxis, Kirchenlehrer und der westgotische Gaius' (n 35) 336.

[41] Aquinas (n 33) [43661] IIª–IIae q 110 a 3 arg 5.

[42] For a comparison of the various theories of canonist moralists, see G Chevrier, *Essai sur l'histoire de la cause dans les obligations* (Paris, Recueil Sirey,1929) 143ff.

[43] Söllner (n 9) 243ff; H Dilcher, 'Der Typenzwang im Mittelalterlichen Vertragsrecht' (1960) 77 *Zeitschrift der Savigny-Stiftung für Rechtsgeschichte – Romanistische Abteilung* 284.

crucial requirement for contractual validity, presenting a significant challenge to formal and abstract contracts. Consequently, Baldus disregarded the formal and abstract nature of *stipulatio* by adopting a causalist approach, asserting that a *stipulatio* lacking a *causa* would be deemed abusive and inherently void.

In light of the foregoing, it is essential to clarify that the concept of *nudum pactum* did not refer to a pact devoid of *causa* but rather to a pact that was no longer dependent on formalities – hence the principle *pactum nudum a solemnitate sed non nudum a causa*. With the concept of *causa finalis* taking precedence in determining the obligatory nature of a promise or contract, the causal element became crucial in assessing its ability to create binding obligations, independent of formalities.

The rising influence of the concept of cause will historically manifest across various legal systems, most notably the French and Italian ones. The German case, as mentioned in Gregor Albers's chapter on the cause in German law, presents unique particularities due to its acceptance of abstraction. While abstraction does not denote an absence of causal control, it signifies a transference of this control to an *ex post* moment.

Accordingly, in this chapter dedicated to the Middle Ages, it is also important to mention instances of resistance to the 'causalism trend' during this period. An interesting question arises regarding medieval Aragonese law, which has provoked inquiries into the acceptance of contractual abstraction during the medieval period. Given its evident interest and the diverse nature of the medieval era, attention is duly afforded to the *promissio sine causa* evident in the Aragonese *Observancias*.

IV. Deviation: *Causa Finalis* and the Case of *Promissio Sine Causa* in the *Observancias* of the Kingdom of Aragon

The decisive role of the Iberian Peninsula in shaping the foundations of European contract law has been already widely acknowledged,[44] with particular emphasis on the legislation of Alfonso XI, recognised for its decisive influence on the evolution of modern contractual theory.

This contribution can be traced, among other sources, to the *Ordenamiento de Alcalá* (1348),[45] namely to the important *Ley Paresciendo*. Initially included in chapter 29 of the original *Ordenamiento de Alcalá*, the *Ley Paresciendo* was subsequently incorporated – though substantially unaltered – into chapter 16 in the revised version of the *Ordenamiento de Alcalá* during the reign of King Pedro I of Castile.[46]

[44] H Coing, *Europäisches Privatrecht*, vol 1 (Munich, CH Beck, 1985) 400.

[45] G Sanchéz, 'Sobre el Ordenamiento de Alcalá (1348) y sus fuentes' (1932) 9 *Revista de Derecho Privado* 353.

[46] The passage from the *Ley Paresciendo* which should be retained had the following content: 'Ordenamiento de Alcalá Capitulo 29: Paresciendo que se quiso un ome obligar a otro por promision, o por algún contracto, o en alguna otra manera, sea tenudo de aquellos a quienes se obligó, e non pueda ser puesta excepción que non fue fecha estipulación, que quiere decir: prometimiento con ciertas solemnidades del derecho, o que fue fecha la obligación del contracto entre absentes; o que fue fecha a escribano público, o a otra persona privada en nombre de otro entre absentes; o que se obligó uno de dar o de facer alguna cosa a otro; mas que sea valedera la obligación o el contracto que fueren fechos en cualquier manera que paresca que alguno se quiso obligar a otro, e facer contracto con él', *Cortes de los antíguos reinos de León y de Castilla publicado por la Real Academia de la Historia* I (Madrid, 1861) 514.

While the significance of Castilian legal texts and other Spanish sources remains uncontested, it is more than reasonable to assert that their importance should not eclipse the relevance of other sources of law. In fact, despite the obvious historical relevance of the *Ley Paresciendo*,[47] the possibility to identify abstract promises in medieval Aragonese law, notably the *promissio sine causa*, warrants significant consideration. Consequently, it is fitting to underscore the distinctiveness of the 'Aragonese abstract promise', and to seek its historical and legal explanation. Specifically, it is of considerable interest to identify signs of the acceptance of abstraction in Aragonese law sources, even during the period of the flourishing concept of cause as *causa finalis*.

The rise of *causa finalis*, which led to the rejection of the possibility of contractual abstraction, has already been highlighted. To this extent, it is pertinent to question why, within the context of the ascendancy of *causa finalis* during the era of the Ius Commune, the recognition of abstract promises was justified in medieval Aragonese law.

The topic of abstraction in Aragonese medieval law underwent scrutiny in at least two studies. The first one, conducted by Rieira Aisa, was published in 1942,[48] followed by a pivotal study resulting from the research of Lacruz Berdejo in 1943.[49] In these historicallegal studies, the authors seek to understand the meaning that results from the *Observancias* of the Kingdom of Aragon (1437),[50] particularly regarding the relevance of the *promissio sine causa*.

In this context, it is important to bear in mind the text of the *Observancia Sexta* (Lib II, *De confessis*): *Item si quis confiteatur in instrumento se debere aliquam quantitatem non expressa aliqua causa, nihilominus condemnatur ad solvendum secundum observantiam Regni quia iudex stat instrumento* (If anyone promises a certain amount to another in a written document without stating the cause, he must nevertheless be ordered to pay according to the rules of the law, as the judge must be bound by the document/*instrumento*). Pursuant to the *Observancia Sexta*, it seems evident that a promisor, through the use of an *instrumento*, would be compelled to pay a specified amount, even in the absence of disclosing the corresponding cause for the payment obligation.

However, other sources of Aragonese law must be considered. It is also important to examine the *Compilación of Huesca* (1247), which contained references to the *promissio sine causa*,[51] and was subsequently complemented by the *Observancias*.

[47] A Cavanna, *Storia del diritto moderno in Europa, Il pensiero giuridica e le fonti*, vol I (Milan, Giuffrè, 1982) 420ff.

[48] L Riera Aisa, 'La promesa abstrata de deuda en el antiguo Derecho de Aragón' (1942) 26 *Revista de Derecho privado* 43.

[49] JL Lacruz Berdejo, 'Notas para el estudio de la *promissio sine causa* en los fueros de Aragón' (Zaragoza, 1 Segunda Semana de Derecho Aragonés, 943) 203–42.

[50] The *Observancia Sexta* is part of the *Observancias del Reino de Aragón*, a compilation of judicial interpretations and customary laws that became fundamental to Aragonese legal tradition. The process of compiling these observances began in the mid-13th century and they had become particularly significant by the 15th century. A major compilation was completed in 1437 under the supervision of Martín Díez de Aux, following a directive from King Alfonso V in 1428. This collection, entitled *Observantiae Consuetudinesque Regni Aragonum*, encompassed both legal customs and judicial precedents.

[51] 'Si quis ad preces alterius hominis promiserit aliquam causam, et promisisse eum posteat peniteat nisi fuerit de voluntatate sua, promisserit dixerit contra illum quod propter servitium, quod ei fecit tempore necesitatis, aut propter adiutorium in pleyto, aut in alia causa, aut per serallam convenit et promisit quod ab eo petit': L Riera Aisa, 'La promesa abstrata de deuda en el antiguo Derecho de Aragón' (1942) 26 *Revista de Derecho privado* 43.

Within this context, particular attention should be dedicated not only to the *Observancia Sexta*, but also to the *Observancia Cuarenta* (Lib IV, *De generalibus privilegis totius regni Aragonum*): *Si quis sine carta promiserit aliquid dare sine causa. Non tenetur dare nisi voluerit, vel nisi iusta causa probetur promissionis* (If anyone, without a written document, promises to give something without cause, they are not obliged to give unless they so desire, or unless a just cause for the promise is proven).[52]

The combination of *Observancias Sexta* and *Cuarenta* gives rise to a significant distinction based on whether the commitment is expressed orally or in writing. In the case of an oral promise, the absence of the cause negates any obligation. Conversely, in the context of a written commitment executed through a formal instrument, an obligation is acknowledged, notwithstanding the omission of the cause of such obligation in the *instrumento*.[53]

Regarding this matter, Rieira Aisa conducted a comprehensive examination of the Aragonese sources, contrasting the viewpoints of several *Fueristas* on the implications of the above mentioned *Observancias*. It is noteworthy that unanimous consensus prevailed regarding the existence of an obligation when a commitment was documented in writing (*instrumento*), irrespective of the explicit mention of the cause of the obligation in the instrument.[54]

Franco de Villalba regarded this matter as highly significant, noting that under the Ius Commune, a promise – even when committed to writing – was insufficient to create an obligation unless its cause was expressly stated.[55] In this regard, Franco de Villalba highlighted the seeming inconsistency between the *Observancia Sexta* and the established principles of the Ius Commune. One of the factors that must be taken into particular account is the value of the *instrumento* in medieval Aragonese law, given the centrality of the principle *standum est chartae*.[56] As argued by Riera Aisa, the central issue revolved around the exemption from the need to prove the cause of the obligation when a commitment/promise was documented in writing, through an *instrumento*, even without explicit mention of the cause. Rieira Aisa then questions whether it would be possible to prove the absence of the cause (demonstrating the crisis of the causal agreement), thereby defeating the force of the *instrumento*, ultimately concluding in the affirmative.[57] From this perspective, it is argued that the *Observancias* relate to the realm of evidentiary rules. This interpretation suggests that the primary function of the *Observancias* was not to enable or address the abstraction of promises without cause.[58] According to Riera Aisa, it is not possible to conclusively assert the 'full and absolute' legal strength of the *instrumento*. Instead, one must acknowledge that, in medieval Aragonese law, it would be possible to demonstrate the lack of cause of the promise, thus challenging the *promissio sine causa* made by the *instrumento*.[59] Thus, in conclusion, Riera Aisa, taking in consideration the *Observancias* above mentioned, argued that

[52] In Lacruz Berdejo (n 49) 225.
[53] Riera Aisa (n 48) 44.
[54] For a comparison of the various positions, see ibid 44; similarly, see Lacruz Berdejo (n 49) 225–26.
[55] See Lacruz Berdejo (n 49) 226.
[56] Riera Aisa (n 48) 46.
[57] ibid 47.
[58] ibid 47.
[59] ibid 47.

there was nothing to prevent the possibility of proof to the contrary (lack of cause) of what is stated in the *instrumento*.[60]

As previously indicated, Lacruz Berdejo played a pivotal role in the discourse regarding the acceptance of contractual abstraction within medieval Aragonese law.[61] Following a comprehensive analysis of the sources of medieval Aragonese law, Lacruz Berdejo concluded that there exists unequivocal evidence within the *Observancias* of the Kingdom of Aragon to substantiate the acceptance of obligatory abstraction in medieval Aragonese law – in his words: 'the mediaeval type of abstract promise which presents more modern technique is, without doubt, that which is regulated in the *Observancias*'.[62]

On this matter, Lacruz Berdejo highlights several historical-legal elements crucial to understanding the potential recognition of obligatory abstraction in medieval Aragonese law. Although the concept of *causa finalis* was acknowledged in medieval Aragonese law, it did not achieve a status of essentiality (*essentialia*). According to Lacruz Berdejo, this implies that *causa finalis* in medieval Aragonese law functioned merely as one of the possible *vestments* of a legal transaction: 'The *causa finalis* in Aragon has not succeeded in transcending the status of a mere "vestment", thus exerting influence on the legal transaction only when the parties have expressly included it in its content.'[63]

Despite the complexity of this topic, Riera Aisa rightly emphasises the necessity of clarifying this issue. According to his analysis, as said, while a formal promise alone could establish obligations, the 'full' effectiveness of the *instrumento*[64] was not accepted. Regarding this topic, as mentioned before, Riera Aisa argued that, in medieval Aragonese law, it was possible to challenge the *promissio sine causa* made by the *instrumento* by demonstrating the absence or illegality of the cause.[65] Riera Aisa's conclusions are based on several factors: the procedural nature of the *Observancias Sexta* and *Cuarenta* and the absence of the *condictio* remedies in Aragonese law demanded a different approach to control the harmful effects of the abstraction of the *promissio sine causa*, precisely through *annullability*. This led Lacruz Berdejo to label Riera Aisa's perspective as the 'theory of annullability'.[66]

[60] Riera Aisa concludes, therefore, that: 'el Fuero de promissione sine causa y las observancias sentaron el principio básico de la posibilidad de existencia en Derecho de Aragón del negocio jurídico abstracto, cuyo convenio causal permanecia ajeno al mismo, pero siempre, naturalmente, existiendo este convenio y correspondiendo al que hizo la promesa la prueba de su no existencia, y quedando, por tanto, en situación de privilegio el que tenía a su favor la promesa escrita': ibid 47–48. There, according to the author, the *Fuero 'de promisione sine causa'* and the *Observancias Sexta* and *Cuarenta* do not allow for the conclusion that it is impossible to provide evidence against the *instrumento*; on the contrary, in this context, it would be possible to demonstrate that the promise made by the *instrumento* lacked a cause. Of great interest, then, is the comparison of this situation with the doctrine of relative abstraction, which seems to be, as supposed, the author's idea about the Aragonese promise. See ibid 48.

[61] Lacruz Berdejo (n 49) 203ff.

[62] 'El tipo medieval de promesa abstracta que presenta técnica más moderna es, sin duda, el que se regula en las Observancias': ibid 224.

[63] 'La causa finalis en Aragón no haya logrado pasar la condición de simple 'vestes', por lo que no influye en el negocio jurídico sino cuando las partes la han incluido en su contenido': ibid 226.

[64] Riera Aisa (n 48) 47.

[65] Lacruz Berdejo (n 49) 239.

[66] ibid 239.

In response to Riera Aisa's theory, Lacruz Berdejo presented counterarguments to demonstrate that, in medieval Aragonese law, the abstract promise could not be *invalidated* due to a lack of cause; instead, its harmful effects could be rectified through other means. The issue, therefore, was not one of *validity*, but rather one of preserving effectiveness or correcting the harmful effects resulting from the abstract obligation. Lacruz Berdejo argued that the medieval Aragonese system anticipated, by several centuries, the foundational philosophy of the German law of obligations' abstraction system as later doctrinally shaped by Otto Bähr.[67] Furthermore, Lacruz Berdejo criticised Riera Aisa's procedural interpretation of *Observancia Sexta*. According to Lacruz Berdejo, the *Observancia Sexta* should be regarded as a '*fuente de obligaciones de derecho material*' (source of obligations).[68] This perspective emphasises the substantive legal obligations created by the *Observancia Sexta*, rather than viewing it merely as a procedural rule.

To reach this conclusion, Lacruz Berdejo asserts that it is essential to consider that the *causa finalis* was not elevated to an imperative element in Aragonese law.[69] On the contrary, the cause element was merely one among various ways that could constitute obligations. Other methods of establishing obligations were possible through different forms, as exemplified by the *promissio sine causa* carried out through the *instrumento*, as mentioned in *Observancia Sexta*.

On the other hand, *promissio sine causa* traced back to the ancient Aragonese *homagium*, historically a sufficient *form* for the creation of obligations.[70] In addition

[67] In this regard, it is important to recall that, diverging from the causalist tradition of other European systems and studying various Roman legal figures, particularly the *stipulatio*, Bähr, as early as 1855, promoted the reconfiguration of the classic problem of *cautio indiscreta* through the prism of the will, thus laying the foundations for obligatory abstraction in the German system: O Bähr, *Die Anerkennung als Verpflichtungsgrund* (Kassel, Oswald Bertram, 1855). In Bähr's view, a declaration of acknowledgement of a debt or the promise of a performance without mentioning the cause could be classified as an abstract obligation and thus constitute an independent basis for bringing proceedings against the debtor (ibid 3), referring to a new basis for the legal relationship ('es kann dem Rechtsverhältniss eine neue Grundlage gegeben werden, welche statt der ursprünglichen processualisch zu wirken vermag') facilitating their procedural position. This significant paradigm shift allowed Bähr to develop the theory of obligatory abstract obligations. (See also B Windscheid, *Lehrbuch des Pandektenrechts* II (Frankfurt am Main, Literarische Anstalt Rütten & Loening, 1887) § 318, 235, fn 4.) Its construction put the creditor in the position of suing the debtor solely on the basis of the abstract promise or debt acknowledgement, given the existence of its own legal basis, which, as has already been said, translated into a facilitation of the procedural position of the creditor (*Klagerleichterung*) (M Rümelin, *Zur Lehre von den Schuldversprechen und Schuldanerkenntnissen des BGB* (Tübingen, Mohr, 1905/06) 276–77; P Marburger, annotation §780, *Staudinger BGB, II, Recht der Schuldverhältnisse, §§ 779–811* (Berlin, Sellier–de Gruyter, 2015) 103). Thus, the titling of the legal claim results directly from an abstract promise or an abstract acknowledgement, representing an advantage for the creditor's position, since it will be up to the debtor to prove that the creditor's position is affected by a legal pathology that requires its legal effectiveness to be limited (N Wielandt, *Die einseitig verpflichtende Schuldzusage* (Oxford, Peter Land, 2010) 31–40; Marburger (idem) 102 et seq). In cases of relative juridical abstraction, the relevance of the (cause of the) obligation is not suppressed. Rather, its relevance is allowed to act on a different level, namely through *condictio*. See O Bähr, *Die Anerkennung als Verpflichtungsgrund* 3ª (1894, reprinted Leipzig, Scientia Verlag Aalen, 1970) §44, 132: 'Damit nun die Anerkennungserklärung in dieser Weise wirke, muss sie vor Allem mit dem Willen, sich zu verpflichten, in Verbindung treten, und zwar mit einem solchen Willen, welcher aus dem ursprünglichen Bestand oder Nichtbestand der Verbindlichkeit nicht mehr die Bedingung seiner Gültigkeit, sondern nur seine Voraussetzung (causa) entnimmt'.

[68] Lacruz Berdejo (n 49) 239.

[69] ibid 240.

[70] ibid 240.

to these arguments, one should consider the literal element of *Observancia Sexta* (what was promised in the instrument was to be fulfilled), and the circumstance that, in the Aragonese system, a considerable level of civil freedom could be observed.[71] Indeed, with respect to freedom of contract, the primary constraints were the general principles of impossibility and natural law. These foundational limits essentially governed the validity and enforceability of contractual agreements, ensuring that obligations arising from contracts were feasible and aligned with the principles of natural justice.[72] Given these considerations, according to Lacruz Berdejo, the validity of the Aragonese abstract promise could not have been challenged solely due to the omission of cause. Instead, only its harmful effects were subject to corrective measures in terms of *ex post* control of its effectiveness. The absence of specific provisions regarding the *condictio* did not preclude this control. Rather, the general principle of *aequitas* provided sufficient grounds to prevent unjust enrichment, ensuring fairness and justice in contractual obligations.[73]

In summary, Lacruz Berdejo's claim for the medieval Aragonese law's role as the precursor to the modern German abstract promise is of significant importance to the history and evolution of European private law, providing valuable insights into the development and understanding of contemporary legal systems.

V. Synthesis

In Roman law, a notable development was the imposition of certain controls over *stipulatio*, an abstract formal contract. These controls were chiefly enforced through procedural defences, which offered protection in cases involving abstract contracts that depended solely on the observance of specific formalities or solemnities, such as *stipulatio*.

During the medieval period, the glossators largely adopted the Roman law framework for contracts. It is often observed that the glossators emphasised a nominal reorganisation of the sources of obligations, centring their classification around the concept of *pactum*. Given the Roman law principle *nuda pactio obligationem non parit* (D. 2,14,7,4), the glossators faced the challenge of determining the legal significance of *nuda pacta* – or naked agreements. Within this context, the *pactum cum vestimento* emerged as a recognised source of voluntary obligations, playing a pivotal role in the medieval contractual system. However, the term *vestimentum* encompassed a wide range of meanings and lacked terminological consistency, creating ambiguity regarding what qualified as a *pactum cum vestimento*.

Within the broader context of the increasing significance of the cause element, a notable medieval development is the widespread recognition of the necessity of identifying the cause of an obligation. This had a direct impact on cases where a promise to pay a sum of money was made without specifying its cause. This development was founded

[71] ibid 240.
[72] ibid 240.
[73] ibid 240.

upon the texts of Paulus (D. 22,3,25,4) and the decision of Justinian (C. 4,30,13). These sources provide that, where a promise to pay a sum not lawfully owed was made in abstract terms (*cautio indebite et indiscrete loquatur*), meaning without a stated basis for the obligation, it was incumbent upon the creditor to establish that the amount claimed was supported by a valid legal cause.

From an Aristotelian–Thomistic perspective, Bartolus and Baldus later offered an innovative interpretation of the concept of *cause*, making significant contributions to its theoretical understanding as *causa finalis*.

The roots of the *causa finalis* concept can be traced back to ancient Greek philosophy, particularly to Aristotle, with its early introduction into medieval juridical thought attributed to Johannes Bassianus. However, as noted above, the concept underwent careful refinement during the fourteenth century through the work of medieval scholars such as Bartolus and Baldus. Both jurists held the conviction that a deep understanding of the ultimate purpose of a phenomenon – a thing – was essential to grasp its ontological essence, nature and attributes.

With the rise of the *causa finalis*, the omission of any reference to the cause gained increasing importance. This shift inevitably led to the rejection of abstraction. The abstract contract, particularly the *stipulatio sine causa*, was marginalised, as it stood in direct opposition to the finalist approach.

Within the medieval framework shaped by Aristotelian–Thomistic thought, the *causa finalis* of an act came to be regarded as an essential element (*essentialia*). In this context, the concept of *cause* became central to determining the validity of a contract. It was during this period that the principle *ex nudo pacto oritur actio* – a shortened form of *ex nudo pacto oritur actio nudum a solemnitate sed non nudum a causa* – also emerged. Here, the term *nudum pactum* does not signify a pact devoid of *causa*, but rather one no longer dependent on formalities. With the ascendancy of *causa finalis* in determining the binding nature of promises or contracts, the element of *cause* became critical for evaluating whether a contract could create valid obligations.

Within this new axiological framework, Baldus argued that *cause* possessed the strength of *vestimentum*, enabling the *pactum* to be 'vested' by its *causa finalis*. Thus, the validity of a *pactum* hinged on its *causa finalis*, making the identification of *cause* indispensable. The explicit mention of *cause* became a fundamental requirement for contractual validity, posing a direct challenge to formal and abstract contracts. As a result, Baldus rejected the formal and abstract nature of the *stipulatio*, adopting a causalist approach by asserting that a *stipulatio* without *causa* would be abusive and inherently void.

In concluding this chapter on the Middle Ages, it is important to recognise that, despite the predominance of causalism, instances of *resistance* also existed. Notably, medieval Aragonese law presents a compelling example of contractual abstraction.

The concept of *promissio sine causa*, as reflected in the Aragonese *Observancias*, is particularly significant for its abstract nature and for its divergence from the causalistic trend. The Aragonese *promissio sine causa* offers valuable insights for understanding modern systems that accept contractual abstraction. It highlights an important lesson: an abstract obligation – such as that embodied in the *promissio sine causa* – does not imply a lack of control or absolute abstraction. As demonstrated, the strength of the *instrumento* (the formal element) in the *promissio sine causa* did not guarantee its absolute validity. Instead, its effects could later be challenged – not on the grounds of invalidity, but to rectify any unjust consequences arising from it. This aspect, while a departure from the prevailing medieval causalism, remains highly relevant, especially for systems that currently uphold abstraction.

It is important to note that abstraction and causality fundamentally differ in the timing of when *cause* is assessed – whether at an *ex ante* moment (in causal systems) or at an *ex post* moment (in systems with non-absolute abstraction). This distinction, which is evident in modern legal systems, was also clearly observable during the medieval period.

3

Causa and Consideration: Motive and Exchange in English Contract Law

DAVID J IBBETSON

For most of its history, English law avoided abstract structures. The common law emerged in the twelfth century as a system of remedies, structured around the writs that initiated litigation. No doubt there were values and principles that lay behind this system, and we can discern traces of these fundamental ideas if we look beneath the remedial system, but if we mean by 'law' that which was needed to be known to frame disputes before courts, this system of remedies, with the legal process associated with them, was fundamental.

We should think of the common law as the system whose origins we can trace back to the middle of the twelfth century, approximately a century after the Norman Conquest, and which has continued largely unbroken since then. The earliest book of the law is the Treatise on the Laws and Customs of England known as Glanvill. Book X of this work deals with the writ of debt, where one person claims money or moveable property from another. Two aspects are important for present purposes. First is the statement that claims in debt can be split into those whose proof is a sealed document and those which are proved by witnesses; provided the document is valid on its face as a debt-creating instrument, the defendant cannot deny the claim in the former situation, but in the latter situation he can produce opposing witnesses or swear an oath (supported by oath-helpers) that the money or goods are not owed. The second aspect is that there needs to be a *causa*:

> When both parties are present in court, there are several *causae* on which the plaintiff may base his claim to the debt. The cause of the debt may be loan for consumption (*mutuum*), sale (*venditio*), loan for use (*commodatum*), letting (*locatio*), deposit (*depositum*), or any other just cause of indebtedness.[1]

The requirement to allege a *causa* applies indiscriminately to cases proved by documents and cases proved by witnesses, but the list of acceptable *causae* is not closed.

[1] *Glanvill* (London, GDG Hall, 1965) X.3.

The evidence of the thirteenth-century plea rolls, the courts' official records, show that it was not restricted to what would have been regarded as contracts in Roman law. We find, for example, agreements to compromise actions, or to pay damages, treated as generating debts.[2] It seems to have meant little more than a recognisable motive, though with a predominant focus on what the Romans (and we) would see as contractual transactions.

I. Documents under Seal

By 1300, it was clear that the requirement of *causa* only applied to situations where proof was by witnesses. According to a notebook of around 1300, where the words *obligatum esse* are used in a writing, they make the writing the *causa* of the obligation.[3] As a matter of social fact, of course, it is unlikely that sealed documents would be made without any reason for doing so; but the legal rule was clear, that it did not matter that no *causa* was alleged, and hence as a matter of law it did not matter that no *causa* existed. The wording of these documents shows them to have been formulated as grants; we may think of them, structurally, as delayed gifts which might need legal process to complete them.

By 1300, there was in existence another action, this time an action explicitly based on agreement, the action of covenant.[4] This, too, was required to be in a sealed document, and by analogy with what had come to be the rule in debt there was no requirement of a *causa*, though, since the action was always based on an agreement by two parties, the transaction which lay at its root would invariably be visible.

It was therefore very well established in the Middle Ages that what amounted to promises of gifts were enforceable at common law, provided that the correct form was used. This remains so today. The only change which occurred was that the requirement of a seal of impressed wax degraded: printed documents might have the place for the seal (*locus sigilli*, or LS) shown, and the practice developed of sticking a disc of gummed red paper on the document in imitation of the red wax. By the twentieth century, it was sufficient that there was simply an LS printed, or indeed in some cases the document said it was a deed. In 1989, the charade of the deed was finally abolished, replaced with a specific form of words laid down by statute stating that the document was intended as a deed.[5]

II. Debts Evidenced by Witnesses

Most of what we think of as the law of contract developed first in the context of the action of debt where there was no deed. Here, the requirement that the cause of the

[2] D Ibbetson, 'The Deed Rule in the Action of Covenant' (2021) 42 *Journal of Legal History* 233, 253, no 121.

[3] 69 Selden Society lxxxviii, no 35.

[4] Sir J Baker, *Introduction to English Legal History*, 5th edn (Oxford, Oxford University Press, 2019) 339–42.

[5] Law Reform (Miscellaneous Provisions) Act 1989, s 1(2).

indebtedness must appear in the plaintiff's claim was not abandoned; a case in 1297 stressed the need to show that the debt derived from 'a certain contract and from a certain cause' ('de certein contract e de certein cause').[6] Neither 'contract' nor 'cause' is further explained here, but there is a hint that it would not be sufficient to say simply that there need be a cause; rather, it needed to be explained as a contract. A discussion in 1338 underlines this movement.[7] In a writ of debt, the plaintiff counted on a covenant – an agreement – that the defendant would pay money to the plaintiff for acting as his attorney. It was objected that this was a covenant that required a sealed deed as evidence, but this was rejected: 'Here you have his service in return for his hire … and you have *quid pro quo*.' Here, it is the fact of the receipt of something in exchange, the plaintiff's labour, which has grounded the debt. These cases may show a leaning towards a model of exchange, but we should not be too dogmatic about this, for in a case of 1329 it was held sufficient to require a defendant to answer that there had been an undertaking to pay the debt of a third party.[8]

Through the fourteenth and fifteenth centuries, there was little doubt that a quid pro quo – something for something – was sufficient to generate a debt, but how far it extended beyond that was uncertain. An anonymous case of 1458,[9] commonly known as *Alice's Case*, shows the conceptual ambiguity. Alice was to marry the plaintiff, and 'in exchange for'[10] the marriage her father agreed to pay the plaintiff 100 marks. The marriage took place but the money was not paid, and an action of debt was brought. The judges of the Court of Common Pleas disagreed as to whether debt lay. Prisot CJ thought not. For him, there needed to be an exchange, either a contract strictly speaking, like a sale, or a retainer, as where a person hired a servant and the servant performed his duties so that there was quid pro quo. Danvers J disagreed and would allow the action: although this was not strictly a contract, it was the same in effect, for the father had quid pro quo in that he was relieved of the responsibility of arranging a marriage for his daughter. Wider than this, though, he said that if a man agreed with a carrier that he would pay him to carry another's goods, debt would lie even though the benefit came to another. The act had been done by his command, and that was sufficient. Moyle J agreed with Danvers. In Danvers's example of the carriage of goods for a third party, there was no quid pro quo for the defendant, nor was there where one said he would pay a physician to treat a sick man, but it was much the same in effect.[11] The case was then adjourned for discussion, and nothing further is heard of it.[12]

Writing in the 1520s, Christopher St German recognised recompense as the principal element making a promise binding at common law, but also adopted the fifteenth-century treatment of marriage and charitable promises, holding that where the person to whom the promise was made had a 'charge' by reason of the promise, enforceability

[6] *La Zuche v Rokeny* (1297) in Sir J Baker, *Baker and Milsom: Sources of English Legal History* (Oxford, Oxford University Press, 2019) 250, 251.

[7] YB 11 & 12 Edw III (RS) 587, ibid 254.

[8] *Anon* (1329) 98 Selden Society 743.

[9] YB M.37 Hen VI, fol 8, pl 18, Baker, *Baker and Milsom* 263.

[10] *Pur* in the French Law Report, so presumably *pro* in the Latin of the formal pleadings.

[11] The other two judges are not reported as having addressed the point.

[12] For discussion of the scope of quid pro quo at this time, see AWB Simpson, *History of the Common Law of Contract* (New York, Oxford University Press, 1975) 148–60.

would follow.[13] St German's generalisation here might have been premature. John Rastell simply contrasted the presence of quid pro quo with an unenforceable *nudum pactum*;[14] and later in the century, the identification of quid pro quo as exchange was treated as axiomatically limiting the scope of the action of debt.[15] It was not until 1602 that it was held that debt would lie in the absence of such an exchange agreement.[16] But by this time, in the absence of a sealed deed, the action of debt had been largely superseded by the action of assumpsit.

III. Assumpsit

The action of assumpsit developed out of the tortious action on the case for the misperformance of an undertaking right at the end of the fifteenth century, offering a remedy for the non-performance of an undertaking or promise.[17] Its basic structure was clear by around 1530, though it was not until about 1570 that it was being precisely delineated. At first, it was very common to allege that the defendant's promise had been given 'pro' a small sum of money, typically a few pence, thereby replicating the quid pro quo of the action of debt. We may well suspect that these allegations of the payment of a small sum were sometimes fictitious, and in 1567 it was observed that they were commonly alleged feignedly in the King's Bench, the court where actions of assumpsit were more common.[18] The language of consideration was coming into use too, though without any single focal meaning.[19] The abstract term for what made the promise enforceable perhaps was *causa*. In *Marler v Wilmer* in 1539, an action was brought in the Coventry mayor's court by an executor who was trying to collect debts owed to his deceased father.[20] The defendant was alleged to have bought goods from the father, after whose death he promised to pay the executor. Assumpsit was brought against the defendant, who demurred, claiming that the plaintiff's action was not well grounded in law. The Coventry court gave judgment for the plaintiff, and the defendant brought a writ of error to the King's Bench. One of the alleged errors is pertinent:

> In narracione illa non apparet quam ob causam predictus Thomas assumpcionem predictam fecisset, nec pro denariis sibi premanibus solutis nec pro recepcione parcelli bonorum predictorum; et sic ex nudo pacto non oritur actio.

[13] *Doctor and Student* 91 Selden Society 230–31, discussed by JL Barton at lv–lix.

[14] *Expositiones Terminorum* (1525) *sub verb* Contract.

[15] Most explicitly in *Baxter v Read* (1585) Dyer 272 in marg, BL MS Lansd 1087, fol 183.

[16] *Lady Chandos v Sympson* (1602) Cro El 880, Baker, *Baker and Milsom* (n 6) 273.

[17] For details, see Sir John Baker, *Oxford History of the Laws of England*, vol VI (Oxford, Oxford University Press, 2001) 839–74.

[18] *Lord Grey's Case* (1567) in Simpson (n 12) 633 (translating the French *fainement* of the manuscript as 'feignedly' rather than Simpson's 'faintly'); *cf* Baker, *Baker and Milsom* (n 6) 528, from a different manuscript: 'it is now alleged so frequently'.

[19] JH Baker, 'Origins of the "Doctrine" of Consideration' in MS Arnold et al (eds), *On the Laws and Customs of England* (Chapel Hill, University of North Carolina Press, 1981) 336.

[20] See D Ibbetson, 'Assumpsit and Debt in the Early Sixteenth Century: the Origins of the Indebitatus Count' [1982] *CLJ* 142.

> In the count it does not appear for what *causa* the aforesaid Thomas made the aforesaid undertaking, neither for pennies paid beforehand nor for the receipt of part of the aforesaid goods; and so *ex nudo pacto non oritur actio*.

There is sophisticated thinking here; and it may be significant that Richard Heywood, Marler's attorney, was related by marriage to two eminent legal families, the Rastells and the Mores.[21] The language of *causa* seems to take us back to the thirteenth century or into the language of the contemporary civil or canon law, where it was motive that mattered; but the examples given of acceptable *causae* point firmly towards the receipt of a benefit, quid pro quo.[22]

By about 1570, the word 'consideration' had come to be used to designate what was required for a promise to be enforceable. That can be thought of in the same way as *causa*. If we look at the meaning of the word, ignoring its specific context in the action of assumpsit, it is very close to motive. The considerations behind doing something were the factors which led to its being brought about.[23] But if we look at the content of consideration, it centred very firmly on the idea of reciprocity or exchange. If we are properly to understand the law, it is this content that matters.

IV. Consideration after 1570[24]

The best starting point to understand the doctrine of consideration as it lay down its roots in the latter part of the sixteenth century is the description by James Altham, in argument in the court of Exchequer in 1588:

> There are three manners of consideration upon which an assumpsit may be grounded: 1 A debt precedent; 2 Where he to whom such a promise is made is damnified by doing anything, or spends his labour at the instance of the promiser; as I agree with a surgeon to cure a poor man (who is a stranger unto me) of a sore, who doth it accordingly, he shall have an action; 3 Or there is a present consideration, etc.[25]

A. The Precedent Debt

The first of Altham's three types, the precedent debt, is the most difficult and must be examined first.

[21] JH Baker, *Reports of Sir John Spelman* 94 Selden Society 56.

[22] See too *Lord Grey's Case* (n 18), where the language of *causa* is used.

[23] See especially Simpson (n 12) 327–74. But Simpson missteps in concluding that the content of consideration was necessarily the same as the conception. But *cf Sidenham v Worthington* (1585) 2 Leon 224, where Periam J defined consideration in assumpsit as 'some cause or meritorious occasion requiring a mutual recompense, in fact or in law', taken from *Calthorpe's Case* (1574) Dyer 334, a case dealing with uses.

[24] Much of the evidence for what follows is derived from a careful study of manuscript law reports and court records. I have tried not to overburden the footnotes with these. Further references can be found in my 'Consideration and the Theory of Contract' in JL Barton (ed), *Towards a General Law of Contract* (Berlin, Dunker & Humblot, 1990) 67.

[25] *Manwood v Burston* (1588) 2 Leon 203.

Perhaps the most difficult question facing the emergent action of assumpsit in the first half of the sixteenth century was whether it could be brought where an action of debt would have lain.[26] The orthodox answer was that it could not: the action on the case, of which assumpsit was a variety, was in theory a purely residual action which could not be brought if another action was available. Litigants, however, wanted to be able to use assumpsit in place of debt, since in debt the defendant could simply swear that the money was not owed (supported by oath helpers whose function was purely symbolic), while in assumpsit trial had to be by jury. In 1532, a majority of the King's Bench had held that the cause of action in assumpsit, the breach of the promise, was different from the contract which was the cause of action in debt,[27] but the reasoning here was open to challenge, and within a few years the practice had developed of basing assumpsit on a promise – for the King's Bench, by the 1550s, even a fictitious promise[28] – made after the time of the contract which created the debt. This was precisely the situation which had arisen in *Marler v Wilmer* in 1539,[29] where one of the grounds for the writ of error was that there was no *causa*. Edmund Plowden, probably the most able lawyer of the early years of Queen Elizabeth's reign, made the same point, that there was no consideration, in 1567, but these questions were avoided, culminating in Altham's statement that the precedent debt was itself consideration.

Probably the correct response to Plowden's doubts was that consideration was not needed. The function of consideration was to ground liability rather than as a purely formal requirement of the action of assumpsit; and, where the promise was to pay a pre-existing debt, liability by definition existed already. These cases, known as indebitatus assumpsit, differed from other cases, which were known as collateral assumpsit, in a number of procedural respects, most notably when it was ruled that the promise had to be separate from the underlying debt in indebitatus assumpsit, whereas in collateral assumpsit this was fatal. However, for all the procedural differences, both sub-types of assumpsit were aspects of the same action, and the simplest course was to say that the precedent debt itself constituted consideration, notwithstanding that its nature was completely different from other types of consideration.

B. The Core of Consideration

Practically all discussions of the nature of consideration arose where there was no precedent indebtedness. In James Altham's terms, these were the detriment suffered by the promisee and the 'present consideration', which we take to be the benefit to the promisor. The second of these was the more basic, the equivalent of the quid pro quo of the action of debt. The repeated allegations of the payment of a few pence 'pro' the defendant's promise reveal this in the formative years of the doctrine; and it is the clear core

[26] Ibbetson, 'Assumpsit and Debt' (n 20). Assumpsit could never be brought where the debt had arisen out of a sealed deed, but here the procedure in the action of debt was very favourable to the plaintiff, so there was no reason to use assumpsit as a substitute.

[27] *Pykeryng v Thurgoode* (1532) 93 Selden Society 4, Baker, *Baker and Milsom* (n 6) 452.

[28] *Note* (1559) 110 Selden Society 420, ibid 456.

[29] See n 20 above.

of consideration in *Lord Grey's Case* in 1567.[30] The detriment to the promisee emerged, probably around 1570, as a parallel form of consideration, a generalised form of the promise to a physician to pay for the treatment of a poor person, which one of the judges in *Alice's Case* had argued fell within quid pro quo and which had been incorporated in this generalised form in St German's *Doctor and Student*.[31] It was perhaps easier to expand consideration than it might have been to expand the quid pro quo of debt: apart from the fact that there was the terminological ambiguity of consideration, there might also have been an element of thinking that the induced detriment as the motive for the promise was equivalent to the loss suffered which might have been enough to justify the use of trespass on the case in its delictual aspect.[32] That said, from the 1570s, the induced detriment married with the benefit consideration, resulting in a strong element of reciprocity between the promisor and promisee. Oliver Wendell Holmes wrote of consideration and promise as 'reciprocal conventional inducements':[33] the promise was given for the consideration, and the consideration for the promise.

Crucial to this idea of consideration was that it should have been of some value. This is revealed in many situations in the case law of the late sixteenth and early seventeenth centuries.[34] Where the consideration was expressed as a forbearance to sue the promisor for a period, it was essential that an action might have been brought in this period; it was argued, therefore, that where the forbearance period fell outside the law terms, it was not sufficient since no action could have been commenced, but this was countered by pointing out that an action might have been brought in a local court. Clearly, the forbearance was not of value if it was only for a minute or quarter of an hour, from which it followed that a forbearance described as being 'for a short time' would not be enough – though less rigorous lawyers were willing to treat it as acceptable if the promisee had in fact forborne for a sufficiently long period. Similar problems arose where the consideration was to do what one was already legally bound to do; in principle, this was insufficient – unless it could be said that the receipt of the actual performance was more valuable than merely having a right that the other party perform. That there was more than a little pedantry in the assessment of value shows just how central an idea it was. If nothing was (broadly) given in exchange for the promise, it was a *nudum pactum, ex quo non oritur actio*.

That there needed to be some benefit does not mean that the value of the consideration had to be equivalent to the value of the promise. Rastell's *Expositio Terminorum*[35] had said expressly that a penny was sufficient quid pro quo for a debt of £20, and it was repeated in the context of assumpsit that it was no part of the court's responsibility to assess the value of the consideration, so long as it had some value.[36] The only qualification here was that where the court was persuaded that the literal meaning of the words of the consideration was different from the substance which had been intended, they might refuse to enter judgment for the plaintiff until they were satisfied that the

[30] See n 18 above.
[31] See n 9 above.
[32] JB Ames, *Lectures in Legal History* (Cambridge, MA, Harvard University Press, 1913) 147.
[33] *The Common Law* (first published 1881, reprinted Cambridge, MA, Harvard University Press, 2009) 265.
[34] For details, see Ibbetson, 'Consideration and the Theory of Contract' (n 24) 74–83.
[35] (1525) *sub verb* Contract.
[36] *Knight v Rushworth* (1596) Cro El 469 (Anderson CJ).

economic substance had been performed. In *Lord Mordaunt's Case*,[37] for example, there was a promise to pay £300 in consideration that the promisee made an assurance of certain lands; after a verdict for the plaintiff, the court refused to enter judgment until it was satisfied that the assurance which had been made had in fact operated to give the promisor an interest in the land.

The requirement that the consideration be of value meant that some easily recognisable motives were not regarded as sufficient to create an actionable obligation. Most important was the 'natural love and affection' which the promisor had for the promisee, as where a father made a gratuitous promise to pay money or transfer property to his son. This was made clear in *Sharrington v Strotton* in 1565, as the nature of consideration settled into its classical form.[38] There was, however, an apparent inconsistency here, for it was held in the Court of Chancery that natural love and affection was sufficient basis for a use or trust, and that such a use or trust could be enforced by the beneficiary.[39] The argument that the consideration for a promise and the consideration to raise a use should be the same was emphatically rejected in *Sharrington v Strotton*, casting light on the problems that might arise in English law, where the 'equity' of the Chancery produced different results from the common law.[40]

Cases of marriage consideration, where money or other property was promised by a bride's father to her future husband, might have been expected to create problems; but, in practice, they did not. There were sufficient hints in the fifteenth-century yearbooks that the marriage here constituted quid pro quo[41] for it to be arguable that by analogy it must constitute consideration. If need be, it could always be said that the father benefited from the marriage, presumably since he no longer had to support his daughter;[42] or that it was a charge to her husband.[43] It was held sufficient that even if the promise had been made after the marriage, the benefit or charge continued.[44] At first, a promise by a stranger in consideration of marriage was said not to be enforceable as there was no benefit to him, though even this came to be explained as being a charge to the husband or by analogy with the enforcement of charitable promises in the fifteenth-century action of debt.[45] It is hard to avoid the impression that these promises were expected to be enforceable, with the explanation why they were enforceable being little more than ex post facto justification.

The requirement that the promise and consideration must each be the cause of the other affected the chronological relationship between them. They had to be parts of the same bargain. It was easy when the performance of the consideration was

[37] (1602) Cambridge University Library MS Ee 3.45, fol 7v.

[38] Plo 298.

[39] See n 54 below.

[40] See further section V below.

[41] See n 9 above. It could still be asserted in the 16th century that this was the case: *Applethwait v Nertley* (1591) Cro El 229, 4 Leon 56.

[42] *Sidenham v Worthington* (1585) 2 Leon 224, Godb 31, Cro El 42; *Beaucamp v Neggin* (1592) Cro El 282; *Harford v Gardiner* (1589) 2 Leon 30.

[43] *Freeman v Freeman* (1614) 1 Rolle 61.

[44] *Hunt v Bate* (1568) Dyer 272, Baker, *Baker and Milsom* (n 6) 529; *Halifax v Barker* (1600) Cro El 741. *cf Marsh v Rainsford* (1588) 2 Leon 611.

[45] *Harford v Gardiner* (1589) 2 Leon 30; *Brown v Garborough* (1588) Goulds 94, Cro El 63; *Whitehead v Attenbridge* (1598) Harvard Law School MS 118b, fol 11.

contemporaneous with the promise, as where they were linked together by the word 'pro'; but such cases were in fact not common. More commonly, the consideration would fall to be performed in the future, in consideration that the promisee would do something. In the pleadings when bringing the action, the promisee would state that the consideration had been performed, thereby establishing the mutuality between consideration and promise.[46] A variant form of this would express the consideration as a promise, hence envisaging a future performance. Provided the consideration-promise was enforceable, and what was promised had value, it was good consideration, and there was no need for performance of the promise to be alleged: consideration and promise were transparently parts of the same bargain.[47] Past consideration, though, was not enough, even if the promise had been motivated by the consideration. The consideration would not have been motivated by the promise: 'it is not any consideration, for he who promised has nothing for his promise'.[48] This was subject to an exception, where the past consideration had been performed at the request of the promisor.[49] The request, it was said, created the necessary link of mutuality between consideration and promise. This made it easy to deal with the situation where one person had worked for another in the expectation of payment, but the amount of the payment had only been fixed later. More importantly, the ability to frame the action in terms of a past consideration on request made it possible to use the same form of pleading in indebitatus assumpsit, where the consideration – the indebtedness – had to be past and collateral assumpsit (where it had not to be). This was an enormous advantage to litigants and their lawyers, since it made it unnecessary to decide whether the antecedent agreement and performance had in fact generated a debt.

V. Contracts in the Chancery

The Court of Chancery had emerged in the fifteenth century, alongside the courts of common law. It was not constrained by the substantive or procedural rules of the common law, so could achieve different results from those which could be achieved at common law. Although the records of the court's decrees and orders only survive from the second quarter of the sixteenth century, the mass of surviving petitions from the fifteenth century enable us to reach provisional conclusions about its activity, on the assumption that a series of petitions on similar alleged facts suggests that the court might have been expected to grant a remedy if those facts were proved. On this basis, there is some evidence that the Chancery might enforce simple gratuitous promises.[50] By the sixteenth century, it seems that the Chancery would require consideration, a rule which was most obviously visible in terms of the creation of uses or trusts of land,[51] but which

[46] *Rogers v Snow* (1573) Dal 94; *Anon* (1582) Godb 13; *Lee v Exelby* (1602) Cro El 888.

[47] eg *West v Stowel* (1578) 2 Leon 154: Baker, *Baker and Milsom* (n 6) 529. Problems might arise where it was envisaged that only one of the mutual promises was intended to become actionable, as in bets or promises to perform arbitration awards.

[48] *Boycott v Gowchman* (1595) Cro El 442, Cambridge University Library MS Ii 5.25, fol 12.

[49] *Hunt v Bate* (1568) Dyer 272; *Sidenham v Worthington* (1585) 2 Leon 224, Godb 31, Cro El 42.

[50] WT Barbour, *The History of Contract in Early English Equity* (Oxford, Clarendon Press, 1914) 163, no 7.

[51] See n 23 above.

probably represents a general understanding. The corollary was that where property was purportedly transferred without consideration, the court would order it to be retransferred to the grantor, the so-called resulting use or resulting trust.[52] 'Consideration' here, though, meant something different from 'consideration' at common law, though it had similar features.[53] What was required was convincing evidence of motive, which would negative any supposition that the promise or agreement was vitiated by error. Hence, that the beneficiary of a promise was a relative, the consideration of blood or 'natural love and affection', though insufficient consideration in assumpsit at common law, was sufficient in the equity of the Chancery.[54]

VI. Indebitatus Assumpsit: The Common Counts

The strict indebitatus count, in the form of 'Defendant, being indebted to plaintiff, promised to pay plaintiff', had a number of advantages. At first, it was argued that all that was necessary was to say that the defendant was indebted, but in the early seventeenth century it was established that it was essential to say how the plaintiff had become indebted, so as to avoid the possibility that the debt had arisen out of a sealed deed or some other transaction which could not be the basis of an action of assumpsit.[55] Still, though, it was only necessary to identify the type of transaction, for example 'for goods sold and delivered, for work done or the like',[56] contrasting with what came to be known as 'special assumpsit', where the consideration had to be described in detail.[57] It was necessary to prove that there had been a debt which had arisen in the way outlined, but an overstatement of the amount owed was not fatal, so a jury verdict that a lesser sum than had been claimed was owed justified judgment for the plaintiff.[58] Wherever there was a debt, provided it was not on a deed (or an enrolled recognisance) or for rent, assumpsit would lie, though the most frequently encountered situations generated standard forms of pleading, known as common counts (including one 'for the use and occupation of land', given by statute in 1738 to remedy the lack of indebitatus assumpsit for rent). Analogous forms, where there was an ascertainable sum but no debt was created, developed: counts for what the plaintiff deserved (*quantum meruit*) or what goods were worth (*quantum valebant*) came into being, but they fell out of use since it was simpler to claim a fixed sum representing the maximum the plaintiff might hope to get, leaving the jury to reduce it as they saw fit.

The most obvious feature of indebitatus assumpsit was its simplicity, raising almost no legal issues on the pleadings. So far as consideration was concerned, if the debt had arisen out of a contract, consideration must have existed in the form of the quid

[52] NG Jones, 'Uses and Automatic Resulting Trusts of Freehold' [2013] *CLJ* 91.
[53] 117 Selden Society 172, 117-3.
[54] ibid 117-[251].
[55] *Woodford v Deacon* (1608) Cro Jac 206, Baker, *Baker and Milsom* (n 6) 499.
[56] E Lawes, *Practical Treatise on Pleading in Assumpsit* (London, 1810) 421–42.
[57] See section VII below.
[58] *Baker v Edmonds* (1647) Aleyn 28.

pro quo received by the debtor.[59] Moreover, normally, no debt would arise until the consideration had actually been performed,[60] again removing potentially difficult questions from the purview of indebitatus assumpsit. We may think of these as the easy cases of contractual liability, cases which provided an effective and efficient remedy without fuelling any conceptual development in the law: the pressures for development emerged in marginal cases excluded from indebitatus assumpsit.

VII. Special Assumpsit

What was known as collateral assumpsit in the sixteenth century came, in time, to be known as special assumpsit. Here, the agreement was laid out in detail, ending with the defendant's promise to perform and the breach. In these cases, since everything was specified, there was the possibility of greater conceptual sharpness and hence the possibility of conceptual development. This development began in the eighteenth century.

The impetus for the change without doubt came from the growth of the natural law school in Germany in the later seventeenth century, especially through the work of Samuel Pufendorf. His *De Jure Naturae et Gentium* was translated into English in 1704, reaching a fifth English edition in 1729. If nothing else, the number of editions published points to its popularity in England. Pufendorf's theory was an essentially promissory theory, traceable back through Thomas Aquinas to Aristotle, based on the virtue of keeping promises.[61] Pufendorf's theory, and even some of his language, was reflected in what might be thought of as the first treatment of the law of contract published in England, the material on contract in the *Treatise on Equity* attributed to Henry Ballow printed in 1737. It was not every promise that generated an obligation, but only promises that had been accepted, thereby erecting a scaffolding of bilateral agreement on a foundation of unilateral promise. Contractual theory, therefore, was based on the act of will of the party or parties. There was no place in Pufendorf's theory for any idea of bargain consideration, so Ballow's treatment of this aspect is based purely on English law rather than on Pufendorf.[62] Written a few years before Ballow, Jeffrey Gilbert's unprinted *Treatise on Property and Contract* had similarly tried to reconcile a treatment of contract as something created by the mutual wills of the parties with the doctrine of consideration, but to do this consideration had to be more or less transformed into evidence of a serious intention to be bound.[63]

The friction between the newer will theory and the older idea of agreed exchange was not the only difficulty in maintaining the idea of consideration. More importantly,

[59] See n 16 above.

[60] Sale of goods was an apparent exception to this. Since the middle of the 14th century, it had been held that property in the goods sold passed at the moment of the agreement (D Ibbetson, 'Sale of Goods in the Fourteenth Century' (1991) 107 *LQR* 480), allowing an action of debt and hence indebitatus assumpsit 'for goods bargained and sold' to be brought.

[61] J Gordley, *Philosophical Origins of Modern Contract Doctrine* (Oxford, Clarendon Press, 1991).

[62] For Ballow's reliance on Pufendorf, see D Ibbetson, *Historical Introduction to the Law of Obligations* (Oxford, Oxford University Press, 1999) 218–19.

[63] M Lobban, *Gilbert on Property and Contract* 134 Selden Society clvii–clxiii.

in practice, the exchange model as it had developed by the sixteenth century did not easily cohere with more modern mercantile practice. The first situation in which the requirement of consideration was watered down was the bill of exchange.[64] If A owed money to B and drew a bill on C, instructing C to pay B, on C's acceptance of the bill, B could bring an action against C. At first, the pleadings would be formulated so as to allege a consideration between B and C, but by the early seventeenth century it could be alleged simply that by 'the custom of exchange amongst merchants used' B could bring an action against C once he had accepted the bill. Still, at this time, the contract between A and B was laid out in the pleadings, but by the middle of the seventeenth century this was no longer necessary: all that was needed was to say that the custom of merchants allowed an action against the acceptor, and by the end of the century this allegation was no more than a very simple formality. The practice might have been for the bill to state on its face 'for value received', but it was held in the King's Bench in 1729 that even these words were unnecessary.[65] It later came to be said that consideration was presumed,[66] a fig leaf to cover up that there was no consideration. A second form of document in use by merchants was the promissory note.[67] Here, there was nothing more than a promise to pay, signed by the promisor, with no semblance of consideration. Early in the eighteenth century, Holt CJ expostulated that if these were to be enforced it would be 'setting up a new form of specialty, unknown to the common law, and invented in Lombard Street'.[68] But Holt's judgments were reversed by statute in 1703,[69] ensuring that promissory notes constituted a new class of contractual document, enforceable without consideration. Another situation was the letter of credit,[70] where a bank would let it be known, or perhaps promise, that they would accept bills drawn on them by a particular person. Once accepted, they were straightforward bills of exchange, but it was open to question whether an action would lie if the bank had promised to accept but was in fact unable to do so. Such a situation arose in *Pillans v van Mierop*,[71] where the drawer of the bill had gone bankrupt by the time the bill was presented for acceptance and the bank therefore refused to accept it. An action was brought by the payee of the bill against the bank. The action succeeded. The easiest justification for this was that there was consideration, insofar as it could be said that the payee (who would typically have provided the credit to the drawer) had acted on the faith of the bank's promise,[72] but the court went further. According to Lord Mansfield CJ, merchants' contracts in writing should be enforced even if there was no consideration; Wilmot J would go further still and

[64] J H Baker, 'The Law Merchant and the Common Law before 1600' [1979] *CLJ* 295, 308–10; J S Rogers, *The Early History of the Law of Bills and Notes* (Cambridge, Cambridge University Press, 1995) 127–37.

[65] *Eveskyn v Merry* (1729) 1 Barn 87.

[66] Bills of Exchange Act 1882, ss 2(4) and 30.

[67] Rogers, *Early History of Bills and Notes* (Cambridge, Cambridge University Press, 1995) 177–86.

[68] *Clerke v Martin* (1702) 2 Lord Raym 757; see also *Buller v Crips* (1703) 6 Mod 29.

[69] Stat 3 & 4 Anne c 9.

[70] Rogers, *Early History of Bills and Notes* (Cambridge, Cambridge University Press, 1995) 199–201.

[71] (1765) 3 Burr 1663. Ibbetson, *Historical Introduction* (n 62) 204–96; Swain, *Law of Contract 1670–1870* (Cambridge, Cambridge University Press, 2015) 90–93; J Oldham, *English Common Law in the Age of Mansfield* (Chapel Hill, University of North Carolina Press, 2004) 84–86.

[72] So letters of credit continued to be enforceable, notwithstanding the rejection of the more extreme aspects of the judgment in *Pillans v van Mierop*. For the later history, see M Lobban, *Oxford History of the Laws of England*, vol XII (Oxford, Oxford University Press, 2010) 754–58.

say that all written contracts, whether or not between merchants, should be enforced even in the absence of consideration. A few years later, Lord Mansfield repeated the view that written agreements, signed by the parties, were enforceable, clearly grounding this on the centrality of the parties' wills,[73] but in the event, this was a step too far, and in *Rann v Hughes*, the House of Lords reasserted the traditional model of exchange consideration.[74]

The doctrine of consideration as exchange was locked in place after *Rann v Hughes*.[75] It was asserted, and defended, through the nineteenth century. In the leading case of *Eastwood v Kenyon*,[76] for example, Lord Denman CJ expressly denied Lord Mansfield's suggestion that all deliberately intended promises created binding obligations, saying that a moral obligation to do something did not automatically generate a legal obligation to do it, even if supported by an express promise to do so. But by the middle of the century, the courts were clear that they would not examine the sufficiency of the consideration. So, in *Brooks v Haigh*,[77] Lord Abinger CB was willing to hold that the handing over of a worthless piece of paper – worthless here because the guarantee it embodied was void – was sufficient consideration. Other cases of the time reinforced the point that any value, however small, was sufficient consideration.[78] Such nominal considerations might easily degenerate into fictions, as had happened in the sixteenth century.[79] Also, in some cases, the courts were inclined to discover consideration where none was visible on the facts as pleaded. In *Shadwell v Shadwell*,[80] for example, an uncle had written to his nephew on his forthcoming marriage promising to pay him £150 per year during his (the uncle's) lifetime. The uncle paid the £150 each year for 12 years, but paid only a small amount in the thirteenth year and nothing for the next five years, at which point he died. The nephew brought an action against his executor for the unpaid arrears. For all that could be seen, and as Byles J held, this was a 'mere kindness', a promise to make a gift; and although the uncle's payment for 12 years showed it was seriously intended, there was nothing in the way of orthodox consideration. Erle CJ and Keating J disagreed: they interpreted the facts as constituting an inducement to the nephew to marry, which might have been a benefit to the uncle, and this was good consideration. Similarly, in *Hicks v Gregory*,[81] the father of an illegitimate child promised to pay the mother £100 per year. As in *Shadwell v Shadwell*, the payment was regularly made until the death of the father, clearly evidencing the seriousness with which it was made. The action was brought after his death, against his executor. The court accepted that, as pleaded, this was in consideration that the mother 'behaved herself' – that she did not engage in what might have been seen as immoral conduct – and so constituted good consideration, though the evidence that this was the father's

[73] *Williamson v Losh* (1775) in Oldham (n 71) 85–86.
[74] (1778) 4 Bro PC, 7 TR 350.
[75] For the 19th century, see Lobban, *Oxford History* (n 72) 358–90.
[76] (1840) 11 Ad & El 438, 450–51; it was still firmly statable in *Dunlop Pneumatic Tyre Co Ltd v Selfridge & Co Ltd* [1915] AC 847, 855.
[77] (1840) 10 Ad & El 323, 334, upholding the decision of Lord Denman CJ at first instance.
[78] Lobban, *Oxford History* (n 72) 373.
[79] See n 18 above.
[80] (1861) 30 LJCP 145.
[81] (1849) 19 LJCP 81.

intention was very thin. As in *Shadwell v Shadwell*, the court went to great pains to discover the consideration, whatever the evidence showed.[82]

The nineteenth-century treatise writers tried to explain the doctrine of consideration at the same time as saying that contract depended on the will of the parties. They did so by saying, as Gilbert had done,[83] that it was evidence of seriousness of intent.[84] But this left a gaping hole in the legal conceptualisation: that consideration was evidence of seriousness of intent did not remotely entail that it was the only possible evidence of intent. And once English law had come to recognise the separate requirement of an intention to create legal relations,[85] it became hard to see any independent doctrinal value to consideration.

VIII. Conclusions

By the end of the nineteenth century, consideration had become an empty shell of its former self. The model of contract based on agreed exchanges had been superseded by a model based on giving effect to the will of the parties. Mercantile contracts had been hived off into a separate category of 'commercial law', where the clear intention of the parties could be upheld. The exchange idea of consideration survived within the general law of contract, but its substance had been eaten away by the acceptability of nominal consideration and the inventiveness of judges in discovering consideration despite the lack of evidence, and text writers could marginalise its significance by seeing it as evidence of serious intention to be bound; moreover, the recognition of the need for there to be an intention to create legal relations deprived the doctrine of consideration of any gatekeeper function in excluding from legal protection simple domestic promises. More to the point, a gratuitous undertaking could be rendered enforceable by the use of a deed, requiring no more than the use of writing with an increasingly minimal formalism and, until 2003, the payment of a tax in the form of stamp duty.[86] By this time too, the Court of Chancery had shown itself willing to give effect to gratuitous undertakings, provided that these satisfied the formal requirements for the creation of a trust,[87] including the use of writing. In addition, the Chancery was beginning to explore the use of ideas of estoppel to give effect to (some) gratuitous undertakings on which the beneficiary had relied to his detriment.[88] It was only the inherent conservatism of the common law and its treatise writers, ever reluctant to abolish a rule which had long outlived its usefulness, that was keeping consideration nominally in its place.

[82] See also *Bainbridge v Firmstone* (1838) 8 Ad & El 743, where the court was willing to assume that the consideration must have been of value to the defendant or he would not have promised.

[83] See n 63 above.

[84] J Chitty, *Practical Treatise on the Law of Contracts*, 2nd edn (London, S Sweet, 1834) 23; Addison, *Contract* (London, W Benning & Co, 1847) 17–18; SM Leake, *Elements of the Law of Contracts* (London, Stevens, 1867) 310.

[85] Ibbetson, *Historical Introduction* (n 62) 233. It first appeared in the textbooks in 1876, explicitly derived from Savigny: Pollock, *Principles of Contract* (London, Stevens, 1876) 2.

[86] Finance Act 2003, part 4.

[87] S Anderson, *Oxford History* (n 72) 256–57.

[88] *Ramsden v Dyson* (1868) LR 1 HL 129.

4

The Rise of the Concept of Cause: Its Codification and Interpretation in France, Italy and Spain (1804–1900)

DAVID DEROUSSIN

The word 'cause' is undoubtedly one of the most polysemous terms in legal language. In Roman law, it was sometimes used to designate the operative facts giving rise to an obligation (*cause efficiente*, in French). These facts were called *causa civilis* when they gave rise to a civil obligation (D. 15,1,49,2) or *causa naturalis* when they gave rise to a natural obligation (D. 2,2,3,7). To the generating facts identified by Gaius (*delictus/contractus*) and then Justinian, Roman law added the service already performed by one the parties (a *datio* or a *factum*), as in the case of innominate contracts, where the performance was considered as the equivalent of the *causa civilis*, able to transform a *pactum* into a *contractus*. At other times, *causa* rather referred to the economic and legal aim the parties wanted to accomplish. For example, the stipulation whose legal purpose was to constitute a dowry for the benefit of the husband was called *stipulatio dotis causa*. Here, *causa* was, in a sense, future-oriented, not past-oriented. These different meanings are still present in the medieval commentaries on the *Corpus iuris civilis*,[1] through the distinction made between the *causa civilis* as the efficient cause of an obligation (in the *pactum cum causa* doctrine) and the *causa* as the *causa finalis*.[2] This distinction was also adopted by the legal doctrine of the Modern Times. As explained by Vinnius, for example, the *causa finalis* is either the intention to give (in donations) or the consideration for which one obliges himself (a thing or a service), but not the personal reason why one agrees. However, the legal doctrine of the Modern Times did not necessarily put the cause at the centre of the very definition of the contract. Scholars of that time (as was the case, in the Germanic

[1] See M Schermaier, 'Die Rolle der causa bei der Überwindung des Typenzwangs durch die mittelalterlichen Juristen' in G Albers, FP Patti and D Perrouin-Verbe (eds), *Causa contractus* (Tübingen, Mohr Siebeck, 2022) 97–152. See also T dalla Massara, 'Come nasce un'idea: la causa del contratto' (2013) 2 *Legal Roots, The International Journal of Roman Law* 353.

[2] See J Gordley, *The Enforceability of Promises in European Contract Law* (Cambridge, Cambridge University Press, 2004) 5; K Kowalski, 'Die causa des Vertrages im Naturrecht der frühen Neuzeit' in Albers et al (n 1) 153–200.

area, of the seventeenth and eighteenth centuries treaties, in which the absence of cause is often compared to a defect in the consent)[3] do not systematically treat the cause as an autonomous requirement for the validity of the contract distinct from the consent or the object. In this respect, Donellus and Vinnius are exceptions. Donellus lists, in a formula which almost announces Article 1108 of the 1804 French Civil Code (CC), the conditions necessary for the validity of contracts in a way that includes, in addition to the *conventio* (considered as the efficient cause of the contract) and the completion of certain formalities (when required by law: *forma obligationis*), what he calls 'finis dandi, acquirendique'. Vinnius considers the *causa finalis* as an element that comes *praeter consensum*, so that the *causa finalis* is not part of the consent, but something distinct from it.[4] The doctrine of natural law also insists on the idea that an agreement, in order to be binding and lawful, must be reasonable, and that a reasonable agreement implies that the parties commit themselves in view of a consideration. Both Grotius (*De iure belli* II, XII) and Pufendorf (*De iure natura* V, XI, IX) are clear on this issue: the reasonable will that is necessary for the formation of the contract consists in making a sacrifice of such a nature that it does not consist of a pure loss. The reasoning is based on what they both call the principle of equality: in onerous contracts, this principle requires everyone to do or give with a view of receiving something in return. However, neither Grotius nor Pufendorf really refers to the technical concept of cause as an autonomous condition. Following in the footsteps of Grotius and Pufendorf, Heineccius[5] also does not explicitly mention the cause in connection with the conditions required for the validity of agreements, citing only the consent, a determined object and, sometimes, forms.

What did contemporary French legal doctrine teach? From the sixteenth century onwards, two trends clearly emerged in France. On the one hand, uncaused *instrumenta* (the written documents that can constitute proof of an obligation) are deemed valid, which means that the cause does not have to be expressly mentioned. On the other hand, any obligation (as a substantive right) must have a cause, and this cause, disconnected from the personal psychology of individuals (Pothier clearly states that a mistake as to the personal motives does not invalidate contracts, just as it does not invalidate legacies),[6] varies according to whether the contract is a unilateral or onerous contract. On this point, both Domat and Pothier agree: Domat clearly distinguishes onerous contracts (ie commutative contracts, which he classifies using the categories designed in Ancient Rome regarding innominate contracts) from unilateral contracts, which shows that the definition of the concept of cause depends on the general economy of the contract. But did they really share the same definition of *la cause*? Regarding unilateral contracts, the answer is yes. Dealing with the category of unilateral contracts, Domat isolates the donation from other unilateral contracts, to say that, in the donation, the will of the donor must have been moved by a reasonable and just reason ('un motif raisonnable et juste'), which may be the desire to reward a service rendered or the sole pleasure of doing good (it is significant that Domat does not use

[3] See, eg J Borcholten, *De Obligationibus et Actionibus Tractatus utilissimus* (Helmaestadi, 1599).
[4] A Vinnius, *Tractatus de pactis*, VIII, 7 (in *Tractatus quinque …*, Venice, 1780).
[5] *Elementa juris naturae et gentium*, 1764, I, XIV.
[6] RJ Pothier, *Traité des obligations* (Paris, Bechet Ainé, 1824) para 20.

the words *animus donandi*). A remunerative donation can therefore be considered as a true donation only if what is given could not be demanded of the donor.[7] If this *motif* really pushed the donor to divest himself, then it operates as a cause ('il tient lieu de cause') and gives the donor's commitment its 'fondement'. This motive may be expressed in the *instrumentum* or not; and when an erroneous motive is mentioned in the *instrumentum*, the donation remains no less valid, because the will to give may have had other reasons than those mentioned. Pothier is more concise, but he says the same: the cause of the donor's obligation consists in his sole will to give without return (the donor prefers the donee to himself, as he explains).[8] In his *Traité des donations*, he calls *libéralité* this will to give.

But when it comes to bilateral contracts, their way of understanding the concept of cause seem to diverge. Bilateral contracts are, says Domat,[9] the legal form of a trade (an exchange) 'où rien n'est gratuity' (in which nothing is free), and in which the commitment (*l'engagement*) of one of the parties serves as a basis (*fondement*) for that of the other. This commitment is precisely what Domat calls *la cause*. In the sales contract, for example, the seller 'gives a thing in exchange of a monetary prize', and the buyer seeks to acquire in order to 'have' and 'possess' the goods.[10] The 'fondement' of an obligation thus consists of the legal effects that the contract (and all contracts of the same kind) allows to be achieved, and not in personal reasons (which, in the example of the sales contract, can vary from one buyer or seller to another). Basically, it is a way of saying that the will is only legally effective if it wants something which represents an interest for the individual and which the legal order admits as being the typical economic function of the contract. Pothier takes a more empirical approach. In his *Traité des obligations*, he mentions the cause for the first time when he defines the obligation: every obligation arises from a cause.[11] Here, he is talking about the efficient cause, *causa obligandi*. Then, he mentions the cause in the chapter devoted to the factors that can void a contract. Alongside error, fraud and violence, he deals here with what he calls 'the lack of cause in the commitment' (*le défaut de cause dans l'engagement*).[12] Two points should be noted here. First, the word 'cause' designates what medieval scholars called the *causa finalis*. This cause, he says, is what the other party gives or undertakes to give, or the risk he assumes.[13] The words used to describe the cause ('ce que l'autre partie lui donne') indeed seem to refer to the thing, the service itself, concretely understood (this may be the reason why Pothier does not refer to the concept of cause when it comes to explaining the termination of the contract for non-performance).[14] Second, to deal with the *cause finale* in relation to defects of consent means that the issue raised by this concept is

[7] J Domat, *Les Loix civiles dans leur ordre naturel* (Paris, 1766) I,X,I,V.
[8] Pothier, *Traité des donations*, para 11, in C Bugnet, *Œuvres de M Pothier*, vol VIII (Paris, 1890) 350.
[9] Domat (n 7) I,I,I,IV.
[10] ibid I,II,II,I.
[11] Pothier, *Traité des obligations* (n 6) para 2.
[12] ibid para 16.
[13] ibid para 41.
[14] ibid para 672. Pothier bases the resolution for non-performance on the existence of an express or tacit resolutory condition (in bilateral contracts), while Domat is content to say that the non-performance of the contract on the part of one of the parties can give rise to the resolution, without seeking to base this resolution on the idea of a tacit resolutory clauss, Domat (n 7) I,I,VI,XI).

only an aspect of the more general problem of the validity of consent. This explains why Pothier does not give a formal list of the conditions required for the validity of conventions equivalent to that of the future Article 1108 CC of 1804: in his eyes, the cause, unlike the object (studied in another chapter of the *Traité*), is not to be considered as an autonomous condition.

So, regarding onerous contracts, the Ancient French legal doctrine did not speak with one voice: some assimilate the cause into the expected thing to be transferred or service to be rendered, others equate the cause with the legal relationship created by the contract between the parties, as if *la cause* was the legal effect produced by the contract, the economic-legal function that it fulfils. Despite these divergences, which moreover the drafters of the CC do not mention, the 1804 CC is, among the modern European codifications, the first that formally includes the concept of cause in the list of the essential conditions for the validity of contracts.[15] The 1865 Italian Civil Code (ICC), which does not really differ from its French model, follows the same path, as does the 1889 Spanish Civil Code (SCC). However, with the exception of the SCC, these codes do not define this concept, so that the scholars' imagination has been given free rein, no doubt because of its *excessive generality*, which makes its meaning *obscure and equivocal*,[16] to such an extent that, in Spain, Bustos Pueche still asserted in 1990 that searching for the meaning of the word *causa* is an obscure and difficult task.[17] The aim of this chapter is therefore to give an account of the way in which the provisions of these codes have been interpreted with a view to formulating an operative concept of cause, from 1804 to the end of the nineteenth century. To choose this end date seems legitimate insofar as, at that time, considering the cause as a specific condition really starts to be challenged and leads either to the renunciation of it being seen as a specific condition (German Bürgerliches Gesetzbuch, BGB) or to the rethinking of the notion in a way that is then presented as more objective. For legal historians (in France, Italy and Spain), and a large part of the legal doctrine as well, such an evolution (from a subjective conception to an objective conception) almost constitutes a master narrative. This master narrative should, however, be challenged.

I. The Provisions of the Codes

That the requirement of a cause should be raised to the level of a condition for the validity of a contract in addition to the exchange of consent relating to a lawful object is not self-evident. Both before (Roman law) and after 1804 (the 1867 Portuguese Civil Code, BGB), many legal systems did not and do not require such a condition, which does not prevent them from assessing the social or moral value of a contract. Yet this is the choice made in France, Italy and Spain.

[15] See D Deroussin, *Histoire du droit des obligations* (Paris, Economica, 2012); AM Garofalo, 'Itinerari della causa dal Code civil del 1804 al Codice civile del 1942' in Albers et al (n 1) 201–46.

[16] CBM Toullier, *Le droit civil français*, vol VI (Paris, Warée, 1824) 170.

[17] J-E Bustos Pueche, 'El derecho civil español en materia de obligaciones y contratos' (1990) 48 *Estudios de Derecho* 154.

A. *La Cause* in the French Civil Code

In the two drafts presented by Cambacérès during the Revolution, the term *la cause* is used only in the sense of efficient cause of the obligation. Of course, only lawful obligations are binding, but *la cause* is not the technical tool by which the lawfulness of the obligation is assessed. Moreover, they do not take the trouble to enumerate, in a special provision, the conditions for the validity of contracts. We have to wait for Cambacérès's speech on the third draft (1796) for the concept of *la cause* to appear, precisely at the moment when Cambacérès quotes the definition of the contract given by Pothier. For the first time, he clearly explains that a cause is required for an agreement to be valid, because a convention without a cause would be a derisive act.[18] But does he really turn the cause into a specific requirement, in addition to consent? It is hard to say, insofar as, having in mind only bilateral contracts, he seems to equate *la cause* with the concrete service or the thing due, so that the *la cause* merges with the *objet* of the obligation.

Compared to these drafts, the one submitted by Portalis to the Conseil d'État more clearly requires *la cause* (a lawful cause) as an autonomous condition separate from the consent and the *objet*. The choice thus made by the Napoleonic legislator calls for some remarks. First, most of the French scholars of the seventeenth and eighteenth centuries already claimed that for a contract to be binding a cause is required: 'dans les conventions où quelqu'un se trouve obligé sans aucune cause, l'obligation est nulle', said Domat.[19] But none of them had made the effort to set out all the conditions required for the validity of the agreements in a single summary including the concept of cause, presented as an autonomous condition. It can therefore be said that the wording of Article 1108 CC ('Quatre conditions sont essentielles pour la validité d'une convention: le consentement de la partie qui s'oblige … Une cause licite dans l'obligation') was not directly borrowed from Domat or Pothier, but appears as the result of the Drafting Committee's effort to combine all the requirement for the validity of contracts in a single introductory article for the detailed study of all of these conditions.

Secondly, do the preparatory works for the CC provide any definition of the technical concept of cause? A part of the answer lies in Bigot de Préameneu's words: the *cause* consists in *the reciprocal interest of the parties or in the benevolence of one of them*.[20] Thus, either the cause is given by the contract itself, as is the case for onerous contracts, or it must be sought in the particular state of mind of the person who gives without receiving anything. Favart only adds that one should not confuse an obligation which has no cause with an obligation whose cause is not expressed. In the first case, there is no obligation; in the second, the obligation subsists and is valid if its cause, although not expressed, can be discovered.[21] The preparatory works do not give further detail, as if all this were self-evident. At first sight, it was. As previously noted, Domat and Pothier both agreed that the cause was not to be sought in the psychology of the parties.

[18] PA Fenet, *Recueil complet des travaux préparatoires du Code civil*, vol I (Paris, Videcoq, 1836) 170.

[19] Domat (n 7) I,I,V,XIII. Domat does not give a list of the conditions required for the validity of contracts and was content to mention these conditions successively in the section entitled *Des conventions qui sont nulles dans leur origine*.

[20] Fenet (n 18) XIII, 228.

[21] ibid XIII, 318.

But Domat and Pothier also shared the view that the concept of cause should be designed according to the nature of the contract, whether onerous or charitable, a view the CC does not make its own, at least expressly. Moreover, the CC does not choose between the two different approaches, one abstract and the other more empirical adopted by Domat and Pothier.

Finally, the provisions the CC dedicates to *la cause* clearly show that *la cause* (more than the object, which Article 1108 only requires to be determined) is to serve as a gateway to control the legality and morality of the contract. According to Article 1131 CC, an obligation without a cause or with a false or unlawful cause cannot have any legal effect.[22] According to Article 1132 CC, an agreement is valid even though the cause is not expressed,[23] and Article 1133 provides that a cause is unlawful when it is prohibited by law or when it is contrary to the public policy or *les bonnes mœurs*.[24] To see the technical concept of cause as a means of controlling the contents of the contract is a choice of legal policy that the Italian and Spanish legislators also make.

B. Provisions of the Italian Civil Code (1865)

In 1837, the Civil Code for Sardinia already placed the *causa* among the conditions of validity of the contract and reproduced Articles 1108, 1131 and 1132 CC.[25] As for the 1865 ICC, it reproduces the structure of the CC. First, in Article 1104, it lists the requirements for the validity of contracts (*requisiti essenziali*), including 'una causa lecita per obbligarsi'. Then, in Articles 1119–22, it deals with the obligation without a cause, or based on a false or an illicit cause, in the same way as the CC does.[26] The only difference lies in Article 1121 ICC, borrowed from the Sardinian Code (Article 1223), according to which the existence of the cause is presumed, as long as the opposite is not proven.[27] But none of these articles takes the trouble to define the concept of cause, and the preparatory works (the Minister of Justice's *Relazione* of November 1863, which insists only on the very few innovative rules proposed by the project)[28] do not give any clue. It seems, however, that the Italian legislator conceived the *causa* as a unitary concept, which explains why, unlike the contemporary French legal doctrine, he chose not to design this concept according to the nature of the contract (onerous/gratuitous). This is a choice the Italian legal doctrine will make after 1865, and that the 1851 Spanish draft Code Civil already made.

[22] Art 1131 CC (1804): 'L'obligation sans cause, ou sur une fausse cause, ou sur une cause illicite, ne peut avoir aucun effet'.

[23] Art 1132 CC (1804): 'La convention n'est pas moins valable quoique la cause n'en soit pas exprimée'.

[24] Art 1133 CC (1804): 'La cause est illicite quand elle est prohibée par la loi, quand elle est contraire aux bonnes mœurs ou à l'ordre public'.

[25] Art 1195 of the Sardinian Civil Code (1837) reproduces Art 1108 CC; Art 1221 reproduces Art 1131 CC; and Art 1222 reproduces Art 1132 CC.

[26] Art 1119 reproduces Art 1131 CC. Art 1122 merely underlines, like Art 1133 CC and in the same terms, that a cause contrary to law, morality or public order is not valid. Art 1120 is the simple translation of Art 1132 CC and therefore states that the contract is valid even though the cause is not mentioned.

[27] The sole purpose of this provision is to formulate a rule of evidence, but in doing so, the ICC usefully supplements the regulations put in place by the CC and settles the doctrinal controversy (that arose in France) of whether it is up to the creditor or the debtor to prove the existence or the lawfulness of the cause of the obligation undertaken by the debtor.

[28] *Relazione sul progetto del terzo libro del Codice civile …* (Turin, 1863).

C. Provisions of the Spanish Civil Code (1889)

The real starting point for Spanish civil codification is the 1851 Draft Civil Code, commonly known as the Proyecto Isabelino (the Project), resulting from the work of the General Commission on Codes established in 1843, of which Garcia Goyena was the vice chairman. This project did not come to fruition, but it deserves to be dealt with here, because it is in this project that the original elements that distinguish the SCC from the CC are already to be found (though Spanish scholars writing after the promulgation of the 1889 SCC readily acknowledge the influence of the CC on the drafters of the 1851 Project).[29] For instance, Article 1000 of the Project provides that the cause is presumed to be lawful until the debtor proves the contrary. According to Goyena, the rule is directly borrowed from Article 1223 of the Civil Code of Sardinia. Unlike the CC, the Project defines the concept of cause. According to Article 997, the *causa* of an onerous contract is the supply or promise of a thing or service made by the other party. Regarding pure charitable contracts, it lies in the mere willingness to donate. Between these two categories, the Project introduces a third and intermediate class of contracts, called *remunerative contracts* (*remuneratorios*). In this kind of contract, the *causa* lies in the service or benefit which is remunerated by the person who has already benefited from it. Declining the concept in three different ways, depending on the nature of the contract, was already in vogue in Spain, according to Garcia Goyena.[30] By adhering to this approach, the 1851 Project clearly departs from the wording adopted by the French and the Italian Civil Codes. Also according to Goyena, these definitions found their inspiration both in the explanations given by Bigot de Préameneu (in line with Pothier) at the time the CC was discussed and in the Louisiana Civil Code of 1824, whose drafters knew Domat, Pothier and Toullier perfectly.[31] What is interesting here is that the Louisiana Civil Code, on the one hand, devotes to the concept of cause (Article 1887 and following) a number of provisions that reproduce almost verbatim the provisions of the CC, but on the other hand emphasises that 'the cause of the contract, in this section, is meant, the consideration or motive for making it' (Article 1890). The words 'cause', 'motive' (and sometimes 'consideration' or even 'purpose') are, in many provisions of this Code, in particular those dealing with the concept of error, systematically used as synonyms, and refer to the factual motive determinant of the will.[32] According to Article 1892, the cause can even consist in the thing to be transferred, which is evidence of the rather empirical and factual approach inherited from Pothier. Assuming that Goyena had personally read the provisions of the Louisiana Civil Code, it is hard to imagine that he did not also have this empirical approach in mind.

The SCC finally passed in 1889 adopts the same order of presentation as the CC (with the exception of Article 1277 SCC, which states the same presumption in favour

[29] See, eg F Clemente de Diego, *Instituciones de derecho civil español*, vol I (Madrid, Librería General, 1929) 48.

[30] On the 1851 Project, see M Reparaz-Padros, *García Goyena y el Proyecto de Código civil de 1851* (Pamplona, 1995); A Garcia Hoyos, *Influencia del Code Napoleónico en el proyecto de Código civil de 1851* (Madrid, Universidad Pontificia Comillas, 2018).

[31] F García Goyena, *Concordancias, motivos y comentarios del codigo civil español* III (Madrid, Imprenta de la Sociedad tipográfica, 1852) 32.

[32] See Art 1772, which requires four conditions for the validity of the contract, including what it calls a *lawful purpose*.

of the creditor as Article 1121 ICC).[33] Article 1261 lists the elements required for the validity of a contract, among which is the *causa*. Then, in *sección 3: De la causa de los contratos* (Articles 1274–77), Article 1274 (which reproduces very faithfully Article 997 of the 1851 Project) adapts the concept of cause according to the nature of the contract. The word *causa* may then have three meanings: in onerous contracts, it refers to the concrete performance expected; in remunerative/compensatory contracts, it refers to the service or benefit already rendered by one party and which the other intends to remunerate; and in purely charitable contracts, it refers to the mere liberality of the donor, so that the cause is no more than a particular form of consent. For the rest, Articles 1131–33 CC are simply translated and combined in Article 1275 SCC (contracts without cause, or with an illicit cause – contrary to laws or morality – cannot have any legal effect).[34]

Despite these detailed provisions, the SCC remains unclear in some places. For instance, what is exactly the *causa de la obligación que se establezca* (the cause of the obligation created by the contract) to which Article 1261 refers? Is it the cause of the obligation or the cause of the contract? Why did the legislator substitute this wording for the clearer wording of Article 985 of the 1851 Project (whose formulation was the simple translation of the French formula: a 'causa lícita de la obligación')? On the one hand, Article 1274, which states that the *causa* consists in the completion of the services promised by the other party, seems to imply that the concept of cause has something to do with the obligations to which each party agrees, rather than with the contract itself. On the other hand, in Articles 1274 and following, which are placed under the heading *De la causa de los contratos*, the word 'obligation' is sometimes considered synonymous with the concept of 'obligatory relation' referred to in Articles 1112 and 1303, so the expression *cause of the obligation* can perfectly well be understood as referring not to the cause of each of the obligations of the parties, but to the cause of the obligatory relation as a whole, eg the contract. Moreover, according to Article 1262, the *consensus in idem* (*el consentimiento*) supposes the perfect correspondence between the offer and its acceptance with regard to the *cosa* (object) and the *causa* which must constitute the contract. Here, the concept of cause seems to apply to the contract itself, and not to the obligation.

D. Final Remarks

First, the SCC, in a more explicit way than the French or Italian Civil Code, uses the concept of cause as a criterion for classifying contracts (Article 1274). That is why it is not univocal, but adapts to the economic structure of the contract. Second, the absence of cause and the presence of false cause are considered together by these three Codes,

[33] The cause, although not mentioned in the *instrumentum*, is presumed to exist and be lawful unless the debtor proves otherwise. This presumption was already admitted by Art 1000 of the 1851 Project, and Goyena located its origin in Art 1894 of the Civil Code for the State of Louisiana.

[34] If the parties expressed a false cause in their contract, the contract is void, unless they can prove that the contract was nevertheless based on another true and lawful cause (Art 1276 SCC). Art 999 of the 1851 Project (based on the Civil Code of Louisiana) preferred a more positive formulation: the contract is valid even if the cause expressed therein is false, as long as it is based on another true cause.

despite the fact that the absence of cause can be observed objectively, whereas, to say that the cause is erroneous, it is necessary to engage in a more subjective analysis. Putting these two issues on the same footing explains why the preparatory works of the CC deals with the false cause with regard to unilateral and abstract contracts only (insofar as the question of false cause does not arise in bilateral contracts, since the mutual obligations of the parties are the cause of each other),[35] and will prevent the nineteenth-century commentators from breaking completely with a subjective analysis.

II. The Interpretation of the Codes, or How to Explain the Specificity of the Concept of Cause?

At the beginning of the twentieth century, faced with the criticisms levelled at the concept of cause, which led the German legislator to get rid of it (at least in relation to the formation of legal acts), many scholars in France, Italy and Spain strove to propose new approaches, which they claimed were more modern, in that they took account of the economic function of the contract and renounced discovering the cause in the psychology of the parties. To emphasise the specificity of such new approaches, they characterised them as more objective, while at the same time characterising previous analyses as subjective. Does such a discourse describe reality, or does it simply serve to disqualify the previous analyses by criticising them in ways they perhaps do not deserve? In order to give credit where it is due, it is necessary to give a faithful account of the way the courts and the legal doctrine understood the provisions of the Codes during the nineteenth century through a series of questions they asked themselves. From the perspective of comparative legal history, this will be an opportunity to see that if a dialogue sometimes takes place between scholars, it is always one way: Italian,[36] and to a lesser extent Spanish, scholars sometimes mention French scholars, but the latter are often indifferent to what is happening in Italy or Spain.

A. Is the Cause Referred to in the Codes the Cause of the Contract or the Cause of the Obligation?

In the eyes of nineteenth-century French scholars, there is no doubt that the Napoleonic legislator actually had *la cause de l'obligation* in mind in Article 1108 CC (as well as in Article 1131 CC, where the words *cause de l'obligation* are expressly mentioned), and that, although Aubry and Rau use the term *cause des conventions* in the first edition of their textbook,[37] in a legal system subject to the principle of consensualism, the cause of the obligation cannot be equated with what the Romans called *causae obligandi*, but only

[35] Fenet (n 18) XIII, 228.

[36] Among many examples, see G Venezian, *La causa nei contratti* (Rome, Cooperativa Editrice, 1892), who considers Pothier as the father of the conception of the cause adopted by the CC and often quotes Toullier, Marcadé, Demolombe and Larombière, among others.

[37] C Aubry and C Rau, *Cours de droit civil français*, vol II (Strasbourg, Lagier, 1839) para 345. In later editions, however, Aubry and Rau prefer the term 'cause de l'obligation'.

with what medieval civilists and canonists called the *causa finalis*. As a consequence, the term *cause du contrat* refers to either the *consensus in idem* (which is, from a technical point of view, the fact that gives rise to the contract) or, from a non-technical point of view (that of the ordinary language), the personal motive which led to bargain.[38] By contrast, French courts, adopting a literal interpretation of Article 1108 CC, which speaks of the 'convention', are interested in the cause of the contract rather than the cause of the obligation, precisely because investigating the cause of the contract is, to them, a means of giving full scope to Articles 1131 to 1133 of the Code. They readily think, for instance, that Article 1133 CC (a cause is unlawful when it is prohibited by law, or when it is contrary to the public policy or moral decency) entrusts them with the mission of assessing the social or economic value of the *negotium*.

In this debate, Italian scholars of the second half of the nineteenth century take the side of their French counterparts. According to Giorgi, for instance, the French and Italian Civil Codes, though they speak of the *cause of the contract*, actually require a cause for the *contractual obligation*. In support of this interpretation, he quotes a decision of the Turin Court of Cassation of 7 January 1870,[39] but also numerous French jurists, as if the proximity between the French and Italian Civil Codes justified that the Italian Code should be read in the light of the French scholars' commentaries. In Spain, on the contrary, the issue remains more controversial, and no consensus seems to emerge among the commentators.

B. How to Define the Cause of an Obligation?

Throughout the nineteenth century, French and Italian scholars taught with one voice that the concept of cause is to be determined by the nature (onerous or charitable) of the contract, since it depends on the direct legal effect the law attaches to the contract.[40] Insofar as, formally, neither the French nor the Italian Civil Code makes such a distinction, it is clearly the burden of the past: scholars choose to follow in the footsteps of the *Ancien régime* legal doctrine. Regarding charitable contracts (*contrats à titre gratuit*), they teach that the cause consists in the sole will to give without expecting anything in return, which is nothing more than the traditional concept of *animus donandi*.[41] Regarding onerous contracts, the *cause* is the answer to the seemingly simple question: why are the parties obliged to do so? Yet, French and Italian scholars face difficulties with giving an unequivocal meaning to the word *cause*, difficulties doubtless due to the varied functions that this concept is called upon to concretely play (either to control the *negotium* with regard to extrinsic criteria – morality – or to verify that an individual

[38] V Marcadé, *Explication théorique et pratique du Code Napoléon*, vol IV (Paris, Cotillon, 1866) para 400.

[39] G Giorgi, *Teoria delle obbligazioni nel diritto moderno italiano*, vol III (Florence, Cammelli, 1885) 527.

[40] In France, see, eg Aubry and Rau, *Cours de droit civil français*, vol III, 3rd edn (Paris, Cosse, 1856) para 345. For an Italian example, see, eg F Tenoesto, *Commentario teorico pratico …* (Turin, 1873) VII, 297.

[41] In France: Merlin de Douai, *Recueil des principales questions de droit* (Paris, Garnery, 1819) I, v° cause des obligations, 579; Marcadé (n 38) para 453; C Demolombe, *Cours de Code Napoleon*, vol XXIV (Paris, Durand, 1868) para 352; G Baudry-Lacantinerie and L Barde, *Précis de droit civil*, vol I (Paris, 1886) 298. In Italy: F Ricci, *Corso teorico-pratico di diritto civile*, vol VI (Turin, Utet, 1886) 53. According to E Presutti, *Giur it*, 1889, IV, 35, such a meaning is commonplace in Italy in the second half of the 19th century.

obliges himself in view of a counterparty or with the conscious aim of depriving himself in favour of another). In France, two different approaches emerge. Some keep to Pothier's empirical approach. Toullier, for instance, states that the cause of an obligation is either what the other party gives or undertakes to give, or the risk he takes on, that is to say, the factual advantage or interest to be provided by one party to the other.[42] Others adopt a more technical approach. Aubry and Rau, finding their inspiration in the commentary published by Zachariae,[43] define the cause as a motive – and not just any motive, but what they call a sufficient legal motive (*motif juridique suffisant*). The cause is therefore not a factual element, existing in nature, but a technical concept shaped by law. By 'motif juridique suffisant', Zachariae, Aubry and Rau mean the legal reason which makes the debtor's obligation legally binding, and this reason is a legal reason in the sense that the law, according to the nature of each contract, presumes this reason to be the one which determined the parties to contract, which amounts to saying that the *cause* is linked to the legal effect of the contract.

Without using the term *motif juridique*, Demolombe[44] also identifies *la cause* with the legal goal directly and immediately pursued by the parties, the one the contract makes it possible to perform. He thus regards *la cause* not as the thing itself or the fact to be accomplished, but as a personal right, a legal relationship between individuals. This abstract approach allows him to link the respective obligations of the parties together, so that the contract then appears less like an exchange of things than the space in which obligations, conceived as legal links, respond to each other.[45]

A few years after, Baudry-Lacantinerie,[46] in the same vein, describes *la cause* as an abstract and formal concept reduced to its legal dimension alone. Taking the example of the sale contract, he concedes that the seller actually intends to obtain the price, but he points out: first, that the fact that the buyer pays because he is subject to a contractual obligation to pay mediates the relationship between the seller and the price; and second, that the cause of the seller's obligation lies in another obligation, that of the buyer to pay the price. Thanks to the concept of cause, the thing or service that is the subject matter of the contract is not seen in itself and concretely, but only through the prism of legal relations.

Such an abstract understanding has the merit to explain that, for the *cause* not to be vitiated, it is not enough that the service to be performed is permitted, but that it must also not be obligatory, because what is already legally binding cannot be the cause of a contractual obligation.[47] However, it is not of great help in understanding what the absence of cause could consist in (the only hypothesis that French scholars think of is that of contracts involving sequential performance, when the expected fact can no longer be performed).[48] Nonetheless, this technical approach is taken up by many

[42] Toullier (n 16) 171.

[43] KS Zachariä von Lingenthal, *Handbuch des französischen Civilrechts* (Heidelberg, 1839) § 344.

[44] Demolombe (n 41) para 345. See also Marcadé (n 38) para 400: the legal *cause* of an obligation is not a thing, but another obligation, that which the other party has contracted. It is thus a legal relationship.

[45] Demolombe (n 41) para 346.

[46] G Baudry-Lacantinerie, *Précis de droit civil* (Paris, 1882) II, para 811.

[47] Marcadé (n 38) para 457.

[48] For example, in a lease contract, the destruction of the rented house during the course of the lease, *cf* Baudry-Lacantinerie and Barde (n 41) para 814.

Italian scholars of the second half of the nineteenth century. Gianturco, speaking the same language as Aubry and Rau, defines the cause as the sufficient legal motive for which the parties bargained: 'il motivo giuridicamente sufficiente che ha indotto le parti a contrattare'.[49] So does Giorgi too (speaking of the 'motivo giuridico'),[50] who quotes not only the writings of French scholars, but also several Italian court decisions, which shows that Italian courts were also sensitive to the French legal thought (which, in the perspective of comparative legal history, is worth noting), and uses the word *motivo* only to insist on the fact that the determining reason which led the individual to contract remains somehow subjective, in the sense that we are dealing with individuals who are thinking subjects. But that does not imply that, technically, it would not be possible to determine in advance what type of cause is required for each of the different categories of contracts. Ricci goes even further and draws the logical consequence of such a statement: if the *causa* of an obligation is the obligation of the other party, then a bilateral contract, which cannot exist without reciprocal obligations, always has a *causa*.[51] If we set aside those less numerous who seem inclined to favour a more factual approach,[52] it is possible to state that most of the Italian scholars of that time give the cause of the obligation an objective dimension,[53] in the sense that the *causa*, defined as the purpose that the law makes the parties' will produce, is always the same for the same type of contract. It is the contract's typical function. This idea highlights the particular economic function of each type of legal act as it is regulated by the law. However, just like their French counterparts, the Italian scholars reconcile this objective dimension with a more subjective approach, which consists not in assimilating the *causa* into the personal motives, but in recalling that a contract is concluded for a certain purpose, and that this purpose must be wanted by the parties themselves and is, in this respect, related to what the parties desired.

In Spain, things are different. The common pre-codification doctrine, based on the authority of the Las Siete Partidas, already asserted that a *causa* or significant reason is required for the validity of contracts, and defined this *causa* as either the reciprocal utility that the parties obtain for each other or the *animus donandi*. The 1851 Project gets scholars used to defining the concept of *causa* in three ways, depending on whether the contract is onerous, remunerative or purely charitable.[54] It seems to have, so to speak, frozen the discussion, so that, even before the enactment of the 1889 SCC, scholars already preferred to define the *causa* in a concrete way. In 1871, Gutiérrez Fernández equated the *causa*, regarding onerous contracts, with 'la prestacion ó promesa de una cosa ó servicio hecho por la otra', the fact or the thing itself which is owed by the debtor, eg the object. Regarding remunerative contracts, he equates

[49] E Gianturco, *Istituzioni di diritto civile italiano* (Florence, Barbèra, 1888) para 56.

[50] Giorgi (n 39) paras 439 and 529.

[51] Ricci (n 41) 53–54.

[52] eg Tenoesto (n 40) VII, 297 equates the *causa* either with the 'prestazione dall'altra parte', the 'liberalità' or the 'obbligazione anteriore'. See also Presutti (n 41) 35: 'la causa dell'obbligazione consist[eva] nella prestazione che l'altra parte ha fatta, o si assume di fare'.

[53] This objective dimension is still clearly highlighted by G Lomonaco, *Delle obbligazioni e dei contratti in genere*, 1 (Naples, Marghieri, 1912) 175.

[54] See, eg B Gutiérrez Fernández, *Codigos estudios fundamentalas*, vol IV (Madrid, Librería Sánchez, 1871) 46.

the cause with the service or the advantage the debtor wants to compensate. In 1886, Montalban also anticipated the wording of Article 1274 SCC, stating that the *causa* of an obligation consists either of: (i) the delivery of the expected thing or the expected service, in the case of onerous contracts; (ii) the (past or future) service or benefit which the contract is intended to compensate/remunerate, regarding remunerative contracts; or (iii) the sole intention to provide a benefit to the other party, in charitable contracts.[55] After 1889, and despite criticism from some (Sánchez Román,[56] for instance, feels that there is no true theory of *causa*, expressed in general terms and valid for all legal acts, in the SCC), it was still difficult for scholars, given the clear wording of Article 1274 (which recalls that of Pothier), not to give way to an approach that looks at the cause in a rather concrete and material way, at least in onerous and remunerative contracts, in which the cause is the performance itself or the service that has been rendered (as explained by Otero y Valentín[57] or Díez de Ulzurrun y Orue, who, moreover, claims that such definitions are consistent with 'the principles of the old law'[58]). It is not therefore surprising to observe that in the Spanish legal literature of this period, references to French legal doctrine are virtually non-existent. Only Pothier, whose *Traité des obligations* has been translated several times into Spanish, is sometimes mentioned, and this is no surprise either.

C. Is the Cause Different from the Motives (*motifs*)?

The question is as simple as it is fundamental: does the word *cause* invite the courts to take into account all the elements which took part in the parties' decision to contract, including subjective and personal ones? Does this word have a technical meaning in the language of the law that is different from its ordinary meaning? In France, with the exception of Delvincourt, who, in 1813, explained that *la cause* consists in any motive which determined the parties to contract,[59] the distinction between *la cause* and *les motifs* quickly became a leitmotif, as it was before the French Revolution. As Toullier points out, the answer to the question 'Why did the parties agree?' has nothing to do with the particular use that the buyer, in the case of a sale contract, wishes to make of the thing he buys, insofar as the cause only consists in the acquisition of ownership.[60] Marcadé also takes the example of a seller: the motive that determined him to sell may be the desire to acquire other things, or many other goals he may have in mind, but all these *motifs* are not to be considered. The law must be interested only in the 'cause immediate' of the obligation, which constitutes its legal cause. This *cause légale* is the obligation under which the buyer contracts to pay him the price, whatever use the seller wishes to make of this money.[61]

[55] *Elementos del derecho civil y penal de España*, vol II (Madrid, Librería Sanchez, 1886) 186.
[56] F Sánchez Román, *Estudios de derecho civil*, vol II (Madrid, Ribadeneyra, 1889–1990) 575.
[57] J Otero y Valentín, *Tratado elemental del derecho del obligaciones* (Valladolid, Viuda de Cuesta, 1893) 52.
[58] C Díez de Ulzurrun y Orue, *Tratado legal de las obligaciones y contratos* (Valencia, 1893) 133.
[59] CE Delvincourt, *Cours de Code Napoléon*, vol II (Paris, Gueffier, 1813) 12. In charitable contracts (Art 1105 CC), it consists in the sole will to give, defined as the opposite of a pecuniary interest.
[60] Toullier (n 16) 170.
[61] Marcadé (n 38) para 400.

This approach is particularly evident among scholars who define *la cause* as a formal and abstract concept. Particularly symptomatic in this regard are Demolombe, who explains that *la cause* referred to in Article 1108 CC is what medieval scholars called the *causa finalis*, and Aubry and Rau, who reproach Toullier and Delvincourt for having yielded too easily to the temptation to assimilate *la cause* into the concrete and personal reasons which led the parties to contract. A few years later, at the time the SCC was drafted, Baudry-Lacantinerie, in turn, took the example of the sales contract to show that the personal reason that leads to buying is a *pur motif* that differs from one buyer to another. Whether they define the cause as *what is owed by the other* or as a legal relationship, French scholars thus take care to distinguish fact from law and share the opinion that, regarding onerous contracts, the cause must be considered entirely from the contract itself and not from its context.

Such a decontextualisation is not limited to onerous contracts. Regarding charitable ones (Article 1105 CC), French scholars all agree that the intention to give must be addressed independently of the events that have concretely determined the donor. This is not to suggest that individual volition is not a subjective process (it is, in the sense that it is performed by a person, *un sujet*), but to insist that it is also an abstract process, which is not legally linked (although it may be in the mind of the donor) to the motives for bestowing the gift. Through the *animus donandi*, the concept of *cause* clearly appears here as a tool which makes it possible to grasp the individual volition objectively and abstractly. As a consequence, the donation is caused, without the judge having to wonder about the donor's concrete reasons. This *animus* cannot be wrongful or immoral in itself, unlike the *motifs*, which are likely to be morally evaluated. Taken to its logical extreme, this amounts to saying that a donation can only be condemned as immoral on the consideration of its object, not on the ground of Article 1133 CC, which is the exact opposite of the solutions adopted by the courts.

It is true, however, that some nineteenth-century lower court decisions adopted the abstract approach advocated by the scholars and, for example, ruled that a contract whose direct object is not the activity of a brothel in itself is lawful, so that the lender was allowed to ask for the repayment of a loan he made to the defendant, provided that the sum was borrowed for the sole purpose of buying the house to be used for the prostitution activities.[62] In the same vein, the Court of Bordeaux rejected the claim by which the buyer, who bought the supplies needed for the reception of his clients in his brothel, asked to be released from the obligation to pay the price on the grounds that the contract had an illicit cause[63] (on the contrary, contracts between the owner of a brothel and his clients, or contracts for the sale of brothels, are always considered null and void for being based on an unlawful cause).[64] Such decisions are based on the idea, consistent with the doctrinal views, that the way in which the buyer finally uses the goods he bought does not reveal *la cause* of his obligation, but his *motifs*, which are not relevant to the validity of the contract.

The French Court of Cassation never shared this view. In her eyes, the word *cause* has no other meaning in law than its ordinary one, and the Court's job is to sort out

[62] Paris, 13 February 1877, S.77.2.233; see also Paris, 14 December 1889, DP.1890.2.189.
[63] 6 February 1885, S.86.2.16.
[64] Civ, 15 December 1873, DP.74.1.222.

the agreements which appear to be acceptable from those which do not, depending on the intentions pursued by the parties. To this end, the Court is naturally led to place the contract in its context. Contracts relating to the operation of a brothel (rental of premises, loan with a view to acquiring the establishment, hiring of staff) are therefore deemed null and void by the Court of Cassation, because of their immoral *motifs*.[65] With regard to onerous contracts, the Court of Cassation even ensures that the lower courts have correctly informed themselves of the reasons which prompted the debtor to undertake his obligation and verified that he did not pursue a goal contrary to the laws.[66] In a famous decision of 1 May 1855, which takes the opposite view of some lower courts, the Court of Cassation states that agency contracts entered into with marriage agencies are based on an illicit and immoral cause, as being contrary to the dignity of marriage.[67] (In Italy, during the same period, some court decisions denied any validity to such an agreement, as being void for immoral cause, eg Cass Turin 25 September 1883;[68] others, on the contrary, saw nothing immoral or illicit in such an agreement, and therefore considered the *causa* of the obligation as lawful;[69] and the Supreme Court of Rome, in a decision of 29 April 1878, placed itself between these extremes, explaining that it is necessary to determine what function was entrusted to the broker before ruling on the validity or nullity of the contract: if the broker is content to put the future spouses in contact, the contract is valid; but if his mission is to influence the consent to the marriage, then the contract is void, because each of the future spouses must be able to express a free consent.)

The French Court of Cassation also adopts an empirical approach regarding charitable contracts. Despite the proof of the *animus donandi*, the donation made for the benefit of a concubine with a view to persuading her to continue her culpable relationship with the donor is declared null and void.[70]

Of the legal doctrine and the Court of Cassation's divergent attitudes, the Italian and Spanish legal doctrines prefer that of the French scholars. Considering that legal science is not capable of probing hearts and minds,[71] most Italian and Spanish scholars of the second half of the nineteenth century claimed that the technical concept of *causa* did not refer to subjective elements. In Italy, a terrific example of this opinion – one of many[72] – is set by Giorgi, who equates the *causa* with the legal basis of the obligation:[73] Pietro, a 'dabben uomo e ricco signore', goes to a gun manufacturer to buy a revolver. Now let us imagine, continues Giorgi, that Pietro, under the influence of jealousy and revenge, shoots his wife's lover. The judge seised of the case may think that the purpose

[65] Cas, 17 May 1841, S.41.1.623; Civ, 15 December 1873, DP.74.1.222.

[66] Req, 21 November 1831, D31.1.360.

[67] Cass civ, 1 May 1855, S.55.1.337.

[68] Quoted by Ricci (n 41) 62.

[69] Ricci quotes two decisions of the Court of Genova, of April 1853 and August 1877, ibid 62.

[70] Cass, 2 February 1853, S.53.1.428; D53.1.157. Scrutinising the intentions of the donor and drawing all the consequences of the moral value of the personal motives for which he made the donation became such a widespread attitude among the courts during the 19th century that in the 20th century, the French legal doctrine forged the technical concept of *cause impulsive et déterminante* from case law.

[71] Giorgi (n 39) para 437.

[72] See Gianturco (n 49) para 56: the *causa* of the obligation is its immediate and final one, which is completely different from the mediate and secondary motive proper to the individual ('quænam occasio debendi').

[73] Giorgi (n 39) 527.

of the purchase was the assassination of the lover, and deduce from this that the *cur contraxit* was illicit. But is the contract entered into by Pietro definitely null and void on the grounds that it lacks an essential element? The answer, according to Giorgi, is no,[74] because the technical concept of *causa* cannot be reduced to a personal purpose. The purchaser of a revolver is obliged to pay the price, insofar as his obligation has a *causa* that lies in the fact that he has entered into a commutative contract by the effect of which he received a thing whose value corresponds to the price he promised to pay (basically, this amounts to basing the respective obligations of the parties to a bilateral contract on the idea of commutative justice, which requires that the exchange of services be completed: 'la giustizia commutativa esige il ricambio dei servigi').[75]

This clear distinction between *causa* and personal motives was, at that time, commonplace in Italy, as it was in France (Ricci quotes a decision of the Court of Turin of 7 January 1870).[76] Still, in 1912, Lomonaco explained that the intention of one who buys a thing with a view to giving it to another constitutes a motive for him, but this motive is not the legal motive which constitutes the cause of the contract of sale.[77] In Spain, Article 1274 SCC is also understood by most scholars as excluding the personal considerations that led the parties to agree. On this point, the explanations given by Clemente de Diego at the beginning of the twentieth century are a good synthesis of the majority position of the Spanish doctrine: of the various reasons explaining why the parties agreed, it is the closest and most intrinsic one, the one which is always the same for all those who carry out the same type of contract and which therefore has an objective dimension that must be considered as the *causa*. The other reasons, remote and subjective, as varied as individuals can be, are of no importance unless they have been incorporated into the declaration of will in the form of a condition, a mode or a presupposition.[78] Even scholars who speak of the *impulso* or *móvil* that determined the act of volition, like Díez de Ulzurrun y Orue, end up, in accordance with Article 1274 SCC, by reducing the *causa* to the contractual performance, therefore to a material element (or, regarding pure charitable contract, to the sole liberality of the donor).[79]

Personal and contingent elements are therefore left at the contract's door. Such a widespread attitude among scholars may be explained from a technical point of view: the distinction between *cause* and *motives* enables the cause to play the role of the technical tool through which the creditor can legally justify the acquisition of his right. Understood that way, the requirement of a cause must be seen in light of the sanction of unjust enrichment. The cause, objectively considered, is nothing less than the element of legal technique whereby the legal effectiveness of a legal act and the protection that the law grants it can be legitimised.[80]

[74] ibid 526. What he calls *cur contraxit* is what a contemporary French scholar would have called *motifs personnels*.

[75] ibid para 437, p 527.

[76] Ricci (n 41) 52.

[77] Lomonaco (n 53) 175.

[78] Clemente de Diego (n 29) 251–52.

[79] Díez de Ulzurrun (n 58) 133.

[80] At the beginning of the 20th century, the idea remained that the *causa*, as a technical concept, was what gives the obligation its justification. According to Clemente de Diego (n 29) 450, the *causa* is the 'fundamento o razón justificativa' for the acquisition of a right.

D. The Cause as an Autonomous Requirement

In the specific case of charitable contracts, the law (in Spain) or the legal doctrine (in France and Italy) equates the cause with the *animus donandi*. With the very marginal exception of a few, such as Laurent,[81] who argues that the *animus donandi* is confused with the donor's consent, all agree to see in this *animus* a distinct concept. Yet, they have great difficulty in giving examples of erroneous cause that are different from the cases in which the donor was mistaken and his consent was vitiated[82] … which may lead to the conclusion that the *animus donandi* is not so different from consent!

Regarding onerous contracts, the question 'Is the cause to be considered as an autonomous requirement?' gave rise to controversy even before the end of the nineteenth century. In France, despite Article 1108 CC (1804) clearly giving the cause the status of an autonomous condition, distinct from the object, a few commentators acknowledged that these two notions are one and the same. Duranton, for instance, takes the assimilation of the *cause* to the promised thing or fact to its logical conclusion and claims that *la cause* is not a specific requirement: a mistake as to it is nothing more than a mistake as to the object.[83] Even more critical, Laurent dares to question the wording of Article 1108, and asserts that *la cause* should not be considered a specific condition for the validity of contracts.[84]

However, most commentators of the CC strive to distinguish *l'objet* from *la cause*. Most of the time, the distinction they draw is, on the face of it at least, quite simple: to speak of *la cause* is to answer the question as to *why* an individual agreed to a convention (*pourquoi*?); to speak of *l'objet* is to answer the question as to *what* he agreed for (*pour quoi?*). But this distinction often falls apart as soon as the details are dissected, even under the pen of those who understand the concept of *cause* from a legal and abstract point of view (*la cause* as the legal reason for the acquisition of a right, as alleged by Domat). For instance, Aubry and Rau (§ 345) concede that *la cause* merges with *l'objet* owed by the other party, insofar as the words *la cause* and *l'objet* describe all faces of the same coin: the *prestation* which is the subject matter of the contract. To speak about the *objet* is to address the contractual obligation independently, in and of itself (*isolément*), whereas speaking about *la cause* is to look at the contractual obligations in relation to each other,[85] in order to grasp the economics of the contract in its entirety. In the same vein, Demolombe also highlights that, regarding mutual contracts, the *cause* of

[81] In Belgium, where the CC was exported, F Laurent (*Principes de droit civil* (Brussels, 1875) vol XVI, para 111) explains that the cause of a gift is nothing else but the consent, since the donor only consents because he has the will to give. In Spain, Otero y Valentín (n 57) 52 teaches the same.

[82] *cf* Merlin de Douai (n 41) 179; Aubry and Rau, *Cours*, vol III (n 40) para 345. For instance, the donor agrees to deliver a thing to another in payment of a legacy to which he believed he was bound by virtue of his father's will, when that will had been revoked: Marcadé (n 38) para 455.

[83] A Duranton, *Traité des contrats*, vol I (Paris, Neve, 1819) paras 299 and 308. Similarly, it is because the object is *extra commercium* that the cause is illicit (para 311). In his opinion, it is therefore only in unilateral legal acts which are not gifts that a cause, understood as a distinct and particular condition, is necessary (para 300).

[84] Laurent (n 81) para 111.

[85] Aubry and Rau, *Cours*, vol III (n 40) para 345: 'La théorie de la cause, en ce qui concerne ces sortes de contrats [bilateral contracts], se rattache donc, d'une manière intime, à celle de l'objet.'

the obligation of one of the parties relates to the object of the obligation of the other, reciprocally.[86]

This confusion becomes even more apparent when it comes to the unlawfulness and immorality of the cause. Dealing with this issue, Toullier only gives examples of illicit objects, or *res extra commercium*.[87] Aubry and Rau simply teach that an obligation needs a lawful cause and that, consequently, the contract is void when the service ('prestation') is contrary to law, public order or morality.[88] Demolombe is even more clear: the question of knowing whether *la cause* of an obligation is lawful or not 'merges with that of knowing whether the object of this obligation is lawful' or not, so that the courts or the legal doctrine are free to deal with the wrongfulness of an obligation either on the ground of Article 1128 CC, relating to the object, or on the ground of Article 1133 CC, relating to the cause.[89]

Such statements are perfectly understandable when the cause is equated with *what is actually owed* (*what is given* or *done* by the other party). But they are less consistent with the idea that *la cause* consists of a pure legal relationship. Besides, these difficulties contrast with the simpler attitude adopted by the courts, according to which *la cause* lies in the commitment made by the other party, so that the obligation is devoid of cause when this commitment does not have, or no longer has, an object, or when its object is unlawful. In line with their more concrete understanding of the concept of *cause*, they have no qualms about rejecting agreements on the ground of Article 1133 CC, where the legal doctrine would have chosen to rely on Article 1128 CC. In economic matters, for example, the Court of Cassation considers as based on an unlawful cause the conventional restrictions on freedom to work imposed in an absolute way, and states that the courts must not save such agreements by modifying them in such a way as to restrict the prohibition, for example, to a single town.[90] Similarly, agreements by which the main manufacturers of a commodity agree to give this commodity prices above or below those which free competition would have determined are void.[91] The assignment of a patent is void for lack of cause when the patented invention is recognised as not having the results promised by the assignor or as not being patentable.[92]

In short, it can be said that the distinction between *l'objet* and *la cause* is the French doctrine's Achilles' heel,[93] which fuelled the anti-causalist criticism that developed in France at the end of the nineteenth century. In Italy, the nineteenth-century legal doctrine faced the same difficulties and shared the same hesitations. Giorgi, for example, replicates Aubry and Rau's reasoning: what is called an object, when it is considered as a *quid facti* endowed with an objective existence external to the minds of the contracting parties, becomes what is called the *causa* of an obligation when it is considered

[86] Demolombe (n 41) para 348. See also Marcadé (n 38) 389, para 453.

[87] Toullier (n 16) 171.

[88] Aubry and Rau, *Cours*, vol II (n 37) para 345.

[89] Demolombe (n 41) para 348.

[90] Cass, 25 May 1869, S.69.1.307.

[91] Cass, 11 February 1879, S.79.1.198; D79.1.345.

[92] Cass, 21 February 1837, S.37.1.186; Cass, 22 August 1844, S.44.1.831; unless the parties have expressly given the assignment a random character, Cass, 22 April 1861S.61.1.735; D61.1.423.

[93] This was already the case with Pothier. When he dealt with the illicit/immoral cause, and though he tried to see in *la cause* and *l'objet* two distinct requirements, he took examples which could perfectly illustrate the hypothesis of an illicit object: Pothier, *Traité des obligations* (n 6) para 43.

subjectively as the determining reason for the will to be bound.[94] So too does Ricci, who states that the *oggetto* and the *causa* of the obligation are basically one and the same thing.[95] Some, such as Gianturco, go so far as to say that, if one were to stick to rational requirements alone, the *causa* should not be considered an autonomous condition for the validity of contracts, because it is included either in consent or in the object.[96]

In Spain, the same ambiguity is already present in Goyena's commentaries on the 1851 Project, where he seems to see the cause as an element not fundamentally separate from consent[97] and refers directly, when dealing with the issue of unlawful cause, to his explanations on the illicit object. Yet, many scholars did not wait for the promulgation of the SCC to give a list of the conditions imposed on the parties, strongly reminiscent of Article 1108 CC. According to Gutiérrez, for instance, four conditions are required for the validity of agreements, including a specific object which forms the subject matter of the obligation (*objeto cierto que forma la materia de la obligacion* and a *causa lícita*).[98] In 1886, Juan Manuel Montalban listed the same elements,[99] as if the difference between the *objeto* and the *causa* of the obligation were obvious. However, most of the examples of cases of immoral cause quoted by Spanish scholars of that time are actually examples of illicit objects (eg the *quota litis* pact). Paradoxically, after 1889, some scholars distanced themselves from the list drawn up by the SCC, which formally refers to the *causa* as a distinct condition. In 1893, Otero y Valentín, making no reference to French nor Italian legal doctrine, claimed that individuals always act for some reasons and that these reasons are so connected to their will (consent) and the object of the contract that they should not be considered, either legally or philosophically, as an autonomous requirement.[100] Making the *causa* an essential condition for the validity of the contract is a mistake, he adds, and this mistake, in his opinion, stems from the fact that, in Roman law, a *causa* was required to transform a *pactus* into a *contractus*. Now that the distinction between *pactus* and *contractus* no longer applies, the requirement of a cause should disappear too.[101] Yet, the word *causa* being mentioned in the list of conditions required by the SCC is considered by most Spanish scholars after 1889 a sufficient reason to keep treating it as an autonomous condition. For instance, between 1889 and 1893, Sánchez Román[102] and Díez de Ulzurrun y Orue[103] clearly taught that the *causa* is a distinct and essential element of the contract.

Beyond the wish to conform exactly to the letter of legal texts, another reason why the nineteenth-century French, Italian and Spanish legal doctrines persisted in the idea

[94] Giorgi (n 39) para 440; see also 606–21.

[95] Ricci (n 41) 53.

[96] Gianturco (n 49) para 56. However, studying positive law, he teaches that *causa* consists in the legally sufficient reason that led the parties to contract. He uses the words 'il motivo giuridicamente sufficiente', reminiscent of those of Aubry and Rau, who he does not quote. He insists on the fact that this *causa* is the immediate and primary final cause of the obligation, the answer to the question *cur debetur*, and that it is completely different from the answer to the question 'quænam occasio debendi', which refers to the internal and subjective motive, the absence of which, if not made a condition, does not invalidate the contract.

[97] Quoted by Otero y Valentín (n 57) 52.

[98] Gutiérrez (n 54) 496.

[99] Montalban (n 55) 181.

[100] Otero y Valentín (n 57) 51.

[101] ibid 53.

[102] Sánchez Román (n 56) 526, para 12.

[103] Díez de Ulzurrun y Orue (n 58) 134.

that the cause must be considered as an autonomous condition is to be found in Domat and Pothier: the binding force of an agreement can only be justified by the existence either of a true intention to give or a reciprocal economic transfer, which is precisely what the concept of cause consists in. *In fine*, all this is linked to the ancient idea (which, in Rome, justified the prohibition of the stipulations in favour of a third party) according to which agreements have no legal existence unless they involve a patrimonial interest, which has nothing to do with the idea of contractual justice (just as English courts accept an inadequate consideration, French, Italian and Spanish scholars do not require that the economic value of one promise corresponds exactly to that of the other promise).

III. Conclusion

Even though one can be amused by the somewhat vain efforts deployed by scholars of the nineteenth century in defining the concept of cause, it should be underlined that those efforts are the testimony of their intention to organise and classify the contractual practices, in order to subsume those practices under a generic concept transposable from one contract to another, provided the contracts are of the same type. To make the cause a distinct condition and to define it both in a subjective and in an objective way (since it is distinguished from personal motives) is revealing of a specific conception of freedom and contract. It amounts to saying that the individual will, even if it agrees with another will, is not in itself normative. To be so, it has to be a reasonable will.[104] Such a requirement brings the continental concept of cause close to the English notion of consideration: both are used to distinguish, among all the agreements, between those which are serious,[105] and deserve to be considered as binding, and those which are not.[106] In France, Toullier, for instance, does not hesitate to say that what the CC refers to as a *cause* is exactly what English courts refer to as *consideration*.[107] By defining obligation as a restriction on individual freedom that can only be legitimate if it has a reason, Ricci basically thinks the same.[108] However, the comparison should not be taken too far, since, as Aubry and Rau point out,[109] the *cause* of the obligation may consist in an obligation previously imposed on the one who is contracting, whereas a past consideration is not, in principle, a valuable consideration. Such a requirement, far from being considered contrary to the widespread (in the nineteenth century) idea that the effects of the contract were to be determined by the private will, is, moreover, considered necessary to guarantee the stability of contracts, which would be totally destroyed if the validity of contracts depended on the appreciation of a personal purpose, that is to say, on something of which it is not possible to have with certainty an extrinsic knowledge.[110]

[104] M Barcellona, *Della causa. Il contratto e la circolazione della ricchezza* (Milan, Cedam, 2015) 14.
[105] All the authors insist that only a lunatic engages without being determined by a cause.
[106] This is basically what F de Castro, *El negocio jurídico* (Madrid, INEJ, 1971) para 214 explains.
[107] Toullier (n 16) 171.
[108] Ricci (n 41) 53.
[109] Aubry and Rau, *Cours*, vol II (n 37) para 345.
[110] Giorgi (n 39) 527.

The abstract approach taken by the legal literature therefore helps to protect the private autonomy from the incursions of the courts, rather than undermining its importance (no matter that such a choice leads to an aporia: if the cause is the cause of the obligation and if contractual obligations presuppose that the contract has been formed, how can the existence of these obligations be considered as a condition for the formation of the contract?).

Such a conception is not, however, only intended to address ideological concerns. It also has technical reasons. Everyone always acts for one reason or another. If all these reasons were capable of constituting a valid cause of an obligation, then the assumption that an obligation is void for lack of cause would become a textbook case, and it should be admitted that the legislator amused himself by formulating a legal rule devoid of any practical significance (unless nullity for lack of cause is to be reduced to hypotheses of error as to cause). To equate the *cause* with something that exists outside the psychology of the individuals makes it easier to understand in which situations an obligation may be void for absence of cause. It offers the advantage of explaining some legal mechanisms which imply a connection between the respective obligations of the parties, such as the rule according to which the subsequent impossibility of occupying the house rented releases the lessee from the payment of the rent.

Behind all this lies the idea that the subjective aim pursued by each party must be objectified either in the legal relationship which unites them or in the services owed, so that, insensibly, the subjectivity of the parties gives way to an objective way of looking at the contract as an instrument to fulfil a determined function.[111] In this perspective, the contract of sale can be described as the exchange of a thing for a price, which is not far from a purely economic and objective analysis. All this suggests that the opposition often evoked between the subjectivist legal orders, supposed to readily resort to the concept of cause, and the objectivist legal orders, supposed to be indifferent to this concept, should be nuanced, insofar as the elaboration of a generic concept of cause, declined for each contractual type, is already a form of objectification of reality. Is there, in this respect, any real difference between what Aubry and Rau taught and what Bonfante stated in 1908 (the cause is not the reason why the party acts, but the reason why the law guarantees a legal sanction, ie the objective essence of the relationship between the parties)?[112] The opposition between the so-called *théorie classique* and the objectivist theories, which develop in the twentieth century, especially in Italy, deserves to be qualified for the same reasons. It is true that a new way of justifying the binding force of contracts (less anchored on the individual will, insofar as a contract is considered as a social fact) led, from the beginning of the twentieth century, to the multiplication of more clearly objective approaches. It then became quite common in Italy, for instance, to define the cause as the economic and social function fulfilled by the contract, whether this conception was added to (as in Scialoja's writings, for example) or substituted for the classical conception (Covielo, Ruggierio). In Spain, Clemente de Diego (a keen reader of von Tuhr), although referring to *el reinado de la autonomía privada*, teaches that any legal act, objectively considered, tends towards an economic-legal purpose which is the

[111] See Barcellona (n 104) 3.
[112] P Bonfante, 'Il contratto e la causa del contratto' [1908] *Rivista di diritto commerciale* 115.

economic and social function in view of which (and for the protection of which) the law grants its assistance to the individual will.[113] However, both of these two approaches (the modern one and the so-called classical one) objectify the subjective goal pursued by each party either in the legal link that exists between them or in the thing or the service to be done, so that taking into account the subjective goal disappears in favour of a more objective understanding of the *negotium*, based on the analysis of the function the contract is supposed to perform. Moreover, all agree that only the closest, intrinsic reason for contracting, which is the same for all those who intend to contract, deserves the name *cause*. The other reasons, as diverse as the individuals themselves, are only relevant to the law if they are incorporated into the declaration of will in the form of a condition, mode or presupposition.[114] Why, then, did some twentieth-century scholars criticise their predecessors for an approach which they considered too subjective? The answer may be that, speaking of the cause of the obligation rather than the cause of the contract, the latter may have given the impression that the cause had to be understood from the point of view of the individuals, and not from the contract itself.

[113] Clemente de Diego (n 29) 251. In this regard, the textbooks published from the beginning of the 20th century give the impression of relative synchronisation of national legal doctrines: *synchronisation* because they evolve at the same pace; but *relative* since the conceptual modifications then proposed will become more established in Italy, and perhaps Spain, than in France.

[114] Clemente de Diego (n 29) 251–52.

5

The Decline of Cause

WOJCIECH DAJCZAK

I. Introduction

The term 'decline of cause' is by itself ambiguous. In this chapter, I use it to represent two phenomena in the evolution of law in continental Europe. The first involves the elimination of the word *causa* from the doctrinal prerequisites for the enforceability of an agreement. The second entails scrubbing the word 'cause' from the statutory definition of prerequisites for agreement enforceability. The common denominator of these two processes could be called the external history of the decline of cause. Recognising these processes, however, must be accompanied by the question of whether the external decline of *causa* has affected the enforceability of agreements and, if so, how? I refer to this as the problem of the internal decline of cause. In other words, it is the question of correlation between the external decline of cause and the field of agreement enforceability.

In this chapter, I will examine the modern use of Roman law (*usus modernus*), which from the sixteenth to the nineteenth century was the framework of legal scholarship in Europe and strongly influenced the legal practice in the German states and the Netherlands; I will also consider codified French and German law, which are presented as different models for approaching the cause of a contract, as well as Polish law. The uniqueness of the Polish 1933 Code of Obligations lies in the fact that it represented a unification of law that replaced foreign laws in force on Polish soil, including the French Code civil (CC) and the German Bürgerliches Gesetzbuch (BGB).

II. The External History of the Decline of Cause

A. Disappearance of the Word *Causa* from Doctrinal Prerequisites for Agreement Enforceability

(i) *The Gradual Decline of* Causa Contractus *in Modern Roman Law*

The clear statement that 'according to Roman law, a contract is an agreement that has a cause' was used until the mid-eighteenth century by numerous Dutch and German jurists to describe the modern use of Roman law.[1] There was, however, a certain inconsistency between this interpretation and the principle, adopted in the late sixteenth century in the *usus modernus*, that every agreement is enforceable by law. Such a change required the resolution of two questions concerning the relationship between cause and agreement enforceability. The first was how to understand *causa contractus* in Roman law. The second was whether and how to incorporate cause into the new doctrine, which followed the principle of enforceability of any agreement. The explanations of *usus modernus* jurists, relating to cause as a factor in the enforceability of an agreement, have for centuries referred to a pattern familiar from Roman law. They were a paraphrase of the ancient opinion of Ulpian that the absence of cause (*nulla sub est causa*) in a reciprocal contract precluded its enforceability.[2] For example, Arnold Vinnius argued that cause is the delivery of an item or the performance of a specific action in order to receive an item or service in return.[3] An attempt to explain cause more deeply within the framework of a contract was made by Franciscus Marquardus in his doctoral dissertation presented at the Catholic University in Dillingen, Bavaria, in July 1681. Marquardus clearly distinguished between the interpretation of cause present in the definition of contract and the use of the word in philosophical reflections on causality. In this way, Marquardus confirmed the position of early modern doctrine that within the definition of a contract, cause cannot be understood otherwise than as the performance of a reciprocal agreement by one of the parties in order for the counterparty to fulfil their obligations.[4] Moving beyond this understanding of cause, Marquardus noted that the parties to a contract constitute the efficient cause (*causa efficiens*) of its effectiveness when the contract is not contrary to natural and positive law.[5]

One generation after Marquardus by, Jean Domat solved this problem in his Christian-based system of natural law by moving in the direction familiar from canon law.[6] Domat's declaration that 'no agreement binds without cause' was combined with the principle of enforceability of all agreements giving benefits to both parties or made with the intention of giving a benefit to another.[7] *Usus modernus* jurists, however, have chosen other ways to legitimise and delimit the principle of enforceability of all agreements.

(a) Moving *Causa* from the Contract Definition to Agreement Interpretation

The first of these paths is illustrated by Georg Struve's explanation that the enforceability of any agreement derives from interpreting the parties' statements as if they

[1] *cf* A Vinnius, *In quatuor libros Institutionum imperialium commentaries*, III,14,9; GA Struve, *Syntagma jurisprudentiae secundum ordinem Pandectarum*, II,14, no 6; JG Heineccius, *Elementa iuris civilis secundum ordinem pandectarum*, II, 14, para 351.

[2] D 14,2,7,4.

[3] Vinnius (n 1) III,14,9.

[4] F Marquardus, *De pactis et contractibus* (Dilingae, 1681) 35.

[5] ibid 78.

[6] *cf* W Decock, *Theologians and Contract Law. The Moral Transformation of the Ius Commune (ca 1500–1650)* (Leiden, Martinus Nijhoff Publishers, 2013) 136.

[7] J Domat, *Les loix civiles dans leur ordre naturel*, Lib I, tit 1, s 1, no 5.

were a Roman verbal contract called *stipulatio*.[8] In the discussion on the boundaries of contractual freedom, jurists of the seventeenth century regarded the absence of cause as fraud – following the example of the Roman *stipulatio*.[9] This line of reasoning is illustrated by David Mevius's commentary on the Constitution of the Bishop of Bremen on unfair usury contracts. Struve's contemporary and a well-known jurist from northern Germany, Mevius explained that loans to which the Constitution applies must have a 'true' *causa debendi*, in order to be almost effective.[10] The lack of this cause in the document, or doubts about the plausibility of the cause, did not automatically affect the enforceability of the agreement, but required proof that a proper *causa debendi* existed and thus the usury transaction was not wrongful.[11] In seventeenth-century *usus modernus*, we find even more general statements, including that the remote cause (*causa remota*) of keeping agreements is the law of nations or that the immediate cause (*causa propinqua*) of contracts is the intentional and voluntary action of the parties.[12] As such, the seventeenth-century doctrine shows a shift away from the enumeration of cause as a formal prerequisite for agreement enforceability and a shift of the concept of cause towards a legal discussion of the limits of the freedom of contract.

(b) Cause Surrogates in Defining and Interpreting the Contract

In the seventeenth century, the debate over the enforceability of agreements also took a new path, emphasising differences from Roman law and a desire for simplicity. The simplification resulting from natural law ideology is illustrated well by Samuel Pufendorf's argument. He based the obligation to perform a mutual agreement on the parties' agreed equivalence of performances, and, like Grotius, did not link this to the concept of cause.[13] Another premise for the simplified approach to the principle of enforceability of agreements came from the insistence of influential German jurists such as Lauterbach,[14] Stryk[15] and Heineccius[16] that loyalty based on German customs, as already attested by Tacitus,[17] justifies the enforceability of all agreements concluded prudently and intentionally. The difference between this approach and the shift of the word 'cause' towards the realm of contract interpretation did not imply a qualitative change.

The disappearance in *usus modernus* of cause as a formal prerequisite for the enforceability of an agreement is confirmed by legal discussions throughout the eighteenth century. An important, innovative contribution to this process came from Daniel Nettelbladt. From the mid-eighteenth century onwards, he had built a legal framework which rendered the principles of the law of nature useful to those applying positive

[8] Struve (n 1) II,14, no 32.
[9] D 44,4,2,3.
[10] D Mevius, *Vollständiger Commentarius von wucherlichen Contracten* (Frankfurt, 1710) 90.
[11] ibid 90.
[12] JF Böckelmann, *Commentariorum in Digesta Justiniani*, II,14 no 17.
[13] S Pufendorf, *De jure naturae et gentium*, Lib V, ch 2, no 9 and ch 3 no 1.
[14] WA Lauterbach, *Collegium Theoretico – Practicum*, vol 1, Lib II, tit 14, no 68.
[15] S Stryk, *Specimen usus moderni pandectarum*, II,14, no 3.
[16] JG Heineccius, *Elementa iuris germanici*, vol 1, para 340.
[17] Tacitus, *Germania*, 24.

law in German countries. Nettelbladt explained, more succinctly than Grotius and Pufendorf, that 'nothing is required for the validity of a contract except an agreement'.[18] He also regarded a valid agreement as the justification (*causa*) for the transfer of property, the absence of which meant an obligation to restitute unjust enrichment.[19]

(c) The Extrasystemic Place of Cause in the Pandectist Conception of the Private Law System

Nettelbladt's system was criticised in the late eighteenth century as a 'metaphysics of law' by Dabelow.[20] However, in his proposed new systematics of law, Dabelow consolidated the exclusion of cause from the prerequisites for agreement enforceability. Dabelow understood contracts as one specific form of legal transaction (*rechtliche Geschäft, negotium iuridicum*), which he defined as 'permitted human behavior which has as its object mutual rights or duties'.[21] In that context, he conceived cause as one element that can be added to the content of a legal transaction to limit its force or effect.[22] Such effects of cause were, however, limited only to cases where it could be shown that the cause indicated is false and that the person who added it would not have entered into the transaction had they known about it.[23] The separation of the systemic justification of the enforceability of agreements from the cause of an agreement became firmly established in the nineteenth century, both in Roman law used in Germany and in the new pandectist theory of private law. Savigny, like Dabelow, identified the contract as one particularly important instance of legal transaction, which produces the effect intended by the parties when the parties' statements are not the result of error or fraud.[24] Otto Bähr justified the enforceability of a simple promise to pay by drawing on the Roman *stipulatio* and the fact that the promise was made and accepted.[25] Bähr also saw grounds for the enforceability of abstract promises in the needs of practice.[26] Siegmund Schlossmann, on the other hand, argued that a broad understanding of the enforceability of agreements resulted from the agreement enforceability principle adopted in the *usus modernus*. Schlossmann also recognised the enforceability of agreements concluded without the intention to benefit.[27] The doctrines of Bähr and Schlossman represented a revival of the German discussion of cause after the 'lazy calm' of the first half of the nineteenth century.[28] Bähr criticised the 'ambiguous, error-inducing view'

[18] D Nettelblatt, *Systema elementare universae iurisprudentiae naturalis usui systematis iurisprudentiae positivae*, vol 2, para 319.

[19] ibid para 303.

[20] C Dabelow, *System des gesammten heutigen Civil – Rechts* (Halle, Hemmerde & Schwetschke, 1796) vol 1, p XII.

[21] ibid para 366.

[22] ibid para 382.

[23] ibid para 406.

[24] FC Savigny, *System des heutigen römischen Rechts* (Berlin, Deit & Comp, 1840) vol 2, para 71 and vol 3, para 114.

[25] O Bähr, *Die Annerkennung als Verpflichtungsgrund* (Cassel, Bertram, 1855) 159.

[26] ibid 286.

[27] S Schlossmann, *Zur Lehre von der Causa obligatorischer Verträge* (Breslau, Jungfer's Buchdruckerei, 1868) 23 and 61.

[28] *cf* G Albers, 'Die causa vom Code civil zum BGB/Zuwendungen tragen statt Verpflichtungen begründen' G Albers, FP Patti, D Perrouin-Verbe (eds), *Causa contractus* (Tübingen, Mohr Siebeck, 2022) 319.

that every agreement requires cause for enforceability. He linked the separation of the validity of a contract from cause to the admission of formal abstract contracts, which became widespread in German legal theory.[29] Schlossmann critiqued Bähr's position, as he understood cause as a concrete economic purpose and contracts as an instrument of economic circulation driven by interests and egoism.[30] However, he believed that cause should be linked not to the validity of a contract, but rather to its effectiveness.[31] Despite the controversy between Bähr and Schlossmann, they spoke with one voice on the tradition of separating the prerequisites for the enforceability of an agreement from cause. Like Bernard Windscheid, on this issue they drew on Roman law.[32] They were unanimous in their view that if a simple promise to pay was made for cause, in the absence of said cause, the promisor would be protected by a plea of fraud (*exceptio doli*) and by an obligation to restitute unjust enrichment.[33] Thus, the jurists who built the new private law system in the nineteenth century, basing it on Roman law, definitively excluded cause from the prerequisites for the enforceability of an agreement. References to cause remained in procedure, evidence and unjust enrichment. The evolution of *usus modernus* and pandectics ultimately resulted in cause not being included among the prerequisites for the enforceability of an agreement in the Austrian and German Civil Codes, drafted under their strong influence.

(ii) Removal of Cause as a Factor for the Enforceability of an Agreement in the French Code Civil

The fathers of the French Code civil, Jean Domat and Robert Pothier, gave its drafters a clear direction in thinking about the cause of a contract, with the former notably saying that 'no agreement binds without a cause'.[34] Pothier explained that 'where an engagement has no cause, or … where the cause for which it is contracted is false', the engagement is void.[35] Consequently, the provisions which listed cause as a prerequisite for the enforceability of an agreement were adopted without controversy. In the efforts leading up to the codification, it was only affirmed succinctly that 'it is difficult to imagine of an obligation without a cause', and it was emphasised that such a regulation of the enforceability of agreements required equity.[36] On the authority of Domat and Pothier, the French Civil Code adopted cause as a prerequisite agreement enforceability in Article 1108 CC but did not define the concept explicitly. This opened up a wide field of interpretation of the Code, which, in turn, sparked a discussion, spanning the nineteenth and twentieth centuries, on the utility of cause. Doubts in this area came from some prominent and influential French jurists. For example, Charles Demolombe

[29] *cf* A Stadler, *Gestaltungsfreieheit und Verkehrsschutz durch Abstraktion* (Tübingen, Mohr Siebeck, 1996) 15; Albers (n 28) 282.

[30] Schlossmann (n 27) 45.

[31] ibid 35.

[32] B Windscheid, *Lehrbuch des Pandektenrechts*, 4th edn (Düsseldorf, Verlagshandlung Julius Buddeus, 1875) 221–25.

[33] Bähr (n 25) 159; Schlossmann (n 27) 59.

[34] Domat (n 7).

[35] R Pothier, *Traité des obligations* (Paris, Debure, 1761) vol 1, nos 42–43.

[36] A Fenet (ed), *Recueil complet des travaux préparatoires du Code civil* (Paris, 1827) vol 13, 52 and 222.

observed that 'the history of the concept [cause] has not only failed to clarify its essence, but has contributed to obscuring it'.[37] Some voiced concerns that a provision introducing cause as a prerequisite for enforceability was theoretically wrong, unnecessary and even dangerous.[38] Referring to doctrinal discussions, Marcel Planiol argued in the first half of the twentieth century that cause was a false and unusable concept. In mutual contracts, he linked falsity to the fact that both obligations arise simultaneously, and saw uselessness in the fact that the absence of the object of the contract already makes it void. In unilateral contracts, he saw the falsity of cause in the fact that the absence of *animus donandi* meant the absence of consent, and argued that the uselessness of cause in unilateral contracts stemmed from the fact that the intention to donate is never wicked.[39] The doctrinal critique of cause was accompanied by a strong recognition of its importance in practice, in particular by the Cour de cassation. Hence, in opposition to the anti-causalists, the *néo-causaliste* movement also arose in doctrine,[40] whose members sought a clearer elucidation of the meaning of cause as a prerequisite for the enforceability of an agreement. In the twentieth century, this search brought about a clear link between the cause and the purpose of the contract (*but*). This did not produce greater uniformity, however, because the assessment of the purpose was either linked to intentions, which give subjective characteristics to the transaction,[41] or was understood more objectively as the result (*interest*) on account of which the obligation arose.[42] In clarifying the meaning of cause, it became important to point to other words or terms that clarified the legal meaning of cause. This direction included Carbonnier's argument that the word 'interest' is probably the most appropriate translation of cause, because cause is the interest of the debtor just as the object of the transaction is the interest of the creditor in a contract.[43] This trend is also evident in the writings of Jacques Ghestin, who, in the second half of the twentieth century, devoted much attention to cause as the premise for the validity of a contract. With regard to mutual contracts, he said that judicial practice excludes the existence of cause when one of the performances is illusory or derisory.[44] He also argued that cause is unlawful when one of the parties wants to achieve an 'immoral or illicit purpose'.[45] The introduction of views in the doctrine that clarified the legal meaning of cause and creative jurisprudence still did not remove the so-called anti-causalists from legal discussion.

In the early twenty-first century, opinions were drafted that framed cause as 'useless'.[46] Likewise, viewing cause as a prerequisite for the enforceability of an agreement was criticised as leading to doctrinal controversy and legal uncertainty.[47]

[37] C Demolombe, *Traité des contrats ou des obligations conventionnelles en général* (Paris, 1868) vol 1, 324.

[38] G Baudry-Lacantinerie, *Traité théoretique et pratique de droit civil* (Paris, Sirey, 1925) vol 2, 551–52, 601–02.

[39] M Planiol, *Traité élémentaire de droit civil* (Paris, 1923) vol 2, 354–58.

[40] *cf* M Giorgianni, *L'evoluzione della causa del contratto nel codice civile francese* (Naples, Jovene editore, 2018) 38.

[41] L Josserand, *Les mobiles dans les actes juridiques du droit privé* (Paris, Dalloz, 1928) 25 and 121.

[42] H Capitan, *De la cause des obligations (contrats, engagements unilatéraux, legs)* (Paris, Dalloz 1927) 5, 42, 347.

[43] J Carbonnier, *Droit civil: Les biens, les obligations* (Paris, Presses universitaires de France, 2004) 2029.

[44] J Ghestin, *Cause de l'engagement et validité du contrat* (Paris, LGDJ, 2006) 8.

[45] ibid 9.

[46] X Lagarde, 'Sur utilité de la théorie de la cause' (2007) 11 *Recueil Dalloz*, 740.

[47] P Remy, 'Réviser le titre III du livre troisiéme du Code civil?' (2004) 4 *Revue du contrats* 1169.

The problem of cause became part of the idea of modernising French contract law on the bicentenary of the entry of the Code civil into force.

(a) Proposal to Remove the Cause from the Code in the Terré and Chancellerie Projects

The first attempt to modernise French contract law in the twenty-first century was made in 2003 by a group of professors and judges of the Cour de cassation, led by Pierre Catala and supported by the L'Association Henri Capitant des amis de la culture juridque française.[48] In the project, unveiled in 2005, cause remained the basis for the enforceability of agreements. The draft proposed to amend Article 1108 CC by replacing the term 'une cause licit dans l'obligation' with 'une cause justifiant l'engagement'. This addressed objections of ambiguity arising from the use of the similar concepts of cause of obligation and cause of contract. A uniform concept of cause, justifying the enforceability of an agreement, was also introduced.[49] The drafting of the provisions contained therein made use of terms familiar from doctrine and judicial practice to clarify the meaning of cause, including the 'purpose of the engagement' (Articles 1126 and 1126-1), to link the existence of cause to the fact that reciprocal performance is not illusory or derisory (Article 1125), and to expressly state that without the intention to make a gift, the gifting act is void (Article 1125-4).[50] Four years after the publication of the Catala project, a team led by Professor François Terré and associated with the Académie de sciences morales et politiques presented a new draft modernisation of French contract law. In this case, the idea of specifying the cause in the statutory regulation was replaced by a proposal to remove the term from the French Civil Code altogether. Such a direction of change was consistent with the move towards a 'denationalisation', or at least a stronger Europeanisation, of French civil law.[51] In Terré's draft, the prerequisites for the enforceability of an agreement, defined as 'un objet certain' and 'une cause licite', were replaced by 'un contenu certain et licite'.[52] The drafters explained that 'nothing prevents one from calling content what others call an object, and purpose what others call cause'.[53] Such a change brought the Terré project closer – from a formal point of view – to the European contract law harmonisation projects, which used the term 'content' in their regulation of the effects of a contract.[54] Following on from the French discussion on cause, a provision was introduced declaring void a contract whose content or purpose (but) is contrary to public policy or good morals (Article 59).[55] A draft reform of contract law prepared in the French Ministry of Justice (Chancellerie) was then presented in 2008.

[48] *cf* V Vogenauer, 'The Avant-projet de réforme: An Overview' in J Cartwright et al (eds), *Reforming the French Law of Obligations. Comparative Reflections on the Avant-project de reforme du droit des obligations et de la prescription* (Oxford, Hart Publishing, 2009) 3–4.

[49] Giorgianni (n 40) 52.

[50] See www.vie-publique.fr/sites/default/rapport/pdf.

[51] Giorgianni (n 40) 17.

[52] C Aubert de Vincelles, 'Les principes généraux relatifs au droit des contrats' in F Terré (ed), *Pour une réforme du droit des contrats* (Paris, Dalloz, 2009) 113–14.

[53] D Houtcieff, 'le contenu du contrat' in Terré (n 52) 187.

[54] See Principles of European Contract Law, www.trans-lex.org/400200/_/pecl/.

[55] *cf* Giorgianni (n 40) 55.

In this text, the word 'cause' was also removed from proposed regulation of the prerequisites for agreement enforceability. Instead, the draft regulation of the contents and effects of contracts uses a term ('interest') previously applied in doctrinal discussion and case law to clarify the legal meaning of cause. The Chancellerie draft says that 'each party should have an interest in the contract that justifies their agreement' (Article 85) and that a contract is void when the consideration is illusory or derisory (Article 86).

French attempts to modernise contract law in the early twenty-first century aimed to overcome the deficits of cause as a statutory prerequisite for the enforceability of an agreement. All these attempts incorporated doctrine and judicial decisions that sought to clarify the legal meaning of the word 'cause'. Solutions more clearly rooted in the French legal tradition have drawn on this *acquis* in their detailed regulation of cause. Projects that took stronger account of attempts to harmonise contract law in Europe rejected the word 'cause' as a prerequisite for enforceability of an agreement, but in various ways recycled the terminology previously used to specify the meaning of cause, introducing it into provisions regulating the effects of a contract. Even these solutions that formally removed cause as a prerequisite for agreement enforceability did not temper the criticism from anti-causalists, who bemoaned that replacing the word 'cause' by the word 'interest' in the draft changes nothing.[56] They proposed a further simplification of the mechanism for the protection of contractual justice.[57]

(b) Removal of Cause from the List of Prerequisites for Agreement Enforceability in the French Code Civil

Cause as a prerequisite for the enforceability of an agreement was removed from the text of the Code civil by the overhaul of contract law in 2016. The prerequisites of 'a certain object forming the matter of the contract' and 'a lawful cause of obligation' were replaced by the prerequisite of 'content which is lawful and certain'. The change was introduced by ordinance, that is, in an extra-parliamentary manner. The 2016 amendment of French contract law ought to be seen in the broader context of the experience of judicial practice and academic debate. However, the extra-parliamentary mode of the overhaul means that the key reasons and aims of the change were presented in a report to the President of the French Republic.[58] In the introduction to the document, it was indicated that the intention was to 'simplify the regulation of prerequisites for the validity of the contract', including those concerning the content of the contract, and to clarify the principles governing contract nullity and termination.[59] The adoption of 'content which is lawful and certain' as a new prerequisite for agreement enforceability was explained by the fact that this term appears in several European law harmonisation projects, but includes what French law calls object and cause. The amendment of the Code civil was explained as a 'modernization aimed at adapting the Code to the evolution of economic

[56] C Larroument, 'De la cause de l'obligation à l'ntérêt au contrat (à propos du projet de réforme du droit des contrats)' (2008) 35 *Recueil Dalloz*, 2441.

[57] B Fauvarque-Cosson, 'La réforme du droit français des contrats: perspective comparative' (2006) 1 *Revue des contrats* 147.

[58] See Journal Officiel de la République Française [11 February 2016].

[59] *Rapport au Président de la République relatif à l'ordonnance no 2016-131 du 10 février 2016 portant réforme du droit des contrats, du régime général et de la preuve des obligations*, 1.

life' and a 'codification of the juridical decisions which – more or less artificially – were linked to the concept of cause'. The report to the French President says that the meaning of the new phrase 'content of the contract' is elucidated by several provisions of the overhauled Code civil, the contents of which include concepts or criteria previously used in doctrine and case law to clarify the legal meaning of cause.[60] The view that the 2016 amendment to the French Civil Code looked to reject the word 'cause' without changing the French approach to the enforceability of agreements is prima facie consistent with the report presented the President of the French Republic.[61] Consequently, there must have been an external decline of cause in France, as the term is no longer listed among prerequisites for the enforceability of agreements. Whether and how this change has affected the limits of enforceability of agreements in France remains an open question. I will return to it later in this chapter in my comparative reflection on what I have called the internal decline of cause.

(iii) The Rejection of Cause in the Polish Unification and Codification of Contract Law

The Kingdom of Poland, first established in the eleventh century, lost its sovereignty in 1795. Its lands were partitioned between Prussia, Russia and the Habsburg Empire. The partitions of Poland gradually led to local laws being replaced by foreign statutes. In the territories incorporated into Prussia, the Prussian Landrecht of 1794 was in force, later replaced in 1900 by the German Civil Code. In the so-called Duchy of Warsaw, allied with Napoleon, the French Code civil was adopted in 1808. After Napoleon's fall, it remained in force in some of the Polish lands, mainly those under Russian domination, as the so-called Franco-Polish law. Across most of the Polish lands incorporated into the Habsburg Empire, the Austrian Civil Code was gradually introduced. In the eastern territories, local law was replaced by the Svod Zakonov of the Russian Empire. Poland regained its independence in November 1918. The Codification Commission, established in September 1919, was tasked with preparing drafts of uniform Polish legislation on civil and criminal law. According to statements from the Commission's chairman, the new code was to be modern and tailored to the Polish national identity. Within that framework, the drafters responsible for codifying contract law had to decide how to regulate the prerequisites for the enforceability of agreements, and put together a document that would replace both the French and German Civil codes, the latter rooted in the doctrine of the German pandectists. The first draft codification of the law of obligations was prepared by a group of academic jurists led by Ernest Till. As a law professor in Lviv (Lwów), the capital of autonomous Galitzia in the Habsburg Empire, Till played an important role in what has come to be known as the pandectisation of the doctrine of Austrian private law, ie its reconstruction inspired by nineteenth-century German private law theory. The so-called Till draft of the general part of the law of obligations, published in 1923, proclaimed the principle of the freedom of

[60] ibid sub-s 3.
[61] *cf* O Deshayes, T Genicon and Y-M Laithier, 'La Cause a-t-elle réellement disparu du Droit français des Contrats?' (2017) 13(4) *European Review of Contract Law* 419.

all contracts that 'are not prohibited by law and not contrary to good morals'.[62] The draft's rationale indicates that public policy and lawful cause were not listed among the prerequisites for the enforceability of an agreement. The abandonment of the first of these prerequisites existing in both French and Swiss law was justified by the fear of uncertainty arising from allowing policy decisions to influence contractual practice.[63] The abandonment of lawful cause, meanwhile, was based on a brief reference to French judicial practice and doctrine. Ernest Till pointed out the discrepancy between the frequent use of enforceability of an agreement in judicial practice and the views of French doctrine, which 'in more recent times mostly considers this factor theoretically wrong on the one hand, and on the other unnecessary and even dangerous'. He recalled Demolombe's opinion 'that the history of this concept [cause] has not only failed to clarify its essence, but has contributed to obscuring it'. Till described the doctrinal divisions of cause as doubtful and controversial. Till saw Article 1274 of the Spanish Civil Code, where the elucidation of cause was supplemented by a statutory definition of the concept as *causa finalis*, the most accurate solution to these doubts without rejecting cause as a prerequisite for the enforceability of an agreement. Such an understanding of cause was, according to Till, evidence of the redundancy of its inclusion in the prerequisites for agreement enforceability, because for mutual contracts, it derives from 'the essence of the synallagmatic relationship', and for a donation, from the intention to transfer property free of charge. In addition to the French critique of cause, Till said that the best proof that cause in Article 1108 CC (as then numbered) 'is misguided' is that 'all more recent legislation (Swiss, German, Japanese, Portuguese, Serbian Russian and Hungarian drafts, etc) omits this factor for the enforceability of agreements'.[64] Till's proposed regulation of enforceability prerequisites was fully accepted by the co-referent of the codification draft, Ludwik Domański, who was an attorney specialising in the Code civil, then in force in central Poland.[65] The Polish Code of Obligations, formulated by the Codification Commission and brought into force in 1934, proclaimed the enforceability of agreements where 'the content and purpose of the contract were not contrary to public order, laws, or good morals' (Article 55). The phrasing of this rule did not repeat verbatim the content of any law previously in force on Polish territories. In the rationale of the final draft text, these differences are described as 'mostly formal',[66] implying their marginal significance. The abandonment of cause as a statutory prerequisite for the enforceability of an agreement is explained by reference to Till's preliminary draft.[67] The reference to Till's opinion on the redundancy of cause as a statutory prerequisite for agreement enforceability was supported by Capitan's view that doubts as to the understanding of cause can be removed if its meaning is linked to *causa finalis*, ie the purpose of the contract.[68] The adoption in Article 55 of the Polish

[62] E Till, *Polskie prawo zobowiązań (część ogólna). Projekt wstępny z motywami* (Lviv, 1923) 10.
[63] ibid 81.
[64] Tibid 81.
[65] *Projekt prawa o zobowiązaniach w opracowaniu koreferenta projektu adwokata Ludwika Domańskiego* (Warsaw, 1927) 21.
[66] R Longchamps de Berier, *Uzasadnienie projektu Kodeksu zobowiązań. Art 1–167* (Warsaw, 1934) 71.
[67] ibid 72.
[68] ibid 73. Longchamps de Berier cites the book H Capitan, *De la cause des obligations (Contrats, Engagements unilatéraux, legs)* (Paris, Dalloz, 1923).

Code of Obligations of the requirement that the purpose of the contract must conform to the law, good morals and public order was consistent with this opinion. The Polish regulation of the enforceability of agreements experienced formal changes following the introduction of the concept of legal transaction into Polish law in 1950, which covered contracts, and the introduction of a provision proclaiming the principle of freedom of contract by the 1990 amendment to the Polish Civil Code (KC). The former introduced the nullity of a legal transaction contrary to the law or the principles of social coexistence.[69] The 1990 amendment, meanwhile, precludes the enforceability of an agreement the content or purpose of which is contrary to the nature of the relationship, the law or the principles of social coexistence.[70]

B. The External Decline of Cause as a Complex Historical Process

In the civil law tradition, we can trace a process called the decline of cause. What I have called the external history of the decline of cause opens up a new perspective on the factors driving it and its essence. The origins of this process trace back to the pre-codification period, but they do not end there. It seems to me an oversimplification to explain the decline of cause as the result of how trivial it seemed to seventeenth- and eighteenth-century jurists that agreements would be enforced by law when the parties seriously intended to be bound by them.[71] The abandonment of cause as a formal prerequisite for agreement enforceability has been a complex process spanning centuries.

(i) The Roman stipulatio *as an Inspiration for the Legal Discussion of Cause from the Seventeenth to the Nineteenth Century*

Seventeenth-century German *usus modernus* jurists – inspired by the Roman *stipulatio* – moved the question of the cause of a contract from the factors determining the enforceability of an agreement to the area of assessing the legal effects of a contract. The shift was supported by the quest for simplicity these seventeenth- and eighteenth-century jurists were on. Such thinking was legitimised by opinions that consent was the same as the accepted allocation of benefits in a contract or by invoking Germanic loyalty in contracts. The transformation found its formal culmination in the recognition that a contract was just one type within the more general concept of legal transaction. This notion became one of the pillars of the theory of private law developed from the end of the eighteenth century and into the nineteenth by German jurists called pandectists. The references to Roman verbal contract (*stipulatio*) formulated within this theoretical framework led to the recognition of the enforceability by law of abstract legal transactions as well. Cause could only remain in the field of assessing the effects of legal

[69] The 'principles of social coexistence' clause was introduced in communist-controlled Poland in 1950, and has remained in use well into the present day.

[70] Art 353^1 KC.

[71] R Zimmermann, *The Law of Obligations. Roman Foundations of the Civilian Tradition* (Oxford, Oxford University Press, 1996) 553.

transactions, in the sense that the lack of a basis for the transfer of property gave rise to an obligation of restitution for enrichment upon the person who obtained it without cause.

(ii) Surrogates of Cause as a Formal Prerequisite for the Enforceability of an Agreement

The systemic exclusion of cause from the prerequisites for agreement enforceability led to the formation in the nineteenth and early twentieth century of the then-modern model, which included two clearly separated areas for the assessment of a transaction. The first was the assessment of the parties' conduct in the formation of the contract (consensus and defects in the declaration of intent). The second was an assessment of whether a contract or its terms could be declared void on the grounds that the contents of the agreement are contrary to the criteria imposed by law (eg good morals, public policy). The example from Poland shows that the choice of this model in one country often inspired its choice in another. Read in this way, the modernity of this model contrasted with the model adopted in the Code civil in 1804 of including cause in the prerequisites for the enforceability of an agreement. The arguments for its rejection were its anachronism and the criticism of cause in French legal doctrine.

(iii) Criticism and Late Overcoming of the Model Adopted in the French Civil Code

In the French critique of cause from the nineteenth century to its removal in 2016, two separate lines of argument can be clearly identified. The first is functionally similar to the reasons for rejecting of cause as a formal prerequisite for agreement enforceability in German theory of private law and in many other jurisdictions. Consistent with the model separating the assessment of the existence of the agreement from the assessment of the content of that agreement were the claims formulated in French doctrine arguing that cause is a useless or false concept. In such a model, the only place for assessing causality could be the assessment of the content of the agreement. This line of criticism of cause also includes the proposal to remove this word from statutory regulation altogether, on the grounds that it does not appear in the drafts of projects harmonising European contract law which emerged in the late twentieth and early twenty-first centuries. Such a statement is reminiscent of the rejection of cause by the drafters of the Polish Code of Obligations in order to make their new code more modern. I would link the second line of argument in the French critique of cause to the fact that the term obscured the idea of linking this prerequisite for the enforceability of an agreement to contractual justice, and, according to Jean Domat, only agreements that would give the benefits expected by the parties were to be enforced by law. Proposals to replace the word 'cause' with the words 'interest' or 'purpose', which are more precise criteria from the perspective of contractual justice, have sought to restore clarity to this link. An earlier example of this approach was the singling out of the purpose of a contract in the Polish 1933 Code of Obligations in assessing its validity and legal effects. The external decline of cause as a result of the 2016 amendment to the Code civil can therefore be described as another instance in the civil law tradition of overhauling contract law within which a formal distinction between the assessment of the conduct of parties at the formation of a contract and the assessment of the content of the contract was adopted (Article 1128 CC). The latter was clearly linked to the assessment of the purpose of the contract from the perspective of contractual justice (Articles 1162 and 1169 CC). Such attempts to modernise have not been clearly accompanied by controversy over the limits of the freedom of contract. The question therefore arises as to whether the external decline of cause makes it possible to identify changes in the boundaries of contractual freedom. Can it be said that the external decline of cause brings about some internal decline of cause, that is, an attenuation of the influence of justice on the limits of agreement enforceability?

III. The Problem of the Internal History of the Decline of Cause

A. The Idea of Causality in the Preparatory Work for Codes in which Cause was not Adopted as a Formal Prerequisite for Agreement Enforceability

It is the task of the lawmakers to define the prerequisites for the enforceability of an agreement in statutory regulation. The removal of cause from these prerequisites was accompanied by references to the principle of causation in contract law. The recognition of this principle in the preparatory works of the drafters of the German Civil Code can be retraced by following the discussion on the enforceability of a promise or an agreement to accept a debt, also when the cause for this promise or agreement is not indicated or is indicated very generally. A provision allowing for such obligations was already in the so-called Dresden draft of 1866, which was the starting point of the German codification of contract law.[72] However, the draft excluded the enforceability of an abstract promise when the debtor proved that he could claim restitution of the payment as unjust enrichment (*wegen ungehöriger Bereicherung*).[73] In the course of the work of the first codification committee of the German Civil Code (1874 –88), it was reiterated that the enforceability of a promise or agreement accepting a debt without specifying the cause for it required written form.[74] In the discussion, it was clarified that the abstract nature of the obligation is not to be understood as the absence or total irrelevance of its cause, but as the case where the cause of the obligation is omitted from the wording of the promise to pay or the contract for payment, or is stated in general terms.[75] The great advantage for the creditor of the enforceability of such promises or agreements was seen in the fact that in the event of an attempt to abuse them to the

[72] Dresden draft, para 922.
[73] ibid para 925.
[74] HH Jakobs and W Schubert (eds), *Die Beratung des Bürgerlichen Gesetzbuches in systematischer Zusammenstellung der unveröffentlichen Quellen. Allgemeiner Teil* (Berlin, Walter de Gruyter, 1985) 556.
[75] ibid 566.

debtor's disadvantage, the latter 'will be forced to unveil and explain the material cause in order to prove that he is not obliged for this cause'.[76] The members of the committee noted that in an abstract obligation, the debtor could refuse to pay when it would lead to unjust enrichment because the debtor's promise was contrary to morality or public policy.[77] In the first Codification Commission, it was considered 'obvious' that in such cases the debtor can raise a plea and no special provision is required.[78] The belief in the exceptional nature of promises and contracts whose content does not explain the cause for the obligation is also evident in the second Codification Commission of the German Civil Code (1890–95). In its second year of work, the committee accepted that there would be a provision in the Code declaring the enforceability of an abstract promise or agreement, but decided that there would be no such provision in the general part of the law of obligations.[79] The second Commission's restrained approach to abstract obligations also reflects the view that 'the cause of the obligation is an essential part' of the legal bond between debtor and creditor.[80]

The view of the authors, who interpreted the enforceability of abstract promises and contracts as an exception to the principle of contractual causality in German law, was therefore made legitimate.[81] The same approach was clearly expressed in the rationale of the Polish Code of Obligations of 1933, which replaced the French, Austrian and German Civil Codes previously in force on Polish territories. Said rationale explains that 'essentially all obligations are causal, as in all codes in force [previously] in Poland'.[82] The admission of several abstract acts in the Polish Code of Obligations was justified, as in Germany, by practical needs. Their list, unlike in Germany, does not include the promise and acceptance of debt without indicating the reasons for these transactions. In addition to the rationale of the Code, Domański explained that the purpose of a contract, in accordance with good morals and public policy, as a prerequisite for its enforceability by law means 'the advantage or use which the parties intend to achieve either jointly or each separately from the transaction'.[83] Domański's argument ran similar to the words of Domat, which the French jurist used to explain the principle that 'no agreement obliges without *causa*'.[84] The clear separation of the removal of cause as a prerequisite for the enforceability of an agreement from the principle of causality was indicated in the report on the February 2016 ordinance modernising the French law of contracts, which was presented to the President of the French Republic. In the section of the report describing the objectives of the reform, it was explained that 'the word cause, which had given rise to various debates, was formally discarded … but the various functions which judicial practice had associated with this word were

[76] ibid 563.
[77] ibid 564.
[78] ibid 575.
[79] ibid 584–86.
[80] B Mugdan (ed), *Die gesammelten Materialien zum Bürgerlichen Gesetzbuch für das Deutsche Reich* (Berlin, Decker's Verlag, 1899) vol 2, 1041.
[81] T Bremkamp, *Causa: Der Zweck als Grundpfeiler des Privatrechts* (Berlin, Dunker & Humblot, 2008) 164; Albers (n 28) 317.
[82] Longchamps de Berier (n 66) 75.
[83] L Domański, *Instytucje kodeksu zobowiązań. Komentarz teoretyczno-praktyczny. Część ogólna* (Warsaw, Ginter, 1936) 27.
[84] Domat (n 7).

retained in law'.[85] The sense of these changes is expressed well by the opinions that the principle of causality can easily be seen in the modernised text of the Code civil.[86] 'What was a seed has not died … French law does not depart from its tradition, it persists in the new terminology.'[87]

German and Polish codification work and the 2016 modernisation of the Code civil unanimously justify the conclusion that the process referred to as the history of the external decline of cause cannot be understood as allowing for the enforceability of agreements that would lead to unfair transfers of assets unjustified by rational egoism or altruism. The mechanism for implementing this principle is different when cause is a formal prerequisite for the enforceability of an agreement and when it is not. But must the effects of these disparate mechanisms be different? The starting point for answering this question will be the presentation of several interpretations of the word 'cause' offered by French judges, the functional continuation of which is provided by several provisions introduced into the Code civil in 2016. I will determine whether analogous legal reasoning can be found in German and Polish case law. I will also investigate the basis for such reasoning provided by the provisions of the Civil Codes of these countries.

B. How to Interpret Unfair or Unreasonable Agreements? A Comparative Look at Judicial Practices

Following the modernisation, four provisions were introduced into the Code civil, clearly inspired by the interpretation of the word 'cause' and thus continuing the function of *causa* as a formal prerequisite for agreement enforceability. Each of these provisions requires separate comparative legal analysis.

(i) Validity of Contract and its True Purpose

Among the leading cases in the interpretation of cause was a 1989 judgment of the French Cour de cassation, which assessed the validity of a contract for the sale of materials intended to assist in the performance of occult activities.[88] The judges held that their assessment cannot be limited to seeing the sale as cause, involving the transfer of ownership of materials, but must be extended to the purpose of the sale of those materials. The purpose of exercising the profession of guessing the future was considered by the Cour de cassation to be illicit and, consequently, such an agreement was declared as not enforceable by law. The essence of this reasoning was incorporated into the new Article 1162 CC, which excludes derogation from public policy either by the stipulations or by the purpose of a contract. A finding of unenforceability for agreements based on such reasoning can be found in German and Polish practice. For example, in 1998,

[85] *Rapport au Président de la République* (n 59) 3.
[86] Deshayes et al (n 61) 429.
[87] N Dissaux and C Jamin, *Réforme du droit des contrats, du régime général et de la preuve des obligations* (Paris, Dalloz, 2016) 57.
[88] Cass civ 1er, 12 July 1989, Bull civ I, no 293/Cass civ 1er.

the German Supreme Court declared the distribution of telephone cards for making erotic calls and the related loan agreement to be void due to the reprehensible purpose of such agreements. The basis of the court's decision was that the contract violated good morals.[89] Another example of a contract assessment focused on its purpose can be found in a 2008 ruling of the Polish Supreme Court, concerning a surety contract. The case involved a claim the transfer of which required the consent of the debtor. In order to sidestep this restriction, the creditor concluded a surety agreement by which the guarantor could step into the place of the original creditor. The Supreme Court held that a surety agreement entered into for such a purpose was contrary to the integrity and loyalty of the original creditor to the debtor. On this basis, the Court concluded that the agreement was contrary to the principles of social coexistence and therefore void.[90] The interpretation of what is illicit, contrary to good morals or contrary to the principles of social coexistence changes over time. However, the reasoning involving the assessment of the purpose of a contract according to these criteria is persistent in the reasoning of French, German and Polish judges. In more recent jurisprudence, this is illustrated by a ruling of the German Supreme Court declaring invalid a donation that led the donor to become entitled to adult social care.[91] In Poland, a clear basis for this reasoning is provided by a provision introduced in 1990, according to which a contract whose content or purpose violates the law, the principles of social coexistence or the nature of the legal transaction is unenforceable.[92]

The protection of contractual justice based on an assessment of the purpose of the contract is one of the fruits of the interpretation of cause. However, analogous possibilities to respond to the abuse of contractual freedom are provided by an assessment of the contract from the perspective of good morals or the principles of social coexistence.

(ii) Validity of Contract and its Economic Irrationality

A well-known French interpretation of cause is the *Vidéo club* case. The eponymous 1996 ruling of the Cour de cassation concerned a contract that a couple entered into with a videotape rental company in order to then rent the tapes out in their municipality. The small population of the municipality, however, meant that the couple's intended economic objective could not be achieved. On this basis, the Cour de cassation held that the videotape rental agreement was not enforceable. The judges explained that the lease had no cause, because the agreement could not have the economic benefit the couple expected.[93] This reasoning is now expressed in Article 1169 CC. According to this provision, a contract is void when what is agreed in return for the benefit of the person undertaking an obligation is illusory or derisory. The question of the relationship between the enforceability of an agreement and its economic sense has also been posed in German and Polish practice outside the field of application of the special rules

[89] BGH, 9 June 1998, XI ZR 192/97.
[90] SN, 4 April 2008, IV CSK 39/08.
[91] BGH, 20 November 2018, X ZR 115/16.
[92] Art 353^{1} KC.
[93] Cass civ, 3 July 1996, no 94-14800, D1997, 500.

on exploitation. Drawing on this reasoning, the German Supreme Court has declared a lease void when the market rent rate has been exceeded more than twice.[94] On a number of occasions, German judges have recognised the nullity of contracts concluded under so-called pyramid schemes (*Schneeballsystem*). For example, in 2021, the German Supreme Court declared null and void a contract for the acquisition of service packages that was intended to produce benefit by inducing further new customers to acquire service packages.[95] In the cases indicated, the reason for nullifying the contract was that it was contrary to good morals (§ 138 BGB). Polish courts, although recognising the link between the enforceability of an agreement and its economic reasonableness, have been restrained in applying similar argumentation. The Polish Supreme Court has said that a gross inequality of benefits will justify the nullity of a contract when it results from unfair use of their stronger position by one of the parties.[96] The basis for this reasoning is that such a contract violates the principles of social coexistence (Article 353^1 KC). Precluding the enforceability of economically unreasonable agreements by interpreting the cause is therefore not the only way to protect this particular aspect of contractual justice. Another basis for its protection is provided by clauses of good morals and principles of public order. Differences in their application are probably expressed by a more liberal or more solidarity-based approach of judges to market transactions.

(iii) Validity of Contract and Contract Terms Removing Debtors' Essential Obligations

Another famous French ruling on the interpretation of cause can be found in the *Chronopost* case, which saw the Cour de cassation deliberate on a parcel delivery contract. Chronopost, a company specialising in rapid parcel delivery, failed to deliver on time a package sent by Banchereau, thereby causing the company significant difficulties. Chronopost, however, refused to pay damages, referring to a provision in the contract that limited Chronopost's liability only to the reimbursement of service costs. The Cour de cassation, in a 1996 judgment, held that if the contract so limited an essential contractual obligation, it would have no cause. Consequently, the court ruled that such a limitation of liability had no legal effect.[97] The reasoning was later incorporated in Article 1170 CC. In accordance with this provision, 'any contract term which deprives a debtor's essential obligation of its substance is deemed not written'. Such an approach is also not unfamiliar in jurisdictions whose laws did not include cause as a prerequisite for the enforceability of an agreement. The German Supreme Court, in its assessment of the validity of a contract from the perspective of good morals (§ 138 BGB), said that the limitation of legal protection in a contract must not go so far as to undermine the essence of that protection, due to its role in preserving the legal order.[98] Similar approaches to contractual justice are illustrated by a 2005 ruling of the Polish Supreme

[94] BGH, 28 April 1999, XII ZR 150/97; BGH, 30 June 2004, XII ZR 11/01.
[95] BGH, 10 June 2021, X ZR 157/20.
[96] SN, 18 March 2008, IV CSK 478/07; SN, 31 March 2016, IV CSK 372/15.
[97] Cass com, 22 October 1996, no 93-18632, D 1997, 121.
[98] BGH, 6 April 2009, II ZR 255/08.

Court, which held that the exclusion of the lessor's liability for late delivery of the leased item is contrary to the nature of the leasing contract and is therefore void.[99]

From a comparative legal perspective, we can see that this reasoning of the French judges referring to cause offered a path to tread to German and Polish judges referring to good morals or the nature of the contract. In each of the jurisdictions considered, we find judgments ruling out the validity of contractual terms limiting contractual liability in a way that the judges considered unfair.

(iv) Validity of Contract and Loss of Cause for Concluding it

In interpreting cause as a prerequisite for agreement enforceability, the Cour de cassation also went beyond assessing only the circumstances at the time the contract was concluded. It ruled that events occurring after the conclusion of the contract could result in the absence of cause as a consequence of its disappearance (*causa finita*). In a 2008 judgment, the Cour de cassation assessed the validity of a debt recognition (settlement of action). In the case, an ex-husband recognised his debt to his ex-wife in the amount of 360,000 francs, and undertook to repay it in instalments. This amount corresponded to the child support that the debtor was obliged to pay to his ex-wife for his minor son. When the son came into his custody, he stopped paying the debt. The court held that the creditor's demand for further payment was unjustified, because the cause of debt's recognition, which was the successive payment of child support, had disappeared.[100] This extension of the function of cause is now expressed in the first sentence of Article 1186 CC, that a contract which has been validly formed lapses if one of its necessary elements disappears. From the perspective of German and Polish law, the failure to achieve the purpose of the contract is linked to the problem of unjust enrichment. The possibility of returning what has been rendered in such a case is understood rather narrowly, and limited to cases where the purpose clearly indicated in the contract has not been achieved.[101] With regard to the situation identified in France as the disappearance of cause, I see more uncertainty from the German and Polish perspective. It remains to be assessed whether the claimant's demand is contrary to good faith (§ 242 BGB) or principles of social coexistence (Article 5 KC) and is therefore an abuse of rights.

(v) Validity of Contract as an Element of Economic Operation

One interesting result of the French interpretation of cause was the enforceability of an agreement falling within the so-called *ensambles de contrats* (contractual link). This problem is illustrated well by a 2006 judgment of the Cour de cassation. The court was confronted with the problem of whether the early termination of a contract between a district heating company and a single consumer affects the validity of the contract between the heating company and its gas supplier. The judges held that when the two contracts form a 'joint economic operation', there would be no cause in the gas sales

[99] SN, 8 December 2005, II CK 297/05.
[100] Cass civ, 30 October 2008, no 07-17646, Bull 2008, I, no 241.
[101] SN, 17 January 2002, III CKN 1500/00; BGH, 6 October 2003, II ZR 63/02.

contract from the moment the heat supply was terminated. In practice, this meant that the heating company's contractual obligation to pay for gas after the termination of the heat supply fell away.[102] This legal reasoning was incorporated into the second sentence of Article 1186 CC, according to which

> where the performance of several contracts is necessary for the putting into effect of one and the same operation and one of them disappears, those contracts whose performance is rendered impossible by this disappearance lapse, as do those for which the performance of the contract which has disappeared was a decisive condition of the consent of one of its parties.

From the perspective of a German or Polish lawyer, this approach to economic rationality seems original. There is a concept of 'linked contracts' in the German Civil Code, but it is limited to cases in which 'the consumer has effectively withdrawn his declaration of intention to enter into a contract for the supply of goods or for the provision of a service', and as such 'he is also no longer obliged by his declaration of intention to enter into a loan contract linked to this contract' (§ 358 BGB). In Polish private law, there is no concept of a group of contracts forming a single business operation. In German and Polish judicial practice, I have not found any reasoning that would introduce the idea of linked contracts for assessing their enforceability as in the French interpretation of cause.

IV. Final Remarks

The question of the decline of cause provides an interesting perspective for looking at the tension between freedom and contractual justice.

This picture becomes clearer when we distinguish between the external decline of cause and the so-called internal causality of contracts. The former involves the removal of the word 'cause' from the formal prerequisites for the enforceability of agreements. The latter, meanwhile, concerns the validity of contracts in which the freedom of the parties would lead to transfers of property not justified by rational egoism or altruism.

The complex process of the external decline of cause, which has been going on for centuries, is not an expression of the internal collapse of causation. The primary drivers of the external decline of cause include the moving of the question of the cause of an agreement from the prerequisites of enforceability to the area of assessing its legal effects, the generalisation and simplification of the prerequisites of enforceability of legal transactions, and, finally, the protection against the ambiguity of the word 'cause' in statutory regulation. Such changes have been accompanied by the belief that the driving principle is the causality of contracts, understood to mean that contracts should not legitimise transfers of property that are so unreasonable as to become unjust.

The comparative analysis above shows that similar reasoning precluding the enforceability of an agreement due to its content has been developed in the judicial practices of France, Germany and Poland. Some differences in the application of these

[102] Cass civ, 4 April 2006, no 02-18277.

legal reasonings arose not from the presence of the word 'cause' solely in the Code civil until 2016, but from the historical variability of the interpretation of good morals or differences between the more solidarity-based or more liberal approaches of judges to market transactions.

Said comparative analysis also shows that the presence of the word 'cause' among the prerequisites for the enforceability of an agreement in France has paved the way for a broader consideration of changes in the economic rationality of contracts in their performance. This applies to cases which, according to German and Polish law, do not meet the statutory prerequisites of an extraordinary change of circumstances, and which involve the breakdown of the purpose of the contract not indicated in its contents or the disruption of an economic operation based on related contracts. Following on from this reasoning, Article 1186 CC shows that the external decline of cause has reinforced the predictability of cases in which the enforceability of an agreement will cease, in order to preclude such economic irrationality that it becomes injustice. Consequently, the external decline of cause in France may inspire the extension of contractual justice protections in countries that do not have the French experience of interpreting the word 'cause'. Inspiration may lead to the introduction of provisions similar to Article 1186 CC. On the other hand, in existing German and Polish law, it may lead to an interpretation in line with the spirit of provisions dealing with good faith (§ 242 BGB) or the nature of the contract (Article 353^1 KC) in contract performance disputes. Speaking of the external decline of cause in France, we can proclaim: *causa* is dead, long live cause.

PART II

National Reports

6

The Role of Consideration in English Law

JOHN CARTWRIGHT

I. Introduction

We have seen in chapter three that the doctrine of consideration has a rich and complicated history. This chapter will step away from the historical origins of the doctrine of consideration and focus on how it works within English contract law today. There is much rhetoric about the significance of the doctrine – which sees consideration as one of the essential building blocks of the notion of contract in English law, therefore emphasising at least its *theoretical* importance. Against this, however, we must ask whether the doctrine plays such a significant part *in practice*. The chapter aims to get to the heart of the role the doctrine plays within the modern law and how far it gives us the key to the notion of contract within English law, and to suggest what, from a comparative law perspective, it tells us about differences between the English contract and contracts of systems of the civil law tradition which do not have the doctrine of consideration.

II. Outline of the Doctrine of Consideration and the Scope of its Operation

A. The Requirement of Consideration

Consideration[1] is one of the requirements for the formation of every informal[2] contract in English law, together with the requirement that the parties have agreed

[1] For a brief account, see J Cartwright, *Contract Law: An Introduction to the English Law of Contract for the Civil Lawyer*, 4th edn (Oxford, Hart Publishing, 2023) 134–46; for more detail, see J Beatson, A Burrows and J Cartwright, *Anson's Law of Contract*, 31st edn (Oxford, Oxford University Press, 2020) 94–119; J Cartwright, *Formation and Variation of Contracts*, 4th edn (London, Sweet & Maxwell, 2024) chs 8 and 9; H Beale (ed), *Chitty on Contracts*, 35th edn (London, Sweet & Maxwell Ltd, 2023) ch 6.

[2] A promise may be binding by virtue of a particular formality – a deed – even if it is not made within an agreement supported by consideration: see Cartwright, *Contract Law: An Introduction* (n 1) 129–31; Cartwright, *Formation and Variation of Contracts* (n 1) ch 7. Some English contract law writers refer to such

(objectively[3]) on sufficiently complete and certain terms which they (objectively) intend to be a contract.[4] If there is no consideration, even if the parties agreed on the terms and intended them to be contractually binding, there is no contract: it is a matter not simply of validity or enforceability[5] of the contract but of its very existence. Sometimes we refer to the contract being 'void' for lack of consideration, but this is not describing a transaction which requires some form of intervention by a court or by the parties to set it aside:[6] to say that a contract is void for lack of consideration means that there is not (and never was) a contract.[7]

In English law, the agreed variation or novation of a contract (changing either its terms or one or more of the parties) or its agreed termination (such as the cancellation of a debt) is effected by a new contract,[8] superimposed on the existing contract: the general rule is therefore that consideration is required not only for the formation of a contract, but also for the (contractual) variation of an existing contract.

The doctrine of consideration focuses on the legal reason for a promise being binding on the promisor within the English law of contract. There are certain other mechanisms provided by the law for both the creation and the variation of legally binding agreements and promises – in particular, the deed[9] and the doctrine of promissory estoppel,[10] both of which operate without the requirement of consideration, but if a contract is to be entered into, it must comply with the doctrine of consideration.

a promise as a (formal) 'contract': see Beatson et al (n 1) 33 and 94; Beale (n 1) paras 1-052, 1-123 and 6-001; ch 3 of this book, by David J Ibbetson. Other writers limit the term 'contract' to agreements supported by consideration, seeing the deed (where it does not formalise such an agreement) as a unilateral act giving binding force to the promise by virtue of its formality: see E Peel, *Treitel on The Law of Contract*, 15th edn (London, Sweet & Maxwell, 2020) paras 1-001 and 3-172. This disagreement need not concern us here as long as the underlying point is understood: that a promise, even if it is not contained in an agreement, or is not supported by consideration, may still be binding on the promisor if it is contained in an instrument executed by him, as long as the instrument satisfies the legal requirements for a deed.

[3] For the objective approach in English contract law, interpreting the communications between the parties, and their resulting agreement, from the perspective of a reasonable person, see Cartwright, *Contract Law: An Introduction* (n 1) 70–71 and 97–105; Cartwright, *Formation and Variation of Contracts* (n 1) paras 3-02–3-08; Beale (n 1) paras 4-002 and 4-211–4-212.

[4] For some types of contract, there may be additional requirements of formality set by law, such as a particular form of writing for contracts for the sale or other disposition of an interest in land: Law of Property (Miscellaneous Provisions) Act 1989, s 2.

[5] In *Dunlop Pneumatic Tyre Co Ltd v Selfridge & Co Ltd* [1915] AC 847 (HL) (see text to n 22 below), Viscount Haldane LC referred to a contract not being enforceable by the party in the absence of consideration. However, the context of the case was not the requirements for the formation of a contract but who can enforce a contract, and in particular the common law doctrine of privity of contract: that a contract can only be enforced by a party to the contract, not by a third party.

[6] The contract being void must not be confused with a contract that is a *nullity* in a civil law system, which requires a court order, or at least a positive step initiated by the parties, to annul the contract; see, eg Art 1178(1) of the French Civil Code (nullity must be declared by a court unless the parties establish it by mutual agreement) and Art 5.59 of the Belgian Civil Code (nullity requires either a court order, the parties' agreement or a written notice by one party to the other). Such a form of nullity equates more closely to a contract being *voidable* in English law, where the contract is valid unless and until it is avoided, but that is the remedy not for the failure to comply with the conditions for the formation of a contract, but for other defects in formation, such as where one party has induced the other's agreement by misrepresentation, duress or undue influence: cf Beale (n 1) para 1-095.

[7] Beale (n 1) para 1-093.

[8] Or by deed: *cf* n 2 above.

[9] See n 2 above.

[10] Cartwright, *Contract Law: An Introduction* (n 1) 146–58; Beatson et al (n 1) 119–35; Cartwright, *Formation and Variation of Contracts* (n 1) ch 10. See further n 13 below.

B. An Outline of the Rules

The basic idea underlying the doctrine of consideration is that, where A makes a promise to B, B can enforce it only if he has done (or omitted to do), or promised to do (or not to do),[11] something for A in return for A's promise: in effect, he must have paid for, or promised to pay for, the promise he is enforcing.

The doctrine can be broken down into the following rules (keeping throughout the example of B enforcing A's promise):[12]

1. Consideration is provided by B when B does (or omits to do), or promises to do (or not to do), something at A's request. The exchange of mutual promises is sufficient to make the contract binding, but B's act, omission or promise cannot be 'in return for' A's promise unless A requested it, either expressly or at least impliedly.[13]
2. To constitute consideration, B's act, omission or promise must be part of a single transaction with A's promise. It is commonly said that 'past consideration' is not sufficient, although this does not mean that the time of performance must be linked, but the promises must themselves be linked and agreed upon contemporaneously. Where B's act appears to be separate from A's later promise, the courts will examine the facts closely to see whether the parties must have understood at the time that the act was to be remunerated.[14]
3. For B's act, omission or promise to count as consideration it must have some economic value: something which is to B's detriment and/or to A's benefit[15] – either is sufficient, but in most cases it is both, such as the mutual exchange (money in return for a good) involved in a contract of sale. However, the act, omission or promise need not be the payment or promise of money, and the courts will not enquire into the balance (or objective fairness) of the parties' transaction: it need not be 'adequate'. It is for the parties to determine the balance of their bargain, as long as there is something promised or given in exchange, and even the promise or payment of a purely nominal sum of money (eg as a token price in a sale contract) or the promise or delivery of a thing of purely nominal value (eg a peppercorn) is sufficient.[16]

[11] An omission ('forbearance') can be consideration, as much as a positive act, if requested by the other party.

[12] For more detail, see Cartwright, *Contract Law: An Introduction* (n 1) 134–46; Beatson et al (n 1) 94–118; Cartwright, *Formation and Variation of Contracts* (n 1) paras 8-11–8-39.

[13] *Combe v Combe* [1951] 2 KB 215 (CA). If B's act or promise is only *in response to* (caused by) A's promise, and not requested by A, B may be said to have *relied on* A's promise – a basis for the enforcement of the promise under the doctrine of promissory estoppel. This is an alternative to consideration in some common law legal systems (notably, in the USA: see, eg *Restatement of the Law (2d) Contracts* (St Paul, Minnesota, American Law Institute, 1981) para 90). However, in English law, promissory estoppel is not a general basis for promises to be binding by reason of the promisee's reliance on the promise: this doctrine applies only in a narrow context, and only for the variation of an existing contract: see Cartwright, *Contract Law: An Introduction* (n 1) 155–56; Beatson et al (n 1) 126–29; Cartwright, *Formation and Variation of Contracts* (n 1) paras 10-19 and 10-38–10-41; Beale (n 1) para 7-062.

[14] *Pao On v Lau Yiu Long* [1980] AC 614 (PC) 629–31.

[15] *Currie v Misa* (1875) 10 Exch 153, 162.

[16] *Midland Bank Trust Co Ltd v Green* [1981] AC 513 (HL) 531; *Chappell & Co Ltd v Nestlé Co Ltd* [1960] AC 87 (HL) 114 (Lord Somervell: 'A contracting party can stipulate for what consideration he chooses. A peppercorn does not cease to be good consideration if it is established that the promisee does not like pepper and will throw away the corn').

4. An act, omission or promise by B which he is already under a contractual obligation to perform in favour of a third party can be good consideration for A's promise,[17] but not (unless A obtains some additional benefit) one which B has a legal obligation to perform,[18] or one which B is already under a contractual obligation to perform in favour of A,[19] because B (being already under the obligation) suffers no additional detriment, and A (being entitled to it already from B) obtains no additional benefit[20] from B's act, omission or promise.

III. The Effect and Practical Operation of the Doctrine of Consideration

A. The Theoretical Effect of the Doctrine

In theory, at least, consideration is a fundamental doctrine of the English law of contract:

> My Lords, in the law of England certain principles are fundamental. One is that only a person who is a party to a contract can sue on it … A second principle is that if a person with whom a contract not under seal[21] has been made is to be able to enforce it consideration must have been given by him to the promisor or to some other person at the promisor's request. These two principles are not recognized in the same fashion by the jurisprudence of certain Continental countries or of Scotland, but here they are well established.[22]

The first of these two 'fundamental principles' – the common law doctrine of privity of contract, which was developed by the courts out of, or as a consequence of, the doctrine of consideration[23] – was reformed by legislation in 1999 so as to allow third parties in defined circumstances to sue to enforce terms of a contract made for their benefit.[24] But the doctrine of consideration itself has not undergone any general legislative reform.[25] What does it bring to the notion of contract in English law?

[17] *New Zealand Shipping Co Ltd v AM Satterthwaite & Co Ltd* [1975] AC 154 (PC) 168.

[18] *Glasbrook Bros Ltd v Glamorgan County Council* [1925] AC 70 (HL).

[19] *Stilk v Myrick* (1809) 2 Camp 317; 170 ER 1168.

[20] In a series of recent cases (not yet entirely settled: see text to nn 48–51) the courts have found consideration in cases where, although B's performance does not in itself directly confer an additional benefit, it may none the less indirectly confer a collateral benefit.

[21] ie not executed as a deed: see n 2 above.

[22] *Dunlop Pneumatic Tyre Co* (n 5) 853 (Viscount Haldane LC).

[23] *Tweddle v Atkinson* (1861) 1 B & S 393, 398; 121 ER 762, 764 (Wightman J: 'no stranger to the consideration can take advantage of a contract, although made for his benefit'; Crompton J: 'the consideration must move from the party entitled to sue upon the contract').

[24] Contracts (Rights of Third Parties) Act 1999.

[25] In 1937, there was a proposal to reform both the doctrine of privity and the doctrine of consideration: Law Revision Committee, Sixth Interim Report, *Statute of Frauds and the Doctrine of Consideration* (1937, Cmd 5449). However, this was not taken forward for legislation by the government, and the reform which was eventually enacted in 1999 was limited to the doctrine of privity. The Law Commission, which proposed the 1999 reform, noted that the doctrine of consideration might be a suitable topic for a future separate review: *Privity of Contract: Contracts for the Benefit of Third Parties* (Law Com No 242, 1996) para 6.17.

Most obviously, the requirement of consideration means that a contract in English law necessarily involves some kind of exchange: one party can enforce a contract against the other because he has himself done, omitted to do or at least promised to do something in return. In that sense, English contract law is based on the *bargain* model – even if (given that the consideration may be small or even nominal) it is for the parties to decide the balance of that bargain without any general control from the court.[26] Limiting the definition of contract in this way means that English law will not recognise as contracts certain transactions that would be contracts in civil law systems which base their notion of contract on the parties' agreement, with or without a doctrine of cause but without the additional requirement of consideration (exchange, or bargain). Sometimes, however, transactions which cannot be contracts because there is no consideration can take effect under other doctrines of English law.

In principle, the doctrine of consideration excludes from the scope of contract promises of gifts and other gratuitous undertakings where nothing is expressly or impliedly requested in return, however seriously the promises and undertakings may have been intended to be binding as a matter of law. Gifts can, of course, be given effect in English law. The gift, once made, is protected under the law of property; and although a promise of a gift is not, in principle, a (legally binding) contract, the parties – at least if they know the law or are legally advised – can make what is in substance a promise of a gift into a (technical) contract by using a token ('peppercorn') consideration,[27] or they can make a wholly gratuitous promise binding by using the formality of a deed.[28] Civil law systems, following the Roman law model, generally categorise certain transactions as 'real contracts',[29] where the delivery of money or some other thing (by way of loan of the money or the thing, or as security for a debt) gives rise to the obligation to restore it, or its equivalent, according to the terms of the loan agreement. And, unlike Roman law, modern systems can recognise as a contract an agreement by one party to make such a loan, even if the loan is to be gratuitous.[30] There is some debate as to how to characterise such transactions in English law. If the loan, or even the promise to make such a loan, is not gratuitous, it can be a contract in English law since the promise to pay interest on the loan of money, or to pay a charge or provide some other benefit in return for the loan of a thing, constitutes consideration for the loan (or for the promise to make the loan). But

However, no such review has been undertaken. For the Law Commission's project in the 1960s for a Contract Code, which (if it had succeeded) might have removed the doctrine of consideration from the English law of contract, see n 62 below.

[26] See n 16 above. There may be control of the bargain for other reasons, or in particular circumstances: the significant imbalance in the bargain may be evidence of some wrongdoing, such as duress or undue influence; or the type of contract might be one where the content is subject to judicial control, such as unfair terms in consumer contracts. But there is no general control over contractual balance – the courts never developed it for themselves within the common law vision of contract, and Parliament has never legislated to give such a broad power to the courts for contracts generally.

[27] See n 16 above. 'Nominal' consideration may even be something mentioned as consideration in the contract, but which is not necessarily in fact paid: *Midland Bank Trust* (n 16) 532. See also *Souglides v Tweedie* [2012] EWCA Civ 1546, [2013] Ch 373 [7] ('one red rose' as consideration for extension of the term of a lease, although the rose was in fact handed over: [16]).

[28] See n 2 above.

[29] See eg Art 1109(3) of the French Civil Code ('Le contrat est réel lorsque sa formation est subordonnée à la remise d'une chose': a contract is real where its formation is subject to the delivery of a thing).

[30] *cf* B Nicholas, *The French Law of Contract*, 2nd edn (Oxford, Clarendon Press, 1992) 40–42.

if the loan is to be purely gratuitous, it seems that the *promise* of the loan is not binding because of the lack of consideration.[31] Where the loan is made by the delivery of the money or the thing, there is an obligation to return it in accordance with the agreement, but whether that obligation is *contractual* depends on whether there was consideration for the agreement. The delivery of possession of a thing (a chattel) on the basis that it is to be returned falls within the peculiar common law category of 'bailment', which can be contractual if there is consideration for the use of the thing but is non-contractual if the bailment is not for consideration, a distinction which depends on the circumstances of the loan and in particular whether the bailment is for the benefit of the bailor (lender) or bailee (borrower).[32] The courts have found consideration by holding that, on the facts, the borrower, by requesting the loan, had received a benefit from it being made or, at least, the lender had suffered a detriment by parting with possession of the thing.[33] It is also generally assumed that in the case of a loan of money without interest, the borrower's duty to repay is contractual.[34]

B. The Practical Operation of the Doctrine

Consideration is a paradoxical doctrine in modern English contract law. There are cases where a court has found that there is no contract for lack of consideration,[35] but in practice the doctrine of consideration appears to be applied very rarely to deny enforceability to a promise or an agreement: in 1977, a judge said that 'A defence of lack of consideration rarely has merit',[36] and in 2017, another judge said that he was 'not aware of any case in the twenty-first century in which a claim founded on an agreement has failed for want of consideration'.[37]

This is not only a contemporary phenomenon. There are some older cases where the courts found consideration rather artificially (it has even been described as 'invented' consideration[38]) so as to make a promise binding, and thereby to provide a remedy, where today there would be no need for such an approach because another area of the law can now provide an appropriate remedy. For example, developments during the second half of the twentieth century in the tort of negligence have diminished the need to stretch the doctrine of consideration (and thereby stretch the scope of the law of

[31] A Burrows (ed), *Principles of the English Law of Obligations* (Oxford, Oxford University Press, 2015) para 1.32; *cf* Beale (n 1) para 42-271 (noting that there is no authority on whether a promise to make a loan of money without interest is, while still executory, unsupported by consideration and therefore unenforceable).

[32] Beale (n 1) paras 36-002 and 36-008; Peel (n 2) paras 3-168 and 3-169.

[33] *Bainbridge v Firmstone* (1838) 8 Ad & El 743; 112 ER 1019.

[34] Beale (n 1) para 42-271 (including an interest-free loan, at least once the money has been paid (see n 31 above) as a contract of loan of money); WW Buckland and AD McNair, *Roman Law and Common Law: A Comparison in Outline*, 2nd edn (Cambridge, Cambridge University Press, 1965) 222 ('In loan of money or other fungibles (*mutuum*) it is obvious that consideration has been given by the lender, who alone can sue on what is essentially a unilateral contract').

[35] eg *Costa v Dissociadid Ltd* [2022] EWHC 1934 (IPEC) [34]–[57].

[36] *Thoresen Car Ferries Ltd v Weymouth Portland BC* [1977] 2 Lloyd's Rep 614 (QB) 619 (Donaldson J).

[37] *Blue v Ashley* [2017] EWHC 1928 (Comm) [58] (Leggatt J).

[38] GH Treitel, 'Consideration: A Critical Analysis of Professor Atiyah's Fundamental Restatement' (1976) 50 *Australian Law Journal* 439, 440.

contract) in cases which can now be remedied by an award of damages in tort.[39] But this is only part of a broader scepticism on the part of the judges about finding that a promise is not supported by consideration where to do so would undermine the apparent intention of the parties that the promise should be binding, a scepticism which has grown stronger and become more explicit in the modern law. It may be that the kind of cases that come before the courts tend to be commercial, or at least cases where it is clear that the parties came to an agreement, and it is not attractive to allow one party to escape the agreement by appealing to the technical doctrine of consideration. Commercial parties will generally make agreements which are in their own interests, and – given that it is for the parties, not the court, to decide whether there is an exchange of value[40] – the courts are reluctant to decide that there is nothing at all of value in return: 'it stands to reason that there was consideration for the lease. It is highly improbable that the claimant, himself an experienced businessman, would have agreed to the one year rent-free period unless there was "something in it" for him.'[41]

Developments in other rules within contract law also contribute to this reluctance to find that there is no consideration and therefore that the contract was void (or, more simply, not formed):[42] the more the courts are able to rely on other rules or principles which have more nuanced application – such as a developed doctrine of duress, which does not prevent the formation of a contract, but only makes it voidable[43] – the more they see the doctrine of consideration as a blunt instrument that they prefer to avoid using. Sometimes judges have been explicit:

> Now that there is a properly developed doctrine of the avoidance of contracts on the grounds of economic duress, there is no warrant for the Court to fail to recognize the existence of some consideration even though it may be insignificant and even though there may have been no mutual bargain in any realistic use of that phrase.[44]
>
> The modern cases tend to depend more upon the defence of duress in a commercial context rather than lack of consideration for the second agreement … the court is more ready in the presence of this defence being available in the commercial context to look for mutual advantages which would amount to sufficient consideration to support the second agreement under which the extra money is paid.[45]

And the language that the courts have used sometimes suggests that they are really looking at whether the parties have agreed on their transaction, rather than focusing on the technical question of whether there is an exchange of valuable benefits: the parties' intention becomes decisive. As always in English contract law,[46] we are concerned

[39] See *De la Bere v Pearson Ltd* [1908] 1 KB 280 (CA); see also the discussion of the case by Lord Devlin in *Hedley Byrne & Co Ltd v Heller & Partners Ltd* [1964] AC 465 (HL) 528 ('today the result can and should be achieved by the application of the law of negligence and … it is unnecessary and undesirable to construct an artificial consideration').

[40] See n 16 above.

[41] *Kishenin v von Kalkstein-Bleach* [2014] EWHC 3416 (Ch) [12] (Deputy Judge Edward Murray).

[42] See text to n 7 above.

[43] See n 6 above.

[44] *Vantage Navigation Corp v Suhail and Saud Bahwan Building Materials LLC (The Alev)* [1989] 1 Lloyd's Rep 138 (QB) 147 (Hobhouse J).

[45] *Williams v Roffey Bros & Nicholls (Contractors) Ltd* [1991] 1 QB 1 (CA) 21 (Purchas LJ).

[46] See n 3 above.

with their objectively determined intention, not their purely subjective intention; but their intention is sometimes referred to explicitly as the determining factor:

> Consideration there must still be but, in my judgment, the courts nowadays should be more ready to find its existence so as to reflect the intention of the parties to the contract where the bargaining powers are not unequal and where the finding of consideration reflect the true intention of the parties.[47]

The last two quotations come from *Williams v Roffey Bros & Nicholls (Contractors) Ltd*,[48] a case which addressed the question in a particular context: the requirement of consideration for the *variation* of an existing contract, where the Court of Appeal held that, as long as the promise by one party (to perform the contract) provided at least *in practice* a benefit in exchange for the other party's promise (to increase the price payable under the contract, with a view to securing compliance with the contract terms), that '*practical* benefit' can be sufficient consideration – even though the party promising to pay more was already entitled to the defaulting party's performance and the latter therefore appeared to be giving nothing in return for the additional payment. This is still a controversial case. It has been criticised by judges in the lower courts,[49] but also applied by the Court of Appeal,[50] although still in the context of the agreement to vary an existing contract. But it has not yet been approved or rejected by the Supreme Court, which, in giving judgment in a case in 2018, declined to take advantage of the opportunity to consider it, noting that the issue is a difficult one which needs careful consideration.[51]

IV. Do the Recent English Cases Herald a Significant New Direction in the Doctrine of Consideration – And How Does it Compare to Approaches in Other Systems?

Legal systems do not often make fundamental changes to their core doctrines in private law, but it sometimes happens. In the civil law world, within the last 35 years, we have seen a radical rethinking of the law of contract in the Netherlands, with a new Civil

[47] *Williams v Roffey Bros* (n 45) 18 (Russell LJ).

[48] ibid.

[49] eg *South Caribbean Trading Ltd v Trafigura Beheer BV* [2004] EWHC 2676 (Comm), [2005] 1 Lloyd's Rep 128 [108] (Colman J: 'But for the fact that *Williams v Roffey Bros* was a decision of the Court of Appeal, I would not have followed it. That decision is inconsistent with the long-standing rule that consideration, being the price of the promise sued upon, must move from the promisee').

[50] *MWB Business Exchange Centres Ltd v Rock Advertising Ltd* [2016] EWCA Civ 553, [2017] QB 604. The context was the agreement to reduce, rather than increase, the payment due under a contract.

[51] *Rock Advertising Ltd v MWB Business Exchange Centres Ltd* [2018] UKSC 24, [2019] AC 119 [18]. The case was decided on another point, so anything said on the doctrine of consideration would not have been part of their decision. The Supreme Court was not prepared to comment on the doctrine of consideration and cases such as *Williams v Roffey Bros* because it might lead to the overruling or substantial modification of older decisions on the requirement of consideration in the variation of a contract (including a long-standing decision of the House of Lords: *Foakes v Beer* (1884) 9 App Cas 605) and such a decision should be taken before a larger panel of Supreme Court judges in a case where their decision would be formally binding under the doctrine of precedent.

Code which moved away from the Napoleonic heritage – and, especially relevant for our purpose, no longer bases the validity of a contract on the doctrine of cause.[52] France has removed *la cause* from the list of requirements for a valid contract,[53] even if it can be debated whether the doctrine of *la cause* (or, at least, its significant effects as they stood within French contract law when it was reformed in 2016 and 2018) are still present in a different form within the reformed code.[54] Belgium, by contrast, has decided to keep *la cause* in its reformed civil code.[55]

In the common law world, consideration remains a totemic doctrine of contract law. Even in jurisdictions where other bases of enforcement of promises have been developed,[56] or where the doctrine of consideration has itself been questioned by the courts,[57] consideration remains the core, and primary, basis for the enforcement of promises within the law of contract.[58] And although we have seen some doubts about the strictness of the application of the doctrine of consideration in the lower English courts, the Supreme Court has shown some hesitation over making any radical changes.[59]

In comparing the possible development of the doctrine of consideration in the common law with the developments in the doctrine of *cause* in the civil law, we need to remember the different sources of law and different approaches to the development of doctrines of private law. The recent formal changes in the Netherlands and France have been by legislation – reform of the Civil Codes – inevitable within the context

[52] The new Dutch Civil Code came into force on 1 January 1992, and made specific provision for certain effects that were formerly dealt with by the requirement of a valid cause ('oorzaak'): J Chorus, E Hondius and W Voermans (eds), *Introduction to Dutch Law*, 5th edn (Alphen aan den Rijn, Kluwer Law International, 2016) 194–95.

[53] French Civil Code, Art 1128, as reformed in 2016, requiring the parties' consent and capacity, together with lawful and certain content, and replacing the original Napoleonic text, which (in Art 1108) required consent, capacity, a certain object and a lawful cause. For further details, see ch 7 of this book, by Olivier Deshayes.

[54] S Rowan, *The New French Law of Contract* (Oxford, Oxford University Press, 2022) 103–04.

[55] New Belgian Civil Code, Art 5.27 (free and informed consent, capacity, a determinable and lawful object, a lawful cause).

[56] Many common law systems still follow the historical practice, inherited from English law, of formality (deeds) as a basis of enforcement of promises where there is no consideration: see, eg JW Carter, *Contract Law in Australia*, 8th edn (Sydney, JW Carter Publishing, 2023) para 6-12; SM Waddams, *Law of Contracts*, 8th edn (Toronto, Thomson Reuters, 2022) §172 (Canada); S Todd and M Barber, *Burrows, Finn and Todd on the Law of Contract in New Zealand*, 7th edn (Wellington, LexisNexis NZ, 2022) para 3.1. Across the different states in the USA, however, the use of deeds has been abolished or curtailed, although promissory estoppel has been developed very significantly to recognise reliance on a promise as an alternative to (bargained-for) consideration: EA Farnsworth, *Farnsworth on Contracts*, 4th edn (New York, Walkers Kluwer, looseleaf) §§ 2.19, 2.23. Promissory estoppel has also been developed more recently as an alternative to consideration in Australia (Carter, *Contract Law in Australia*, ch 7) and New Zealand (Todd and Barber, *Burrows, Finn and Todd on the Law of Contract in New Zealand*, para 4.6), although these developments are not as extensive as in the USA. Other common law systems are still closer to the English approach in allowing promissory estoppel (reliance) in the context of the variation of existing contracts but not as a general alternative to consideration in the enforcement of promises generally: in Canada, see Waddams, *Law of Contracts*, ch 5. See also n 13.

[57] In Singapore, see *Gay Choon Ing v Loh Sze Ti Terence Peter* [2009] SGCA 3, [2009] 2 SLR(R) 332 [92]–[118], a detailed critique by the Singapore Court of Appeal, although no formal change has been made to the law in Singapore where consideration remains a standard requirement for the formation or variation of a valid contract: *Gay Choon Ing v Loh Sze Ti Terence Peter* at [64]; *Ma Hongjin v SCP Holdings Pte Ltd* [2020] SGCA 106 [3], [59], [60].

[58] In the USA, see Farnsworth (n 56) ch 2, esp §2.02 ('Among the limitations on the enforcement of promises, the most fundamental is the requirement of consideration').

[59] See text to n 51 above.

of systems based on the requirement of legislation for the creation or reform of the fundamental rules of contract law. Judicial interpretation can go beyond the legislative text – sometimes very far – and in France there were some significant judicial developments in the operation of the doctrine of *la cause* before the legislator intervened with the reforms of 2016 and 2018.[60] But judicial interpretation of the code has its limits. In the common law, by contrast, the doctrine of consideration is a creation of the common law – the case law – and is not based in a legislative text. The UK Parliament could introduce specific legislation,[61] or even a general code of contract law,[62] reforming or even abolishing the doctrine of consideration. However, that is so unlikely to happen in the foreseeable future that we can discount it. Unless there is a demonstrable problem with the operation of the existing law, it is not in Parliament's interest to spend time on reform, nor even to ask the Law Commission to apply its resources to a project with a view to possible reform. Any reform must therefore rest on the courts, and although they can mould the rules of the existing doctrine of consideration,[63] and even introduce new, other doctrines alongside consideration to deal with its perceived defects,[64] the English courts are conservative – and the Supreme Court, in particular, is generally reluctant to make significant change to well-established common law doctrines. The fact that in the current circumstances the courts might not have chosen to introduce established doctrines in their accepted form is not a good enough reason for abolishing them: legal certainty requires continuity, and it is for Parliament, not the courts, to rewrite well-established and fundamental common law rules and doctrines.[65]

We have seen that there has been some evidence that, whilst not formally departing from the requirement of consideration for the formation of a contract, the modern English judges may focus on the parties' intentions to be bound to the terms they agreed

[60] See eg J Rochfeld, 'A Future for *la cause*? Observations of a French Jurist' in J Cartwright, S Vogenauer and S Whittaker (eds), *Reforming the French Law of Obligations* (Oxford, Hart Publishing, 2009) ch 4.

[61] *cf* the reform of the doctrine of privity of contract by the Contracts (Rights of Third Parties) Act 1999 Act; see n 24 above.

[62] In the 1960s, the English and Scottish Law Commissions contemplated a general reform of contract law by means of a Contract Code, although the project was abandoned in 1972 and the English Law Commission preferred thereafter to address issues of reform through specific legislation targeted at particular issues. See J Cartwright, 'The English Law of Contract: Time for Review?' (2009) 17 *European Review of Private Law* 155, 168–69. The draft text was later published; it did not include a requirement of consideration for the formation of a contract (a necessary reform for the proposed unification of the contract laws of England and Scotland, given that consideration is not a requirement in Scots law): H McGregor, *Contract Code Drawn up on Behalf of the English Law Commission* (Milan, Giuffrè, 1993) 3.

[63] As in the development of 'practical benefit' as sufficient consideration for variation of a contract in *Williams v Roffey Bros* (n 45).

[64] eg the development in English law of the doctrine of promissory estoppel in the variation of a contract since the decision of Denning J in *Central London Property Trust Ltd v High Trees House Ltd* [1947] KB 130 (KB) and its clarification by the Court of Appeal in *Combe v Combe* (n 13).

[65] See eg *Cavendish Square Holding BV v Makdessi* [2015] UKSC 67, [2016] AC 1172 [36] (Lord Neuberger and Lord Sumption: 'We rather doubt that the courts would have invented the rule [against penalty clauses] today if their predecessors had not done so three centuries ago. But this is not the way in which English law develops, and we do not consider that judicial abolition would be a proper course for this court to take'); *cf Beswick v Beswick* [1968] AC 58 (HL) 72 (Lord Reid, arguing that reform of the doctrine of privity of contract (text to n 24 above) should be made by legislation rather than the courts, although 'if one had to contemplate a further long period of Parliamentary procrastination, this House might find it necessary to deal with this matter').

rather than making a traditional, strict application of the doctrine of consideration.[66] Should this be taken further by some process of reform? Would the shift to the parties' (objectively determined) intention as the test for the existence of a contractual obligation, in place of the doctrine of consideration, be a natural step for English law to take – by legislation, even if it would be a step too far for the Supreme Court? It would certainly be so radical as to change the basis of contract in English law.

In English law, a promise is not binding just because the defendant had a good reason for making the promise, whether a good moral, social or economic reason – it is not, in other words, a version of a civilian doctrine of cause.[67] Nor, in English law, is a promise binding just because the defendant had a serious intention to be bound to fulfil the promise, an approach which, in various forms, other systems in the civil law world use where they have not developed, or have rejected, the doctrine of cause. There is a fundamental difference of perspective. The civil lawyer asks why the defendant's promise should be binding from the *defendant's perspective*. There are situations in which English law may ask a similar question – notably in justifying why a deed is binding on a party: the formal commitment to the instrument is the basis of its binding force, even if the undertaking it contains is entirely unilateral and gratuitous from the defendant's perspective. However, the modern English law of contract is not based on formality, but on other reasons for the defendant to be bound to his promise – reasons which focus not so much on why the defendant should be bound to keep his promise, but on the *claimant's perspective*: why should the claimant be entitled to enforce the promise? What has the claimant done to earn it? Under the doctrine of consideration, I can sue you under a contract not because you made me a promise, however well-intentioned and serious that promise may be, but because you asked me to do, to omit to do or to promise to do something in return for your promise. By my act, omission or promise I have earned in law the right to hold you to your promise. Even the doctrine of promissory estoppel, developed in the modern law of common law jurisdictions to supplement the doctrine of consideration,[68] has a similar emphasis: it is the claimant's (reasonable) reliance on the promise that grounds and therefore justifies the claim.

It may well be that the courts generally see a coincidence between cases where there is a shared common intention between the parties and the presence of consideration, and they have even moved in their thinking to the idea that intention would be a better focus, giving effect to a core notion of what contract should be about – to the extent that they sometimes mould the doctrine of consideration, or interpret the facts of a case, to try as far as possible to ensure that intention and consideration coincide. They

[66] See section III.B above.

[67] This was made clear in *Thomas v Thomas* (1842) 2 QB 851; 114 ER 330, where the civilian notion of cause was discussed (and Art 1131 of the French Civil Code as it then stood was cited), but Patteson J rejected the argument that it was the motive of the defendant (the promisor) in making the promise that gave the promise binding force in English law, as the consideration is viewed from the claimant's perspective: 'Motive is not the same thing with consideration. Consideration means something which is of some value in the eye of the law, moving from the plaintiff: it may be some benefit to the plaintiff, or some detriment to the defendant; but at all events it must be moving from the plaintiff' (859, 333–34).

[68] See n 56 above.

might even revisit some aspects of the rules determining in which situations consideration is required in order to make a promise or agreement binding – such as deciding that, whilst consideration is required for the formation of a (new) contract, the parties' agreement to adjust its terms (the variation of a contract) is sufficient without fresh consideration.[69] But it would be step too far to abolish consideration as a fundamental requirement of the formation of a contract in English law. It would remove one of the building blocks of the common law of contract and would change fundamentally the basis of promissory liability in English private law.

[69] This approach was adopted in the Uniform Commercial Code §2-209 in the USA, but not yet by the English courts as the rule for a contractual variation. *cf Combe v Combe* (n 13) 220 (Denning LJ: 'The doctrine of consideration is too firmly fixed to be overthrown by a side-wind. Its ill-effects have been largely mitigated of late, but it still remains a cardinal necessity of the formation of a contract, though not of its modification or discharge); for other references, see Cartwright, *Formation and Variation of Contracts* (n 1) para 9-24.

7

The End of *La Cause* (a French Perspective)

OLIVIER DESHAYES

I. Introduction

La cause was known to be an idiosyncratic feature of the French law of contract. It has prima facie disappeared from the Code civil. The authors of the 2016 ordinance reforming the law of contract tracked down all the previous occurrences of *la cause* and erased the word. Notably, *la cause* is no longer referred to by the provisions on validity of contracts.

The change in terminology is striking. But does it really mean that the French law of contract has shifted from a cause-based approach to a cause-free approach? The answer is undoubtedly no. *La cause* has not come to an end in France. Many, if not all, of the functions played by the notion remain, now being taken care of by a set of specific provisions drafted without using the word *cause*.

In fact, this is exactly what the French legislator purported to do: replacing the general, and rather mysterious, requirement that a contract be based on a cause by as many specific rules as this general requirement had given birth to in case law. The *Rapport au Président de la République* on the 2016 ordinance, which serves as explanatory comments on the reform, is very clear on that point. It refers to the 'formal abandonment of the concept of cause' (*abandon formel du concept de cause*) and adds that this abandonment has been decided 'while at the same time enshrining in the law the various functions … which the courts have assigned to it'.[1] This is why a vast majority of scholars talk of a mere 'removal of the reference to *cause*'[2] or change of 'flag'.[3] In a

[1] *Rapport au Président de la République relatif à l'ordonnance n° 2016-131 du 10 février 2016 portant réforme du droit des contrats, du régime général et de la preuve des obligations*, www.legifrance.gouv.fr/jorf/id/JORFTEXT000032004539. This solution was suggested as the lesser evil by J Ghestin, 'Observations sur le projet de réforme du droit des contrats' in J Ghestin (ed), *Les Petites Affiches, Numéro Spécial* (12 February 2009) No 31. On alternative solutions, also see G Wicker, 'La suppression de la cause et les solutions alternatives' in *La réforme du droit des obligations en France, 5e Journées franco-allemandes* (Société de Législation comparée, 2015) 107ff.

[2] F Ancel and B Fauvarque-Cosson, *Le nouveau droit des contrats, Guide bilingue à l'usage des praticiens* (Paris, LGDJ, 2019) 180 (in French) 378 (in English).

[3] R Cabrillac, *Droit des obligations*, 15th edn (Paris, Dalloz, 2022) 96.

suggestive formula, tainted with regrets, François Terré, Philippe Simler, Yves Lequette and François Chénedé say that *cause* has not been eradicated but instead 'pulverised' (*pulvérisée*, ie fractioned into smaller pieces).[4]

In this chapter, I will analyse how the transition from a single general requirement on cause to multiple specific rules has been implemented in the French law of contract. I will also try to assess whether it has been effective in terms of upholding the same solutions while making them clearer.[5] But there is more to talk about. Indeed, the French legislator's decision to formulate rules for the various functions formerly performed by *la cause* provides a unique opportunity to answer a question that is crucial from a comparative perspective: what exactly is the role of *la cause* in the French law of contract? Now that the once-opaque black box is open, we might understand more easily what *la cause* is performing and, consequently, we might find an answer to the question why some legal systems do not use *la cause*. Maybe they use it without knowing they do? Or maybe they have alternative tools to achieve the purpose that *la cause* serves in France? If so, then the differences between systems based on *la cause* and other systems would be proved not fundamental.

By now, it should be apparent that the term 'end' in the title of this chapter does not refer to the vanishing, death or disappearance of *la cause*. Rather, it refers to the function, the purpose, the role of the notion.

Before delving into detailed analysis, a few things should be mentioned.

First, the general requirement I alluded to earlier, which is now replaced by multiple specific rules, is the one that was provided for by the former Article 1131 of the Civil Code. This provision stipulated that, for a contract to be valid, it must be based on a cause that exists, that is not false and that is not unlawful (*illicite*): 'An obligation without a cause or with a false cause or with an unlawful cause cannot have any effect.'[6] It is worth noting that, despite appearances, these conditions were not considered to be three separate ones. The requirements that *la cause* exists and that it is not false are merged together (see below). Therefore, a traditional presentation by a French lawyer would only highlight two conditions relating to cause: *la cause* must exist and it must be lawful.[7]

Second, the Civil Code gave no definition of *la cause*. It did not take long to figure out that the term refers, in the context of the formation of contracts, to the reason why the contract is concluded or the obligation is undertaken (*cause finale*). But it did take quite a long time before scholars and judges agreed on the way to define *la cause* more precisely. There have always been two options. The reason why a party enters a contract can be found either in its personal remote motive (*la cause subjective*, also known as the *cause lointaine*, *causa remota* or *cause du contrat*) or in the standardised and immediate reason why a party to a similar contract normally enters such a contract (*la cause*

[4] F Terré, P Simler, Y Lequette and F Chénedé, *Droit civil, Les obligations*, 13th edn (Paris, Dalloz, 2022) 403: 'le législateur … a fait le choix, non pas d'éradiquer mais de pulvériser la cause en divers instruments de contrôle de la rationalité et de la moralité des volontés contractuelles'.

[5] For a pessimistic conclusion, see T Genicon, 'L'avenir de la cause en droit français des contrats' in G Albers, FP Patti and D Perrouin-Verbe (eds), *Causa Contractus: Auf der Suche nach den Bedingungen der Wirksamkeit des vertraglichen Willens* (Mohr Siebeck, Tübingen, 2022) 715ff.

[6] Note: the translations of provisions of the French Civil Code abrogated by the 2016 ordinance are those of DW Gruning, *Traduction du Code civil français en anglaise* (Poitiers, Juriscope, 2014).

[7] See J Rochfeld, 'Cause' in *Répertoire de droit civil* (Paris, Dalloz, 2012).

objective, also known as the *cause immédiate* or *cause de l'obligation*). After decades of debates, it was admitted both by scholars and by judges that *la cause* should be defined differently depending on the condition under scrutiny. In other words, the meaning of cause varies depending on whether the question pertains to (i) the existence or (ii) the lawfulness of *la cause* (see below). This polysemy is one of the reasons why the French doctrine of cause was sometimes regarded as complex. It certainly played an important role in the choice made by the authors of the 2016 Ordinance to split what relates to the existence of *la cause* and what relates to the lawfulness of *la cause* in different texts and to scrupulously avoid using the same words. Indeed, as we will see, the word *cause* has not simply been replaced by another one, but by multiple formulations directly naming what *la cause* represents in the specific context of each provision.

This having been said, we can now dive deeper into *la cause*. One could expect a two-part presentation, as *la cause* had first to exist and then to be lawful (see above). However, upon reading comments about French law from foreign jurists (especially English and German ones, whose domestic laws of contract have not true equivalent to *la cause*), I realised that proceeding in that manner would cause something important to be overlooked. Indeed, there seems to be a misunderstanding about the requirement *la cause* has to exist. The reason for this might be that French scholars tend to skip the question that foreign observers typically expect to be addressed under this heading and jump directly to a sub-question which may not seem connected to *la cause* for someone unfamiliar with the specifics of French law. To put it more simply, it seems that foreign jurists – or at least some of them – tend to concentrate on the requirement that every obligation be based on a cause. For them, controlling that a cause exists more or less amounts to identifying the cause and denying abstract obligations. For better or worse, French jurists do not pay much attention to that question. They usually take for granted that the obligation cannot be an abstract one and that the cause is already identified. They usually address another issue: that with the cause being identified, the contract is null and void if, at the time of its conclusion, the cause was only apparent, a chimera. For them, controlling the existence of the cause involves verifying if the elected cause can be achieved or if, for some reason that already exists at the time the obligation is entered into, it is entirely delusive. Since there are two different issues, I will deal with each of them separately. Therefore, I have divided the remainder of the chapter into three sections, starting with what is easy and ending with what is not: the lawfulness of the cause (section II), the existence of *the* cause (section III) and the existence of *a* cause (section IV). In each part, I will first describe the reasoning based on *la cause* that was applicable before the 2016 reform (the old French Law of Contract), followed by a presentation of the provisions that replace it (the new French Law of Contract), and finally I will provide some comments for the comparative lawyer.

II. The Lawfulness of the Cause

A. The Old French Law of Contract

When controlling the lawfulness (*licéité*) of *la cause*, inquiring into the personal motives of one party (*cause subjective*) instead of scrutinising only the immediate reason of that party's decision to enter the contract (*cause objective*) has advantages: it expands the scope of the control and maximises the chances the unlawful contract is nullified.

French law adopted this view long ago. Before the 2016 reform, *la cause* was indeed defined, when assessing its lawfulness, as the very reason that pushed a particular party to enter a particular contract: *la cause subjective*.

The only question was: if one party enters a contract driven by an unlawful reason or goal without the other one knowing, is the contract void[8] (*nul*) or is it valid? Overturning its own jurisprudence, the Cour de cassation decided in a 1998 case that it is void.[9]

B. The New French Law of Contract

The word *cause*, as we already know, has disappeared from the Code civil. But the rule that an unlawful contract is void has, of course, been upheld. Moreover, the 1998 ruling was also enshrined in the Code. New Article 1162 states that: 'a contract cannot derogate from public policy[10] [*ordre public*] either by its stipulations or by its purpose, whether or not this was known by all the parties'.[11]

As one can see, the reference to cause has simply been replaced by a reference to the purpose (*but*) of the contract. No real modification of the law should derive from such a minor change. Indeed, *cause* and *but* are two equivalent notions.[12]

C. Comments for the Comparative Lawyer

There is not much to say here from a comparative perspective. Hopefully, every legal system operates a certain control on the lawfulness of the contracts. It need not use the notion of cause to achieve this. As Reinhard Zimmermann puts it, 'there is no difference between … a statement to the effect that an unlawful contract is void and … that a contract without lawful cause is void'.[13]

[8] We use the term 'void' as an equivalent for *nul*. However, it needs to be said that French law – particularly since the 2016 reform – officially knows no automatically void contracts. It certainly holds every contract that is not valid for 'void' (*nul*) but, at the same time, it decides that such a contract will disappear only after it is made void by a judge (or after both parties have acknowledged its nullity). The English concept that would correspond the most is, hence, voidable.

[9] Cour de cassation, Civ 1ère, 7 October 1998, *Recueil Dalloz* (1998) 56.

[10] On the one hand, *ordre public* in France is not limited to what is prohibited by statute law. Therefore, courts can rely on this notion to nullify a contract even if the purpose of the parties has not been identified by a legal text as being unlawful. On the other hand, not every illegal act is contrary to *ordre public*. Only those acts that contravene some founding principles and consequently need to be erased fall under this qualification. For instance, the fact that lending money is a monopoly of banks (and similar entities listed in the Monetary and Financial Code) does not imply that the contract concluded by an unauthorised lender is necessarily void. In fact, the Cour de cassation ruled that such contracts are valid, with the consequence that the lender cannot ask for immediate reimbursement.

[11] Translations of the new provisions of the Civil Code quoted in this chapter are those commissioned by the French Ministry of Justice and drafted by J Cartwright, B Fauvarque-Cosson and S Whittaker. They are accessible at www.legifrance.gouv.fr.

[12] Henri Capitant strongly advocated in favour of the synonymy: see H Capitant, *De la cause des obligations*, 2nd edn (Paris, Dalloz, 1924) 3.

[13] R Zimmermann, *The Law of Obligations, Roman Foundations of the Civilian Tradition* (Oxford, Oxford University Press, 1996) 553.

Nevertheless, referring to the cause or to the purpose (*but*) of the contract – as France now does – adds a little something: it clearly enables the legal system to nullify a contract that is in itself (ie if you solely look at its content, at its 'stipulations') perfectly harmless but is nonetheless a way for one or both of the parties to achieve an unlawful goal. Lending money, for instance, is not a problem per se; lending money to finance an illegal activity is unlawful.

III. The Existence of *the* Cause

The situation being examined here needs to be described precisely. It is the one of a contract whose economic rationale is apparent. In other words, I will focus only on cases where the reason – at least the immediate reason, *causa proxima* – why an obligation has been undertaken is clear, known and taken into account by the law. For instance, an obligation to pay a sum of money has been undertaken as a counterpart for the transfer of ownership of a good (contract of sale); or the same obligation has been undertaken as a counterpart for a service (service contract, *contrat d'entreprise*); or a payment is made without any counterpart, as a pure gift (*contrat de donation*). In these examples, the contract is a nominate one. But it does not really matter whether it is or not. What matters is the fact that the economic rationale is known and taken into account. One could say that these contracts are self-evidently caused or inherently caused (which resembles the German *Kausale Schuldverträge*).[14] There is therefore no point asking if the undertakings of the parties have *a* cause. They certainly have one. Nevertheless, French law does not stop here, and this is probably where it departs the most from German and English law: it requires that *the* chosen cause each party has in mind really exists at the moment the contract is concluded.

A. The Old French Law of Contract

When assessing the existence of the cause under former Article 1131 of the Civil Code, there were reasons not to search as deeply into the mind of the parties as was done when controlling the lawfulness of *la cause* (see above). Indeed, if a party were able to void a contract based solely on the fact that a certain external factor, which it had considered while entering into the agreement, did not exist at that moment, then the other party would be in a precarious position. Personal motive should remain outside the boundaries of the contract unless the parties have agreed otherwise. For the sake of legal certainty, when assessing the control of its existence, *la cause* is therefore defined as being the immediate and standard reason for entering a given type of contract: *la cause objective*.

This was certainly true in France regarding onerous contracts. In such contracts, *la cause objective* was always the reciprocal undertaking, the counterpart one party

[14] H de Page talks of the cause being 'inscribed in the very structure of the contract' ('inscription de la cause dans la structure même du contrat'): H de Page, *L'obligation abstraite en droit interne et en droit comparé* (Brussels, Bruylant, 1957) 58.

receives in return for the obligation it undertakes (ie the English consideration).[15] The assessment of the existence of such a *cause* only involved verifying that the expected consideration really existed at the time of the conclusion of the contract in the sense that it *could* move from one party to the other, that it was not a chimera. If, for instance, someone entered into a contract of sale and agreed to pay the price, the contract was voidable for lack of cause if the buyer could receive nothing in return (eg the good did not exist or the seller was not the owner of the good). Similarly, the Cour de cassation ruled that a contract entered into by a company and a member of its board stipulating that the board member should perform a certain task and would receive in return a 'management fee' was voidable for lack of cause if the board member was already under the obligation to perform the said task: once again, there is no real counterpart to the price agreed upon.[16]

Two remarks can be made here. First, the lack of cause of one's contractual obligation is characterised when the expected counterpart or consideration is illusory (ie has no consistency at all). But courts also agreed to nullify contracts for lack of cause when the counterpart had some value but was considered derisory.[17]

Second, the requirement the cause exists served, in onerous contracts, to ensure that each party could receive the benefits that are expected to flow from the given type of contract entered into. If, for instance, a contract of sale is concluded, then there should be a transfer of ownership of a good in favour of the buyer. If no such transfer could occur for a reason that existed before the conclusion of the contract, then the contract is a nullity.[18] The Cour de cassation, in the remarkable – though much criticised – 1996 decision *Chronopost*, decided to push the control further in that very direction. It ruled that if a stipulation of a contract (a liability waiver clause in the case) deprives the essential obligation (*obligation essentielle*) that typically arises out of such contract of its substance, then the contract lacks cause. Surprisingly (given the ground on which the solution was based), the Cour did not invalidate the contract as a whole; rather, it ruled that the stipulation is deemed not written. The solution was upheld in later case law, but the reference to cause disappeared.

What about gratuitous contracts? How did the requirement that there be a cause apply to them? On that matter, judges followed a different path. They soon realised that limiting their control to *la cause objective* would be deceptive. Indeed, where a party undertakes an obligation or transfers the ownership of a good with the intention of gratifying the other party (*donandi causa*), controlling the existence of *la cause objective* amounts to verifying that this liberal intention existed. It adds nothing to controlling whether there is an intention to enter the gratuitous contract. Furthermore, the

[15] J Ghestin advocated that this *cause* is not abstract: it is the consideration modeled by the agreement of the parties and not a standardised consideration applicable to every contract of the same type. See J Ghestin, G Loiseau and YM Serinet, *La formation du contrat*, vol. 2: *L'objet et la cause – Les nullités*, 4th edn (Paris, LGDJ, 2013) 588ff.

[16] On this scenario, see T Genicon, 'Dialogues entre la cause et la consideration: à propos de la promesse rémunérée d'exécuter une prestation déjà due' in *Mélanges en l'honneur du Professeur Camille Jauffret-Spinosi* (Paris, Dalloz, 2013) 447ff.

[17] It should be noted that a derisory consideration is not simply one of small value, it is one whose value is so small that it is tantamount to no counterpart at all.

[18] It needs to be said that the condition cause exists was assessed at the time obligation is entered into (as with any other condition set forth for the validity of a contract).

argument put forward to limit the control of the existence of *la cause* to *la cause objective* in onerous contracts (that is, protecting the other party and legal certainty) does not seem as strong when it comes to gratuitous contracts. This is because the beneficiary of a gratuitous contract does not require the same level of protection as a party to an onerous contract. Since the beneficiary gives nothing in return for what it receives, it was argued that the beneficiary can be deprived of the benefits of the contract without triggering the same objections.

Indeed, French judges have agreed, in some rare cases involving a gratuitous transfer of ownership (*libéralité*), to verify whether or not the donor's consent was given based on a full knowledge of the facts. This amounts to controlling the existence of *la cause subjective*, the personal motive. For example, if someone donates their property to a friend under the belief that they have no living heirs but it is later discovered that they did have an heir at the time of the donation, the donation is voidable for lack of cause.

B. The New French Law of Contract

All the above-mentioned solutions were upheld in 2016.

With regard to onerous contracts, Article 1169 of the Code civil now provides that 'An onerous contract is a nullity where, at the moment of its formation, what is agreed in return [*la contrepartie convenue*] for the benefit of a person undertaking an obligation is illusory or derisory'. Even the *Chronopost* decision was enshrined in the Code. Article 1170 indeed states that 'Any contract term which deprives a debtor's essential obligation of its substance is deemed not written'.

With regard to gratuitous contracts, Article 1135 now states that 'mistake about the motive for an act of generosity [*libéralité*] is a ground for nullity where, but for the mistake, the donor would not have made it'.

On these points, as one can see, the reform did not bring any change to the pre-existing law.[19] Did it clarify it? To a large extent, yes. Solutions are now straightforward: one can read them in the Code without having to distinguish between *cause objective* and *subjective* or between onerous and gratuitous contracts.[20]

Nevertheless, the reform also raises some questions. This is mainly because, instead of a general rule, applicable to every contract, there is now a set of specific provisions (one dedicated to onerous contract and one dedicated to *libéralités*) that do not embrace all scenarios.

What about, for instance, gratuitous service contracts? They do not fall within the scope of Article 1135, for this text is limited to *libéralités* (ie gratuitous transfer of ownership). Will the judge nevertheless be able to invalidate such a contract on the

[19] With one possible minor exception: since the lack of cause of *libéralités* is now seen as a matter of mistake (Art 1135), nullity will logically require that the mistake be excusable (*excusable*). Such a requirement did not seem to exist before.

[20] Inquiring into the way judges who sometimes used *la cause* to push forward the control on validity of contract could keep on doing so using other rules or notions, see J Rochfeld, 'The Abolition of the Cause: A Clean Slate and New Bases for Court Intervention (Standard-Form Contracts, Dependence, Error)?' in B Fauvarque-Cosson and G Wicker (ed), *La réforme du droit français des contrats*/[December 2017] *Montesquieu Law Review* Special Issue: *The Reform of French Contract Law* 87.

grounds that the debtor committed a mistake relating to its own motive? Scholars are divided. Some of them consider that Article 1135 should be applied to gratuitous service contracts.[21] Others suggest seizing the opportunity to build a slightly different regime for them.[22]

And what about contracts that are not evidently onerous but clearly are not *libéralités* either, such as a guarantee (*cautionnement*) or an acknowledgement of a pre-existing debt? Should they fall within the scope of Article 1169 or should they be left orphan of a text imposing there be a cause? The *Rapport au Président de la République* on the 2016 ordinance gives an answer to this. It indicates that the reference to 'onerous contract' in Article 1169 shall not be construed as pointing only towards bilateral commutative contracts – for which an 'agreed counterpart' (*contrepartie convenue*) is easily found and equates to the English consideration. The text, it is said, also embraces aleatory contracts (*contrats aléatoires*) and onerous unilateral contracts (*contrats unilatéraux à titre onéreux*,[23] such as option contracts (*contrat de promesse de contrat*) and maybe guarantees). However, some scholars are sceptical about this interpretation of the text and suggest, once again, seizing the opportunity to advocate for alternative reasonings.[24]

C. Comments for the Comparative Lawyer

The requirement that the cause exists for the contract to be valid is probably the most surprising feature of the French doctrine of cause, at least for jurists not used to the notion of cause. Some foreign jurists would probably find it easier to address issues dealt with by *la cause* using other notions.

This is particularly true of defects in consent and notably mistake. Some arguments are indeed in favour of that position. The first is that when the 2016 legislator enshrined in Article 1135 of the Code civil the solution that an erroneous personal motive (*cause subjective*) could be a ground for nullity of *libéralités*, it did so by adding a new text on mistake (indeed, Article 1135 deals with mistake, *erreur vice du consentement*). A second argument is that a pure lack of cause is never seen. If the cause is lacking (ie is illusory), then it must be because the party who pursued that cause made a mistake or was forced to enter the contract.[25] Indeed, some French scholars suggested before 2016

[21] See O Deshayes, T Genicon and YM Laithier, *Réforme du droit des contrats, du régime général et de la preuve des obligations*, 2nd edn (Paris, LexisNexis, 2018) 228; F Chénedé, *Droit des obligations et des contrats*, 3rd edn (Paris, Dalloz, 2023) 123, 301.

[22] G Wicker, 'De la survie des fonctions de la cause: ébauche d'une théorie des motifs' (2020) 34 *Recueil Dalloz* 1906.

[23] 'L'ordonnance codifie la jurisprudence actuelle de la Cour de cassation sur la nullité des contrats à titre onéreux lorsque, au moment de la formation du contrat, la contrepartie convenue est inexistante ou dérisoire, étant observé que le champ de cet article dépasse celui des contrats synallagmatiques et commutatifs, de sorte qu'y sont également soumis les contrats aléatoires et les contrats unilatéraux à titre onéreux (art 1169)'.

[24] See Chénedé (n 21) 123.311ff. The solutions would not be different, but the reasoning would.

[25] This is precisely why it was largely admitted before 2016 that the requirements that the cause exist and that it not be false were not two separate ones (see the introduction of this chapter). A false cause implies that a mistake has been committed about the cause, leading one party to believe that the elected cause is not illusory whereas in fact it is. Requiring that there be no false cause (*fausse cause*) consequently adds nothing

that cause should be jettisoned. The notion, they said, is useless; provisions on defects in consent suffice.[26]

There is an answer to this[27] – and quite a convincing one, in my opinion. If one limits the discussion to onerous contract, the fact that there can be no real consideration moving from one party to the other (even though the type of contract entered into entails one) does not call for a sanction because the consent is defective. Instead, there is a sanction because it is unjust for the party receiving nothing to remain bound by the contract. It is a question of commutative justice. Therefore, the nullity of the contract need not be submitted to the conditions applicable to defects in consent. Not only is the party claiming for nullity relieved from the duty to prove that its consent was defective, but it will also succeed in its claim even though the conditions set forth by the law regarding defects in consent are not fulfilled. In France, mistake, for instance, will lead to the annulment of contract only if the mistake is excusable (*erreur excusable*).[28] No such condition is required on the ground of lack of cause.[29] And there is a good reason for this. When the law sets the conditions under which a defect in consent can lead to the nullity of the contract (especially mistake), it searches for an equilibrium between the protection of the interests of the victim of the defect and those of the other party. No such equilibrium matters in case of lack of cause, for the party who gives nothing never deserves to keep what it received from the other party.

Some legal systems might also prefer to address the issue raised by the initial lack of cause in onerous contracts as a matter of unseriousness of the consent to be bound by the contract. They would argue that the party who claimed it would provide a consideration had no real intention to be bound by the contract where that consideration did not exist. This is indeed an acceptable alternative to *la cause*. But it is doubtful it can replace it in every situation, for it requires that the party pretending it would provide a given consideration knew that that consideration could not be provided. Moreover, it misses what is essential in the doctrine of cause. Nullifying a contract for the initial lack of a cause in onerous contracts is not, as I have already said, a matter of verifying that consent exists and is not defective: it is a matter of commutative justice. Regardless of consent, in a contract which entails a consideration moving from one party to the other, if the consideration cannot be provided for a reason that already existed at the time the contract was concluded, then the contract is null and void.

There is a far better competitor to *la cause* (ie a functional equivalent) in onerous contract. If it is true that the lack of cause is characterised when, at the time of the

to requiring that the cause exists (ie is not illusory). See P Malaurie, L Aynès and P Stoffel-Munck, *Droit des obligations*, 12th edn (Paris, Defrénois, 2022) 383, 353: 'il n'y a pas de différence entre l'absence de contrepartie et la fausse contrepartie' ('there is no difference between the absence of consideration and false consideration'); *contra* JR Binet, 'De la fausse cause' (2004) 4 *Revue trimestrielle de droit civil* 655.

[26] X Lagarde, 'Sur l'utilité de la théorie de la cause' (2007) 11 *Recueil Dalloz* 740; L Aynès, 'La cause, inutile et dangereuse' (2014) 240 *Droit et patrimoine* 40; C Grimaldi, 'Les maux de la cause ne sont pas qu'une affaire de mots' (2015) 14 *Recueil Dalloz* 814.

[27] See Genicon, 'Dialogues entre la cause et la consideration' (n 16) 493; see also H, L and J Mazeaud, *Leçons de droit civil*, vol 2, 2nd edn (Montchrestien, Paris, 1962) 254.

[28] The solution now lies in Art 1132 of the Code civil. It existed in case law before the 2016 reform.

[29] See Cour de cassation, Civ 1ère, 10 May 1995, reproduced in H Beale, B Fauvarque-Cosson, J Rutgers, D Tallon and S Vogenauer, *Contract Law*, 2nd edn (Hart Publishing, Oxford, 2010) 5.10.

contract, there is no real consideration offered by one party, then why not treat this as a problem of performance of the contract? For instance, in a sales contract, if the good no more exists on the date of the agreement, why not say the sale is valid and simply grant the buyer the remedies for non-performance of the seller's undertakings?[30]

Once again, this is a perfectly acceptable alternative. In such a situation of initial impossibility, French law holds that the contract is voidable for lack of cause,[31] but other legal systems – the German one in particular, if I understand correctly – would reason in terms of non-performance. This makes a difference, though not a big one in the context of our discussion. Indeed, in both cases, the legal systems come a similar conclusion: the party which receives nothing should be granted an action. Henri Capitant did not hesitate to see remedies for non-performance in onerous contracts as a piece of the doctrine of *la cause*, which, in his opinion, embraced many other solutions than the requirement, set forth for the validity of contracts, that the cause exists.[32] Non-performance could, conversely, easily 'absorb' some of the issues raised by the lack of cause.

However, it is doubtful rules on non-performance could totally replace the requirement that *la cause* exists at the time the contract is concluded. Let us take the example of the contract concluded between a company and one of its board members (see above). Without *la cause*, there would be no action for the company who undertook to pay management fees, even though it receives nothing other than what was already due. In such a case, indeed, the problem does not arise from the non-performance of an obligation; rather, it arises from the fact that the board member gives nothing new or real in return for the management fees. Well, there could, in fact, be an action for the company, but it would have to be based on a totally different ground: unjustified enrichment.

Precisely, unjustified enrichment is another competitor to *la cause*. A legal system could opt not to invalidate an onerous contract for initial lack of *cause* and instead grant an action for repayment to the party which performed its obligation receiving nothing in return. But again, this would not make a big difference. Indeed, in both cases, the party which has performed its obligation would not be left without an action. However, to a French jurist, the reasoning based on unjustified enrichment does not appear any better than the reasoning it is accustomed to. Why would a legal system persist in considering a contract valid if, at the moment it is concluded, it is already possible to say that the expected consideration to one's undertaking does not really exist? Why would it do so while finally granting an action for repayment on the grounds that this payment was unjustified? It even seems that in some legal systems – notably

[30] On this matter, see C Witz, 'L'impossibilité initiale de la prestation doit-elle être sanctionnée par la nullité du contrat?' in *Mélanges en l'honneur de Pascal Ancel* (Brussels, Larcier, 2021) 663ff.

[31] The nullity of the contract may also be based on the impossibility of the subject matter (*contenu*) of the contract (Civil Code, Art 1163: the performance which is the object of the obligation must be possible). This is another reason *la cause* is said to be useless by its opponents. This is particularly true among 19th- and early 20th-century scholars: F Laurent, *Principes de droit civil français*, vol 16, 2nd edn (Brussels, Bruylant, 1876) 111; M Planiol, *Traité élémentaire de droit civil français*, vol 2, 8th edn (Paris, LGDJ, 1921) 1037ff. For a recent presentation suggesting that *la cause* was not the ground on which nullity of contracts was based in case of initial impossibility of performance, see S Fulli-Lemaire, 'Le role passé de la cause au stade de la formation du contrat' in Albers et al (n 5) 407ff.

[32] Capitant (n 12) 259ff.

the German one, if I understand correctly again – unjustified enrichment allows the party receiving nothing not to perform its obligation (instead of having to perform and then be granted an action for repayment). If this is correct, then the difference between nullifying the contract on the ground of *la cause* and treating it as valid is tantamount to nothing: indeed, in both cases, the party receiving nothing is free not to perform. But let us not go too fast. It is not certain that the question under scrutiny here (the initial lack of cause) would be seen as one triggering the application of the provisions on unjustified enrichment in legal systems where this notion plays a large role. These provisions are, on the contrary, of crucial importance when another question is examined: that of existence of *a* cause.

IV. The Existence of *a* Cause

The situation being examined here is different from the previous one. Let us suppose that an obligation has been undertaken without the debtor giving any reason or without the law taking that reason into account. The obligation, one might say, stands by mere virtue it has been agreed upon, the economic rationale remaining in the dark. By way of simplification, one might say the undertaking exists without a cause.

Two different scenarios are possible. In the first one, the debtor undertakes an obligation without saying why. It is clear there is a cause or reason, unless the debtor is insane. The problem is: that reason remains unknown. We will refer to this as a case of undisclosed cause.

In the second scenario, the parties want or the law provides that an undertaking is valid regardless of its cause. In other words, no defence relating to why the obligation has been undertaken can theoretically be raised by the debtor. We will refer to this as a case of abstract obligation.

A. The Old French Law of Contract

Before the 2016 reform, the fact that the cause was not disclosed was not in itself a ground for nullity. Indeed, after former Article 1131 of the Code civil required every contract be based on a cause, former Article 1132 provided that: 'An agreement is nevertheless valid, although the cause is not expressed.' It was for the party who claimed a contract is not valid to disclose the cause of the obligation and then demonstrate why the contract is void (eg the contract is gratuitous and applicable formalities were not accomplished; the contract is onerous and the expected consideration is illusory). If one looks closely, this means that the undertaking without an expressed cause was not null and void per se, but it was not considered an abstract obligation either.

Precisely, regarding abstract obligations, French law was not as decidedly opposed to it as one might think. It is true that the requirement that every contract be based on a cause (Article 1131 of the Code civil) seemed incompatible with the idea that an obligation could be valid regardless of why the consent has been given. But on the other hand, French law did and still does make room for valid and enforceable payment obligations regardless of the lack of a good underlying reason for such obligations.[33] It does so, as do many other legal systems, where it wants to protect the creditor, giving him the right to be paid without having to care about the economic rationale of the debtor's undertaking. That happens particularly – if not only – where more than two parties are involved, the law wanting to protect the creditor against defences arising from the relations between that debtor and a third party (in France, *lettre de change*, *délégation*, *garantie autonome*, etc). This shows that requiring, as a general condition for the validity of a contract, that there be a valid cause does not lead to prohibiting every abstract obligation.[34]

B. The New French Law of Contract

As surprising as it may be from a foreign point of view, the 2016 ordinance remained silent about these issues. Not only did it remain silent about the solution once provided for by former Article 1132 (undisclosed cause), but it also said nothing about abstract obligation. Indeed, it erased the general requirement a contract be based on a cause and did not replace it. More surprisingly, maybe, most French scholars did not pay much attention to this. For sure, this was not the most important part of the French doctrine of cause. But perhaps another reason is that, in the minds of many, upholding the solutions did not require a text be added to the Code.

This is certainly true as regards undisclosed cause. The Civil Code used to say that undertakings without an expressed cause or reason were not a problem. The fact that the new texts say nothing about them does not turn them into a problem.[35]

The same may be said about abstract obligations. Just because the Code is silent on the matter does not mean that parties are now free to enter such obligations. On the contrary, there are strong reasons to believe that nothing has changed. First, the ordinance intended to clarify the requirements based on *la cause* and not to change the law. Second, the above-mentioned requirement that *the* cause has to exist logically implies that the obligation in the first place has *a* cause, an identified one taken into account by the law. It would indeed be very surprising if the parties could bypass the control of the existence of *the* cause by simply pretending their undertakings are two disconnected abstract obligations. Third, on an even more general level, allowing parties to freely undertake abstract obligations would allow them to bypass all the rules applicable to the given type of contract they, in fact, entered into (whether a sale, a service contract, a donation, etc). Fourth, the French law of unjustified enrichment could not apply between the creditor and the debtor in case of valid abstract obligations. Indeed, the provisions of the Civil Code grant no action when the alleged enrichment arises out

[33] See M Vivant, 'Le fondement juridique des obligations abstraites' (1978) 9 *Recueil Dalloz* 39.

[34] On that matter, see the new Belgian law of obligations: cause is still a condition for the validity of a contract, but at the same time, the possibility to enter abstract obligations is enounced (Art 5.54: 'Un contrat conclu sans cause est frappé de nullité relative, à moins que la loi admette qu'il puisse exister sans cause. Les parties peuvent également convenir d'abstraire le contrat de sa cause, à moins que la loi l'interdise', which translates as 'A contract concluded without cause is subject to relative nullity, unless the law admits that it can exist without cause. The parties may also agree to abstract the contract from its cause, unless the law prohibits it').

[35] See Chénedé (n 21) 123.321.

of the performance of a valid obligation (see Article 1303-1). Hence, if abstract obligations were to be considered valid as a general rule, the debtor could never argue for repayment of what it has performed, even in cases where it received nothing in return and had no intention of gratifying the other party. As Thomas Genicon demonstrated,[36] this would give rise to 'perfect' or pure abstract obligations (as will be detailed later), which is not satisfactory and would have no equivalent elsewhere on the planet, at least on such a scale.

Despite those strong arguments, some scholars prefer to emphasise the absence of a requirement that a contract be based on a cause and argue that every obligation is now, to a certain extent, abstract under French law.[37] It brings, they say, French law closer to German law.[38] With all due respect, such a presentation is highly problematic. It blurs both what French law on that matter is and also what German law is. The mere fact it exists could be seen as an indication that the reform is not totally satisfactory in terms of clarifying the law. But it also needs to be said that this presentation comes from scholars who were decidedly opposed to the doctrine of *la cause*.[39]

It is true, however, that the abandonment of the general requirement that every contract be based on a cause might give a clean slate to rethinking the place or role of abstract obligations in the French law of contracts.

Whereas, until 2016, French jurists felt in a way compelled to find a cause in every contract, they could now think differently where this search has proved to be uneasy. This is the case in situations involving more than two persons. Let us take the example of a guarantee (ie the contract by which a guarantor undertakes to pay the debtor's obligation vis-à-vis the creditor). The contract is concluded between the guarantor and the creditor, but there is a third personinvolved: the debtor. The contract seems neither onerous (as the guarantor receives no consideration from the creditor) nor gratuitous (as the guarantor does not act to gratify the creditor). In the 1972 *Lempereur* case,[40] the

[36] Genicon, 'L'avenir de la cause en droit français des contrats' (n 5) 715ff, espec 728; 'L'acte abstrait en droit français après la réforme du droit des contrats: l'impossible consécration' in *Mélanges Teyssié* (Paris, LexisNexis, 2019) 961ff.

[37] L Aynès, 'La disparition de la cause du contrat, Rapport français' in P Ancel and A Prüm (ed), *Réformer le droit des contrats? Analyse comparée autour du droit luxembourgeois* (Larcier, Brussels, 2020) 217ff, spec 221: 'Depuis la réforme de 2016, l'absence de cause n'est plus une source de nullité du contrat. D'une certaine manière, tous les engagements contractuels sont devenus abstraits', the translation of which could be: 'Since the 2016 reform, lack of cause is no longer a source of nullity. In a way, all contractual obligations have become abstract'.

[38] See Malaurie, Aynès and Stoffel-Munck, *Droit des obligations* (n 25) 380: 'l'ordonnance a décidé de ne plus faire de l'existence de la cause (…) une condition de validité de l'engagement, qui serait appréciée distinctement du consentement. Cette réforme simplifie le droit français, le rapproche de plusieurs droits étrangers, en particulier allemand, et restaure une certaine sécurité contractuelle', the translation of which could be 'the ordinance no longer makes the existence of cause (…) a condition for the validity of a contract, to be assessed separately from consent. This reform simplifies French law, brings it into line with several foreign legal systems, particularly German, and restores legal certainty of contracts'. On the same page, the authors have to admit that 'la cause n'est plus une condition de formation du contrat (…). Mais un contrat à titre onéreux est nul si la contrepartie convenue est 'illusoire ou dérisoire' (Art 1169); ce qui correspond à ce que l'on appelait jusqu'à la réforme l'absence de cause', the translation of which could be 'cause is no longer a condition for the validity of a contract (…). But an onerous contract is void if the consideration agreed is 'illusory or derisory' (Art 1169); this corresponds to what was known until the reform as the absence of cause'.

[39] See Aynès, 'La cause, inutile et dangereuse' (n 26) 40 .

[40] Cass. Com., 8 november 1972, n°71-11879. See the same solution adopted *in* Cass. Com., 17 may 2017, n°15-15746.

Cour de cassation ruled that *la cause* of a guarantee lies in the relations between the creditor and the debtor, this cause being the credit offered by the former to the latter. Consequently, if no real credit is offered to the debtor, then the guarantee is void for lack of cause. One could argue that such a ruling distorts the notion of cause. If a cause were to be found, it should be in the relations between the guarantor and the debtor. Indeed, here lies the answer to the question why the guarantor has accepted to secure the debt. It is understandable, though, that the lack of such a cause cannot be a defence for the guarantor in its relations with the creditor. The protection of the creditor comes at a price. In the end, instead of distorting the requirement that there be a cause, some scholars suggest that it would be more convincing to hold that a guarantee is an abstract obligation. This position is not new,[41] but it is put in a new light by the abrogation of former Article 1131 of the Code civil.[42] It is foreseeable that the abstract nature of obligations inscribed in other three-party operations (*délégation*, *garantie à première demande*, etc) will also, in the near future, be put back on the table.

In contracts involving only two parties, there seem to be, on the contrary, no real reason or desire to challenge the need for a cause. This is particularly true of the assignment of rights (*cession de créance*). Given the formulation of the new Article 1321 of the Code civil ('Assignment of rights is a contract by which the creditor (the assignor) transfers, whether or not for value, the whole or part of his rights against the assignment debtor to a third party (the assignee)') it could theoretically be argued that the contract of assignment is abstract. But this view is not shared by a number of scholars who insist on the fact that the assignment of rights always has the nature of a donation, a sale or another onerous act, and shall consequently be submitted to the rules applicable to the type of contract it corresponds *in casu* (among which the cause requirement exists).[43]

C. Comments for the Comparative Lawyer

The issue of undisclosed cause is of less importance than that of abstract obligation. It suffices to say that no legal system would benefit from a rigid rule obliging the parties to disclose their intention, the reason of their undertaking. It would indeed amount to making the mention of the cause a formality, with little to gain. The solution consisting in allowing the judge to freely search what the rationale of the undertaking really is seems to be the best one in every respect. It also provides a solution for the case where the debtor lies about the real reason why the contract is concluded.

[41] See Capitant (n 12) 184. Admitting that *cause* lies in the expected consideration regardless of whether such consideration benefits to the one entering the obligation or to a third party and concluding that personal guarantee is not abstract obligation, see Ghestin, Loiseau and Serinet, *La formation du contrat* (n 15) 872ff.

[42] See F Chénedé, 'La cause de l'obligation de la caution, Analyse rétro-prospective' in *Les coutures du droit, Mélanges en l'honneur de Philippe Théry* (LGDJ-Paris, Dalloz, 2022) 167ff.

[43] See A Benabent, *Droit des obligations*, 20th edn (Paris, LGDJ, 2023) 714; *adde* O Deshayes, 'La cession de créance, contrat 'à titre onéreux ou gratuit'' in *Mélanges en l'honneur de Pascal Ancel* (n 30) 303ff.; L Andreu, 'La 'vente' de la créance' in H Boucard, J Lete, RN Schütz, and E Savaux (eds), *Les recodifications du droit de la vente en Europe* (Poitiers, Presses Universitaires Juridiques, 2021).

More generally, one should keep in mind that identifying the cause or reason of one's undertaking and deciding whether or not this cause or reason should matter from a legal point of view is not something to be put in the parties' hands. It is necessary for the legal system to keep control over this, for on the cause or reason depends the structure of the contract, its nature and therefore the identification of the applicable rules.

This is why abstract obligations seem to play a secondary role in legal systems: they are not a normal situation. Their domain is limited. Moreover, legal systems use other brakes to ensure that they do not lead to unjust solutions. First, a formality is often required (a deed in English law, a written undertaking in German law). Second and foremost, no system admits pure or perfect abstract obligations – that is to say, obligations that are valid and enforceable by the mere virtue of having been agreed upon, and offering no defence or action for repayment to the debtor that is related to why the obligation was entered into.[44] At least, no system admits such abstract obligations on a large scale. That would foster unlawfulness and lead to potentially unjust contracts being validated and enforced without any subsequent action for the debtor. What legal systems do is admit the validity of some abstract obligations while at the same time offering an action to the debtor if it has in the end enriched the creditor with no reason (a sort of *conditio sine causa*). In other words, abstract obligations in the real world are only temporarily abstract (Thomas Genicon suggests calling them 'imperfect' abstract obligations, *acte abstrait imparfait*).[45] To put it like Henri de Page, the action on the ground of *la cause* is simply *postposé* (postponed),[46] and takes the form of a claim based on unjustified enrichment.[47]

But one should be careful here. It is indeed misleading to say that the actions on the ground of *la cause* are simply postponed. Literally, from a French perspective, it would mean that a debtor under an abstract obligation could, after performance, only raise a claim based on the initial lack of cause (illusory cause) or on the unlawfulness of the cause. Yet, this is only a part of what the debtor can invoke. It can raise all arguments showing that there was no reason justifying the payment in the end, whether or not those reasons existed on the day the obligation was entered into.

This last remark shows that when it comes to abstract obligations, the cause is not quite the same concept as that examined earlier. Indeed, the word is not used to refer to a specific condition set forth by some legal systems for the validity of a contractual obligation; rather, it is used to refer to the justifying reason of an obligation, assessed after the obligation is entered into and whose absence enables the debtor to claim for reimbursement. It could be defined as the reason that justifies in the eyes of the law that a person can keep what it received from somebody else. It certainly has the same roots as the French *cause*, but resembles more the German *Rechtsgrund* in that it can be assessed after the obligation is entered into.

[44] On the debate among German scholars as to whether, in case of abstract obligation (*abstraktes Schuldversprechen*) the parties could waive the right for the debtor to invoke the lack of cause, see T Rüfner, 'La disparition de la cause du contrat, Rapport allemand' in Ancel and Prüm (n 37) 239ff, spec 14.

[45] Genicon, 'L'acte abstrait en droit français des contrats' (n 36) 7ff.

[46] de Page (n 14) 32.

[47] Legal systems which do not rely on *la cause* tend to develop a strong law on unjustified enrichment. See, eg M Fromont and J Knetsch, *Droit privé allemand*, 2nd edn (Paris, Montchrestien, 2017) 432–33.

This might explain the discrepancy between what French scholars usually talk about when they refer to *la cause* (a particular condition for the validity of contracts) and what foreign observers sometimes expect to be addressed under the same heading (see above). For French lawyers, *la cause* is first and foremost a technical tool to be used to ascertain the validity of contracts.[48] It is not as directly related to the issue of abstract obligations in their mind as one would think, and therefore not directly related to the issue of unjustified enrichment that arises with it. To make the connection, it is necessary to view cause not simply as a tool, but as a broad underlying concept that can be found beneath different rules or solutions, all of which aim to preserve commutative justice by taking into account the reason of one's undertaking.

As a conclusion, I will summarise the similarities and differences between legal systems as to the use they make of cause (the notion, not the word) in the following way. No legal system can work without taking into account the reason why a debtor undertakes an obligation. Cause, in this respect, is a universal feature. It is used to assess the lawfulness of the debtor's undertaking. It is also irreplaceable for preventing an unjust enrichment of the creditor at the expense of the debtor where there is no valid reason (being said that this reason could not just be: the debtor agreed). Finally, it is also irreplaceable for identifying the set of rules that applies to an obligation (is the contract a sale or a service contract, etc). What differentiates legal systems is the mere fact that some of them also use cause as a technical tool, to assess the validity of a contractual obligation, requiring that the reason a person has chosen to undertake an obligation (the expected counter-performance in onerous contracts or the personal motive in gratuitous contracts) really existed at the time the contract was concluded. They admit, in other words, that a contract is void if the 'why?' that supports the undertaking is lacking, right from the beginning. Other systems use alternative tools to cope with this difficulty. A thorough analysis would probably prove that, in the end, the solutions are quite similar.

[48] As already mentioned, Henri Capitant had a broad understanding of what *la cause* performs in the French law of contract, going so far as to consider that remedies for non-performance of onerous contract are a part of the doctrine of *la cause*.

8

The Functions of the Notion of 'Cause' in Spanish Law

ANTONIO LEGERÉN-MOLINA

I. Introduction

Essential requisite of the agreement, instrument to control, intrinsic element of the contractual obligation, requirement of justice … These are all some of the terms used in Spanish contract law in relation to 'cause'. The absence of an official definition in the Código Civil (Spanish Civil Code, SCC), the vagueness of the regulation and the ambiguity of the term itself explain the variety of theories on this notion.[1]

That lack of conceptual unity is aggravated by the functions it has developed in the Spanish legal system. In fact, this concept has been used to resolve very different problems, and sometimes with little connection between them. In particular, the existence of cause required by Article 1275 SCC – 'contracts without cause or with an unlawful cause have no effect' – has been used, among other things to: (i) recognise the binding nature of an agreement; (ii) declare the nullity of absolutely simulated transactions; and (iii) solve the problems of frustration of the basis of the business or of supervening alteration of the circumstances. The lawfulness also required by the transcribed article has made it possible to use the cause as an instrument to control the morality or lawfulness of the contracts. Finally, the veracity of the cause demanded by Article 1276 SCC – 'the expression of a false cause in contracts will give rise to nullity, if it is not proved that they were based on another true and lawful cause' – has made it possible to use this notion to resolve what concerns the relative simulation.

As can be seen, defining the essence or functions of cause in Spanish contract law is not an easy task and there is no unanimity on the subject; furthermore, it is possible to find anti-causalist authors.[2] Moreover, the Spanish Supreme Court itself has

[1] Statements confirmed by, eg SCJJ 19-02-2009, 5-02-2020 or 22-06-2021.

[2] See E Núñez Lagos, *El enriquecimiento sin causa en el Derecho español* (Madrid, Reus, 1934) 23–36. Their main arguments are that the cause is confused with the consent in contracts for true generosity and with the object in 'onerous' contracts, and that the examination of the illegality of the cause implies entering into the analysis of the particular motives of the subject, which is forbidden. On the contrary, that is, clearly distinguishing cause from consent, see RM Roca Sastre, 'La causa en el negocio jurídico' in Roca Sastre and Puig Brutau, *Estudios de Derecho Privado* (Madrid, Revista de Derecho Privado, 1948) 51; and distinguishing the

recognised on several occasions that 'the doctrine of cause is one of the most confusing in civil law'[3] and its 'legal discipline … is one of the most obscure issues and full of equivocal polysemies in the law of obligations and contracts'.[4] The main objective of this chapter is therefore to examine and clarify such functions, mainly in the light of case law. Thus, references to doctrinal debates and the historical context of the rules will be brief and incidental.

II. Historical Context

Unlike several European Codes – eg the German Bürgerliches Gesetzbuch (BGB), the Austrian Allgemeines bürgerliches Gesetzbuch – the Spanish Civil Code followed the French Civil Code (Code civil) of 1804 and included a notion of cause that was tributary of Pothier's.[5] If the French Civil Code included the 'lawful cause in the obligation' within the 'four conditions … essential for the validity of a convention' ('dans l'obligation', Article 1108 of the Code civil), Article 985 of the Spanish Project of Civil Code drafted in 1851 (the García Goyena Project) stated that 'for the validity of contracts the following requirements are indispensable … 4th. Lawful cause of the obligation'. This is a norm which, with very few variations, was incorporated into Article 1261 of the current Spanish Civil Code (of 1889) and has remained unchanged to this day: 'There is no contract unless the following requirements are met: 1st Consent of the contracting parties. 2nd Certain object which is the subject matter of the contract. 3rd Cause of the obligation that is established.' In this article, the cause refers to the obligation, which, thus configured, is an essential element of the contract.[6]

From the text of Article 1261, it can be deduced that the original concept of cause in the Spanish Civil Code included the two prisms recognised by Pothier: one objective, the other subjective. The first makes the agreements binding: when a promise has a reason for its existence, consisting of the contractual obligation of the other party or the spirit of liberality, it acquires a binding nature, and can consequently be judicially claimed. The Spanish Supreme Court has confirmed in numerous judicial decisions that the cause in the objective sense is the 'true cause'.[7]

The second dimension 'widen[ed] the horizons of the classical and legal conception'[8] and allowed the cause to be used as an instrument to control the common purpose of the parties. Thus, there is an objective concept – cause as contractual obligation – and

cause from the object of the contract, as well as from its content, see H Clavería Gosálbez, *La causa del contrato* (Bologna, Real Colegio de España, 1998) 134. Perhaps this state of affairs explains the lack of technicality that is sometimes observed both in doctrine and, unfortunately and especially, in case law.

[3] SCJ 23-11-1961.

[4] SCJ 24-04-2013.

[5] RJ Pothier, *Traité des obligations*, Part I, ch I, s I, Art II, 9 in *Oevrs*, Title I (París, 1835) 9.

[6] See SCJ 14-01-1935. 'The requirement of the contract is not the cause, but that the obligation established therein has a cause': FA Sancho Rebullida, 'La causa de la obligación', *Estudios de Derecho civil*, vol I (Pamplona, Eunsa, 1978) 148; see also L Díez-Picazo, *Fundamentos del Derecho Civil Patrimonial*, vol I, 6th edn (Cizur Menor, Thomson Civitas, 2007) 272.

[7] See eg SCJ 20-01-1965.

[8] SCJ 14-12-1940.

a subjective one – cause as a common purpose. Both perspectives find their basis in Articles 1274 and 1275 SCC and have been recognised – explicitly or implicitly – by the Supreme Court on many occasions.[9]

Both dimensions include some of the functions that will be examined below: those contained in section III.B (the cause as an element to control the reality of the agreement and its binding nature) within the objective thesis, and those reflected in section III.C (the cause as a common purpose sought through the contract) within the subjective thesis. In addition, in section III.D (the cause as an element of control of the relative simulation of the contract), a function indirectly linked to the objective thesis will be analysed. And in section III.E (the cause as an element of control of the reasonableness of the business), another so-called 'objectivist' function will be examined.

III. Functions of the Cause

A. Introduction

As already mentioned, the functions of the cause recognised by Spanish doctrine and case law will be described below. It seems that the search for solutions to a series of problems of a very different nature, which are not directly resolved by the law, has found in the cause a *mouldable* notion or tool. This, together with the absence of a legal definition, has led to the existence of different explanations of it. Be that as it may, the functions mentioned below are not merely theoretical questions: they have an unquestionable transcendence in contractual practice, as will be seen from the decisions cited.

B. Cause as an Element to Control the Reality of the Agreement and its Binding Nature

(i) Introduction

The functions mentioned in the title of this subsection come closest to the objective or classical concept of cause, which is the one literally contained in the Spanish Civil Code.[10] According to it, every attribution of property must have an antecedent reason – a cause – that justifies it, since no one gives, owes or is obliged for nothing. That justifying reason or cause for which the debtor is obliged is not 'aimless', but serves, seeks or pursues an immediate goal. According to this objective concept of cause, the *finis operis* is always the same for each type of contractual obligation. It is, as jurisprudence uses to

[9] See eg SCJ 17-03-1956 and SCJ 23-11-1961.

[10] This has been made clear in case law on numerous occasions: see, eg SCJJ 24-03-1930, 8-02-1943, 18-05-1953, 14-06-1963, 8-07-1974, 1-04-1982, 31-01-1991, 25-02-1995, 28-07-1998, 17-12-2004, 11-02-2011 and 15-02-2012. However, jurisprudence has evolved towards a more eclectic thesis or a dualist approach, recognising the subjective dimension of the cause (see, eg SCJ 19-11-1990 and SCJ 29-03-1993). Some supporters of the classical thesis are Albaladejo, Lacruz, Sancho Rebullida, De La Cámara and Lalaguna; see also the list of authors examined by Clavería Gosálbez (n 2) 80–94.

say, an 'objective and immediate goal pursued in each contract'.[11] It is objective because such an aim can be assessed independently of 'any introspection of personal psychological motivation', and it is immediate because it is the 'primary reason for legal action'.[12] It should also be legally 'acceptable': it must be approved or typified by the law. In short: the objective concept of cause refers to a 'scheme of the relationship established between the parties, covered by the law with legal sanctions characteristic of typicity'.[13]

The legal support for the functions of the cause of the obligation studied in this section lies, basically, in Article 1274 SCC:

> [I]n onerous contracts, the provision or promise of an object or service by the other party shall be deemed to constitute the cause applicable to each contracting party; in remunerative contracts, the service or benefit which is remunerated, and in contracts for true generosity, the mere liberality of the benefactor.

Although the cause is mentioned in the context of contracts – 'in contracts' – it is 'for each contracting party', which clearly shows that it refers to the obligation. According to some scholars, this norm must be interpreted taking into account its historical origin: although 'for onerous contracts' is contrasted with those 'for true generosity', it is more correct to oppose 'bilaterality' – whether onerous or gratuitous transactions – with 'unilaterality'.[14]

Thus, in bilateral or synallagmatic contracts, the reason for the contractual provision to which a person is obliged – the reason or cause of one's obligation – is the provision or promise obtained from the other party. The provisions or promises of both parties act as the mutual cause for both contractual obligations – eg the lessee is bound by the thing to be used and the lessor by the rent to be paid; there is an interdependence between them, a key element of any contract. In fact, in the case of a sale without economic counter-performance, there is no cause, since the mere will to be bound is not sufficient.[15] In these contracts, the cause is the exchange of the thing for the price.[16] On the other hand, in the case of remunerative contracts, the cause will be 'the service or benefit which is remunerated', and in the case of contracts for true generosity, the 'mere liberality' – eg a gratuitous loan.[17]

[11] SCJ 17-07-2008; in the same sense, see SCJ 14-03-1930 or SCJ 19-02-2009. It should be noted that these judgments incorrectly refer to the cause *of the contract*, whereas Art 1274 SCC refers to the cause of *the obligation*, which, thus configured, is an essential element *of the contract*. For slightly more correct terminology, see SCJ 27-02-1954 and SCJ 16-06-2011. On cause as 'final cause', see, eg Roca Sastre (n 2) 49; J Melich Orsini, 'La causa en la teoría del contrato y sus diversas funciones' (1984) I *Anuario de Derecho civil* 3, 4–6.

[12] See Sancho Rebullida (n 6) 153, 154 and 157.

[13] SCJ 14-01-1935.

[14] See Sancho Rebullida (n 6) 148. On some occasions, the case law seems to follow this interpretation (eg SCJ 17-01-1985). However, there are more decisions which suffer from a lack of precision: for example, it is mentioned that the 'exchange of services' – and therefore no longer the counter-performance – is the cause of both 'onerous' contracts (see SCJ 17-07-2008) and 'synallagmatic' contracts (see SCJ 19-06-2009). Unfortunately, most decisions use the first terminology – 'onerous' – which is technically less correct (see SCJJ 18-05-1953, 26-05-1973 or 28-12-2007). In the doctrinal field, see Sancho Rebullida (n 6) 154; Díez-Picazo (n 6) 265; B Rodríguez-Rosado, *Fiducia y pacto de retro en garantía* (Madrid, Marcial Pons, 1998) 71.

[15] See SCJ 27-06-1996 and SCJ 28-12-2007.

[16] With similar terms, see SCJJ 24-02-1959, 25-04-1960, 24-04-1984 or 10-03-2011. Regarding dation in payment of debt and the bargain where the price is substituted for the payment of debts, see SCJ 25-05-1965 and SCJ 12-04-1975. And for bank loans, see SCJ 26-04-2022 and SCJ 19-05-2022.

[17] See SCJ 5-10-1984.

As can be seen, the classical concept of the cause of any contractual obligation – which comes from Domat and Pothier[18] – does not take into account the subjective motives or the individual will that leads each party to the contract: Article 1274 SCC objectively typifies the reasons that explain the various agreements excluding the personal and particular motives that led the parties to get bound. The cause in Article 1274 SCC 'comes to mean the goal pursued in each contractual hypothesis (counter-performance, service to be remunerated, liberality) outside the merely subjective intention or purpose of the contracting parties (internal motive)'.[19] It is not a question of 'the psychological force of the imponderables determining an individual will which is oriented towards the achievement of a certain goal'.[20]

The cause of the contractual obligation is then something objective – *finis operis*, not *finis operantis* – which does not arise from subjective motives, but is independent of them.[21] Therefore, a standard reason which does not vary is established for each type of agreement. Finally, since Article 1274 SCC refers to the cause of the *obligation* and not of the *contract*, there will be as many causes in an agreement as there are obligations. Consequently, in the case of bilateral contracts, it is not possible to speak of a single cause of the contract, even if, as has been said, the case law is not always precise.

One consequence of the foregoing is that there can be no contractual obligation without an antecedent reason, be it, for example, a provision or promise, or the spirit of liberality.[22] There is no contractual obligation without cause; it would be an unenforceable obligation and its performance would be repeatable. Nor is there a contract or legal transaction without a contractual obligation:[23] as an example, the objective thesis seems to be the basis of the denial of the obligatory donation in Spanish law included in SCJ 10-05-2019. Similarly, there would be no reason to attribute a right to the wife that was already legally hers.[24] Nor is there cause if the contract is simulated, concealing the obligation to pay a credit which has already been extinguished.[25]

Having explained the objective thesis so far, the two main questions it raises concern to the abstract contracts (subsection ii) and to the absolute simulation (subsection iii).

(ii) Abstract Contracts

The Spanish legal system is causal.[26] For this reason, it does not generally allow, even on the basis of the autonomy of the will,[27] abstract transactions, ie those in which, provided there is an intended transfer, the conveyance of the title or the payment takes place

[18] SCJ 19-06-2009 explicitly mentions the origin in Pothier. See n 5. Regarding Domat, see *Les lois civiles dans leur ordre naturel*, Part 1, Book 1, Title I, s I (Paris, 1969) 4–6.
[19] SCJ 8-07-1997.
[20] SCJ 14-01-1935.
[21] See SCJ 2-02-1955 or SCJ 25-05-1965. In particular, on the *finis operantis*, see SCJ 8-07-1974.
[22] It should not be forgotten that the cause is not the requirement of the contract but that the obligation(s) contained in it have a cause; see Sancho Rebullida (n 6) 148.
[23] See SCJ 14-11-2008.
[24] See SCJ 14-02-2005.
[25] See SCJ 18-06-1957.
[26] arg ex Art 609 SCC.
[27] See Art 1255 SCC.

'abstracted' from the effectiveness of the antecedent cause. Although there has been no contract or obligation, the *traditio* would produce legal effects, which do not prevent the transferor from having a personal action against the acquirer. In the Spanish legal system, no such effect will be produced: only a possessory transfer will have taken place, and a real action will be brought to recover what has been delivered. The first system gives greater security to the acquirer; the second, to the transferor.[28]

The *only* abstraction legally permitted in Spain is that of Article 1277 SCC, which has only a procedural nature: it merely involves a reversal of the burden of proof as to the existence and lawfulness of the cause when it is not expressly contained in the contract.[29] This article is not therefore an open door to an abstract system.[30] Although it establishes a rebuttable presumption of the existence and lawfulness of the cause, proof of its non-existence – or of the contractual obligation itself – leads to the declaration of the nullity of the agreement.[31]

The jurisprudence is unanimous in denying the existence of an antecedent reason in any 'enrichment without cause' – which obliges to restitution[32] – and cannot be considered as an abstract contract.[33]

That is not the case with the 'acknowledgement of debt', where case law has been hesitant. At first, it was admitted as an 'abstract' business,[34] considering that such a contract had a 'constitutive' effect on the contractual obligation in cases where the cause was not mentioned 'at all' or it was 'merely general'.[35] This doctrine was subsequently corrected and the above-mentioned constitutive value was denied: the 'acknowledgement of debt' is not an autonomous basis of the contractual obligation, and consequently Articles 1275 and 1277 SCC apply with regard to the existence of a cause and the presumption of such existence.[36] In other words, the 'acknowledgement of debt' is *procedurally abstract* but *substantively causal*; the absence of a cause, if it is the case, can be proved.[37]

Finally, other contracts of a certain abstract nature recognised by case law are the 'guarantee on first demand' and, in some cases, the 'bill of exchange'. The former is characterised by the fact that it leads to the creation of 'an immediate warranty obligation which loses its accessory character to the main obligation (unlike the personal security)'. Thus, the guarantor's obligation 'is independent of the obligation of the guaranteed party and of the initial contract'.[38] With regard to the latter, this only occurs in some cases, as has been pointed out: 'in the absence of the cases mentioned above, the bill of exchange

[28] In favour of the admissibility of 'abstract transactions' in Spain, albeit in a 'procedural' and not 'material' sense, see B Pérez González and J Alguer, *Translation and notes of Ennecerus-Kipp-Wolff, Tratado de Derecho Civil*, vol I-2, 35th German edn, 1st Spanish edn (Barcelona, Bosch, 1944) 87–89.

[29] See SCJ 23-02-2005.

[30] See SCJ 9-07-2019. See also Clavería Gosálbez (n 2) 233.

[31] See SCJ 3-11-1981. In the doctrine, see F De Castro, *El negocio jurídico* (Madrid, Civitas, 1985) 291; Rodríguez-Rosado (n 14) 84. The 'procedural abstraction' of the cause is the name given to the aforementioned reversal of the burden of proof.

[32] See Art 1895 SCC.

[33] See, eg SCJ 18-06-1957, where the creditor, after having paid a debt, demanded payment again from the joint and several guarantors of the debt.

[34] See SCJ 26-10-1962 and SCJ 15-02-1989.

[35] SCJ 8-03-1956; see also SCJ 13-02-1998.

[36] See SCJ 1-03-2016.

[37] See SCJ 9-07-2019.

[38] SCJ 4-03-2014. In the same sense, see SCJJ 27-09-2005, 1-10-2007, 26-10-2010, 17-07-2014, 19-05-2016 or 5-04-2019.

acts as a causal title in the relations between drawer and drawee, between endorser and endorsee … and as an abstract title in the others'.[39]

In view of the above, it should be noted that the Spanish legal system is causal. The only exception – contained in Article 1277 SCC – is of a procedural nature. In any case, the absence of cause entails the declaration of nullity, and consequently the ineffectiveness of any transfer or payment.

(iii) Absolute Simulation

The objective concept of cause also makes it possible to exclude apparent transactions in which a (non-existent) agreement is absolutely simulated. The parties agree to create only a mere appearance: 'the business purpose is completely non-existent'.[40] In other words, 'the appearance of a contract is created, but, in truth, there is no desire for it to come into existence and have legal life'.[41] It is often pointed out that in such a case the contract is null and void for lack of cause.[42]

According to the Spanish Supreme Court, simulation

> has been structured by the most established doctrine, and as opposed to the thesis that it can be a manifestation of discrepancy between the real and the declared will – a vice of the will – it is subsumed as an event that can be included in the cause of the agreement; that is to say, a simulation which implies a defect in the cause of the agreement, with the sanction of Articles 1275 and 1276, and therefore with the mandatory declaration of nullity, unless the existence of another true and lawful cause is accredited.[43]

Although this is true, in my opinion it is not only a question of (lack of) cause, since there is also a lack of will to negotiate.[44] There is a clear will *not intending any contract*: there is no consent – in the legal sense – nor subject matter that could give rise to a valid contract, and this absence is also clearly reflected in the cause.

The main difficulty with absolute simulation is proving it. The parties simulating the agreement usually have a 'natural determination' to 'make the vestiges of the simulation disappear and to make it appear that the contract is true and an effective reflection of reality'.[45] As a result, it is usually difficult to obtain direct and complete proof; it is very common to rely on indications and presumptions.[46] For example, in SCJ 20-10-2005, the evidences used to prove simulation was the lack of conveyance of possession of the property, the absence of proof of payment, the proximity of the transfer and the expiry of the bills of exchange on which the seizures were based, against which a third party's claim to ownership was filed and which was unsuccessful due to the simulation. In any event, its determination is a matter of fact that falls within the discretion of the court of first instance.[47]

[39] SCJ 25-11-2014.
[40] SCJ 26-07-2004.
[41] SCJ 4-04-2012; in the same sense, see SCJJ 17-02-2005, 22-02-2007 or 18-03-2008.
[42] See SCJ 22-06-2021. Emphasising that the simulation is based on a non-existent cause, see Díez-Picazo (n 6) 257.
[43] SCJ 26-07-2004.
[44] *cf* M De La Cámara, 'Meditaciones sobre la *causa*' (1978) 527, *Revista Crítica de Derecho Inmobiliario* 637, 666–67; Rodríguez-Rosado (n 14) 79.
[45] SCJ 3-11-2004 and SCJ 4-04-2012.
[46] See SCJ 11-02-2005 or SCJ 28-05-2007.
[47] See SCJ 4-04-2012.

With regard to what is of interest here, there is a total absence of cause in absolute simulation. The disproportion between the value of what was sold and what was delivered does not render the agreement null and void by reason of simulation, even if it is an indication to be taken into account in such a finding.[48] Nor are the unlawful objectives pursued by the parties, unless they have made them the 'cause' of the agreement itself: if they are not integrated and are not part of the contract, they will be no more than particular motives of the apparent contract which do not provide it with a cause.[49]

Proof of the simulation – direct or by presumption – implies that the apparent agreement is deprived of all validity and effectiveness.[50] It is null and void because it does not exist and, in application of Article 1303 SCC, any provisions must be restituted in order to return the situation to the previous one.[51] Neither Article 1300 SCC nor Article 1306 SCC can be invoked, as both presuppose the existence of a cause – with a defect – and this does not occur in an absolute simulation.[52] As a consequence of the absolute nullity, the action for its recognition is imprescriptible and can be sued by the parties.[53]

An analysis of the case law shows that the absolute simulation is quite often carried out with a fraudulent purpose – of the creditors, of the forced heirs, of the rights of the heirs, etc – and the lack of cause is one of the usual ways of challenging such transactions. In fact, in the case of fraud, there are several ways of challenging the bargain: (i) absolute simulation for lack of cause when there was only appearance but the agreement was not intended; (ii) unlawful cause, when the business was intended – it is not attacked by means of simulation – but there was an unlawful common purpose;[54] and (iii) by means of the rescissory or *pauliana* action.[55]

The absence of cause has been used, inter alia, in transactions carried out in fraud of rights: of the trustee;[56] of the owners of the assets that were intended to be set

[48] See SCJ 30-11-1972.

[49] See SCJ 3-05-2016 or SCJ 22-06-2021.

[50] See SCJ 22-11-1963.

[51] See SCJ 14-11-2008.

[52] See SCJ 22-06-2021.

[53] See SCJ 3-05-2016. As regards the possibility for the parties to challenge the apparent agreement, there has been a development in case law. If it was initially not accepted (see SCJ 17-01-1963 and SCJ 13-11-1970), it was later accepted as it is not affected by the prohibition of Arts 1305 and 1306 SCC (see SCJ 16-01-2013 or SCJ 24-04-2013).

[54] In order to overcome the non-existence of a cause at all in the case of absolutely simulated contracts, the jurisprudence indicates that the unlawfulness is related to the 'cause of the simulation' and not to the cause of the contract. See, eg SCJ 2-05-1964 and SCJ 24-04-2013, from which it can be concluded that there are absolute simulations with a lawful purpose and others with an unlawful purpose. In any case, causal unlawfulness is important for determining the basis on which third parties can stand for the exercise of an action of annulment (see SCJ 24-04-2013). Some examples of the use of the causal illegality route rather than absolute simulation can be found in SCJ 26-04-1962, concerning fraud on creditors; or in SCJJ 12-04-1946, 24-03-1950, 4-04-1961, 20-10-1961 or 6-02-2020, concerning fraud on the rights of forced heirs.

[55] Alluding to the various channels mentioned in the text, see SCJ 3-11-2015; A Carrasco Perera, *Derecho de contratos*, 2nd edn (Cizur Menor, Thomson Reuters Aranzadi, 2017) 723–24. The action for rescission is not the only way of dealing with a bargain in fraud of rights, even if it is subsidiary to a possible action for annulment (see SCJ 22-11-1963 or SCJ 11-05-2007). Such a variety of possibilities makes it possible, for example, to challenge the transaction by other means if the time limit for exercising the right of rescission has already expired (see SCJ 27-03-2007).

[56] See SCJ 12-02-1966.

aside;[57] of the forced heirs;[58] of the heirs;[59] or of the creditors.[60] In the context of a sale, a relatively simple way of proving simulation is the absence of a price: a transfer of assets takes place without any provision in return.[61] Other examples where the simulation was also used were in relation to donations that fraudulently intended to remove assets from the debtor's estate;[62] or a dissolution of the community of property combined with a donation in order to place assets beyond the reach of creditors.[63]

(iv) Some Concluding Remarks

From the foregoing, it can be seen that the requirement of a cause for all obligations as well as the legal determination of the one that corresponds to the different agreements[64] minimises or eliminates the cases of 'contract without cause' – *rectius*: those whose contractual obligations do not have a cause.[65] However, even if the objective thesis serves this purpose and has been applied in case law, as has been seen, it is not free from objections: (i) it does not offer a concept of cause, but several, different, 'incongruous and inharmonious' criteria; (ii) the distinction between 'remunerative' and 'contracts for true generosity' in Article 1274 SCC is 'false, contrived and arbitrary';[66] (iii) this thesis does not easily apply to unilateral transactions, which proves that Article 1274 SCC relies on subjective motivations – the liberality of the benefactor – to explain the transfers in contracts 'for true generosity'; (iv) the standard reasons accepted by Article 1274 SCC do not cover all possible transactions – for example, in the case of a free loan, a reason of liberality on the part of the lender coexists with an onerous reason on the part of the person who must repay the loan; and (v) it creates a certain conflict with the unlawfulness of the cause: if the latter is only objective, the unlawfulness can only derive from the subject matter of the contract, and not from the personal will of the parties, which would not be covered by the provision – an element already covered by Article 1271 SCC:

> [A]ll things that are not out of trade of men, even future things, can be the subject matter of a contract … They can also be the subject matter of a contract all services which are not contrary to the law or to morality.

[57] See SCJ 28-12-2007.
[58] See SCJ 20-05-1959.
[59] See SCJ 19-12-1960.
[60] See SCJ 18-05-2007.
[61] See SCJ 12-02-1966 and SCJ 1-07-2011.
[62] See SCJ 27-02-2001 and SCJ 21-12-2009 (ECLI:ES:TS:2009:7691). See also SCJ 11-01-2007; R Durán Rivacoba, *Donaciones encubiertas* (Barcelona, Bosch, 2009).
[63] See SCJ 21-10-2009.
[64] See Art 1274 SCC.
[65] See Art 1261.3 SCC. Pointing out that there cannot be contracts without cause of the obligation, see Rodríguez-Rosado (n 14) 80. Thus, it does not seem easy that the existence of a cause is an autonomous assumption, since its absence leads either to simulation or to the absence of an object. Also, the expression 'contract without cause' is sometimes used to allude to the problem of the 'cause of the attribution': see Díez-Picazo (n 6) 281.
[66] Díez-Picazo (n 6) 265.

This is one of the reasons why it is possible to identify a different meaning of cause;[67] as the case law has sometimes pointed out, the objective dimension of the cause 'cannot explain the possibility of the existence of an unlawful cause, since this is incompatible with the typical and predetermined aim of any legal transaction'.[68]

C. Cause as the Common Purpose Sought Through the Contract

(i) Introduction. Distinction between Motive and Cause

Among other reasons, the inability of the objective thesis to challenge the lawful agreements of the parties whose motives were unlawful or immoral led the doctrine and case law to develop a subjective explanation of the cause, which can be grounded in Article 1275 SCC: 'contracts … with an unlawful cause do not produce any effect. The cause is unlawful when it is contrary to the law or morality.' If the classical conception did not take into account the particular intentions of the parties but only the objective typified reasons indicated in Article 1274 SCC, this is the aim of this new thesis: the door is opened to the assessment of the will of the contracting parties. The cause then refers to the subjective intention or common purpose – only the main or determining purpose about which there is common knowledge by the parties, even if the participation is not common, since the purpose intended by each of them individually may differ from that of the other.[69]

By focusing on the specific common intention or purpose of the contracting parties, the subjective notion of 'cause' no longer refers to each contractual obligation but to the contract as a whole: to what the parties specifically intended or sought to achieve by it[70] – that is, to the coinciding individual motive that acts as the 'driving cause' of the parties; in other words, the common motives that led the parties to enter into the bargain.

At this point, it is necessary to briefly mention the traditional distinction between the 'particular and subjective motives' and the 'cause' itself.[71] As far as what matters now is concerned, the purely subjective motives or impulses of the parties are irrelevant unless they are included in the declaration of will of the bargain; then they acquire

[67] It has also been said that it is possible to achieve similar effects to those obtained with the objective thesis of cause without giving autonomy to this notion, and by redirecting the effects linked to it to the subject matter of the contract as well as to the specific contractual consent. In this sense, see JL Lacruz et al, *Elementos de Derecho civil*, vol II-I (Madrid, Dykinson, 2003) 421–22.

[68] SCJ 24-04-2013 and SCJ 10-06-2015.

[69] On knowledge and shared participation, see P Saborido Sánchez, *La causa ilícita: delimitación y efectos* (Valencia, Tirant lo Blanch, 2005) 112–19.

[70] The unlawfulness cannot be related to the counter-performance. If it were, it would refer to the unlawfulness of the subject matter, which is already covered by Art 1271 SCC; see Rodríguez-Rosado (n 14) 85–86. Anyway, in many cases it is not easy to distinguish the illicit cause from the illicit subject matter; see MJ Marín López, 'La *causa* del contrato' in Bercovitz Rodríguez-Cano (ed), *Tratado de contratos*, vol I, 3rd edn (Valencia, Tirant lo Blanch, 2020) 750. On the confusion between the unlawfulness of the cause and the unlawful object, see SCJ 31-10-1955.

[71] See eg SCJ 30-01-1960 or SCJ 24-11-1978.

legal relevance.[72] The case law reflects this, but different terms are used to refer to: (i) their irrelevance – except in the case of their incorporation;[73] (ii) that they are an extra-bargain reality – except for their incorporation;[74] or (iii) their character outside the cause – unless they are integrated in it.[75]

With regard to what is at stake here, in contrast to the objective nature of the cause ex Article 1274 SCC, the case law has recognised the possibility of including such subjective motives in the cause, giving rise to the so-called 'causalised motives', or 'specific cause'.[76] Another way of giving legal significance to certain motives is to include them in one of the clauses of the contract, as a condition or as a mode.[77]

Such incorporation will make them legally relevant as an element of the contract.[78] Thus, if they have become the 'practical or empirical, specific and common purpose, pursued with the conclusion of the contract and determining that conclusion, they are elevated to the category of cause of the contract';[79] in short, they become a 'specific cause'. In such cases, the 'reason is causalised, but the cause is motivated'; it becomes more tangible.[80] If, however, it is not possible to identify this particular coincidental purpose, the cause is considered only from an objective point of view, limited to the typical purpose of the bargain in question.[81]

Accordingly, it has been held that

> for the subjective motives of the parties to have legal effects … it is necessary that they have been recognised by both contracting parties and have been made a determining condition of the agreement concluded, acting as an impulsive or determining cause.[82]

However, in order for this to be the case, it is necessary that such purpose or motives must be 'recognised by both contracting parties and externalised or, at least relevant'.[83]

In view of the transcribed text and the difficulties of verifying or 'objectifying' this reality, it is understandable that there is no clear criterion in the case law for recognising the determining value of the particular motives or how such an elevation can be made. Thus, while some judgments require an express character – in particular, those alluding to the condition or mode – others accept their incorporation into the cause without the need for an express mention; and there are even rulings that recognise the 'condition not

[72] See SCJ 6-06-2002.

[73] See SCJ 21-12-2009 (ECLI:ES:TS:2009:8109).

[74] See SCJ 19-06-2009.

[75] See SCJ 19-02-2009.

[76] See SCJ 11-07-1984 and SCJ 1-04-1998.

[77] See SCJJ 30-12-1985, 11-04-1994 and 14-11-2008. Recognising this duality of possibilities – 'causalised motives' or their incorporation as a clause, condition or mode – see SCJ 21-12-2009 (ECLI:ES:TS:2009:8109). By way of example, in SCJJ 21-04-2006, 24-01-2013 and 3-10-2013, the possibility to build was not recognised as a 'specific cause' or as a condition, as it was proved that the buyer knew of the non-buildable situation or was aware of the procedure and assumed this risk.

[78] See SCJ 19-06-2009.

[79] SCJ 23-03-2021 and SCJ 22-06-2021.

[80] *cf* M Alonso Pérez, 'El error sobre la causa' in VVAA, *Estudios de Derecho civil en honor del Profesor Castán Tobeñas*, vol III (Pamplona, Eunsa, 1969) 57.

[81] arg ex Art 1274 SCC.

[82] SCJ 30-12-1978. For the 'transformation' of the particular motive into an 'impulsive cause', see SCJJ 27-12-1966, 22-11-1979 or 3-02-1981.

[83] See eg SCJ 11-04-1994 and SCJ 10-06-2015; in a similar sense, see SCJ 8-06-2006.

developed' by the parties – which connects with the thesis of the German presupposition and the basis of the transaction.[84] These various possibilities also raise the question of whether the inclusion of such subjective elements is only a matter of the cause of the contract or whether it also affects the consent to the legal transaction. There are different opinions with no clear trend or tendency.[85]

The subjective conception of the cause – which understands it as a 'decisive reason or motive that induces one to negotiate' – presupposes that no one enters into a bargain without a reason or motive.[86] Consistently, the 'non-existence' of cause is not possible – a person always enters into a contract for or because of something – and therefore the regulation of contracts without a cause or the examination of the non-existence of cause from the 'motives' that induced the signing of the contract makes no sense. In this context, the subjective concept of cause has served the case law: (i) to control the unlawfulness and morality of the bargain (subsection ii); (ii) to allow the termination of the contract when the circumstances of its perfection have disappeared (subsection iii); or (iii) to solve the problems of serious supervening alteration of circumstances (subsection iv). I will consider each of these separately.

(ii) Cause as an Element to Control the Lawfulness and Morality of the Bargain

The subjective explanation of the cause has also made it possible to use that notion as an element of control over the lawfulness and morality of the agreements; that is, they are adjusted to 'social ethics' and to the rules of conduct required by the legal system. The very text of Article 1275 SCC seems to allow this when it states that 'contracts … with an unlawful cause do not produce any effect' and points out that 'the cause is unlawful when it is contrary to the law or morality'. Unlike the absolute simulated cases in which there was no cause, in these cases there is a cause but it is vitiated by unlawfulness – or 'clumsiness'.[87] In this context, unlawfulness involves a 'harm to a general interest, legal or moral'.[88] The cause is, therefore, the technical tool for declaring the ineffectiveness of a bargain when the shared purpose – or at least, the purpose externalised and recognisable by the other contracting party – is unlawful or immoral. Such a contract has an unlawful cause: the unlawfulness 'rests' on the immoral or unlawful common purpose of the parties.[89] Thus, case law usually requires that the unlawfulness of the purpose pursued by the transaction is common to the parties.[90]

[84] See SCJ 19-02-2009.

[85] Thus, L Martínez Velencoso, *La alteración de las circunstancias contractuales* (Madrid, Thomson Civitas, 2003) 105 refers in general terms to those authors who consider that it is not a problem of cause but one of interpretation of the contractual will. Likewise, reorienting the 'causalisation of the motive' to the presupposition or basis of the business, see Lacruz et al (n 67) 432–36.

[86] *cf* M Albaladejo, 'La causa' (1958) 4 *Revista de Derecho Privado* 316.

[87] See SCJ 22-06-2021.

[88] SCJ 14-12-1940.

[89] See SCJ 13-03-1997 and SCJ 27-03-2007.

[90] See eg SCJ 11-12-2001 or SCJ 23-03-2021. Considering the purpose of only one of the parties as sufficient, see P De Pablo Contreras, 'Los requisitos del contrato' in VVAA, *Curso de Derecho civil*, II-I, 5th edn (Madrid, Edisofer, 2018) 383, who relies on Arts 1305 and 1306 SCC.

As can be seen, and in contrast to the objective dimension of the cause, this notion is now linked to the subjective aims of the parties.[91] It is, therefore, not something objective and invariable. The intention, the purpose, the common motive is elevated – in the legal sense – to the cause of the contract, and impresses on the will 'the [in this case] unlawful and reprehensible finalistic direction of the agreement'.[92] Although the particular motivations of each party, as long as they are lawful, are irrelevant from a legal point of view – unless they are elevated as to be a 'specific cause' or are configured as a condition or mode – this is not the case when the common purpose is unlawful or immoral.[93] In these cases, contracts are relevant to the legal system because of this – unlawful – intent.[94]

And that happens although the parties do not have a positive intention to infringe the law: it is sufficient that the common purpose which impels them to enter into the bargain and is elevated to the status of cause in the legal sense is incompatible with the law or morality.[95] However, if the agreement contains an element of an unlawful nature, this does not make the cause unlawful.[96] What must be unlawful is the cause – in this case, the intent. When that happens, the bargain is null and void: it 'do[es] not produce any effect', according to Article 1275 SCC. Causal unlawfulness thus implies absolute nullity – not mere voidability[97] – without the four-year limitation period for prescription.[98] Moreover, such nullity also produces some specific consequences contained in Articles 1305 and 1306 SCC.[99] It must also be noted that not every nullity for contravention of the law entails the application of Article 1306 SCC. Indeed,

> the application of Article 1306 SCC requires a 'clumsiness' on the part of the person causing the nullity, a moral reproach or a breach of the public economic order, a causal nullity justified by the repression of the content of the contract, which cannot be identified with the nullity of all prohibited transactions.[100]

As has been said, such unlawfulness is more likely to occur when the parties deviate from the typical content of a contract – in the case of that which is typical but prohibited by law, the mere invocation of the law is sufficient to declare its ineffectiveness – or, within it, the consent falls on unlawful obligations, conduct or things,[101] or on lawful provisions but with an unlawful purpose.[102]

The case law shows that the courts have declared the unlawfulness of the *cause of the contract* when the common motives of the parties were immoral or unlawful, without

[91] See SCJ 19-11-1974.

[92] SCJ 20-07-2006. In the same sense, see SCJJ 8-02-1963, 30-03-1979 and 27-03-2007.

[93] See SCJ 24-04-2013. That SCJ points out that if 'the purpose pursued is unlawful, such protection will not be granted and that purpose is elevated to the category of unlawful cause determining the total nullity of the legal transaction'.

[94] See Sancho Rebullida (n 6) 63.

[95] See Marín López (n 70) 750–51.

[96] See SCJ 8-02-1958 and SCJ 5-02-2020.

[97] See SCJ 31-01-1963.

[98] See SCJ 29-04-1961.

[99] See SCJ 23-11-1961 and SCJ 22-06-2021.

[100] SCJ 27-09-2017.

[101] See Art 1271 SCC.

[102] See Art 1275 SCC. See De Pablo Contreras (n 90) 383.

the need to carry out a specific examination of the *cause of each obligation*. By way of example, the Spanish Supreme Court judgment SCJ 18-09-2019 declared the causal illegality of a contract that had an unlawful purpose or was contrary to social morality. Causal unlawfulness has also been declared: where the defendants had been convicted of embezzlement in respect of the donation considered to be unlawful;[103] where the loan concealed a gambling debt;[104] when the casino intended to recover the losses of a customer who had gambled with money lent by the casino itself, in breach of a legal prohibition;[105] when the intention was to evade compliance with a decision ordering the payment of the maintenance;[106] or in the case of a maintenance contract entered into with the intention to fraud the forced share.[107]

On the other hand, the following have not been considered unlawful: an alleged commission clause in a leasing contract designed to secure the position of the financier;[108] lobbying, provided that it does not involve criminal conduct;[109] the establishment of a usufruct by a company in order to ensure the enjoyment of an asset by one of the partners, without any fraudulent purpose;[110] or franchising, where the franchisor fixes the prices.[111]

From these or other rulings, it can be deduced that a cause is unlawful if it is contrary to public order and unjustifiably harms or damages third parties.[112] Contracts will then have an immoral cause if they are contrary to the ethical rules in force or, using Díez-Picazo's words, to those required 'by the normal coexistence of people considered to be honest'.[113] Of course, the determination of what these rules are requires an appropriate assessment by the courts, since they are mutable and are not linked to any religious beliefs.

This being the case, there seems to be an increasing tendency to consider that the illegality or immorality of a transaction can be declared without recourse to the cause. Indeed, it is argued that such a declaration could be made on the basis of Article 1255 SCC – 'the contracting parties may establish the agreements, clauses and conditions they deem convenient, provided that they are not contrary to the law, morality or public order' – or even on the basis of Article 1271 SCC with regard to the lawfulness of the subject matter of the contract – the services cannot be contrary to 'the law or to generally accepted principles of morality'.[114] Be that as it may, it is important to remember that recourse to the unlawfulness of the cause of the contract always addresses a problem of the *structure of the contract* itself.

[103] See SCJ 27-03-2007.
[104] See SCJ 3-02-1961.
[105] See SCJ 10-10-2008.
[106] See SCJ 26-11-1955.
[107] See SCJ 15-02-2022.
[108] See SCJ 7-02-2000.
[109] See SCJ 11-06-2012.
[110] See SCJ 17-03-2015.
[111] See SCJ 28-07-2021.
[112] See Marín López (n 70) 751.
[113] Díez-Picazo (n 6) 283.
[114] In this sense, see Sancho Rebullida (n 6) 152–53. In view of the precepts transcribed in the text, recourse to the cause to control the 'private autonomy' must be the 'last resort'; see De Pablo Contreras (n 90) 383.

(iii) Cause as a Set of Circumstances Surrounding the Contract

A second section of case law in which the subjective dimension of the cause has been used focuses on the circumstances of the contract: the cause here refers to the circumstances surrounding the agreement, the existence of which was crucial or decisive for the parties – even if this is not always explicitly stated – for the perfection of the bargain. Therefore, its frustration or supervening disappearance justifies the release from the contract: what was the presupposition for concluding the contract no longer exists. The circumstances have changed in such a manner that the *contract itself* has been transformed *in such a way* that it no longer fulfils its original purpose: the initial relationship of equivalence, the original meaning of the exchange of services, has been broken. The set of circumstances implicitly or explicitly accepted as the natural sphere of development of the agreement – and which form the basis of the business – have been altered in such a form that the contract cannot be recognised as such; it has been deprived of its original meaning.

The recourse to the cause in these cases belongs to what has come to be called the 'continuing influence of the cause', a term coined by De Castro:[115] it is not enough that the cause exists at the time of the perfection of the contract – when it is examined to determine whether it is defective or not – but must be maintained throughout its performance.[116] Of course, there is no unanimity on this point. Likewise, it is been said that the content of the cause, like consent and capacity, is exhausted 'once its mission has been fulfilled' in the creation of the contractual bond.[117]

Thus, the disappearance or frustration of the common purpose or assumption envisaged by the parties will lead to the modification, ineffectiveness or termination of the contract.[118] Reference should be made, inter alia, to SCJ 21-07-2010, in which the Spanish Supreme Court held that a bargain to transfer an option right to a company had no cause if the property that was the subject of that right did not obtain the expected urban development classification, which was the reason for the company to acquire that right. In particular, the Spanish Supreme Court stated that

> the cause must not only be present at the initial moment of the formation of the contract but must also accompany it during its performance, so that the supervening absence of the cause entitles the affected contracting party to request the modification of the contract or even its termination, which is particularly the case where two contracts are linked, as is the case here,

[115] See De Castro (n 31) 313–26.

[116] See eg SCJ 20-04-1994.

[117] See F Candil, *La cláusula rebus sic stantibus* (Madrid, Librería Jiménez, 1946) 80–81. The same opinion can be found in SCJ 14-12-1940: 'the prolongation of the theory of cause, beyond the moment of the formation of the contract … does not find any support in our current civil law'.

[118] The cases mentioned in the text logically recall the theses of 'frustration' and 'disappearance of the basis of the business', and even of the supervening impossibility of performance. Alluding to the first, though not necessarily linking it to the cause, see SCJ 5-06-1989, and in particular SCJ 9-12-1983 and SCJ 27-10-1986, both relating to the impossibility of carrying out projects of an architect for the lack of appropriate authorisations. In relation to the 'basis of the business', see eg SCJ 23-11-1962 and SCJ 14-12-1993 – neither of which links such a doctrine to the supervening disappearance of the cause. And linking both elements, see SCJ 21-07-2010 and SCJ 26-04-2013. Finally, connecting the supervening impossibility to the cause, see eg SCJ 23-06-1997. A non-exhaustive survey of the case law shows that it is not always easy to distinguish the above-mentioned concepts and that the jurisprudence itself has not always been technically correct in its demarcation.

> since the inoperability of one of them entitles the affected party to request the termination of the other contract, since its cause has supervened and disappeared.[119]

As can be seen, this 'continuing influence of the cause' is particularly relevant in the case of related contracts: it is understood that if one becomes ineffective, the cause of the one that had its raison d'être in the other disappears.[120]

Besides, in contrast to the 'continuing influence of the cause', there is now a growing tendency to link the frustration or disappearance of the basis of the transaction to the consent. In other words, termination is invoked when the cause which motivated the contract and which the parties had accepted as an implicit condition disappears or is frustrated.[121] One of the reasons for this is to avoid a strict application of the notion of the cause, which necessarily entails the ineffectiveness of the contract, when the contracting parties, faced with the termination of the bargain, may prefer its continuation, to which they add the *commodum representationis*.

(iv) Alteration of Circumstances

A third application of the subjective thesis of the cause has made it possible to link it to the principle of *rebus sic stantibus*. According to this principle, it is possible to modify what has been agreed in the event of an unforeseen and supervening alteration of circumstances of such a relevant nature that the burden or cost of the services for one of the parties is increased in an extraordinary manner. The change in circumstances must result in a real collapse of the contractual equilibrium. In this case, one of the arguments used in relation to the notion of cause is that if the extraordinary imbalance created is not corrected, unjust enrichment will occur, thus violating the element of justice implicit in any contract. By way of example, the Spanish Supreme Court judgments SCJ 18-01-2013 and SCJ 30-06-2014, inter alia, mention the cause related to such modification.[122]

Although some case law connects the *rebus* clause with the 'continuing influence of the cause', for some time now a different basis has been recognised: the *rebus* clause is an exceptional remedy based on contractual good faith to exempt a party from a risk not assigned in the contract or to mitigate its consequences, and not a matter of the supervening disappearance of the cause.[123] At the same time, other scholars and case law redirect the application of the *rebus* clause to contractual consent. Likewise, the *rebus* becomes independent of the cause and is mostly linked to the good faith of the contract and the obligations derived from it.[124] Indeed, it is currently considered that one of the obligations inherent in good faith is to renegotiate the bargain if there has been a serious alteration of circumstances.

[119] See also SCJ 20-04-1994.

[120] See eg SCJ 20-07-2012.

[121] On the link with consent, see H Clavería Gosálbez, 'Comentario a la STS 17-01-1985' (1985) 7 *Cuadernos Civitas de Jurisprudencia civil* 2293; Rodríguez-Rosado (n 14) 90.

[122] Mentioning the cause – albeit indirectly – in relation to the alteration of circumstances, see SCJ 23-11-1962. On the contrary, ie pointing out that the alteration of circumstances does not affect the cause, see SCJ 5-06-1945.

[123] See eg SCJ 23-04-2012.

[124] See Arts 7 and 1258 SCC or SCJJ 10-02-1997, 21-05-2009, 17-01-2013 and 18-07-2019.

D. Cause as an Element to Control the Simulation of the Contract

So far, the analysis has focused on the functions of cause directly linked to the objective conception (the reality of the agreement and its binding nature, abstract contracts and absolute simulation) and to the subjective conception (lawfulness and morality of the agreement, the set of circumstances surrounding the contract and the supervening alteration of the circumstances of the contract). The function to be analysed now is linked, albeit *indirectly*, to the first thesis. As noted above, the objective conception requires the existence of a cause in every contractual obligation, since there is no such obligation without a cause, just as there is no contract without an obligation. But what happens if the cause externalised by the parties differs from that which actually animates the agreement?

In cases of relative simulation, the contracting parties manifest a common purpose – in what is of interest here, a lawful one – but internally they harbour a different one; in other words, they externalise a 'false' cause, eg they agree on a sale that conceals a donation.[125] In such a situation, Article 1276 SCC only imposes the need to search for an authentic cause with the requirements of lawfulness and existence: 'the statement of a false cause in contracts shall entail the nullity thereof, unless it is proven that they were based on another true and lawful cause'. The cause of the simulated bargain does not exist – it is a 'false' cause – but, unlike in cases of absolute simulation, there is another cause – true and lawful – in the dissimulated bargain.[126] The debtor must prove the falsehood and the creditor the existence of a true cause.

In line with this, the case law has recognised the effectiveness of the disguised cause that meets the requirements of Article 1276 SCC.[127] And jurisprudence has recognised the validity of the bargain concealed behind another appearance in the case of sales hiding movable donations – not gifts of real estate, which require a public deed[128] or a maintenance contract.[129] In any case, as with absolute simulation, relative simulation must be duly proven.

Such simulation – now relating to the cause, not to the contract as a whole – may also affect the subject matter of the legal transaction, eg its value. For this reason, it has been proposed that the use of the cause be redirected as an element for controlling the relative simulation of contracts towards consent. This is because the latter is projected onto the subject matter and the cause,[130] and the relative simulation directly affects the will of the parties and their consent. In such cases, there is a defect of consent which is also reflected in the cause.[131]

[125] See SCJ 4-04-2012.
[126] Alonso Pérez (n 80) 19: 'falsehood reflects in the Civil Code a special form of absence of cause'.
[127] See eg SCJ 6-10-1977.
[128] See SCJ 14-04-2011.
[129] See SCJ 14-03-2019.
[130] See Art 1261 SCC.
[131] See Rodríguez-Rosado (n 14) 82. Against this, and stressing that simulation is only a defect of cause, see Díez-Picazo (n 6) 257.

One last thought: it is necessary to distinguish between 'false cause'[132] and 'falseness of the cause'.[133] In the first case, 'false' is contrary to the true, and occurs with the simulation and with the untrue cause; its existence leads to nullity and the action for its declaration is imprescriptible.[134] The second, which is closer to error – the parties having stated a cause which is false although they believe it to be true – gives rise to an action for annulment, which can be exercised within four years from 'the consummation of the contract'.[135]

E. Cause as an Element to Control the Reasonableness of the Bargain

Together with the objective and subjective theses, the 'objectivist' one, developed by Italian authors, has also been accepted in Spain.[136] According to this view, the cause refers to the socio-economic function performed by an agreement. It is no longer a question of the subjective intention that the contracting parties may have, but of the function that the bargain they have entered into plays in the social context. Consistently, the legal system protects contracts because it legally 'objectifies' a priori the function they perform, and this function is considered to be positive for society: the sale will develop a social function of exchange of a thing for a price, the mortgage a function of guarantee … The *positive* socio-economic functions they perform justify the protection afforded to such transactions by the legal system – they are worthy of protection and defence[137] – and explain the general raison d'être to which they respond. In my view, case law is wrong when it refers to the economic and social function within the objective category of cause. The objective cause is the counter-performance itself, and the function is something else and cannot be reoriented to that objective sense.

Moreover, this explanation even distinguishes between a subjective dimension – the social function sought by the parties – and an objective one – the assessment of this intention by the legal system. Accordingly, the parties agree to sell on the basis of the general function of 'exchange' recognised by the legal system; a different question – and irrelevant at this point in the explanation – is the specific subjective motive of this bargain, unless, as has been said, it has been elevated to a 'specific cause'.

In line with the function of the cause now under discussion, case law has criticised fiduciary transactions for lacking an economic and social function that justifies them, since the parties alter the original and natural objective and economic purpose of the

[132] See Art 1276 SCC.
[133] See Art 1301 SCC.
[134] See eg SCJ 29-11-1989.
[135] See Art 1301 SCC.
[136] One of the main supporters of this thesis is E Betti, *Teoría generale del negozio giuridico*, 2nd edn (Turin, UTET, 1960) 171–209, in particular 181–82. Pointing out the gaps in Betti's thesis, see C Scognamiglio, 'Contratti in generale' in G Grosso and F Santoro (eds), *Trattato di Diritto civile*, IV-II, 2nd edn (Naples, Casa Editrice Francesco Vallardi, 1966) 122.
[137] See SCJ 16-06-2011 or SCJ 22-06-2021.

type of contract in question.[138] The transfer of assets by way of guarantee or for mere management is not considered correct and does not correspond to the transaction concluded.[139] It should not be forgotten, however, that there are some decisions which recognise the validity of the trust contract, stressing its differences with the simulated contract.[140]

One of the problems with this thesis is that it may lead to confusion between the notion of cause and the function performed by a contract. It also raises a relevant problem because, in addition to the limits to the autonomy of the will established in Article 1255 SCC, if such a thesis were accepted, another would be imposed consisting of the existence of a *reasonable* socio-economic function – a criterion that is not anchored in the rules that the Spanish Civil Code dedicates to the cause.[141] The only possible limits are those established by law;[142] to allow any other without a clear legal basis would also constitute an unjustified restriction on private autonomy.[143] Finally, this thesis also prevents or restricts atypical businesses, ie those that the legislator has not positively included in the regulation and for which there is no specific function that the law wishes to protect.

IV. Final Remarks

A number of conclusions can be drawn about the functions currently performed by the notion of cause in the Spanish legal system. Firstly, the Spanish system remains causal. Since the approval of the SCC in 1889, the cause has been and still is part of the legal system, and is regulated in that legal body. However, the vagueness of the regulation explains to a large extent the ambiguity and lack of certainty in this matter and the consequent imprecision from which judicial decisions often suffer. Be that as it may, in the absence of a change in the law that would definitively abolish it, the notion of cause must continue to be applied in legal transactions, since it is not possible to defend the validity of an abstract system. An analysis of the judgments also reveals its undeniable practical importance.

Secondly, and partly as a result of the above, the notion of cause has undergone a 'hyperinflation' of functions: it is used for simulation; its 'continuing influence' has been used to declare the supervening ineffectiveness of contracts; it constitutes an element to control the 'morality' and 'lawfulness' of the bargain, etc. Perhaps because the general clause of 'good faith' was not enshrined in the law until 1974,[144] the jurisprudence has developed a *mouldable* notion of the cause, applying it to resolve a wide variety

[138] See SCJ 4-07-1998 and SCJ 5-04-1993.

[139] In this sense, see the Resolution of the former General Directorate of Registries and Notaries of 10 March 2004, Official Journal of 14 April 2004.

[140] See SCJ 25-02-1988 and SCJ 13-02-2003.

[141] *cf* Arts 1274–77 SCC.

[142] See Arts 1255 and 1275 SCC.

[143] This view is shared by Rodríguez-Rosado (n 14) 98.

[144] See Art 7.1 SCC.

of situations that are not always related. Maybe this was the most appropriate way to proceed at the time, which explains the maintenance of a dualistic view of the cause, comprising the objective and subjective dimensions.

In view of this situation, I believe that a possible revival and strengthening of the cause requires that it be maintained as a basic requirement of the contractual obligation, and that it must be formulated in precise terms.[145] From the outset, there are two options. The first is to amend the law to limit its functions, as has been done in other legal systems. The second is to consolidate the jurisprudential trends that transfer some of the functions traditionally performed by the cause to other figures.

In particular, in my opinion, recourse to cause should be maintained in cases of relative simulation[146] and also, albeit as a last resort insofar as it concerns the structure of the contract, in those of absolute simulation; that is to say, when one particular bargain cannot be challenged by means of consent. Likewise, and also as a last resort, I believe that recourse to the notion of cause should be maintained with regard to the unlawfulness or immorality of the transaction, when Articles 1255 SCC – on the limits of the autonomy of the will – and 1271 SCC – on the subject matter of the contract – cannot be resorted to.[147]

In accepting such functions, the cause should not be used in cases of frustration or disappearance of the basis of the business, nor in those of unforeseen supervening alteration of the circumstances. The most appropriate legal basis for such situations is consent and good faith,[148] and the appropriate legal remedy is termination and modification, depending on the case.[149] Similarly, I consider that the explanation of the 'socio-economic' function of the cause should not be maintained, as it is unnecessary. If, for example, the prohibition of trust or obligatory donation were to be sought, this would have to be indicated positively by means of a legal reform.

Finally, whether by legislative amendment or by case law, the application and the content of cause and good faith must be coordinated. It would not make sense to empty the cause because of its ambiguity, uncertainty and poorly defined profile and to reintroduce such difficulties in another open concept such as good faith. In general, the texts of unified law suppress the cause as a requirement of the contract and elevate the general clause of good faith to an evaluative parameter of the entire contract.[150]

In my opinion, the notion of cause can still be a useful tool for introducing criteria of justice into the contract that would otherwise have no place. For this reason, given the existing tradition in Spain, it would be advisable not to abolish it, but to subject it to a 'purification' of its functions. But legal trends are still trends, and it seems that Spain will follow them sooner or later.

[145] In the 2016 reform, France deleted the cause (Art 1128 Code civil). Italy still considers it to be an essential requirement of the contract (see Arts 1324 and 1343–45 Codice civile).

[146] See Art 1276 SCC.

[147] See §§ 134 and 138 BGB and Art 1162 of the French Code civil.

[148] See Arts 7 and 1255 SCC.

[149] See § 275, 313 II and 1186 BGB and Art 1195 of the French Code civil.

[150] See Art 2:201 of the Principles of European Contract Law, Art II.-4:101 of the Draft Common Frame of Reference or Art 3.1.2 of the Unidroit Principles of International Commercial Contracts.

V. Table of Cases

SCJ 14-03-1930 (ECLI:ES:TS:1930:1059)
SCJ 24-03-1930 (ECLI:ES:TS:1930:1823)
SCJ 14-01-1935 (ECLI:ES:TS:1935:2523)
SCJ 14-12-1940 (RJA 1135/1940)
SCJ 8-02-1943 (ECLI:ES:TS:1943:17)
SCJ 5-06-1945 (ECLI:ES:TS:1945:173)
SCJ 12-04-1946 (ECLI:ES:TS:1946:67)
SCJ 24-03-1950 (ECLI:ES:TS:1950:358)
SCJ 18-05-1953 (ECLI:ES:TS:1953:1633)
SCJ 27-02-1954 (ECLI:ES:TS:1954:951)
SCJ 2-02-1955 (ECLI:ES:TS:1955:149)
SCJ 31-10-1955 (ECLI:ES:TS:1955:2880)
SCJ 26-11-1955 (ECLI:ES:TS:1955:133)
SCJ 8-03-1956 (ECLI:ES:TS:1956:280)
SCJ 17-03-1956 (ECLI:ES:TS:1956:169)
SCJ 18-06-1957 (ECLI:ES:TS:1957:1286)
SCJ 8-02-1958 (ECLI:ES:TS:1958:1378)
SCJ 24-02-1959 (ECLI:ES:TS:1959:904)
SCJ 20-05-1959 (ECLI:ES:TS:1959:1008)
SCJ 30-01-1960 (ECLI:ES:TS:1960:2002)
SCJ 25-04-1960 (ECLI:ES:TS:1960:1914)
SCJ 19-12-1960 (ECLI:ES:TS:1960:818)
SCJ 3-02-1961 (ECLI:ES:TS:1961:43)
SCJ 4-04-1961 (ECLI:ES:TS:1961:1585)
SCJ 29-04-1961 (ECLI:ES:TS:1961:1735)
SCJ 20-10-1961 (ECLI:ES:TS:1961:326)
SCJ 23-11-1961 (ECLI:ES:TS:1961:2064)
SCJ 26-04-1962 (ECLI:ES:TS:1962:2826)
SCJ 26-10-1962 (ECLI:ES:TS:1962:2503)
SCJ 23-11-1962 (ECLI:ES:TS:1962:208)
SCJ 17-01-1963 (ECLI:ES:TS:1963:2345)
SCJ 31-01-1963 (ECLI:ES:TS:1963:2768)
SCJ 8-02-1963 (ECLI:ES:TS:1963:2188)
SCJ 14-06-1963 (ECLI:ES:TS:1963:2798)
SCJ 22-11-1963 (ECLI:ES:TS:1963:2684)
SCJ 2-05-1964 (ECLI:ES:TS:1964:4055)
SCJ 20-01-1965 (ECLI:ES:TS:1965:2)
SCJ 25-05-1965 (ECLI:ES:TS:1965:836)
SCJ 12-02-1966 (ECLI:ES:TS:1966:2005)
SCJ 27-12-1966 (ECLI:ES:TS:1966:1927)
SCJ 13-11-1970 (ECLI:ES:TS:1970:261)
SCJ 30-11-1972 (ECLI:ES:TS:1972:2448)
SCJ 26-05-1973 (ECLI:ES:TS:1973:17)
SCJ 8-07-1974 (ECLI:ES:TS:1974:172)
SCJ 19-11-1974 (ECLI:ES:TS:1974:2818)
SCJ 12-04-1975 (ECLI:ES:TS:1975:1710)
SCJ 6-10-1977 (ECLI:ES:TS:1977:833)
SCJ 24-11-1978 (ECLI:ES:TS:1978:208)
SCJ 30-12-1978 (ECLI:ES:TS:1978:140)
SCJ 30-03-1979 (ECLI:ES:TS:1979:137)
SCJ 22-11-1979 (ECLI:ES:TS:1979:4656)
SCJ 3-02-1981 (ECLI:ES:TS:1981:51)
SCJ 3-11-1981 (ECLI:ES:TS:1981:186)
SCJ 1-04-1982 (ECLI:ES:TS:1982:1359)
SCJ 9-12-1983 (RJ 1983/6925)
SCJ 24-04-1984 (ECLI:ES:TS:1984:18)
SCJ 11-07-1984 (ECLI:ES:TS:1984:1324)
SCJ 5-10-1984 (ECLI:ES:TS:1984:219)
SCJ 17-01-1985 (ECLI:ES:TS:1985:1431)
SCJ 30-12-1985 (ECLI:ES:TS:1985:1694)
SCJ 27-10-1986 (ECLI:ES:TS:1986:5780)
SCJ 25-02-1988 (ECLI:ES:TS:1988:1267)
SCJ 15-02-1989 (ECLI:ES:TS:1989:9061)
SCJ 5-06-1989 (ECLI:ES:TS:1989:15601)
SCJ 29-11-1989 (ECLI:ES:TS:1989:9739)
SCJ 19-11-1990 (ECLI:ES:TS:1990:8375)
SCJ 31-01-1991 (ECLI:ES:TS:1991:515)
SCJ 29-03-1993 (ECLI:ES:TS:1993:19239)
SCJ 5-04-1993 (ECLI:ES:TS:1993:17422)
SCJ 14-12-1993 (ECLI:ES:TS:1993:8668)
SCJ 11-04-1994 (ECLI:ES:TS:1994:22215)
SCJ 20-04-1994 (ECLI:ES:TS:1994:22229)
SCJ 25-02-1995 (ECLI:ES:TS:1995:10090)
SCJ 27-06-1996 (ECLI:ES:TS:1996:3927)
SCJ 10-02-1997 (ECLI:ES:TS:1997:855)
SCJ 13-03-1997 (ECLI:ES:TS:1997:1819)
SCJ 23-06-1997 (ECLI:ES:TS:1997:4436)
SCJ 8-07-1997 (ECLI:ES:TS:1997:1364)
SCJ 13-02-1998 (ECLI:ES:TS:1998:960)
SCJ 1-04-1998 (ECLI:ES:TS:1998:2172)
SCJ 4-07-1998 (ECLI:ES:TS:1998:4474)
SCJ 28-07-1998 (ECLI:ES:TS:1998:5025)
SCJ 7-02-2000 (ECLI:ES:TS:2000:826)
SCJ 27-02-2001 (ECLI:ES:TS:2001:1453)
SCJ 11-12-2001 (ECLI:ES:TS:2001:9672)
SCJ 6-06-2002 (ECLI:ES:TS:2002:4087)

SCJ 13-02-2003 (ECLI:ES:TS:2003:948)
SCJ 26-07-2004 (ECLI:ES:TS:2004:5536)
SCJ 3-11-2004 (ECLI:ES:TS:2004:7075)
SCJ 17-12-2004 (ECLI:ES:TS:2004:8207)
SCJ 11-02-2005 (ECLI:ES:TS:2005:794)
SCJ 14-02-2005 (ECLI:ES:TS:2005:820)
SCJ 17-02-2005 (ECLI:ES:TS:2005:964)
SCJ 23-02-2005 (ECLI:ES:TS:2005:1128)
SCJ 27-09-2005 (ECLI:ES:TS:2005:5571)
SCJ 20-10-2005 (ECLI:ES:TS:2005:6375)
SCJ 21-04-2006 (ECLI:ES:TS:2006:2352)
SCJ 8-06-2006 (ECLI:ES:TS:2006:3277)
SCJ 20-07-2006 (ECLI:ES:TS:2006:4457)
SCJ 11-01-2007 (ECLI:ES:TS:2007:822)
SCJ 22-02-2007 (ECLI:ES:TS:2007:826)
SCJ 27-03-2007 (ECLI:ES:TS:2007:1970)
SCJ 11-05-2007 (ECLI:ES:TS:2007:3227)
SCJ 18-05-2007 (ECLI:ES:TS:2007:3233)
SCJ 28-05-2007 (ECLI:ES:TS:2007:3422)
SCJ 1-10-2007 (ECLI:ES:TS:2007:6417)
SCJ 28-12-2007 (ECLI:ES:TS:2007:8652)
SCJ 18-03-2008 (ECLI:ES:TS:2008:1558)
SCJ 17-07-2008 (ECLI:ES:TS:2008:5983)
SCJ 10-10-2008 (ECLI:ES:TS:2008:5227)
SCJ 14-11-2008 (ECLI:ES:TS:2008:7242)
SCJ 19-02-2009 (ECLI:ES:TS:2009:586)
SCJ 21-05-2009 (ECLI:ES:TS:2009:3068)
SCJ 19-06-2009 (ECLI:ES:TS:2009:5729)
SCJ 21-10-2009 (ECLI:ES:TS:2009:6181)
SCJ 21-12-2009 (ECLI:ES:TS:2009:7691)
SCJ 21-12-2009 (ECLI:ES:TS:2009:8109)
SCJ 21-07-2010 (ECLI:ES:TS:2010:3901)
SCJ 26-10-2010 (ECLI:ES:TS:2010:5777)
SCJ 11-02-2011 (ECLI:ES:TS:2011:720)
SCJ 10-03-2011 (ECLI:ES:TS:2011:1065)
SCJ 14-04-2011 (ECLI:ES:TS:2011:2688)
SCJ 16-06-2011 (ECLI:ES:TS:2011:4296)
SCJ 1-07-2011 (ECLI:ES:TS:2011:4843)
SCJ 15-02-2012 (ECLI:ES:TS:2012:1689)
SCJ 4-04-2012 (ECLI:ES:TS:2012:2139)
SCJ 23-04-2012 (ECLI:ES:TS:2012:2866)
SCJ 11-06-2012 (ECLI:ES:TS:2012:4403)
SCJ 20-07-2012 (ECLI:ES:TS:2012:5768)
SCJ 16-01-2013 (ECLI:ES:TS:2013:345)
SCJ 17-01-2013 (ECLI:ES:TS:2013:1013)
SCJ 18-01-2013 (ECLI:ES:TS:2013:679)
SCJ 24-01-2013 (ECLI:ES:TS:2013:198)
SCJ 24-04-2013 (ECLI:ES:TS:2013:2753)
SCJ 26-04-2013 (ECLI:ES:TS:2013:2247)
SCJ 3-10-2013 (ECLI:ES:TS:2013:4956)
SCJ 4-03-2014 (ECLI:ES:TS:2014:849)
SCJ 30-06-2014 (ECLI:ES:TS:2014:2823)
SCJ 17-07-2014 (ECLI:ES:TS:2014:3157)
SCJ 25-11-2014 (ECLI:ES:TS:2014:4766)
SCJ 17-03-2015 (ECLI:ES:TS:2015:1860)
SCJ 10-06-2015 (ECLI:ES:TS:2015:2967)
SCJ 3-11-2015 (ECLI:ES:TS:2015:4471)
SCJ 1-03-2016 (ECLI:ES:TS:2016:790)
SCJ 3-05-2016 (ECLI:ES:TS:2016:1892)
SCJ 19-05-2016 (ECLI:ES:TS:2016:2307)
SCJ 27-09-2017 (ECLI:ES:TS:2017:3381)
SCJ 14-03-2019 (ECLI:ES:TS:2019:865)
SCJ 5-04-2019 (ECLI:ES:TS:2019:1126)
SCJ 10-05-2019 (ECLI:ES:TS:2019:1452)
SCJ 9-07-2019 (ECLI:ES:TS:2019:2388)
SCJ 18-07-2019 (ECLI:ES:TS:2019:2556)
SCJ 18-09-2019 (ECLI:ES:TS:2019:2816)
SCJ 5-02-2020 (ECLI:ES:TS:2020:306)
SCJ 6-02-2020 (ECLI:ES:TS:2020:311)
SCJ 23-03-2021 (ECLI:ES:TS:2021:1079)
SCJ 22-06-2021 (ECLI:ES:TS:2021:2493)
SCJ 28-07-2021 (ECLI:ES:TS:2021:3191)
SCJ 15-02-2022 (ECLI:ES:TS:2022:608)
SCJ 26-04-2022 (ECLI:ES:TS:2022:1623)
SCJ 19-05-2022 (ECLI:ES:TS:2022:2072)

9

The Attempt to Suppress *Causa* in German Contract Law

GREGOR ALBERS*

I. A Forgotten Element of Private Law

Most German lawyers would assert that the French concept of *cause du contrat* has no place in German private law. They might proudly recount that German law recognises so-called 'abstract' contracts (*abstrakte Verträge*): in the law of property as well as in the law of obligations, certain agreements produce specific legal effects, without any regard to the social or economic context of the transaction. This can be the case for an agreement aiming at a transfer of title, but also for the creation of a unilateral obligation. The parties' naked will alone produces the desired effect. When pressed on the matter, the proud champion of abstraction would explain that the effect is only a preliminary one: the aggrieved party can rely on the law of unjustified enrichment, using it as a shield or as a sword to rectify any untoward consequences of abstraction. If a party can show, for instance, that there was no legal reason to transfer title or create the obligation in question, neither title nor the relevant obligation can be enforced against the other party, and the previous situation must be restored.

But did Germany thereby really get rid of *causa*? In the main part of this chapter (section II),[1] I will explore why German contract law does not ask for a *causa* from the point of view of the history of legal doctrines. At the end of the eighteenth century, there was already a consensus amongst legal scholars in Germany that the limitations of the Roman contractual system had been overcome and *causa* no longer played a part in the formation of contracts. But the Code Napoléon (Code civil, French Civil Code) sparked the debate anew. I will argue that it was only because of this debate that German law embraced the concept of 'abstract' obligations. Ironically, the very concept was heavily inspired by the French Code, otherwise the great promoter of cause.

* I am deeply grateful to Birke Häcker for her insightful advice and her generosity in proofreading an earlier version of the text.

[1] The chapter draws heavily on my more extensive study 'Die causa vom Code civil zum BGB. Zuwendungen tragen statt Verpflichtungen begründen' in G Albers, FP Patti and D Perrouin-Verbe (eds), *Causa contractus* (Tübingen, Mohr Siebeck, 2020) 263–321.

For in its Article 1132, the Code civil affirmed the validity of a contract whose cause was not expressed. Article 1132 aimed at promissory notes and acknowledgements of debt which did not indicate details of the obligation (*cautio indiscreta*). Reconnecting these practical problems with the concept of cause, the article provided a starting point allowing German scholarship to answer such questions by applying the doctrine of formal or 'abstract' contracts. This doctrine had recently been developed by a new reading of the Roman sources. While it seems that *causa* was thus eliminated as a requirement of contract, the very idea of abstract contracts made *causa* reappear in the law of unjustified enrichment.

In the final part of this chapter (section III), I will comment on the result of this development. In my view, German law today suffers from attempts to suppress *causa*. In contract law, we tend to overestimate how much can be explained by interpreting the parties' will as such. But we lack understanding of the importance of contract types and we underestimate their importance. Here, we might profit from building on the tradition of cause of contract. At the same time, we risk forgetting that the law of unjustified enrichment must be fit to control any obligation for its legal basis. It cannot be limited to claiming back what has been paid or performed on obligations which later turn out to be invalid. Therefore, we must continue to reflect on the connection between the *causa* of contract and the grounds that justify a given enrichment.

II. The Triumph of the Formal Promise

Around the year 1800, German scholars affirmed that the Roman *causa* of contract no longer had a place in the modern (German) common law (*Gemeines Recht* or *ius commune*). It was only after being confronted with the French Code of 1804 that hidden conflicts rose to the surface: at first glance, the Code seemed to require more of a contract, by asking for a legitimate cause. But at second glance, it turned out that the new French rules were less restrictive than the former practice. By constructing a new foundation for the solution aspired to in the Code, German legal scholarship pushed *causa* further away from the realm of contract law while reaffirming its importance in the realm of unjustified enrichment.

A. A Deceptive Consensus

To require *causa* for the validity of a contract was considered a peculiarity of ancient Roman law which had not been maintained by modern law as it could not be justified: this seemed to be the general agreement amongst natural law theorists since Grotius,[2] amongst civilian lawyers since Wesenbeck[3] and amongst legislators since the Codex

[2] See K Kowalski, 'Die causa des Vertrages im Naturrecht der frühen Neuzeit' in Albers et al (n 1) 153–200 (182–83).

[3] M Wesenbeck, *Commentarii in Pandectas Juris Civilis et Codicem Justinianeum olim dicti Paratitla* (Lugdunum Batavorum 1649) D 2,14 no 9, 80–87; *cf* K.-P Nanz, *Die Entwicklung des allgemeinen Vertragsbegriffs im 16.–18. Jahrhundert* (Munich, Schweitzer, 1985) 85–94.

Maximilianeus Bavaricus Civilis of 1756.[4] To consider just one prominent example, one can turn to the commentary on the digests by Christian Friedrich Glück:

> According to German law, therefore, every contract is binding which has been entered into by persons who can bind themselves … concerning a permitted object … free from coercion and cunning, and under this condition there is no longer any promise today which would be a pactum nudum in the Roman sense.[5]

Glück's definition contains three of the four elements required by Article 1108 Code civil (in its original version): consent, capacity and object.

> Article 1108 Code civil 1804: Quatre conditions sont essentielles pour la validité d'une convention: le consentement de la partie qui s'oblige; sa capacité de contracter; un objet certain qui forme la matière de l'engagement; une cause licite dans l'obligation.

Causa had not been left out by accident. Stressing the inexistence of *pacta nuda*, Glück alludes to Roman contract law that only recognised a *numerus clausus* of contract types, and he underlines that every agreement is a valid contract, regardless of any *causa*.[6]

While the absence of *causa* from contract law seemed established, the writings on procedural law and on the rules of evidence hint at a different story. It was generally accepted that in court, claims were not considered well founded if they merely referred to an accepted promise made by the defendant. The claimant had to disclose the context of the promise, in other words, he had to refer to its cause.

The situation becomes understandable if one takes into account the relevant provisions of ancient Roman law, in which the word *causa* makes various appearances in different contexts.[7] Best known is the passage where Ulpian cites Aristo's opinion that an agreement, even if not falling into one of the typical contracts, could give rise to an action for non-performance, provided that it contained a bargain and the claimant had already fulfilled his part of the deal. In such a case, the *synallagma* was to be considered a sufficient *causa* to justify the effects of the agreement.[8] One might speak of *causa conventionis*. This is the meaning of *causa* which dominates modern debates and seems to be the direct ancestor of the requirement of contract established by the French Code. But this meaning cannot be detached from other appearances of the word. One must keep in mind the role *causa* plays in the Roman law of unjustified enrichment.

[4] *Codex Maximilianeus Bavaricus Civilis*, Teil IV, cap 1, § 3. For further examples and exceptions, see Albers, 'Die causa vom Code civil zum BGB' (n 1) 265–68.

[5] *Ausführliche Erläuterung der Pandecten nach Hellfeld*, vol 4.1 (Erlangen, 1796) 280–1: 'Nach teutschem Recht ist daher jeder Vertrag verbindlich, welcher von Personen, die sich … verbindlich machen können, über einen erlaubten Gegenstand … frey von Zwang und List ist eingegangen worden, und unter dieser Voraussetzung gibt es heut zu Tag kein Versprechen mehr, welches im römischen Sinn ein pactum nudum wäre.'

[6] On the position of Roman law, *cf* n 8 below.

[7] For further indications, see G Albers, 'History of a Notion' in Albers et al (n 1) 19–36 (19–24). See also ch 1 of this book, by Francisco Andrés Santos.

[8] Ulpian 4 *ad edictum* D 2,14,7,2: *Sed et si in alium contractum res non transeat, subsit tamen causa, eleganter Aristo Celso respondit esse obligationem. ut puta dedi tibi rem ut mihi aliam dares, dedi ut aliquid facias: hoc συνάλλαγμα esse et hinc nasci civilem obligationem*; in English: 'But even if the matter does not fall under the head of another contract and yet a ground exists, Aristo in an apt reply to Celsus states that there is an obligation. Where, for example, I gave a thing to you so that you may give another to me, or I gave so that you may do something, this is, Aristo says, a synallamga and hence a civil obligation arises' (A Watson trans, Philadelphia, The Digest of Justinian, 1985).

A performance rendered *sine causa* – without cause – could be reclaimed by means of a *condictio*. Only later was the lack of *causa* for the performance described as the 'cause' of the reverse claim (*causa condictionis*),[9] much like the unjust factor English law uses to explain unjust enrichment claims. The law of unjustified enrichment had a specific application in the field of the formal oral promise, the *stipulatio*. This type of contract allowed for the creation of a unilateral obligation that could have any object the parties desired. Although the obligation was considered as binding without regard to the economic or social context of the promise, that obligation itself could be the object of a *condictio* if it enriched the creditor unjustly. If the promisee tried to enforce it in court (*in iure*), the promisor would complain to the *praetor* that the stipulation was made without due cause or that it had lost its cause later. The *praetor* would include a corresponding exception in the formula (*exceptio doli*), and the judge would acquit the promisor after checking the facts. The *causa* that a *stipulatio* needed to avoid being subject to the consequences of unjustified enrichment can be called *causa stipulationis*.[10]

It had always been common in Rome to draw up written evidence of a *stipulatio*. With time, the focus shifted more and more from the oral act to the document.[11] This made specific rules for *causa stipulationis* necessary. It was those peculiar rules that shaped German law around 1800.

The first rule regarding loans: when a Roman granted a loan, the recipient would often promise repayment by means of a *stipulatio*. This was considered more reliable, and it was also a way to agree on the payment of interest. Occasionally, a document proving such a *stipulatio* was issued before the actual loan was paid out, and in some cases, a fraudulent or forgetful creditor – or his innocent heir – used it to reclaim a loan never given. In such a case, the defendant would ask for the *exceptio pecuniae non numeratae* ('the defence of money not paid') to be inserted into the formula.[12] Although the sources are not explicit, one can assume that the onus of proof for paying out the

[9] S Hähnchen, *Die causa condictionis. Ein Beitrag zum klassischen römischen Kondiktionenrecht* (Berlin, Dunker & Humblot, 2003).

[10] JG Wolf, *Causa stipulationis* (Cologne, Böhlau, 1970); A Wacke, 'Zur Causa der Stipulation' (1972) 40 *Tijdschrift voor Rechtsgeschiedenis* 231.

[11] See G Albers, 'Zum Versprechen als Verpflichtungsgrund in der Spätantike: Urkunden, Kirchenväter und der westgotische Gaius' (2018) 135 *Zeitschrift der Savigny-Stiftung für Rechtsgeschichte: Romanistische Abteilung* 334, 345–47, with references.

[12] Ulpian 76 *ad edictum* D 44,4,2,3: *Circa primam speciem, quibus ex causis exceptio haec locum habeat, haec sunt, quae tractari possunt. si quis sine causa ab aliquo fuerit stipulatus, deinde ex ea stipulatione experiatur, exceptio utique doli mali ei nocebit: licet enim eo tempore, quo stipulabatur, nihil dolo malo admiserit, tamen dicendum est eum, cum litem contestatur, dolo facere, qui perseveret ex ea stipulatione petere: et si cum interponeretur, iustam causam habuit, tamen nunc nullam idoneam causam habere videtur. proinde et si crediturus pecuniam stipulatus est nec credidit et si certa fuit causa stipulationis, quae tamen aut non est secuta aut finita est, dicendum erit nocere exceptionem*; or in Watson's translation (n 8): 'With regard to the first point, as to the cases in which this defense has application, the following are the matters which can be discussed. If someone without good cause stipulated something from another and then sues him in terms of that stipulation, the defense of fraud will surely bar him; for even though he has committed no fraud at the time that he stipulated, nevertheless, it must be said that he was acting fraudulently at the time of joinder of issue, if he perseveres in claiming in terms of that stipulation, and also if he had a good cause when the stipulation was made, but seems to have no proper cause now. Consequently, even if a person intending to give a loan stipulated for the money and then did not give the loan, then, although there was a definite cause for the stipulation but it has either not eventuated or been completed, it will have to be said that the defense will avail.'

loan lay on the lender. That was the understanding around 1800, when scholars argued that the law would otherwise require the borrower to prove that he did not receive the loan. Such proof of negative facts was practically impossible and was therefore to be avoided.[13] The second rule related to documents that did not reveal *why* a specific promise had been made: when the question arose in court whether an obligation proven by such a *cautio indiscreta* unjustly enriched the promisee, the burden of proof was again shifted onto the creditor. In this case, the sources are unambiguous.[14]

These rules served to protect defendants against promises given carelessly as well as against fraudulent claimants and fabricated evidence. They were still considered good law when German scholars insisted on the absence of *causa* from contract law. In view of the practical relevance of the burden of proof, this affirmation made a rather theoretical point: what did it even mean to emphasise that any wilful promise with a legitimate object constituted a valid contract, quite irrespective of its context and purpose, if in practice this very context had to be disclosed and proven in court in order to base a claim on it?

It took roughly 60 years for someone to notice how these practical issues cast a shadow on the doctrine of contract. In an article published in 1864, Hermann Witte remarked on 'the binding force of the will in the law of obligations according to today's scholarship':

> It is only in the last 20 years that the problems to be solved here have been approached with fresh vigour, and … this fresh battle of wits must be far preferred to the rotten peace which could only be achieved by superficial concealment of the difficulties.[15]

The debate to which Witte was referring will be portrayed in the following sections.

B. An Irritating Encounter with the French Code

The debate that ultimately led to Germany embracing the abstract contract and the attempt to suppress *causa* once and for all might – as unlikely as it seems – have actually been sparkled by the French Code itself and its provisions on cause. Taking a closer look at those rules, one can observe a similar inconsistency as in German law, but in reverse form.

[13] F Cropp, 'Über literarum obliatio, cautio indiscreta und pecunia non numerata' in GA Heise and F Cropp (eds), *Juristische Abhandlungen*, vol I (Hamburg, 1827) 325–86 (§ 19).

[14] Paulus 3 *quaestionum* D 22,3,25,4 : *sin autem cautio indebite exposita esse dicatur et indiscrete loquitur, tunc eum, in quem cautio exposita est, compelli debitum esse ostendere, quod in cautionem deduxit, nisi ipse specialiter qui cautionem exposuit causas explanavit, pro quibus eandem conscripsit: tunc enim stare eum oportet suae confessioni, nisi evidentissimis probationibus in scriptis habitis ostendere paratus sit sese haec indebite promisisse*; in Watson's translation (n 8): 'If, however, a deed is said to be executed for what is not owing and the cause is not stated in the deed, the creditor must show that the debt in the deed is owing, unless the party who executed it specifically explains the cause for his doing so. In that case, he must stand by his admission, unless he can show by very clear proof in writing that he promised what was not owing.'

[15] H Witte, 'Die bindende Kraft des Willens im Obligationenrecht nach der Lehre der heutigen Wissenschaft' (1864) 6 *Kritische Vierteljahresschrift* 330, 330: 'Erst seit einigen 20 Jahren ist man mit frischer Kraft an die hier zu lösenden Probleme herangegangen, und … dieser frische Kampf der Geister [muß] dem faulen Frieden weit vorgezogen werden, der nur durch oberflächliche Verdeckung der Schwierigkeiten erzielt werden konnte.'

While Article 1108 Code civil, as stated above, required the existence of a legitimate cause for any contractual obligation, Article 1132 Code civil affirmed that cause need not be expressed: 'La convention n'est pas moins valable, quoique la cause n'en soit pas exprimée.'

The drafters of the Code intended this provision to have a very practical meaning, as evidenced by the explanation given by Bigot de Préameneu:

> Ainsi, lorsque, par un billet, une personne déclare qu'elle doit, elle reconnait par cela même qu'il y a une cause légitime de la dette, quoique cette cause ne soit pas énoncée. Mais la cause que l'acte exprime ou fa présumer, peut ne pas exister ou être fausse; et si ce fait est constaté par des preuves que la loi autorise, l'équité ne permet pas que l'engagement subsiste.[16]

According to Préameneu, a written declaration to the effect that one owes a debt should allow others to presume that the obligation was based on a valid cause, even if none was mentioned in the document. The other party should then be burdened with proving, if applicable, that the cause did not exist or was false. The provision apparently aimed at abolishing the Roman rule for *cautio indiscreta* that burdened the creditor with the proof of *causa*.

The Code civil thus presented a mirror image of Witte's 'rotten peace': while German lawyers claimed not to need *causa* for a valid obligation, the courts in practice required it, whereas the French Code purported to require a cause while at the same time stating that there was no actual need to present it in court.

I freely admit that this interpretation of the Code civil was not universal. Quite the contrary. Old debates on *cautio indiscreta* were perpetuated under the Code.[17] Some held that Article 1132 Code civil merely rebutted an extreme position according to which an obligation would be invalidated by being put into writing without mentioning its cause. According to this interpretation, the rule did no more than clarify that the creditor was allowed to prove the required cause by other means. Clinging to the Roman solution, this opinion threatened the practical relevance of written statements of debt. But its representatives attenuated the consequences by lowering the bar for what was to be considered a sufficient reference to cause. Alexandre Duranton was one of the scholars who distinguished between a promise and an acknowledgement of debt: cause could be presumed when a party confirmed a pre-existing obligation, even if no further indication was given (eg *je dois*, *je reconnais devois*), but not if the document was phrased so as to create an unprecedented obligation (eg *je compterais*, *je promets payer*). Moreover, a *billet* signed by a merchant should be presumed to have been signed for his business and thus to have a valid cause.[18]

But others like Philippe-Antoine Merlin argued that the Code had disposed of the Roman rule for *cautiones indiscretae* and that the burden of proof for lack of cause lay

[16] FJJ Bigot de Préameneu, 'Exposé des motifs de la loi sur les contrats ou les obligations conventionnelles en général' in *Code civil des Français, suivi de l'exposé des motifs, sur chaque loi, présenté par les orateurs du Gouvernement …*, vol. 5 (Paris, Firmin Didot, 1804) 15.

[17] See the overview of the older debate given by P-A Merlin, *Recueil alphabétique des questions de droit qui se présentent le plus fréquemment dans les tribunaux*, 3rd edn (Paris, Garnery, 1819) sub voce *causes des obligations*, § I; A Duranton, *Cours de droit français suivant le Code civil* (Paris, Alex-Gobelet, 1830) nos 352–55.

[18] On acknowledgements, see Duranton (n 17) no. 353 (acknowledgements that allow to infer the economical contexts) and no 354 at the end (other acknowledgements); on merchants see no 354.

with the debtor.[19] After some uncertainty among lower courts, the Cour de cassation ruled in favour of such a presumption of cause in 1848:

> Attendu qu'il résulte de cette disposition de la loi que, bien que la cause ne soit pas exprimée dans une obligation, il y a présomption qu'elle existe et qu'elle est vraie et licite, à moins que le contraire ne soit prouvé.[20]

This way, the Cour bolstered the predisposition of the Code to create a tension between the conceptual necessity of *la cause* and its practical irrelevance. The mirror image of the tension in German law was perfected. As in Germany, the tension did not draw much interest for quite some time. In the twentieth century, Henri Capitant proposed to resolve it by recognising that the admission of the presumptive effect of the *billet non causé* naturally led to allowing for an obligating effect of promises unsupported by a cause. Following the lead of the then new German Code, he wanted to introduce the concept of abstract obligations.[21] His ideas might now celebrate a late success as the doctrine of cause has been suppressed in the French Code by the 2016 reform of the law of obligations.[22]

At the beginning of the nineteenth century, the then freshly enacted French Code had sparked similar ideas in what was subsequently to become Germany. Interest in the Code had been boosted by the fact that it had come into force in parts of the former *Reich*.[23] Dealing with the French requirement of *la cause*, German scholars pursued strategies of ignorance, submission or adaptation.[24] A perfect example is Karl Salomo Zachariä. He tried out all three strategies in the first three editions of his manual on French private law. In the first edition, dating from 1808, Zachariä boldly stated that the Code was mistaken to count cause among the requirements of contract, as all agreements were to be considered valid contracts under French law. Apparently, the Code had mixed up contract law and unjustified enrichment. Article 1132 is barely mentioned; the problem is ignored.[25] In the second edition, dating from 1811, Zachariä gave up his resistance and submitted to the French legislation by presenting its content without much comment. By referring to the preparatory works, he briefly interpreted Article 1132 as a presumption of *causa*.[26] From the third edition onwards, Zachariä pursued a strategy of adaptation: citing Duranton and others, he took the position that the Code did not contain a rule on the burden of proof, which therefore had to remain with the creditor.[27] By reinstalling the Roman rule, he tried to bring

[19] See Merlin (n 17).

[20] Cour de cassation, 16 August 1848, *Sirey* 1849 I 113 (115) (with a critical comment by L-M Delville). See also Cour de cassation, 17 December 1849, *Sirey* 1850 I 117.

[21] H Capitant, *De la Cause des Obbligations. Contrats, Engagements unilatéraus, Legs*, 3rd edn (Paris, Dalloz, 1923) nos 164–74 (366–89).

[22] On the reform's potential consequences for abstract obligations under French law, see T Genicon, 'L'avenir de la cause en droit francais des contrats' in Albers et al (n 1) 727–30.

[23] See, eg the contributions in R Schulze (ed), *Französisches Zivilrecht in Europa während des 19. Jahrhunderts* (Berlin, Duncker & Humblot, 1994); R Schulze (ed), *Rheinisches Recht und Europäische Rechtsgeschichte* (Berlin, Duncker & Humblot, 1998).

[24] For a more extensive discussion of the reception of the cause that came with the reception of the Code in German territories, see Albers, 'Die causa vom Code civil zum BGB' (n 1) 271–78.

[25] KS Zachariä, *Handbuch des Französischen Civilrechts* (Heidelberg, 1808) § 172 (263–65).

[26] KS Zachariä, *Handbuch des Französischen Civilrechts*, 2nd edn (Heidelberg, 1811) vol 2, § 278 (267–68).

[27] KS Zachariä, *Handbuch des Französischen Civilrechts*, 3rd edn (Heidelberg, 1827) vol 2, § 345 (285–87).

back the old law.[28] A similar shift of position could later be found in two decisions of the Rhineland Court of Appeal in Cologne.[29]

Ignorance, submission, adaption: no matter how they dealt with it, German scholars had to face the wording of the Code, and were forced to analyse the relationship between Article 1108 and Article 1132. Comparing it with Roman law, they could no longer ignore the possible link between *causa* as a requirement of validity for atypical contracts (*causa conventionis*) and lack of *causa* as defence against abstract promises (*causa stipulationis*), and they had to connect the alleged abolition of *causa* with the practical problem of declarations of debt that did not state their cause (*cautio indiscreta*). Working with the French Code could lead to a new understanding of modern Roman law. This seems to have been what happened in the case of Bernhard Windscheid: in his early work on the invalidity of legal acts according to the French Code, he criticised the idea of cause as a requirement of contract, which he took as result of a faulty reading of the Roman law of unjustified enrichment. For this very reason, he lamented the authority and practical application of the Roman rule on *cautio indiscreta*, and he applauded the French legislator for abolishing it by the Code's Article 1132.[30] But at that time, in 1847, this was not the dominant position.

C. Unleashing the Promise

In the middle of the nineteenth century, many scholars had chosen the opposite approach to reconcile contract doctrine with the burden of proof in the case of *cautio indiscreta*: they embraced the Roman rule that it was on the creditor to prove *causa*, and thus returned to the idea that *causa* was a requirement of contract. This holds true for Georg Friedrich Puchta,[31] Carl Friedrich Ferdinand Sintenis,[32] Heinrich Rudolph Gneist[33] and Carl Friedrich Gerber.[34] At the Eighth Assembly of German Jurists

[28] His successors Aubry and Rau were blamed for the inconsistency of their position by Capitant (n 21) 381, fn 1.

[29] In a decision rendered on 22 November 1832, the court upheld that Art 1132 of the Code was based on a presumption of cause (*Rheinisches Archiv* 17, part I, 199). By contrast, the court decided on 5 July 1848 that the creditor had to prove cause, as general rules applied. The victorious appellant had not only relied on scholars of French law, but also on the Roman rule (*Rheinisches Archiv* 43, part I, 133). An anonymous critic denounced that the court thus adopted an interpretation of the Code determined by Roman law and only upheld by Zachariä and his translators (*Rheinisches Archiv* 43, part II B, 14); this was an exaggeration (see, eg Duranton (n 17)). For more on the application of the Code in the Rhineland, see my article 'Französischer und deutsche Privatrechtsdiskurse im ersten Band des Rheinischen Archivs' in an upcoming volume edited by Carsten Fischer and Hans-Peter Haferkamp (Cologne, Böhlau).

[30] B Windscheid, *Zur Lehre des Code Napoleon von der Ungültigkeit der Rechtsgeschäfte* (Düsseldorf, Verlag von Julius Buddeus, 1847) 312–14.

[31] GF Puchta, *Pandekten*, 3rd edn (Leipzig, Verlag von Johann Barth, 1845) §§ 250 and 257.

[32] CFF Sintenis, *Das pracitsche gemeine Civilrecht*, vol 2: *Das Obligationenrecht* (Leipzig, Tauchnitz, 1847) § 96.

[33] HR Gneist, *Die formellen Verträge des neueren römischen Obligationenrechts in Vergleichung mit den Geschäftsformen des griechischen Rechts* (Berlin, 1845) 111–230.

[34] CF Gerber, *System des Deutschen Privatrechts*, Zweite Abtheilung (Jena, Verlag von Friedrich Wanke, 1848) § 158. On their positions, see Albers, 'Die causa vom Code civil zum BGB' (n 1) 281, fns 88–90 and 288–90.

(Deutscher Juristentag), which took place in Heidelberg in 1869, Rudolf von Jhering remembered the opinion his teachers at that university held in 1836/37:

> Thirty years ago … when I was studying here, the old theory of *cautio indiscreta* still prevailed undisputedly: the doctrine that a promissory note which did not state the reason for the debt was completely worthless; or, to put it more generally, that our common law today does not know any abstract, but only individual or material contracts.[35]

Later, he added: 'That *causa* was part of any legal act appeared as natural to any lawyer as the fact that humans are of female or male sex.'[36]

But at the time of Jhering's studies, a new, different opinion was just about to arise. It was based on the concept of formal or abstract contracts (*formelle, abstrakte Verträge*).[37] The term had been coined by Friedrich Carl von Savigny in 1816 to describe certain Roman acts that were not defined by their cause and purpose (*Zweck und Grund*), but by their specific form.[38] But it was the Brunswick judge Friedrich Liebe[39] who first developed the concept in his book dedicated to the relation between Roman *stipulatio* and simple promises.[40]

Liebe was convinced that under natural law, an accepted promise had by itself no binding effect:

> The promise itself is no different from any indifferent conversation. It contains the declaration of a party's will. But everyone can change his will until it is acted upon, and what happens cannot be undone. It is not conceivable what difference it is supposed to make that the will was directed at something beneficial for another, and that the latter agreed to it. To make and pronounce resolutions which one does not carry out may be contrary to morality and violate the *constantia*, but it does not violate the legal order … The actual element on which legal validity can be based therefore lies outside the promise itself, and is to be sought in the circumstances under which it appears in the individual case … Then, in addition to the simple will, we also have a legal ground for the same.[41]

[35] R Jhering, in *Verhandlungen des achten deutschen Juristentages*, vol 2: *Stenographische Berichte* (Berlin, 1870) 95: 'Vor 30 Jahren … als ich hier studirte, herrschte noch unbestritten die alte Theorie der cautio indiscreta, die Lehre, daß ein Schuldschein, welcher nicht den Schuldgrund nenne, völlig werthlos sei, oder allgemeiner ausgedrückt, daß unser heutiges gemeines Recht keine abstrakte, sondern lediglich individuelle oder materielle Verträge kenne.'

[36] Jhering, in *Verhandlungen des neunten deutschen Juristentages*, vol 3: *Stenographische Berichte* (Berlin, 1871) 88: 'Dem Juristen war es so natürlich, zu einem Rechtsgeschäfte gehören [!] die causa, wie die Thatsache, daß der Mensch weiblichen oder männlichen Geschlechts ist.'

[37] See in particular H Kiefner, 'Der abstrakte obligatorische Vertrag in Praxis und Theorie des 19. Jahrhunderts' in H Coing and W Wilhelm (eds), *Wissenschaft und Kodifikation des Privatrechts im 19. Jahrhundert*, vol 2: *Die rechtliche Verselbständigung der Austauschverhältnisse vor dem Hintergrund der wirtschaftlichen Entwicklung und Doktrin* (Frankfurt am Main, Vittorio Klostermann, 1977) 74–89. For more references, see Albers, 'Die causa vom Code civil zum BGB' (n 1) 283, fn 94.

[38] FC von Savigny, 'Ueber den Literalcontract der Römer, mit Zusätzen abgedruckt' in *Vermischte Schriften*, vol 1 (Berlin, Veit und Comp, 1850) 206–07. On Savigny's further contribution to the matter in his *Obligationenrecht* from 1852, see Albers, 'Die causa vom Code civil zum BGB' (n 1) 290–93.

[39] On Liebe, see T Henne, 'Friedrich von Liebe. Verwaltungsjurist und Politiker 1809–1885' in J Rückert and J Vortmann (eds), *600 Jahre Niedersächsische Juristen*, 2nd edn (Halle, Universitätsverlag Halle-Wittenberg, 2021) 207–09.

[40] F Liebe, *Die Stipulation und das einfache Versprechen. Eine civilistische Abhandlung* (Braunschweig, Verlag von GCE Meyer, 1840). See also Albers, 'Die causa vom Code civil zum BGB' (n 1) 284–88.

[41] Liebe (n 40) 76–77: 'Das Versprechen an sich unterscheidet sich von einem gleichgültigen Gespräche nicht. Es enthält die Erklärung des Willens einer Partei: seinen Willen aber kann Jeder ändern, bis er zur That

The legal ground – the *causa* – that any promise needed consisted of a counter-performance rendered by the promisee, or at least his promise to render one. Having received the counter-performance or at least the counter-promise, the promisor harmed the promisee wrongfully by withholding his own performance.[42] Liebe thus reconstructed contractual liability based on reliance and tort, in a manner that is reminiscent of the way in which the old action of *assumpsit* was able to cover the field of contract law,[43] and foreshadows thinkers like Siegmund Schlossmann,[44] Lon L Fuller, Grant Gilmore or Patrick S Atiyah.[45]

Unlike normal, so-called substantive contracts (*materielle Verträge*), formal contracts such as the Roman *stipulatio* were effective independent of any *causa* by virtue of a command of positive law. However, they were subject to control by the law of unjustified enrichment. If none of the reasons justifying a benefit were present, they were subject to a *condictio*. As a model for this kind of preliminary effect, Liebe cited transfer of ownership by the Roman *mancipatio*. The reasons that could justify a benefit were *causae* in the sense of the law of unjustified enrichment. This category was broader than the category of *causae* that were necessary to give force to a promise (as we have seen, Liebe accepted only a counter-performance or its promise). As a justification for keeping a benefit already bestowed, the intention to donate could be sufficient.[46] If modern law sanctioned the binding force of all kinds of promises, irrespective of the Roman contract types, these promises needed to be considered formal contracts in the sense of the Roman *stipulatio* to allow at least for an ex post control by the tools of unjustified enrichment.[47] The provisions of the Code civil could supposedly be interpreted in such way.[48]

The theoretical success of the idea of formal contracts depended on the fitness of the law of unjustified enrichment. And the law of unjustified enrichment rose to the task: around 1850, Bernhard Windscheid and Albrecht Erxleben developed the general principle that a claim or defence of unjustified enrichment is founded whenever a performance or an obligation fails its purpose.[49] They conceived this remedy

geworden, und das Geschehene nicht ungeschehen zu machen ist. Was hiervon der Umstand, daß der Wille auf etwas einem Andern Vortheilhaftes gerichtet war, und dieser sich damit einverstanden erklärt hat, ändern soll, ist nicht einzusehen. Es mag dem Sittengesetz widersprechen, und die constantia verletzen, Entschlüsse zu fassen und auszusprechen, die man nicht ausführt, aber das Rechtsgesetz ist dadurch nicht verletzt … Das eigentliche Moment, auf welchem eine rechtliche Gültigkeit beruhen kann, liegt sonach außerhalb des Versprechens selbst, und ist in den Verhältnissen zu suchen, unter welchen es im einzelnen Fall erscheint … Alsdann haben wir außer dem einfachen Wollen auch noch einen Rechtsgrund für dasselbe.'

[42] See references in Albers, 'Die causa vom Code civil zum BGB' (n 1) fns 109–13.

[43] See, eg B Häcker, in Albers et al (n 1) 335–42; ch 3 in this book, by David J Ibbetson.

[44] S Schlossmann, *Der Vertrag* (Leipzig 1876); on which see T Dalla Massara, *Il consenso annichilito. La critica radicale del contratto in Siegmund Schlossmann* (Bologna, il Mulino, 2021); G Albers, 'Contract Nihilism in Europe? On Tommaso Dalla Massara's Reading of Siegmund Schlossmann' (2023) 19 *European Review of Contract Law* 90.

[45] On the possibility that the continental legal debate on *causa* could contribute to the mostly Anglo-American debate on contract theory, see G Albers, 'Why Cause of Contract Again, and How?' in Albers et al (n 1) 9–12.

[46] Liebe (n 40) 82; for further references, see Albers, 'Die causa vom Code civil zum BGB' (n 1) 286. On the problem of whether an abstract promise constitutes a valid donation in modern German law, see below at n 78.

[47] Liebe (n 40) 90–93; see Albers, 'Die causa vom Code civil zum BGB' (n 1) 287–8.

[48] Liebe (n 40) 94.

[49] B Windscheid, *Die Lehre des römischen Rechts von der Voraussetzung* (Düsseldorf, Verlag von Julius Buddeus, 1850); A Erxleben, *Die condictiones sine causa* (Leipzig, Verlag der Dieterischen Buchhandlung,

(*Leistungskondiktionen*) as a means of protecting the purposes a person pursues when incurring a detriment in favour of another. This part of unjustified enrichment can thus be considered an appendix to contract law.

Nevertheless, the concept of formal contracts would probably not have had its impact on the German law of obligations without Otto Bähr,[50] who examined it from the practical angle of acknowledgements of debts ('I declare and confirm that I owe …'). In his 1855 book, he analysed such acknowledgements not as acts with relevance for procedural law or for the law of evidence alone,[51] but as genuine sources of obligation.[52]

Bähr once again started with the Roman *stipulatio* and compared it with the transfer of property by *traditio*. He followed Savigny's new doctrine that *traditio* was effectuated by an agreement directed exclusively at the transfer, which was therefore not in any way conditional on a pre-existing obligation or any other motive for the transfer.[53] While *traditio* was thus naturally independent from its *causa*, obligations were normally created by contracts that included an agreement on the purpose of the transaction.[54] From this rule, the parties could make an exception by using the *stipulatio*; in this way, they detached the obligation from its *causa* (*Abstraction von der causa*).[55] But what constituted *causa*, and what was the consequence for an abstract act if its *causa* was defective? Bähr followed Windscheid's theory of presupposition' (*Voraussetzungslehre*):

> If *traditio* transfers property independently of its legal basis, and *stipulatio* creates a right of claim independently of its legal basis, then this is a product of the will, which in the first case isolates the enrichment from its legal basis *naturali ratione*, in the second case by virtue of an artificial process of abstraction. But this will, even if superficially completed, is nevertheless, in the absence of *causa*, internally an unfinished one; the relationship exists 'with the real will (*wirklicher Wille*), but against the proper will (*eigentlicher Wille*) of the transferor' [quoting Windscheid]. The latter is therefore granted a personal right to reclaim the asset transferred.[56]

1851/53). For more details, see Albers, 'Die causa vom Code civil zum BGB' (n 1) 293–94, fn 157; on Windscheid, see below at n 57.

[50] On Bähr, see B Binder, *Otto Bähr (1817–1895). Richter von universellem Geist, Mittler zwischen Dogmatik und Praxis* (Frankfurt am Main, Peter Lang, 1983).

[51] For such an interpretation (*Beweisvertrag*), see A Bruns, 'Das constitutum debiti' [1861/62] *Zeitschrift für Rechtsgeschichte* 1126.

[52] O Bähr, *Die Anerkennung als Verpflichtungsgrund. Civilistische Abhandlung* (Cassel, Verlag von Oswald Bertram, 1855). See also Albers, 'Die causa vom Code civil zum BGB' (n 1) 295–98.

[53] Bähr (n 52) § 4 (13–16). On this new doctrine, see F Ranieri, 'Die Lehre der abstrakten Übereignung in der deutschen Zivilrechtswissenschaft des 19. Jahrhunderts' in Coing and Wilhelm (n 37) 90–111. See also B Rodríguez-Rosado, *Abstraktionsprinzip und redlicher Erwerb als Mittel zum Schutze des Rechtsverkehrs* (Frankfurt am Main, Peter Lang, 2009).

[54] Bähr (n 52) § 5 (16–30).

[55] ibid § 6 (20–23, 22).

[56] ibid § 18 (62): 'Wenn Tradition das Eigenthum, Stipulation ein Forderungsrecht unabhängig von ihrem Rechtsgrunde übertragen, so ist dies ein Product des Willens, welcher dort naturali ratione, hier kraft eines künstlichen Abstractionsprocesses die Vermögenszuwendung von ihrem Rechtsgrunde isolirt. Aber dieser Willen ist, wenn auch äußerlich vollendet, doch bei Ermangelung der *causa* ein innerlich unvollendeter; es besteht das Verhältnis 'zwar mit dem wirklichen, aber gegen den eigentlichen Willen des Uebertragenden'. Letzterem ist deshalb ein persönliches Recht auf Rückforderung des übertragenen Vermögensobjects verliehen.' The reference is to Windscheid, *Voraussetzung* (n 49) 2.

In Windscheid's diction, the 'real, but not proper will' qualifies a decision based upon a false assumption in that it can be nullified by the erring party because the underlying erroneous assumption was discernible to the other.[57]

What good is an obligation that can be reclaimed? When a creditor asks his debtor to acknowledge the debt, he intends to improve his position for a later trial. Such an improvement already lay in the fact that it was subsequently up to the debtor to raise the issue that an obligation created by his acknowledgement lacks *causa*. But according to Bähr, the practical effect of an acknowledgement should go further: firstly, on a level of fact finding, the acknowledgement hinted at the existence of a *causa*;[58] and secondly, a *condictio indebiti* should only be available in case of an excusable mistake.[59]

Under the 'modern' law of Bähr's time, this practical effect had a wider range of application, for parties who wished to detach the effects of their agreement from its *causa* were no longer confined to a specific act like the Roman *stipulatio*. They could now obtain such an effect by bills of exchange, statements of account, promissory notes and other acknowledgements of debt.[60]

While Bähr aimed at the practical effect of such acknowledgements, his position drew part of its strength from his sharp analysis of the different ways in which an obligation could depend on its *causa*. In his conclusion on the matter, Bähr commented on the then popular view:

> It is postulated not seldomly in theory and practice that any contract, to support a claim, needs to have a cause (*causa*). In its ambiguity, this phrase is very much suited to confound any clear insight. If one took it to mean that a simple promise could never exist on its own but were always subjectively determined by a reason (*Rechtsgrund*), this would be correct, but in that sense, one should not count it among the requirements, no more than one would say that it was a requirement of a triangle that its angles amount to two right angles. – If one wants to say that in the area of material contracts the simple promise can only be valid in connection with its reason (*Rechtsgrund*), then this is also correct … Finally, if one wants to express with that sentence that the validity of formal contracts is dependent on the objective existence of their *causa*, this is only very relatively true, namely insofar as the existence of the *causa* becomes important for the effectiveness of those contracts as determined by the Roman law of exceptions.[61]

[57] On the influence of this theory on German law of unjustified enrichment and contract (in particular by means of the doctrine of basis of contract, *Geschäftsgrundlage*), see G Albers, 'Der Einfluss unerwarteter Ereignisse auf den Vertrag nach deutschem Recht' in Albers et al (n 1) 575–88 and 609–32.

[58] Bähr (n 52) § 18 (66–67).

[59] ibid §§ 19–21 and 25–26.

[60] ibid § 41 (155–58).

[61] ibid § 42 (158–59): 'Man hört nicht selten in Theorie und Praxis den Satz aufstellen, jeder Vertrag müsse, um klagbar zu sein, eine causa haben. Dieser Satz in seiner Vieldeutigkeit ist sehr geeignet, die klare Einsicht zu beirren. Verstände man darunter, dass das einfache Versprechen niemals für sich bestehen könne, sondern subjektiv immer durch einen Rechtsgrund bestimmt werde, so wäre das richtig; nur sollte man in diesem Sinne die causa nicht zu den 'Erfordernissen' zählen, so wenig man sagen wird, es sei ein Erforderniss jedes Triangels, dass seine Winkel zusammen zwei rechte ausmachen. – Will man damit sagen, im Gebiet der materiellen Verträge könne das einfache Versprechen nur in Verbindung mit seinem Rechtsgrund Geltung finden, so ist auch dies richtig … – Will man endlich mit jenem Satz ausdrücken, die formellen Verträge seien in ihrer Gültigkeit von dem objectiven Bestande ihrer causa abhängig, so ist dies nur sehr relativ wahr, insoweit nämlich, als der Bestand der causa im Sinne des römischen Exceptionenrechts für die Wirksamkeit jener Verträge von Bedeutung wird.' For a critical appraisal of the triangle analogy, see G Albers, FP Patti and D Perrouin-Verbe, 'Future of Causa' in Albers et al (n 1) 705–713 (705–06).

It is remarkable that the seminal German book on the matter of abstract promises returns to the French Civil Code. Bähr provides a footnote to name representatives of the popular misconception that *causa* was a necessary element of every contract. While he mentions the Code civil among the misguided, he notes that the article on the *billet non causé* makes up for the mistake: 'This sentence has even strayed into the *Code civil* (art 1108). There, however, it is neutralised by article 1132: La convention n'est pas moins valable, quoique la cause n'en soit pas exprimée.'[62]

Bähr's book enjoyed spectacular success.[63] In 1869, the Eighth Assembly of German Jurists discussed the question whether a future common German law of obligations should incorporate the binding force of a contract acknowledging a debt.[64] Such a framing of the problem was in line with an older conception of acknowledgements according to which they constituted a specific type of contract.[65] This doctrine was one way to support the position of those interpreters of the Code civil who held that a document made sufficient reference to its cause if it stated the debt as being already owed.[66] But the assembly reconsidered the problem from Bähr's perspective. Jhering gave a talk[67] and urged his audience to phrase the question differently: should the future German law of obligations recognise the power of the will to oblige 'abstractly', that is, without regard for its cause (*Soll das künftige deutsche Obligationenrecht die abstrakt verpflichtende Kraft des Willens anerkennen oder nicht*)? He pleaded passionately in favour, arguing that such a power flowed naturally from individual private autonomy.[68] The matter was adjourned, and in the following year, the Juristentag adopted the resolution that a contract should be actionable even if it was exclusively directed to the 'owing of a debt' or to any performance, without naming any grounds for such an agreement.[69]

The suggestion was taken up by the Bürgerliches Gesetzbuch (BGB, the German Civil Code) of 1896. The German Civil Code recognised the binding force of a promise intended to create an obligation 'by itself' (*selbständig*). The only requirement was that such a promise be in writing:

> For the validity of a contract by which performance is promised in such a way that the promise is to establish the obligation by itself (*selbständig*) (promise of debt,

[62] Bähr (n 52) § 42, para 1 (158): 'Auch in den Code civil (art 1108) hat sich jener Satz verirrt. Er wird aber dort wieder neutralisirt durch art 1132: La convention n'est pas moins valable, quoique la cause n'en soit pas exprimée.'

[63] For its early reception in legislation, see Albers, 'Die causa vom Code civil zum BGB' (n 1) 300–04.

[64] 'Soll das künftige gemeinsame deutsche Obligationenrecht die verbindliche Kraft des Anerkennungsvertrages aufnehmen … ?'.

[65] See, eg Bruns, who, while conceptualising a procedural contract on proof (n 51), assigned the function of a specific type of obligating contract to the modern version of the Roman *constitutum debiti* (93–97 and 110–21).

[66] See n 18 above.

[67] See n 36 above.

[68] Jhering, *Verhandlungen des achten deutschen Juristentages* (n 35) 104: 'Es ist die Idee der Freiheit, der Autonomie des subjectiven Willens, die hiebei zur Frage kommt, eine Idee, auf die unser ganzes Privatrecht gebaut ist. Aus dieser Idee ergiebt sich als Konsequenz von selbst die abstrakt verpflichtende Kraft des Willens, und es bedarf besonderer Gründe, um diese Konsequenz abzuwehren.' For a full citation and comment, see Albers, 'Die causa vom Code civil zum BGB' (n 1) 306.

[69] See the resolution, *Verhandlungen des neunten deutschen Juristentages* (n 36) 106–08: 'Ein ohne Angabe des Schuldgrundes ausschließlich auf das "Schuldig sein" oder auf die Leistung eines Gegenstandes gerichteter Vertrag ist klagbar.'

> *Schuldversprechen*), written issuance of the promise is required, if no other formality is prescribed.[70]

Writing was required to allow the judge a more thorough examination of the promisor's intention, so that it can be ascertained whether he really wanted to detach the act of promising from its underlying cause (*Abstraktionswillen*). It is therefore an inconsistency that the requirement of writing does not apply to merchants.[71]

The German Code followed the doctrine of formal contracts – and the proposal of the Juristentag –[72] also insofar as it wanted the defence against such a promise to be governed by the rules of unjustified enrichment. In the central norm on unjustified enrichment (§ 812 BGB), the redactors explicitly affirmed that this was the standard by which acknowledgements of debt should be controlled:

> (1) A person who obtains something by performance of another person … without legal grounds is under a duty to surrender to that person what has been obtained … (2) The acknowledgement of the existence or non-existence of an obligation is considered a performance.[73]

But the control the BGB was intended to exercise over abstract promises and acknowledgements of debt was stronger than that devised by the theorists of the nineteenth century. The German Code ensured that *causa* ultimately had a firm grip on every obligation on account of two decisions it made.

First, nothing in the law of mistake or unjustified enrichment could any longer nourish the idea that a promise or acknowledgement could only be undone if it had been given in consequence of an *excusable* mistake.[74] Legal acts can be avoided for mistakes, no matter how ill-founded they are; and a claim or defence of unjustified enrichment is only excluded if the aggrieved party positively *knew* of the lack of *causa* at the time of performance.[75] Only in situations involving more than two parties can the technical construction of abstraction deprive the promisor of his defence in a more final way: he

[70] § 780 BGB 1900: 'Zur Gültigkeit eines Vertrags, durch den eine Leistung in der Weise versprochen wird, daß das Versprechen die Verpflichtung selbständig begründen soll (Schuldversprechen) ist, soweit nicht eine andere Form vorgeschrieben ist, schriftliche Erteilung des Versprechens erforderlich.'

[71] See G Albers, 'Das nicht so abstrakte Schuldversprechen. Eine Inkonsequenz des BGB und ihre Folgen' (2020) 73 *Juristenzeitung* 114, 116–17.

[72] According to the second part of the resolution (n 69), a defence could only be based on an issue with an underlying obligation if such issue could give rise to a counterclaim by the promisor against the promisee 'Die Zulässigkeit von Einreden aus diesem Vertrage selbst richtet sich nach den allgemeinen Rechts-Grundsätzen. – Einreden aus dem unterliegenden Verpflichtungsgrund gegen die hiervon abgelöste Verbindlichkeit sind nur soweit zulässig, als sie selbständige Gegenforderungen oder ein Rückforderungsrecht Seitens des Schuldners gegen den Gläubiger begründen.'

[73] § 812 BGB: '(1) Wer durch die Leistung eines anderen oder in sonstiger Weise auf dessen Kosten etwas ohne rechtlichen Grund erlangt, ist ihm zur Herausgabe verpflichtet. Diese Verpflichtung besteht auch dann, wenn der rechtliche Grund später wegfällt oder der mit einer Leistung nach dem Inhalt des Rechtsgeschäfts bezweckte Erfolg nicht eintritt. (2) Als Leistung gilt auch die durch Vertrag erfolgte Anerkennung des Bestehens oder des Nichtbestehens eines Schuldverhältnisses.'

[74] For Bähr's opinion on the matter, see n 59 above.

[75] See §§ 814, 815 BGB. *cf* Ulpian (26 *ad edictum*) D 12,6,1,1: *Et quidem si quis indebitum ignorans solvit, per hanc actionem condicere potest: sed si sciens se non debere solvit, cessat repetitio*; in Watson's translation (n 8): 'If someone mistakenly pays what is not due he can recover by this *condictio*. However, if he knows the money is not owed, the payment is not recoverable.'

might have no excuse against his creditor, but only a claim against a third party to be liberated from the obligation.[76]

Second, the redactors of the German Code distinguished between actual performances which immediately diminish the patrimony of the performing party and mere obligations to suffer such a diminution in the future. There are several situations under German law where a promise cannot be enforced, but actual performance once rendered cannot be claimed back: such is the case with gift promises that are not notarised, with the fee of marriage brokers, with gambling debts, with any obligation after the statute of limitations has expired and with the performance of illegal or immoral contracts. On can refer to these situations as giving rise to so-called *obligationes naturales* (*Naturalobligationen*).[77] In all these cases, an abstract promise is not equated to actual performance; the promisor cannot be forced to honour it. In some of these cases, the BGB even gives up the formal structure of abstraction by declaring the promise as void (as in §§ 518(1), 2nd sentence, 656(2) and 762(2) BGB); in other cases, the effect is obtained in accordance with the principle of abstraction by means of unjustified enrichment (§§ 817, 2nd sentence and 821 BGB).[78]

Words remain words, and the unwillingness of the law to enforce a certain type of commitment cannot be changed by an additional abstract promise or an acknowledgement of a concomitant debt. In accordance with this intention of the redactors, the bond between abstract promises and acknowledgements of debt and their *causae* should be regarded as being even a bit stronger than admitted by the dominant view. The rule that a performance cannot be reclaimed by the party who knew that there was no legal grounding for it[79] should not be understood as hindering a promisor from defending himself against the obligation arising from his promise. A fortiori, doctrine and courts are mistaken to believe that there is a type of unilateral acknowledgement of debt with the power to finalise the legal situation (so-called *Feststellungswirkung*), depriving the acknowledging party of the defence that the obligation does not exist: such power should be privy to settlements, and a settlement requires consideration – otherwise it should be regarded as a gift promise requiring notarisation.[80]

III. Suppressed Problems

Those who deny *causa* a role in modern German contract law might be inclined to interpret the decision in favour of abstract promises as implying its abolition. But this would be wrong. At most, one can regard that decision as an attempt to suppress

[76] See G Albers in beck-online.GROSSKOMMENTAR BGB, https://beck-online.beck.de/Home, 1 April 2024, § 780, n 47, 118–125.2.

[77] See G Schulze, *Die Naturalobligation* (Tübingen, Mohr Siebeck, 2008).

[78] See A von Tuhr, *Zur Lehre von den Abstrakten Schuldverträgen nach dem BGB* (Leipzig, Verlag von CL Hirschfeld, 1903) 8 = in *Festschrift für Schultze*, Leipzig 1903, 25–50, 32; Albers, 'Das nicht so abstrakte Schuldversprechen' (n 71).

[79] See n 75 above.

[80] *cf* § 779 BGB: mutual concessions (*gegenseitiges Nachgeben*). On the matter, see G Albers, 'Schuldanerkenntnis als Schenkungsversprechen: Gegen Kondiktionsausschluss und einseitigen Feststellungsvertrag' (2020) 75 *Juristenzeitung* 776; H Ehmann, 'Zu den Arten der Rechtsgründe von Leistungen und Leistungsversprechen. Von der causa-Lehre zur Zwecklehre' in Albers et al (n 1) 801–06.

causa:[81] banning it from the realm of contract, it would now have to limit its rule to the realm of unjustified enrichment. Within the field of unjustified enrichment, *causa* cannot be avoided, and we still need to face it comprehensively. This implies that the task of unjustified enrichment cannot be reduced – as a part of the doctrine would like – to claiming back performances made in pursuance of supposed claims that turn out to be (or to become) non-existent. Moreover, even in the field of contract law, *causa* still lurks in the shadows, as a true suppression has only taken place in the special case of the wholly abstract promise.

A. Protecting Purposes by Unjustified Enrichment

Modern doctrine tends to under-equip the law of unjustified enrichment regarding performances. Sometimes, every performance is presented as fulfilment of some obligation, and the function of unjustified enrichment is thus reduced to reclaiming a performance if it turns out that an obligation had been invalid or is terminated (*objektiver Rechtsgrundbegriff*). But obligations cannot be the true starting point, as they themselves can be the object by which one party enriches the other without sufficient justification.

The law of unjustified enrichment must be fit to control whether an obligation itself has a sufficient cause. It must be able to explain *why* a buyer's obligation to pay the agreed contract price does not unjustifiably enrich the seller, no less than it must explain if and why the seller may keep an obligation created by an abstract promise given by the buyer as additional security.

A general criterion for deciding whether a performance or a promise brings about an unjustified enrichment can only be provided by a doctrine that focuses on the intentions of the parties (*subjektiver Rechtsgrundbegriff*).[82] The enrichment lacks justification if the purpose of the transaction fails. For payments and securities, this is indeed the case if the original debt did not exist. But the promise to pay the price achieves its purpose by urging the seller to deliver the goods or to make a valid promise to deliver later. Such a comprehensive approach to unjustified enrichment – in other words, to the purposes of performances and promises – could even provide a framework within which rules on the avoidance of obligations or rescission of contracts could be regarded as providing special remedies for unjustified enrichment.[83] It has been pointed out by Birke Häcker that such a framework could comprise the rules for avoiding a contract or other legal act on the ground of mistake.[84] In this way, the law of unjustified enrichment would regain the scope reserved for it by Bernhard Windscheid and his theory of presupposition (*Voraussetzungslehre*).[85]

[81] On the – different – attempt to suppress cause from the Code civil by the reform of the *droit des obligations*, see Albers, 'Why Cause of Contract Again (n 45) 3–4 (with references) and ch 14 of this book, s II.A(i), by Birke Häcker.

[82] For a fervent argument in favour of the subjective approach, see Ehmann (n 80).

[83] See ibid 868–69; Albers, 'Die causa vom Code civil zum BGB' (n 1) 575–88.

[84] B Häcker, *Consequences of Impaired Consent Transfers* (Tübingen, Mohr Siebeck, 2009) 171–74; ch 14 of this book, s III.D.

[85] See nn 49 and 57 above.

B. A Persistent Distinction in Contract Law

But even if we equip our law of unjustified enrichment well, we still need to reflect on *causa* in contract. In private law in general, we need to distinguish between 'causal' and 'abstract' transactions. In contract law, there can be no doubt, if only because abstract promises need to be in writing according to § 780 BGB.

It is often overlooked that the existence of a specific provision on abstract promises urges German law to maintain a concept of 'abstract' contracts and, in consequence, also a concept of non-abstract, ie causal, contracts.[86] A promise that 'establishes the obligation by itself (*selbständig*)'[87] is considered exceptional by the BGB. All other promises do not apparently oblige on their own, but appear to oblige because the legal order endorses the purposes they pursue.[88]

In this way, *causa* is connected to the problem of different *types* of contracts.[89] When an agreement fits into one of the traditional contract types, a promise thereby given is most certainly not abstract. But apart from the typical contracts, one has to go back to broader categories of purposes, like liberality, exchange, payment and security.[90]

The differences can become blurred, particularly as regards unilateral promises: is the promise to pay €1000 made as a gift promise, as part of an atypical exchange or as a security? And is this purpose incorporated into the promise, so that it becomes a 'causal' contract – which, if the purpose fails, might be void or offer some specific remedy? Or is the promise intended to be detached from its purpose, so that it is 'abstract' and has a preliminary binding effect without regard to its purpose, although it can be challenged by way of unjustified enrichment if the purpose fails? These questions – with their huge implications, as gift promises require notarisation, abstract promises at least writing – are often answered in a mechanical way, by following traditions and case law, without facing the key theoretical question of what is actually necessary for a promise not to be 'abstract'.

C. Delineation of Contract

Reflecting on the relationship between intention and types of contracts brings the realisation that the legal system categorises and assesses the intention of the parties according to the purposes they are pursuing in order to decide which legal consequences have to be applied. Dispositive and cogent rules connected to different types determine large parts of contract law. This leads to the question of how much can really be explained by the will of the parties.

If one contrasts the content of the parties' agreement with their purposes, the purposes appear to be the more important part. This becomes particularly clear

[86] As pointed out correctly by T Bremkamp, *Causa. Der Zweck als Grundpfeiler des Privatrechts* (Berlin, Duncker & Humblot, 2008) 167.

[87] See n 70 above.

[88] See s II.A(i) of ch 14 of this book, by Birke Häcker.

[89] As emphasised in Italy by G Ferri, *Causa e tipo nella teoria del negozio giuridico* (Milan, Giuffrè, 1966). On contract types in German law, see D Leenen, *Typus und Rechtsfindung* (Berlin, Duncker & Humblot, 1971).

[90] See Ehmann (n 80) 756–820.

whenever lawyers evaluate whether an agreement is carried by the parties' so-called 'intention to create legal relations' or whether it remains in the merely social sphere. That 'intention' is a legal construct and inferred from surrounding circumstances. The legal order is aimed at serving the purposes of the parties, not necessarily their will.[91]

The attempt to suppress *causa* as a requirement of contract exposes our tendency to under-equip the law of unjustified enrichment and has left open questions in the law of contract. Refocusing on *causa* in the sense of the purposes pursued by the parties can lead to the discovery that private law is less about protecting the content of the parties' will than about protecting the purposes they pursue through their will. This should not take anything away from private law as a system that realises private autonomy: the rules which govern the interactions between individuals should be defined by the purposes they set, not by the public purpose to implement some policy.

[91] Such a position had been developed by O Lenel, 'Parteiabsicht und Rechtserfolg' (1881) 19 *Jahrbücher für die Dogmatik* 154; however, it was rebutted by W Flume, *Allgemeiner Teil des Bürgerlichen Rechts. Das Rechtsgeschäft*, 3rd edn (Berlin, Springer, 1979) § 4, fn 5. See G Albers, 'Quali requisiti per la volontà? Per una riflessione italo-tedesca sullo scopo pratico perseguito dalle parti e l'effetto giuridico dell'atto' in T Dalla Massara and G Rametta (eds), *Il volere che si fa norma. Quaderno primo: dialoghi tra giuristi e filosofi* (Bologna, Il Mulino, 2024) 33–43. Italian doctrine has developed interesting approaches to the matter; see also ch 10 in this book, by Francesco Paolo Patti.

10

The Evolution of *Causa* in Italian Contract Law: From State Control to Contractual Autonomy

FRANCESCO PAOLO PATTI

I. Introduction

There are some aspects that make the history of *causa* in the Italian legal system quite peculiar in the continental European context. At the textual level of the Italian Civil Code, in Article 1325, *causa* is identified as one of the essential elements of the contract, together with 'the agreement', 'the subject matter' and, where required by law, 'the form'. The absence of *causa* leads to the invalidity of the contract in accordance with Article 1418 of the Italian Civil Code.

One difference compared to the French legal tradition is immediately apparent. The *causa* is not in reference to the obligation (*la cause de l'obligation*)[1] but to the contract in itself. This difference is due to historical developments within Italian doctrinal legal thinking, which led to a departure from the French origins. The separation between the two legal systems was sealed with the enactment of the Italian Civil Code of 1942, when *causa* was conceived as an instrument to control the contractual autonomy of the parties. This control mechanism is based on value judgements that have evolved over time and are a distinctive feature of Italian contract law.

The distance from the French model is even greater since the reform of French contract law of 2016.[2] The French Civil Code abandoned the concept of *causa* with the aim of modernising the legal system and making it more appealing in the international context.[3] It is questionable whether the mere erasure of a concept can extinguish hundreds of years of legal thinking and have a real impact on legal practice. What is

[1] See ch 7 of this book, by Olivier Deshayes.

[2] See L Aynès, 'The Content of Contracts: Prestation, Objet, but No Longer la Cause?' in J Cartwright and S Whittaker (eds), *The Code Napoléon Rewritten. French Contract Law after the 2016 Reforms* (Oxford, Bloomsbury Publishing, 2017) 137. For a general overview, see G Albers, 'History of a Notion' in G Albers, FP Patti and D Perrouin-Verbe (eds), *Causa contractus. Auf der Suche nach den Bedingungen der Wirksamkeit des vertraglichen Willens* (Tübingen, Mohr Siebeck, 2022) 19 and 29.

[3] B Fauvarque-Cosson, J Gest and F Ancel, 'The Process of Elaboration of the Reform of the Law of Contract' in Cartwright and Whittaker (n 2) 17.

remarkable, however, is that the *causa* is more alive than ever in the Italian legal system. It is often present in case law, as it plays a key role in the decision-making process of judges.[4] The *causa* is also much debated by scholars, who sometimes denounce the excessive interventionism of the courts, which can alter the terms of the contractual agreement and undermine the certainty of commercial contract law.[5]

All in all, due to the developments in case law of the last two decades, one can say that in the Italian legal system the *causa* is not only an instrument to evaluate if a contractual promise is enforceable, but has become a tool to potentially assess the fairness and the justice of the contract.[6] The aim of this chapter is to shed light on the historical background of the Italian legal system, to explain the interplay with French legal thinking and the reasons that have led to recent developments in the case law. It will therefore begin with a historical overview by referring to the *causa* in the two Italian Civil Codes of 1865 and 1942 (section II). After an account of the current legal regime (section III), it will focus on some examples taken from case law in order to clarify the broad function of *causa* in contract law (section IV). In the light of the criticisms made by some Italian scholars, the chapter will conclude with some remarks on the future of *causa* (section V).

II. From the Civil Code of 1865 to the Civil Code of 1942

The Italian theoretical framework concerning *causa* between the two Civil Codes of 1865 and 1942 should be presented in two stages.[7] The first stage (section II.A) should distinguish the evolution of the concept during the late nineteenth and early twentieth centuries. The second stage (section II.B) should focus on its culmination in the work of Emilio Betti and its finalisation in the Civil Code of the Fascist era, which was heavily influenced by Betti's theses in many aspects.

A. Departure from the French Model: The Italian Doctrine of *Causa*

The desire to emancipate itself from French legal culture, while adapting its interpretative and reconstructive outcomes to Italian sensibilities and needs,[8] along with the

[4] See CM Bianca, 'Causa concreta del contratto e diritto effettivo' [2014] *Rivista di diritto civile* 251.

[5] On the use of *causa* in case law, see V Roppo, 'Causa: una storia di successo? Dialogo (non reticente, né compiacente) con la giurisprudenza di legittimità e di merito' [2013] *Rivista di diritto civile* 957. The interventionism of judges does not only affect the area of *causa*: for a general overview, see N Lipari, *Il diritto civile tra legge e giudizio* (Milan, Giuffrè, 2017) 235–65; AM Benedetti, 'Interventismo giudiziario e contratto' [2022] *Pactum* 349.

[6] See J Gordley and H Jiang, 'The Lost Doctrines of *Causa* and the Incoherence of Contemporary Contract Law' (2023) 98 *Tulane Law Review* 1023, revisiting, through a historical assessment, the moral foundation that inspired the doctrine of *causa*.

[7] For a comprehensive account, see AM Garofalo, 'Itinerari della causa dal Code civil del 1804 al Codice civile del 1942' in Albers et al (n 2) 201.

[8] As is well known, the Italian Civil Code of 1865 was in fact a translation of the French Civil Code, with a few additions and modifications: so, it was obvious that Italian jurists would refer to French interpretations and reconstructions (all the more so since the commentaries of the *École de l'exégèse* had been largely

influence of Romanist discourse and German scholarship,[9] led Italian legal scholarship at the end of the nineteenth century to partially diverge from French legal doctrine. The concept of *causa* in contract law provides an excellent vantage point to observe this phenomenon. Although Articles 1104 and 1119–22 of the Italian Civil Code of 1865 largely replicated the legal regime of the French cause[10] with minimal variations,[11] only a portion of Italian legal doctrine remained aligned with French interpretations. Other scholars profoundly distanced themselves from the French approach, employing highly innovative methods and arriving at dogmatic reconstructions that diverged significantly from the *École de l'exégèse*.

It is worthwhile examining these different positions separately, beginning with those most closely aligned with the French theses (section II.A(i)), then exploring the more distinct and original perspectives adopting a more functionalist approach (section II.A(ii)).

(i) The Anchoring of the Causa *to the Obligation*

Until the penultimate decade of the twentieth century, Italian legal doctrine had not even considered the possibility that, alongside the cause of the obligation, one might also speak of a cause of the *negozio giuridico*. Generally, the literature, following the lead of French scholars, concurred that in contracts involving pecuniary interest, the *causa* of the obligation lies in the performance that the other party has made or undertakes to make, and in contracts involving gratuitous promises, in the *animus donandi*. However, this consensus evaporated when it came to 'scientifically defining the *causa*'.[12]

As in France, an anti-causalist movement was gaining traction in Italy during those years, with Giorgi as its leading proponent. According to Giorgi, the concept of *causa* was entirely superfluous, as it merely duplicated other elements of the contract: consent (absent in cases of false *causa* and simulation) and the subject matter (lacking in instances of defective cause).[13] Consequently, Giorgi argued that *de iure condendo* the provisions concerning *causa* could justifiably be removed from the Civil Code.

Such a view remained isolated and, like the similar arguments made by the French anti-causalists, did not prevail among practitioners, nor among scholars. In this context, the notion of *causa* referring not only to the obligation, but also to the *negozio giuridico* was more and more accepted. However, the Civil Code of 1865 effectively linked *causa*

translated into Italian and were also used in practice). Nonetheless, Italian peculiarities inevitably had to lead to a revision, in method and merit, of what had been imported from France.

[9] See also G Tarello, 'La "Scuola dell'esegesi" e la sua diffusione in Italia' in *Scritti per il XL della morte di PE Bensa* (Milan, Giuffrè, 1969) 241.

[10] GB Ferri, 'Tradizione e novità nella disciplina della causa del negozio giuridico (dal cod civ 1865 al cod civ 1942)' [1986] *Rivista del diritto commerciale* 127, 130.

[11] The Italian Civil Code specified, in Art 1121, that 'the cause is presumed until the contrary is proved' (*la causa si presume sino a che non si prova il contrario*) in order to overcome the uncertainties on the reversal of the burden of proof in promises without expression of cause that had sometimes arisen in France.

[12] See E Presutti, 'Alcune idee intorno alla causa dell'obbligazione nei contratti (art 1119 a 1122 cod civile)' (1889) IV *Giurisprudenza italiana* 33, 35.

[13] G Giorgi, *Teoria delle obbligazioni nel diritto moderno*, vol III, *Fonti delle obbligazioni – Contratti*, 7th edn (Florence, Eugenio e Filippo Cammelli, 1925) 621.

to the obligation. Thus, only by associating *causa* with the obligation would the law be respected.[14]

Regarding the transformation of the notion of *causa*, these movements preferred to frame it around the 'determining motive' (*movente determinatore*) and the subjective 'justifying reason' (*ragione giustificativa subiettiva*), and linked it not to the obligation, but to the 'utility' (*utilità*) that each party hoped to derive from the contract.[15] Alternatively, they considered the 'motive or end' (*motivo o fine*), which referred to the purpose set by the will itself, a concept whose scope varied depending on whether the contract was lawful or unlawful.[16]

Despite the turbulence in Italian scholarship, where some authors distanced themselves from the French legal tradition, the interesting 1927 project for a Franco-Italian Code of Obligations[17] did not propose any real innovation in the field. Articles 10 and 27–29 of the Franco-Italian project followed the tradition of reproducing the text of the Italian Civil Code. There is not much to say about this project, which was later abandoned, except that it was strongly criticised by the person who later became the most important advocate of the cause as a function, namely Emilio Betti.[18]

(ii) Causa *as Function of the Legal Transaction (*negozio giuridico*)*

The thesis of the *causa* as a function of the legal transaction (*negozio giuridico*), first proposed by Scialoja and not accepted by the majoritarian view in the Italian doctrine, completely rejected the idea of the *causa* of the obligation. The underlying reason of the innovative thesis was the disruptive power of the embraced systematic method, which was significantly different from the French one and less bound to the letter of the law. The connection to the legal transaction led to a different conceptualisation of the *causa*, as Vittorio Scialoja – in his lectures on the *negozio giuridico*[19] – proposed for the first time to identify the *causa* in the typical function of the legal transaction.

The focus was on the *negozio giuridico* rather than the contract, given the prominence of the *Rechtsgeschäftslehre* in German legal thinking at the time (to which Scialoja was much indebted). The function of the legal transaction showed typical traits linked to the idea of an 'objective purpose', but Scialoja stressed the importance of the individual will that he considered part of the agent's mind.

In any case, the *causa* was no longer described from the point of view of each contracting party, but became 'common to the whole legal transaction'; it was no longer centred on obligations or performances, ie on legal forms and structures, but on the function, a concept that could be understood from an economic and social perspective.

[14] S Malvagna, 'Il problema della causa nei contratti' [1934] *Rivista di diritto civile* 118, 213.

[15] E Battistoni, *La causa nei negozi giuridici (dal diritto intermedio al codice civile italiano)* (Padua, Cedam 1932) 24–30, 147–48.

[16] A Motta, *La causa delle obbligazioni nel diritto civile italiano* (Turin, Bocca, 1929) 139–43.

[17] See G Chiodi, 'Innovare senza distruggere: il progetto italo-francese di codice delle obbligazioni e dei contratti (1927)' in G Alpa and G Chiodi (eds), *Il progetto italo francese delle obbligazioni (1927). Un modello di armonizzazione nell'epoca della ricodificazione* (Milan, Giuffrè, 2007) 223.

[18] See E Betti, 'Il quarto libro nel progetto del codice civile italiano' (1938) I *Rivista del diritto commerciale* 537, 541–43.

[19] V Scialoja, *Negozi giuridici. Corso di diritto romano nella R. Università di Roma nell'a.a. 1892–1893 raccolto dai Dottori Maffei e Giannini*, 5th edn (Rome, Società Editrice del Foro Italiano, 1950) 90–91.

Scialoja's thesis radically changed not only the concept, but also the role of the *causa* itself, and thus the modalities to assess private autonomy. In Scialoja's view, the *causa* corresponded to a synthetic representation of the contract, which, as such, reminded the parties and the judge that the product of private autonomy had to be considered in the light of social categories introduced and specified by the legal system (according to canons of normality and reasonableness). Within the Italian scholarship of the last years of the nineteenth and the early twentieth century, Scialoja's thesis became increasingly popular, as shown by the growing number of authors who took it up and specified it further.

First of all, scholars argued that through the *causa* it was possible to ascertain whether the parties really intended to be legally bound.[20] In this way, without abandoning the idea of the *causa* as the 'justifying reason of legality' (*ragione giustificatrice della giuridicità*), the concept assumed the role of synthesising certain deontological and reconstructive profiles of the contract: through the *causa*, the judge could assess whether the contract was capable of producing effects. Hence, the idea of the *causa* was as an arrangement of interests and, as such, as a way of looking at the contract in order to interpret it and, therefore, to identify its effects.

Secondly, the concept of *causa* has been interpreted in various ways as a tool to assess the validity of contractual agreements, based on the premise that the legal system acknowledges certain types of contracts. This has highlighted the significance of these contractual types, while also emphasising the broader utility of contracts in general.

B. Emilio Betti and the Civil Code of 1942

The provisions on *causa* in the new Italian Civil Code of 1942[21] can only be fully understood through the lens of Emilio Betti's studies. A key provision of Article 1325(2) of the Italian Civil Code identifies the *causa* as one of the essential requirements of the contract. According to Article 1418(2) of the Italian Civil Code, nullity of the contract results from the lack of one of the requirements indicated in Article 1325.

These provisions are further intertwined with Article 1322(2), which allows parties to enter into contracts outside traditional types, provided they aim to achieve interests deemed worthy of protection by the legal system. Additionally, Articles 1343–45 clarify that a *causa* is illicit if it violates mandatory rules, public order or morality; if it serves as a means to circumvent a mandatory rule; or if the contract is concluded exclusively for an illicit motive common to both parties. In such cases, under Article 1418(2) of the Italian Civil Code, the contract is deemed null due to the illicit nature of the *causa* or the motives as indicated in Article 1345 of the Italian Civil Code.

[20] See B Dusi, *Istituzioni di diritto civile* (Turin, Luigi Pierro, 1922) 165–68 (the opinion remained unchanged even after the approval of the new code: see B Dusi, *Istituzioni di diritto civile*, vol I (4th edn, Turin, Giappichelli, 1944) 125), considering *causa* 'the justifying reason for the legal efficacy of the transaction', in the sense that 'not every agreement of will – which could also be entirely arbitrary and capricious – can be capable of this, but only the one that realises an *end*, an *intention*, that is deemed by the law to be worthy of legal protection. The agreement, eg of two friends to go on a trip together, may imply an obligation of courtesy, but is not a contract.'

[21] See s III below.

It is widely and correctly believed that the Civil Code of 1942 embraced the concept of *causa* as a function, as proposed by Emilio Betti, although the author himself expressed some dissatisfaction with the final drafting of these provisions.[22] Furthermore, it is well known that subsequent legal scholarship and case law have consistently interpreted these provisions through the lens of Betti's writings, even when they have partially diverged from his views. Therefore, any examination of the *causa*-related provisions in the new Code of 1942 must be closely aligned with the theories of the renowned scholar.[23]

(i) The Definition of Causa

For Betti, *causa* represented the 'socio-economic function' (*funzione economico-sociale*) of the contract,[24] or in other words, the 'social interest function of private autonomy'. Betti's definition closely followed that of Scialoja, with the notable addition of the term 'social'. This addition should be understood in the context of Betti's broader theoretical perspective, which posited that private autonomy did not originate within the legal system but outside of it – in the realm of commercial trade. In this view, certain life interests were typified through trade practices, giving rise to contractual types that eventually imposed themselves on the legal system. These types were sometimes explicitly recognised and regulated by law, and at other times were validated through judicial interpretation.[25]

The term 'social' was intended to emphasise that every contract must be understood in its true 'sense'. For Betti, this social comprehensibility was closely linked to the need for strong typification.[26] In his theoretical framework, the importance of *causa* was intertwined with the practical purpose of the contract, serving as the foundation for interpreting and constructing the contract.[27] The *causa* was directly influenced by the parties' practical intentions, becoming activated in the specific context of the contract (*in concreto*).[28] Therefore, the classification of the contract – and the identification

[22] See, eg M Brutti, *Vittorio Scialoja, Emilio Betti – Due visioni del diritto civile* (Turin, Giappicelli, 2013) 163.

[23] Betti had already set out his theses on the subject of cause before 1942. The most complete elaboration of his theories, however, can be found in some texts published later, under the new Civil Code of 1942: E Betti, 'Teoria generale del negozio giuridico' in F Vassalli, *Trattato di diritto civile* (Turin, Utet, 1943) 112–15, 234–38; F Vassalli, 'Causa del negozio giuridico' in *Novissimo Digesto italiano*, vol III (Turin, Utet, 1967) 32–34. The socio-economic function was expressly mentioned in the official presentation report of the new Italian Civil Code (Relazione al Re del Ministro Guardasigilli, no 613): 'the causa required by the law is not the subjective purpose, whatever it may be, pursued by the contracting party in the concrete case, but is the socio-economic function which the law recognises as relevant to its purposes and which alone justifies the protection of private autonomy' (*la causa richiesta dal diritto non è lo scopo soggettivo, qualunque esso sia, perseguito dal contraente nel caso concreto, ma è la funzione economico-sociale che il diritto riconosce rilevante ai suoi fini e che sola giustifica la tutela dell'autonomia privata*).

[24] Thus already E Betti, *Diritto romano*, vol I, *Parte generale* (Padua, Cedam, 1935) 210.

[25] Betti, *Teoria* (n 13) 191 and 193; E Betti, 'Der Typenzwang bei den römischen Rechtsgeschäften und die sogenannte Typenfreiheit des heutigen Rechts' in *Festschrift Leopold Wenger*, vol I (Munich, CH Beck, 1944) 249, published in Italian translation by D Marcellino Pacitti under the title 'La tipicità dei negozi giuridici romani e la cosidetta atipicità del diritto odierno' (1966) 1 *Annuali della Facoltà di giurisprudenza dell'Università di Macerata* 5, and later re-edited in D Marcellino Pacitti, *Diritto Metodo Ermeneutica. Scritti scelti* (Milan, Giuffrè, 1991) 325.

[26] Betti, *Teoria* (n 13) 171 and 193.

[27] ibid 85–87 and 171.

[28] ibid 178–80.

of its *causa* – had to be grounded in the parties' actual goals, allowing for a concrete evaluation while rejecting excessive formalism.

Despite innovative doctrinal interpretations, the concept of *causa* as a mechanism for directly regulating aspects of the contract primarily had a negative function: it could invalidate a contract in cases where the *causa* was absent, unrealisable, unworthy or illicit.

Differently, understood as the typical function of a contract, *causa* was not a tool for selecting and regulating specific aspects of the contract (like the *cause de l'obligation*), but rather provided an understanding of the contract's overall and inherent 'sense'. As such, while *causa* as a typical function was crucial for interpreting the contract, it did not directly govern the contract itself.

(ii) Lack of Causa

In Betti's interpretation, the absence of a *causa* primarily concerned situations where a promise stood alone, effectively 'abstracted' from any agreement that had its own distinct 'meaning' and specific function.[29] These were generally cases involving pure promises, for which the new Italian Civil Code eliminated the need to reference either the French theory of the *instrumentum* (which lacks mention of cause but includes a reversal of the burden of proof) or the German theory of the *Abstraktionswille*.[30] According to Article 1988 of the Italian Civil Code, the promise of payment (and acknowledgement of debt) effectively shifts the burden of proof, requiring the other party to demonstrate which obligation the promise (or acknowledgement) pertains to and identify any associated defects.[31]

(iii) The 'Unrealisability' of the Causa *(*causa irrealizzabile*)*

As in nineteenth and early twentieth century France, in Italy, the expression 'lack of cause' was understood to mean 'falsity of the cause'. This concept of *faussité de la cause*, when reconsidered through the lens of the theory of cause–function, evolved into the idea of the 'unrealisability of the typical function'. Betti referred to this unrealisability as 'unattainability',[32] which was specifically governed by the combined provisions of Articles 1325(2) and 1418(2) of the Italian Civil Code. To assess the concrete unrealisability of a *causa*, one needed to 'fill in' the typical *causa* in light of the specific contractual intent. For instance, the *causa* of a novation was indeed a typical *causa*, but it represented a framework to be completed based on the obligation to be novated and the new obligation being created. This approach allowed for the verification of whether the novation had a valid *causa* particularly by confirming the existence of the obligation to be novated.

This reasoning also clarifies Betti's response to a common criticism directed at him. According to the 1942 Italian Civil Code, a contract was illegal when its *causa* was illicit.

[29] ibid 188.
[30] See ch 9 in this book, by Gregor Albers.
[31] Betti, *Teoria* (n 13) 182 and 194–96.
[32] ibid 389.

Critics of the theory that envisaged a typical *causa* argued that, under this theory, it would be impossible to identify contracts with an illicit *causa*, as the typical *causa* had to be inherently lawful. However, by accepting Betti's thesis outlined above, one must first evaluate how the typical cause was applied in practice.[33] When the typical cause was infused with specific content, it could indeed prove to be unlawful – consider, for example, a corrupt agreement.

(iv) The Causa *Unworthy of Protection*

Betti's theory also explored the concept of the *causa* unworthy of legal protection, further extending the social dimension of legal action. He argued that social considerations should play a role in determining whether an agreement should be legally binding. This perspective connects with the dual aspects of the 'social function' that were mentioned earlier.[34]

Specifically, Betti contended that the social function of a contract was not limited to the creation and establishment of contractual types through their emergence in legal practice. It was also necessary for each individual contract to address a stable need in life that the legal system deemed worthy of protection – essentially, one that was beneficial to society.

The requirement for a 'suitable' or 'worthy' *causa*, as Betti termed it, varied between typical and atypical contracts (see Article 1322 of the Italian Civil Code).[35] In the case of typical contracts, the legal system had already conducted part of the assessment, leaving to judges only a specific review 'in concreto'. For atypical contracts, however, the entire assessment was left to the judge.

Betti's interpreters have often found it challenging to distinguish between the review of a contract's merits and the assessment of its unlawfulness. Both are heteronomous evaluations, but the outcomes of the assessments are different: the former leads to legal ineffectiveness due to a lack of recognition by the legal system, while the latter results in nullity. According to Betti, these evaluations concern different situations. Illegality arises when there is a conflict between the contract and the legal system, whereas unworthiness occurs when the contract, although not in conflict with the legal system, does not serve interests that promote societal development. However, it remains difficult to understand why, in such cases, the contract is not already considered unlawful, particularly if its cause conflicts with public policy.

C. Other Ways of Addressing *Causa*

Betti's theories had a significant influence on the Italian Civil Code, and their success was, in part, facilitated by the prevailing political regime and the state's *dirigiste*

[33] ibid 386.

[34] See s II.B(i) above.

[35] Betti, *Teoria* (n 13) 389. See also s III.E below.

approach at the time.[36] The notion that *causa* required private autonomy to be continually subjected to state scrutiny, ensuring the social acceptability of contracts, was later challenged by other leading scholars in the decades following the implementation of the 1942 Civil Code.[37] To depart from the ideological traits that surrounded the concept of *causa*, legal scholars tried to underline the practical functionality of *causa* or to undermine its importance within the theory of contract law.

(i) Mitigation of State Control

Based on a comparative-historical methodology, Gino Gorla proposed a neutral approach, whereby *causa* was considered not as a *dirigiste* instrument for implementing the ideologies of prevailing political views, but as a guarantee of the seriousness of the contractual relationship.[38] Gorla observed that not all contracts with economic interests significantly impact the issues of production and distribution of wealth in a way that is practically relevant to the social utility. According to Gorla, the state cannot (and should not) absorb and control every aspect of individuals' lives.[39] The author stated that such an interventionism potentially endangered contractual freedom and legal certainty, the pillars of the contractual regime.[40]

Even Michele Giorgianni, though adopting a more traditional perspective, advocates for a minimalistic interpretation of *causa* as a means of controlling the justification for the transfer of assets from one individual to another. Giorgianni did not consider the social impetus characteristic of Betti's approach to be necessary: in his view, the *causa* is the synthesis of the effects of the legal transaction, within which its justificatory reason can be found.[41]

(ii) The Individual Economic Function

Giovanni Battista Ferri's elaborations on the distinction of *causa* and contractual type are usually considered another milestone of the Italian doctrine.[42] A common criticism of Betti's thesis was the theoretical difficulty in distinguishing the *causa* from the contractual type, which is recognised by the legal system through the establishment of a specific regime for the contract (sale, loan, mandate, etc).[43] In other words, if a contract of sale stipulates an exchange of goods for a price, how could the *causa* be anything other than what the law prescribes? In response, Ferri proposed defining *causa*

[36] On Betti's political commitment and his relations with fascism, see M Brutti, 'Emilio Betti e l'incontro con il fascismo' in I Birocchi and L Loschiavo (eds), *I giuristi e il fascino del regime (1918–1925)* (Rome, Roma Tre-Press, 2015) 63.

[37] For an overview, see F Bartolini, 'La causa del contratto dal Codice civile del 1942 ai giorni nostri' in Albers et al (n 2) 247.

[38] G Gorla, *Il contratto. Corso di diritto privato svolto secondo il metodo comparativo e casistico*, vol I, *Lineamenti generali* (Milan, Giuffrè, 1954) 223–25.

[39] ibid.

[40] ibid 226.

[41] M Giorgianni, 'Causa (dir priv)' in *Enciclopedia del diritto*, vol VI (Milan, Giuffrè, 1960) 547 and 562–64.

[42] GB Ferri, *Causa e tipo nella teoria del negozio giuridico* (Milan, Giuffrè, 1966).

[43] See also s II.B(i) above.

not as the 'socio-economic function' of the contract, but as its 'individual economic function'. His aim was to adopt a concrete perspective, focusing on the economic transaction undertaken by the parties within the specific contractual relationship. The contract should be considered rational (and worthy of protection) not by reference to external and abstract values, but in relation to the objectives that the parties intend to achieve. The role of the contractual type was just to standardise and organise different contracts to default rules, but each contract had to be assessed on the basis of the individual interests of the parties. In the years to come, the role of *causa* became even more practical, and through the works of Massimo Bianca heavily influenced the Italian case law.[44]

III. The Understanding of the New Textual Layer: The Provisions on *Causa*

It is clear that *causa* is a concept that primarily lives and breathes in the doctrinal works of prominent Italian jurists. However, the regulatory implications and their impact on the effects of the contract are far from negligible. First and foremost, it is necessary to examine the provisions of the Civil Code concerning the *causa*, which constitute a condition for the validity of the contract, placing the Italian Civil Code in a unique position within the European context. In order to provide a remedy for a party or to protect general interests, the legal system provides for a verification of the contract through the *causa*. If it fails, the contract is considered invalid. The court must look at the *causa* of the contract to see whether it is present or missing (section III.A), and whether it is lawful or unlawful (section III.B). In these hypotheses, the *causa* is understood as a summary of the economic arrangement in order to ensure a remedy for a party (lack of *causa*) or to check the conformity of the contract with the general interests of the legal system (illicit *causa*). Other peculiar provisions cover the circumvention of a legal prohibition (section III.C), the illicit motive (section III.D) and the control of atypical contracts (section III.V).

A. The Missing *Causa*

According to Articles 1325(2) and 1418(2) of the Italian Civil Code, the absence of *causa* renders a contract null. The *causa* is considered missing when it is lacking *in concreto*, meaning that the agreed-upon terms can actually not be realised.[45] This defect may also arise if the subject matter of the contract is impossible to achieve. However, our legal system requires that attention be given to the defect of *causa* when the contract's flaws are not evident through other structural elements. Thus, the absence of *causa* is the result of an examination from a functional and residual perspective.

[44] See s IV below.

[45] See, among many, U Breccia, 'Causa' in M Bessone (ed), *Trattato di diritto privato*, vol XIII.3, *Il contratto in generale* (Turin, Giappichelli, 1999) 3, 5–7.

(i) Illusory Causa *(*causa illusoria*)*

The *causa* is considered missing, primarily, when it is inherently unrealisable in reality. Some scenarios addressed by the law provide guidance on understanding typical cases.

For instance, in insurance contracts, if the risk ceases to exist before the contract is concluded, the contract is invalid (Article 1895 of the Italian Civil Code). Here, the *causa* lies in the exchange of a premium for the assumption of certain risks by the insurer. If the risk does not exist, the agreed-upon exchange cannot be realised, rendering the contract null.

Similarly, under Article 1234(1) of the Italian Civil Code, novation is ineffective if the obligation to be novated does not exist. Another example is found in Article 1876, where a life annuity contract in favour of a third party who had already died before the agreement was made is null.[46] The nullity arises because the *causa*, which centres on the annuitant's survival risk, is impracticable if the annuitant is already deceased.

Beyond these examples provided by the law, courts have also identified cases where the *causa* is deemed illusory. This often occurs when an individual attempts to acquire a right or service for a consideration, despite already possessing that right or being entitled to the service by law or contract.[47]

In the landmark judgment where the Supreme Court of Cassation first adopted the theory of *causa concreta*, the case involved a party obliged to perform activities they were already contractually obligated to do. Consequently, the contract was declared null, and the other party was not required to perform the stipulated consideration.[48]

*(ii) Derisory Cause (*causa derisoria*)*

Causa is also considered absent when it is derisory – that is, when, in a contract of exchange, the benefit to one party is so insignificant compared to the benefit to the other that a genuine exchange cannot be said to exist. However, the concept of *causa* does not allow for a general review of the fairness of the exchange terms; for causation to be considered absent, the imbalance must be absolute, making it impossible to recognise the transaction as a true exchange.

The Court of Cassation has clarified that only a price that is utterly worthless, merely nominal or symbolic can result in the nullity of a sale due to the absence of one of its essential elements. In contrast, a price significantly lower than the market value, but not entirely without worth, raises questions about the adequacy and equivalence of the consideration, and pertains to interpreting the parties' intentions or potentially identifying a different *causa* for the contract.[49]

[46] See A Magazzù, 'Novazione (dir priv)' in *Enciclopedia del diritto*, vol XXVIII (Milan, Giuffrè, 1978) 823.

[47] See, eg Cass 27.7.1987, no 6492, *Rep Foro it*, 1987, Contratto in genere, no 365.

[48] See Cass 8.5.2006, *Giur it*, 2007, 2203.

[49] Cass 19.4.2013, no 9640, *Rep Foro it*, 2013, Sale, no 32. See also Cass, 4.11.2015, no 22567, *Foro it*, 2016, I, 151.

B. The Illicit *Causa*

Article 1343 of the Italian Civil Code states that a *causa* is unlawful when it conflicts with mandatory rules, public order or morality. An unlawful *causa* results in the nullity of the contract, as outlined in Article 1418(2) of the Italian Civil Code. In this context, legal doctrine refers to such agreements as 'illicit contracts', while contracts that violate a mandatory rule (under Article 1418(1) of the Italian Civil Code) are considered 'illegal'.[50]

The first category of illicit contracts under Article 1343 of the Italian Civil Code involves contracts that contradict mandatory rules. This issue arises from a causal perspective when the contract's purpose involves an agreement that is expressly forbidden by law. Common examples include agreements that violate the prohibition of fiduciary covenants (*divieto del patto commissorio*) (Article 2744 of the Italian Civil Code), succession pacts (*patti successori*) (Article 458 of the Italian Civil Code), usurious agreements (pursuant to Article 644 of the Criminal Code, as amended by Law no 108/1996) or an agreement in which a public official receives monetary compensation for performing official duties in violation of Article 318 of the Criminal Code. Differently, when the conflict with mandatory rules concerns the broader content of the contract, it is classified as an 'illegal contract'.

*(i) Public Order (*ordine pubblico*)*

Although the concept has been extensively developed in both legal scholarship and case law, contrariety to public order generally refers to actions that conflict with the fundamental principles of the legal system. Recently, principles of constitutional significance, which embody the core values of the legal system, have gained increasing importance. Public order may come into play in situations where no specific legal prohibition exists, but the purpose of the contract contrasts constitutionally recognised principles or the principles underlying a set of mandatory rules.[51] In addition, Article 117 of the Constitution allows for the consideration of international regulations and principles, including those found in the European Convention on Human Rights.

In the framework thus outlined, a significant role must be attributed to the inviolable personality rights.[52] An example dealt with by case law concerns a contract concluded on the occasion of a maternity surrogacy: the contract was found to be null for conflict with both public order and good morals.[53]

Public order is sometimes qualified as 'political', with reference to the principles that govern the existence and functioning of the powers of the state and the freedoms granted to individual citizens, or 'economic', when it comes to the principles that govern the production and circulation of wealth (eg the rules concerning competition in the market).

[50] See E Navarretta, 'Della causa del contratto' in E Gabrielli (ed), *Commentario del codice civile* (Turin, Utet, 2011) 573, 658ff; E Betti, *Teoria* (n 13) 116–18.

[51] Navarretta (n 50) 667.

[52] See G Resta, 'Contratto e diritti della personalità' in V Roppo (ed), *Trattato del contratto*, vol VI, *Interferenze* (Milan, Giuffrè, 2006) 3, 13–15.

[53] Trib Monza, 27.10.1989, *Foro it*, 1990, I, 298.

In the context of the theory of illicit contracts, public order has not gained any practical significance.[54] Indeed, the cases in which jurisprudence resorts to public order are residual, as generally the nullity of the contract concerns a conflict with a mandatory rule. However, the role of public order should not be underestimated: the concept is intended to capture cases that were not expressly regulated through mandatory rules. Public order should therefore target contracts that are socially harmful or dangerous, even if they do not correspond to any case precisely described by mandatory rules.[55]

*(ii) Good Morals (*buon costume*)*

In contrast, good morals express, in general terms, the fundamental canons of public and private honesty accepted in the social conscience. A contract contrary to good morals is also referred to as an 'immoral contract'. From this classification derives the applicability of Article 2035 of the Italian Civil Code, according to which a performance may not be repeated (the rule is usually traced back to the adage *in pari causa turpitudinis melior est condicio possidentis* or *nemo auditor propriam turpitudinem alligans*). Traditionally, it is said that the justification for the rule lies in the observation that the one who executed the performance is in an equally reprehensible position as the one who received it. Therefore, the legal system should provide no protection in the presence of immoral contracts. Today, such a motivation is no longer considered rational,[56] and it seems preferable to consider the rule of Article 2035 of the Civil Code as an instrument to increase the effectiveness of the violated mandatory rule.[57]

Acts contrary to good morals are considered to be those that offend sexual dignity or professional ethics, and more generally, those that are condemned by the social conscience at a given moment in history. Many cases affect situations where the contract is intertwined with criminal offences, such as the exploitation of prostitution[58] or the sale of drugs in which the drug dealer, as a guarantee of payment for the prohibited substances, obtained possession of certain gold items.[59]

Indeed, cases in which courts ascertain the existence of an immoral contract are rare.[60] But it has been argued that contrariety to mandatory rules does not prevent an autonomous assessment of the immorality of the contract in order to apply the aforementioned Article 2035 of the Italian Civil Code,[61] and it follows that, although it is rarely used in case law, the concept of good morals has autonomous operative value, aimed at activating the rule of *soluti retentio*.

[54] But see the decision Cass 7.6.2024, no 15986, De Jure: if the substantial financing provided was used by the borrower for illegal activities, it is determined that the *causa concreta* of the two contracts contradicts public order, rendering them null.

[55] V Roppo, 'Il contratto' in G Iudica and P Zatti (eds), *Trattato di diritto privato* (Milan, Giuffrè, 2011) 384.

[56] ibid 390.

[57] See FP Patti, 'In pari causa turpitudinis, cinquant'anni dopo' in *Liber amicorum Pietro Rescigno in occasione del suo 90esimo compleanno*, vol 2 (Naples, Editoriale Scientifica, 2018) 1537. From a general perspective, see G Magri, *Dallo scambio immorale allo scambio illecito. I nuovi confini dell'irripetibilità della prestazione indebita* (Turin, Giappichelli, 2022) 5–15; E Bargelli, 'Invalidità del contratto e restituzioni nelle intersezioni fra le fonti del diritto' [2024] *Rivista di diritto civile* 568.

[58] Navarretta (n 50) 665.

[59] Cass 14.10.2011, no 40051, *Rep Foro it*, 2011, Estorsione, no 22.

[60] For a review, see Patti (n 57) 1540–45.

[61] Cass 7.7.1981, no 4414, *Foro it*, 1982, I, 1769.

From various perspectives, legal doctrine has supported the 'legalisation' of the concept of morality, merging it with the notion of public order.[62] Today, there is a well-established school of thought that, based on differing arguments, considers morality to be encompassed within public order.[63] This view is opposed by a more traditional stance, which holds that morality is shaped by extra-legal values that are historically conditioned.[64]

C. The Contract that 'Circumvents the Law' (*in frode alla legge*)

Article 1344 of the Civil Code states that a *causa* is also illicit when a contract is used as a means to circumvent the application of a mandatory rule. This provision covers situations where parties employ a type of contract that is legally permitted but introduce specific clauses or combine multiple contracts to achieve a result prohibited by the mandatory rules.[65] Differently than what happens in cases of simulation (*simulazione*), the parties do not intend an outcome different from what is stated in the contract; rather, they aim precisely for the result that arises from applying those contractual clauses. The Court of Cassation refers to this as the indirect attainment of a result forbidden by law.[66]

The case of 'contratto in frode alla legge' further demonstrates the limitations of an approach focused solely on contract types defined by the law, particularly when examining the functional aspects of a contract. This concept also highlights the significance of the concrete *causa* in our legal system.[67] While, in an abstract sense, the contract may align with legally acceptable forms, in a concrete sense, considering the actual purpose and interests of the parties, it constitutes an unlawful act. Evidence of fraud against the law must be based on objective elements, and the interplay between *causa* and contract interpretation is particularly relevant in such cases.

A common example in case law is a sale agreement with a repurchase or retrocession clause between a debtor and creditor, intended to allow the creditor to acquire definitive ownership of an asset if the secured debt is not paid. Such contracts are often deemed null and void for fraudulently evading the prohibition against fiduciary covenants (*divieto del patto commissorio*) under Article 2744 of the Italian Civil Code.[68]

[62] GB Ferri, *Ordine pubblico, buon costume e la teoria del contratto* (Milan, Giuffrè, 1970) 260–63.

[63] G Panza, *Buon costume e buona fede* (Naples, Jovene, 1973) 184ff; F Galgano, 'Il negozio giuridico' in *Trattato di diritto civile e commerciale Cicu-Messineo* (Milan, Giuffrè, 1988) 247.

[64] See F Di Marzio, *Contratto illecito e disciplina del mercato* (Naples, Jovene, 2011) 64–67; S Patti, 'Interpretation of the General Clauses "Public Policy" and "Good Morals" in European Contract Law' (2014) 22 *European Review of Private Law* 611.

[65] See U Morello, 'Negozio giuridico (negozio giuridico (negozio in frode alla legge)' in *Enciclopedia giuridica Treccani*, vol XX (Rome, Treccani, 1990) 1ff; more recently, see C Cicero, 'Frode alla legge' in *Digesto delle discipline privatistiche, sezione civile, aggiornamento* (Turin, Utet, 2014) 263ff.

[66] Cass 26.3.2012, no 4792, *Rep Foro it*, 2012, Contratto in genere, no 483.

[67] *cf* Bianca, 'Causa concreta' (n 4) 269ff, claiming that in applying Art 1344 of the Italian Civil Code it is not sufficient to consider the content of the contract and the contractual type in which it should be framed on the basis of the declarations of the parties, but it is necessary to ascertain what is the real, concrete interest that the contract is intended to realise. On *causa concreta*, see also s IV below.

[68] V Cass 9.5.2013, no 10986, *Vita not*, 2013, 719ff; Cass 3.6.1983, no 3800, *Foro it*, 1984, I, 212. See also Cass 19.5.2004, no 9466, *Contratti*, 2004, 979.

D. The Illicit Motive

A motive (*motivo*) refers to the individual interest of a party. Generally, the legal system follows the principle that motives are irrelevant, although the contracting parties may override this by incorporating a condition into the contract (Article 1353 of the Italian Civil Code).[69] Thus, motives typically remain outside the contract because they do not form part of its justifying reason.[70] For instance, in a sales contract, a buyer's desire to use the purchased item as a wedding gift for a friend is a motive limited to the buyer's personal sphere. Even an unlawful motive held by one party does not impact the contract's validity, as the law aims to protect the other party's reliance on the contract's validity. For example, a loan remains valid even if the borrower intends to use the funds to commit a crime. In most cases, an unlawful motive is also irrelevant, even if the other party is aware of it.[71]

Traditionally, Italian doctrine contraposes the objective and legally relevant element of *causa* with motive, which is subjective and generally considered irrelevant to the legal system. While this distinction is still widely accepted in both scholarship and case law, there are situations where motives undeniably become relevant, and others where it becomes difficult to distinguish motive from *causa concreta*.

Motives are particularly significant in acts of liberality, for instance gifts, where there is a transfer of assets to someone without any consideration. Such actions are believed to be driven mainly by personal reasons, or motives. A genuine exception to the principle of the irrelevance of motives is found in Article 1345 of the Italian Civil Code concerning illicit motives – those that contradict mandatory rules, public order or good morals, or aim to circumvent a mandatory rule. A contract is invalid if an illicit motive is shared by both parties and is the sole reason for entering into the contract.

It is unsurprising that the leading proponent of the theory of *causa concreta* considers the scenario governed by Article 1345 of the Italian Civil Code to be a legal example of *causa concreta*.[72] Motives always reflect the interests of the parties. When these shared interests reveal an objectively identifiable purpose, distinguishing between a common motive and a concrete *causa* becomes impossible.

E. *Causa* and Interests Worth of Protection

The provision of Article 1322(2) of the Italian Civil Code deserves special attention. Pursuant to the provision, 'the parties may also enter into contracts that do not belong to the types governed by specific regulations, provided that they are aimed at realising interests worthy of protection according to the legal system'. Initially, this rule was interpreted as excluding the legal recognition of contracts that were not advantageous

[69] C Scognamiglio, 'Motivo (del negozio giuridico)' in *Digesto discipline privatistiche, sezione civile*, vol XI (Turin, Utet, 1994) 466.
[70] Roppo (n 55) 358.
[71] ibid 394.
[72] Bianca, 'Causa concreta' (n 4) 259.

to the legal system, which, at the time, was governed by the corporatist principles of fascism.[73]

Following the fall of the Fascist regime, legal doctrine largely disregarded Article 1322(2) of the Italian Civil Code, viewing it as a redundant check on the legality of the *causa* already explicitly required for atypical contracts.[74] However, over time, this provision has gained increasing significance in determining the legitimacy of contracts not expressly regulated by the Civil Code, such as the autonomous *Garantievertrag*.[75]

In some instances, case law has gone further, suggesting that a contract cannot be worth of protection if it places one party in a position of indefinite subordination to the other, grants an unfair and disproportionate advantage to one party without any corresponding benefit to the other or compels a party to act in a manner contrary to constitutionally imposed duties of solidarity.[76] In these cases, the legal scrutiny aligns with the generally accepted direct application (*Drittwirkung*) of constitutional principles.

For example, in a contract that is clearly commutative,[77] a clause rendering it aleatory in practice has been considered not worth of protection.[78] Similarly, clauses that limit liability or define the contract's subject matter in a way that contradicts the underlying interests of a certain type of contract have been excluded from contractual agreements for not being worth of protection (which closely aligns with the rationale of Article 1170 of the French Civil Code[79]).

Despite these judicial interpretations, the doctrine remains highly fragmented on the correct interpretation of Article 1322(2) of the Italian Civil Code. Some scholars argue that a review aiming to assess whether the contract is worthy of protection has no place within the legal system, advocating a more formalistic view of private autonomy.[80] On the other hand, some scholars broadly support the described assessment, infusing private autonomy with principles of solidarism and functionalism.[81]

[73] *cf* Betti, *Teoria* (n 13) 389ff. See also F Piraino, 'Meritevolezza degli interessi' in *Enciclopedia del diritto, I tematici*, vol I (Milan, Giuffrè, 2021) 667, 670.

[74] See GB Ferri, *Causa e tipo nella teoria del negozio giuridico* (Milan, Giuffrè, 1966) 406.

[75] See Cass, sec un, 1.10.1987, *Giur it*, 1988, I.1, 27. On the 'contratto autonomo di garanzia', see GB Portale, 'Il contratto autonomo di garanzia' in F Barachini (ed), *Lezioni pisane di diritto commerciale* (Pisa, Pisa University Press, 2014) 29.

[76] See Cass 19.1.2018, no 1465, *Foro it*, 2018, I, 452.

[77] V Cass, sec un, 17.2.2017, no 4224, *Nuov giur civ comm*, 2017, 1214.

[78] See, eg the court decisions on *claims-made* insurance policies and, in particular, Cass, sez un, 24.9.2018, no 22437, *Nuova giurisprudenza civile commentata*, 2018, 78. On this matter, *cf* Sara Landini, 'The Worthiness of Claims Made Clauses in Liability Insurance Contracts' (2016) 2 *Italian Law Journal* 509.

[79] According to Art 1170 of the French Civil Code, 'toute clause qui prive de sa substance l'obligation essentielle du débiteur est réputée non écrite'. The provision was inspired by the famous *Chronopost* case, decided in the 1990s by the French Cassation Court: see Cass civ 22.10.1996, no 93-18632, *Bull civ*, IV, no 261. For more information, see S Fulli-Lemaire, 'Le rôle passé de la cause au stade de la formation du contrat Le rôle passé de la cause' in Albers et al (n 2) 407 and 419.

[80] *cf* Roppo (n 55) 345–47, who justifies this view by stating the need to avoid *dirigiste* control over private autonomy.

[81] See AM Garofalo, 'Fisiologia e patologia della *causa* contrattuale. Profili generali e applicazioni specifiche' in G Perlingieri and L Ruggeri (eds), *L'attualità del pensiero di Emilio Betti a cinquant'anni dalla scomparsa* (Naples, Edizioni Scientifiche Italiane, 2019) 681, 729–31; E Minervini, *La 'meritevolezza' del contratto. Una lettura dell'art 1322, comma 2, c.c* (Turin, Giappichelli, 2019) 46–48.

IV. The Emergence of the *Causa Concreta* in Italian Case Law

As seen, the concept of *causa concreta* has been referenced in case law related to rules on nullity and the preliminary assessment of a contract's effectiveness. Courts have also employed *causa concreta* as a tool to interpret contracts more specifically in light of the parties' interests. In such instances, judges do not follow the rules set out in section III, but instead use the notion of *causa concreta* to apply different contractual remedies. It is now essential to delve into the theoretical basis of this approach and to illustrate the types of arguments judges use with examples from case law.

A. The Theoretical Foundation: The Effectiveness of Contract Law

The increasing role of the concept of *causa* as a kind of argumentative stratagem to solve contractual disputes rests predominantly on the functional approach of Cesare Massimo Bianca, who described the *causa* as 'the practical function of the contract, the interest that the contract has to satisfy'.[82] In order to apply contractual remedies with specific normative goals, judges have first to properly understand the interests that the contract aims to fulfil. Bianca's legal thinking is not formalistic in nature; rather, it looks at the effectiveness of contractual remedies and the impact on the positions of the contracting parties.

The described approach has been adopted by Italian judges in a huge number of judgements that increasingly refer to the *causa concreta* as a way to outline the practical purpose that the parties wanted to achieve with the contract. To understand the methodology that characterises Italian case law, it is necessary to present some examples.

B. Examples of *Causa Concreta* in Case law

(i) Contractual Interpretation

The *causa concreta* plays a role in the interpretation of the contract. This practical application of the theory of the *causa concreta* aims to promote a functional interpretation in light of the contract's practical purpose.[83] Recent case law has aligned with this innovative approach, emphasising the necessary connection between the criteria for contract interpretation set forth in Articles 1362 et seq of the Civil Code and the

[82] CM Bianca, *Diritto civile*, vol 3, *Il contratto*, 3rd edn (Milan, Giuffrè, 2019) 3: 'La causa è la funzione pratica del contratto, cioè l'interesse che il contratto è diretto a soddisfare.'

[83] ibid 434, Bianca saying that 'The meaning of what the parties have agreed upon cannot be adequately determined without considering the practical reason for the transaction, that is, its *causa concreta*' (*il significato di ciò che le parti hanno concordato non può … essere adeguatamente accertato se non si tiene conto della ragione pratica dell'affare, ossia della sua causa concreta*).

achievement of the contract's practical purpose.[84] The identification of this connection, which some argue could be based on the reference to the 'nature' of the contract mentioned in Article 1369 of the Italian Civil Code,[85] has the clear merit of encouraging the interpreter to consider the contract's purpose – a requirement that is also evident in European law model rules, where reference to the 'purpose of the contract' is frequent.[86]

(ii) Supervening Impossibility

Cesare Massimo Bianca asserts that the basis for termination due to supervening impossibility is the essential importance of the performance (which has become impossible).[87] The author considers such performance crucial for the fulfilment of the contract's *causa concreta*.[88] While impossibility relates to the obligation, the *causa concreta* pertains to the contract. Any supervening event should therefore be evaluated in light of the interests that the contract was intended to satisfy. The theory of *causa concreta* connected to the supervening impossibility has also been recognised by the Court of Cassation, moving beyond earlier approaches that confined the concept of *causa* solely to the initial formation of the contractual relationship.[89] In some rulings that have sparked considerable debate among scholars, the Court of Cassation has linked the concept of *causa concreta* to the provisions of the Italian Civil Code regarding supervening impossibility.

Firstly, in the context of an 'all-inclusive' touristic package, the Court of Cassation held that the inability to use the service results in the termination of the contractual relationship due to the frustration of the *causa concreta*, in the event of a dengue hemorrhagic fever outbreak at the travel destination.[90] The Court clarified that the

[84] In particular, see Cass 22.10.2014, no 22343, *Foro it*, 2015, I, 2118, which states that the criteria for interpreting contracts as set out in the civil code must be used 'to ascertain the meaning of the agreement in accordance with its practical reason or *causa concreta*, and that any overly technical interpretation of the literal expressions that conflicts with this and renders the actual contractual purpose desired by the parties unachievable should be excluded'. For a detailed discussion, see D Achille, 'La funzione ermeneutica della *causa concreta* del contratto' [2017] *Rivista trimestrale di diritto e procedura civile* 37; D Achille, 'Metodo dell'interpretazione contrattuale e diritto effettivo' [2017] *Rivista di diritto civile* 155; see also the critical remarks by S Pagliantini, 'Le stagioni della causa in concreto e la c d interpretazione abusiva del contratto: notarelle critiche su regole e principi (del diritto dei contratti)' [2016] *Contratti* 604; observations by M D'Auria, '*Causa* in concreto, operazione economica e procedimento ermeneutico contrattuale: spunti di riflessione' [2015] *Corriere giuridico* 1382.

[85] See Roppo (n 55) 452, who connects the 'nature' of the contract to its *causa concreta*. *Contra* A Gentili, *Senso e consenso*, vol II (Turin, Giappichelli, 2016) 599.

[86] See the detailed references in GB Ferri, 'L'"invisibile" presenza della causa del contratto' [2002] *Europa e diritto privato* 897, 905–07; Achille (n 84) 60.

[87] CM Bianca, *Diritto civile*, vol 5, *La responsabilità*, 3rd edn (Milan, Giuffrè, 2021) 400.

[88] ibid.

[89] An example in this regard is the decision Cass 10.1.1964, no 53, *Giust civ*, 1964, I, 574, affirming that the requirement of *causa* must be considered fulfilled by the exchange of obligations. Subsequent non-performance or the supervening impossibility of one of the performances leads to the termination of the relationship according to principles different from those governing the element of *causa*. In the same vein, indicating that a defect concerning the *causa* results in the nullity of the contract and does not pertain to events occurring after the conclusion of the contract, see also Cass 17.5.1976, no 1738, *Rivista del diritto commerciale*, 1977, II, 341.

[90] Cass 24.7.2007, no 16315, *Foro it*, 2009, I, 214.

'touristic purpose' does not consist of interests that remain within the buyer's subjective intent, which drives them to enter into the contract, but rather becomes (even implicitly) 'objectified' in this type of contract, constituting the interest that the contract is actually designed to satisfy, thereby characterising its *causa concreta*.[91] The *causa concreta* serves to define the nature of the contract, determining the essentiality of all activities and services instrumental to achieving the primary vacation purpose – that is, the physical and psychological well-being that full enjoyment of the holiday as an opportunity for leisure and relaxation is intended to provide. Since the creditor's interest (in accordance with Article 1174 of the Italian Civil Code) can no longer be established, the performance does not become impossible, as would be required by the combined provisions of Articles 1463 and 1256 of the Italian Civil Code, but rather 'unusable'.[92]

The Court of Cassation adopted the same approach with reference to the termination of a lodging contract for two spouses at a hotel, where the supervening event was the death of one of the spouses the day before the stay was to begin.[93] The Court correctly highlighted that it was not the hotelier's performance that had become impossible, but rather its enjoyment. This led the judges to focus on the synallagmatic structure of the contract and, therefore, on the *causa concreta* of the contract. According to the judges, the *causa* assumes relevance as a criterion for 'adjusting the contractual relationship, considered in its dynamic-effective aspect',[94] allowing for consideration of events that negatively impact the creditor's interest (in this case, the touristic interest), which has been objectified within the causal element of the contract, to the extent that – based on normal criteria, considering the concrete circumstances of the case – 'it is established that its realization has become impossible'.[95]

C. Critical Assessment

In the above-described case law, the reference to the *causa* seems to pursue the goal of understanding the set of interests the contract seeks to satisfy. In this regard, the *causa concreta* might be viewed as a unifying element within the general framework of contract law – a mechanism that serves to protect the parties in situations where the exercise of private autonomy fails to achieve its intended purpose.[96] In this context, however, the *causa* does not appear indispensable; for the protection of the contracting parties, the application of ordinary rules of contractual interpretation, starting with the search for the parties' common intention, might suffice.

Indeed, it cannot be denied that arguments related to the *causa contractus* often simplify legal reasoning and lead to solutions that overlook the normative data and the

[91] ibid 214.
[92] ibid 214.
[93] Cass 20.12.2007, no 26958, *Contratti*, 2008, 786.
[94] ibid 786.
[95] ibid 787.
[96] See C Scognamiglio, 'La causa concreta: una proposta dottrinale di successo' [2020] *Rivista di diritto civile* 588.

conditions upon which certain legal effects are triggered.[97] Ultimately, judicial decisions often disregard a rigorous examination of the cases in which the legal system contemplates supervening events and defines criteria for managing contractual risk. Moreover, in legal doctrine and court judgments, the *causa concreta* frequently assumes merely a descriptive function, useful for identifying the specific interests the contract sought to realise. In this regard, the reference is certainly helpful, but in many cases, the same results achieved through reliance on the *causa concreta* could be reached by applying the ordinary principles of contract interpretation[98] or other essential elements of the contract as the subject matter (*oggetto*).[99]

By relying on a general concept like that of the *causa*, rather than examining in detail the conditions for the effectiveness of legal remedies, the judicial method reflects yet another manifestation of the phenomenon described as the 'crisis of the legal category' (*crisi della fattispecie*),[100] referring to the frequent recourse to principles or general concepts to resolve judicial cases. The most significant problem of this methodology seems to be the uncertainty regarding the outcome of judicial cases. As noted, considering the various legal institutions potentially applicable in such situations, the element of the *causa concreta* does not appear capable of providing any particular advantage.

V. Conclusion

The concept of *causa* in Italian contract law has undergone a significant evolution, distinguishing it from its French origins and shaping it into a unique element of legal discourse. Initially borrowed from French law, the Italian understanding of *causa* has diverged considerably over time. This divergence is evident not only in the textual formulation of the second Italian Civil Code of 1942, but also in the theoretical and doctrinal elaborations that have marked its development from the nineteenth century to the present day.[101]

Historically, *causa* was incorporated into the Italian Civil Code as a mechanism to control the contractual autonomy of the parties, reflecting the socio-political environment of the Fascist era. During this time, legal scholars like Emilio Betti emphasised the social function of contracts, arguing that the *causa* must align with interests deemed worthy of protection by the legal system.[102] This perspective was inherently tied to the state's role in regulating economic relationships to ensure that they served broader social purposes, thus providing a means of state intervention in private transactions.

[97] For criticism to the methodology adopted by Italian Courts with reference to *causa contractus*, see Roppo (n 5) 957; M Girolami, *L'artificio della causa contractus* (Padua, Cedam, 2012) 8ff; M Martino, 'La causa in concreto nella giurisprudenza: recenti itinerari di un nuovo *idolum fori*' [2013] *Corriere giuridico* 1441.

[98] See E Navarretta, 'Le ragioni della causa e il problema dei rimedi. L'evoluzione storica e le prospettive nel diritto europeo dei contratti' [2003] I *Rivista del diritto commerciale* 979, 989.

[99] Roppo (n 5) 964; Girolami (n 97) 40–42.

[100] N Irti, 'La crisi della fattispecie' [2014] *Rivista di diritto processuale* 36. For a different approach, see C Castronovo, *Eclissi del diritto civile* (Milan, Giuffrè, 2015); Lipari (n 5) 173. For a general overview, see G Christandl, 'Percorsi metodologici della civilistica italiana. Una breve storia a partire dal XIX secolo' [2020] *Rivista di diritto civile* 43, 62–63.

[101] See s II.A above.

[102] See s II.B above.

Betti's theory gave *causa* a socio-economic dimension, aligning private autonomy with social utility, which fitted well with the corporatist ideology of the time.

However, the concept of *causa* has gradually shifted from being an instrument of state control to one that supports contractual autonomy. This transformation has been driven by both doctrinal reinterpretations and practical applications in case law. Legal scholars have increasingly viewed *causa* as a reflection of the actual intentions and interests of the contracting parties, rather than as a state-imposed standard.[103] This shift is evident in the emergence of the notion of *causa concreta* – the practical function or purpose of a contract as defined by the parties themselves.[104] By focusing on the specific interests the contract seeks to satisfy, the Italian legal system has moved towards a more flexible and functional understanding of *causa* that respects the parties' autonomy and their freedom to shape their legal relationships. In practice, Italian courts have adopted this functional approach by using *causa concreta* to interpret contracts in light of their practical purposes.[105] The courts have applied the concept to resolve a variety of contractual disputes, particularly in cases involving supervening impossibility or the interpretation of ambiguous terms.[106]

Nevertheless, this shift towards recognising contractual autonomy has not eliminated all concerns regarding the use of *causa*. While the modern interpretation of *causa* appears to be more neutral and oriented towards facilitating the parties' intentions, there is still a risk that it could be manipulated to serve certain political or ideological ends. The concept remains sufficiently flexible to allow for varying interpretations that could potentially undermine private autonomy. For example, if courts overemphasise the social function of *causa*, they might impose value judgements that reflect contemporary moral or political ideologies, rather than strictly adhering to the parties' agreed terms.

This risk is particularly relevant in light of the ongoing efforts towards the harmonisation of European contract law. The notion of *causa* in Italian law, with its unique characteristics and historical baggage, may not easily align with the principles underlying other European legal systems that emphasise freedom of contract and predictability.[107] In fact, the flexibility and adaptability of *causa* could be seen as both a strength and a weakness – providing a useful tool for interpreting contracts in a fair and context-specific manner, while also allowing room for judicial discretion that may not always align with the principles of European harmonisation.

In conclusion, the evolution of the concept of *causa* in Italian contract law reflects a broader trend away from its origins as a tool of state control and towards a more flexible and autonomy-oriented interpretation. This shift has enhanced the concept's role in safeguarding the parties' freedom to contract and their ability to define their own legal relationships. However, the inherent flexibility of *causa* also means that it remains a

[103] See s III.C above.
[104] See s IV above.
[105] See s IV.B above.
[106] ibid.
[107] See E Hosemann, 'Freedom of Contract' in N Jansen and R Zimmermann, *Commentaries on European Contract Laws* (Oxford, Oxford University Press, 2018) 30, 49–51, discussing the symbolic function of provisions on freedom of contract within European model rules and in Art 1102 of the French Civil Code.

potentially powerful instrument that could be used to impose specific political or moral viewpoints, potentially at the expense of private autonomy and the goal of European legal harmonisation.

Ultimately, while *causa* is no longer primarily a tool for state intervention, it has not entirely shed its capacity to serve as a mechanism for judicial or political control. Its future will depend on how Italian courts and legal scholars continue to balance the need for contractual freedom with the desire to protect public interests and maintain legal certainty. As such, *causa* remains a dynamic and contested concept that reflects the ongoing tensions between autonomy and regulation, individual freedom and social control, in the evolving landscape of contract law.

PART III

Cross-Sectional Studies

11

Cause, Consideration and the Enforceability of Promises

BRUNO RODRÍGUEZ-ROSADO

I. Formalism, Causalism and Consensualism: The Formation of Three Contractual Schemes

A. The Roman Formalistic System

Gaius' well-known classification of Roman types of contract divided them into real, verbal, literal and consensual, depending on whether they were perfected by delivery, by the use of certain words, by the fact of being in writing or by the mere exchange of consents (Gai. 3,89). Contrary to what might be supposed, given the existence of various possible contractual forms, the system was characterised by its formalistic nature: consensual contracts constituted a closed list, so that, as a rule, the mere exchange of consents did not give rise to a contract, but to a mere pact or agreement which did not produce obligations. Apart from real or literal contracts (also formal in themselves, but limited in their application), the most common way of producing an obligation was through the verbal contract, the stipulation; its mere formality permitted the parties to bind themselves.[1]

B. The Medieval Alliance between Causalism and Consensualism

The authors of medieval civil law inherited this system and did not feel legitimised to change it. A mere promise (*the promissio simplex*) was not enough to bind the promisor,

[1] On the classification of Roman contractual types, see M Kaser, *Das römische Privatrecht*, vol I (Munich, CH Beck, 1971) 524–27.

it needed a *stipulatio*, now transformed into a written document.[2] However, the authors of canon law took the opposite view. They were not bound by Roman texts, but rather by the authority of Holy Scripture and their own sources. The Gospel of Matthew had established the obligation to keep one's word without the need for it to be reinforced by oaths or formulas (Matt. 5,37), and theologians accordingly abided by the conscientious obligation to fulfil any promise.[3] Consequently, a simple promise was sufficient to bind the promisor without the need for any form, and a special action, called a *condictio ex canone*, was granted to enforce performance. This is what Johannes Teutonicus defended, and his view was followed by later decretalists, such as Bernard of Pavia and Cardinal Hostiensis.[4]

This led to a serious divergence between civil law, faithful to the Roman principle of *ex nudo pacto non oritur actio* (a naked agreement does not beget an action), and canon law, which asserted the opposite. And the divergence threatened to spread to the civil world, as the canonical doctrine began to gain ground. Castile adopted this latter system in 1348; and commercial practice was also favourable to that freedom of form.[5]

Baldus de Ubaldis tried to approximate the two positions. Ever since Roman law, it had been stated that the *stipulatio* could be paralysed with an exception (*exceptio doli*, and in case of loan *exceptio non nummeratae pecuniae*) if the cause for the promise was non-existent. The cause was therefore an element that contributed to reinforce the Roman *stipulatio*. Baldus thought that the canonical doctrine would be more acceptable for civil lawyers if the obligatory character of the simple promise was reinforced by a cause, by a reasonable motive that lent obligatory force to the promise: in the same way that the stipulation would only be binding in civil law if it were supported by a cause, in canon law a simple promise would only be binding if it had a cause.[6] His point of view was accepted by canonists, and the cause, adopted from the *stipulatio*, thus became a necessary element of the canonical *promissio simplex*.[7] Later, from the beginning of the sixteenth century, this canonical point of view was accepted in the civil world as well, so that the idea was consolidated in the various European legal systems that the simple agreement, without the need for form, and provided that it was supported by a cause, was sufficient to bind the parties. Even innominate contracts, for which Baldo had preserved the real character, were now understood as consensual.[8] The rule *ex nudo*

[2] A Söllner, 'Die causa im Kondiktionen- und Vertragsrecht des Mittelalters bei den Glossatoren, Kommentatoren und Kanonisten' (1960) 77 *Savigny Zeitschrift – Romanistische Abteilung*, 182, 212; R Zimmermann, *The Law of Obligations* (Oxford, Oxford University Press, 1996) 538–45, 551.

[3] See extensively JP de Oliveira Geraldes, 'Sobre equidade, causa e promessa simples' [2022] *Revista de Direito Comercial* 102-5-07, with texts by Thomas Aquinas and other authors. More briefly, Söllner (n 2) 241–42. See also ch 2 in this book , by JP de Oliveira, 22–23.

[4] See the texts in Söllner (n 2) 243–44; see also H Dilcher, 'Der Typenzwang im Mittelalterlichen Vertragsrecht' (1960) 77 *Savigny Zeitschrift – Romanistische Abteilung* 281, 284.

[5] For Castile, see Ordenamiento de Alcalá, Title XVI, single rule (Lex 'Paresciendo').

[6] Baldo's main texts are found in his commentary on the canon Antigonus (X. 1,35,1), the passage that fundamentally supported the actionability of the naked agreements in canon law: Baldo de Ubaldi, *ad tres priores libros decretalium commentaria* (first published Lyon, 1585; Aalen, Scientia Verlag, 1970) 122.

[7] Söllner (n 2) 254–56; Dilcher (n 4) 300; M Schermaier, 'Die Rolle der causa bei der Überwindung des Typenswangs durch die mittelalterlichen Juristen' in G Albers, F Patti and D Perrouin-Verbe (eds), *Causa contractus. Auf der Suche nach den Bedingungen der Wirksamkeit des vertraglichen Willens* (Tübingen, Mohr Siebeck, 2022) 139. Also ch 2 in this volume, by JP de Oliveira, 20–24.

[8] Several of Baldo's texts exclude the possibility of unnamed contracts being perfected by mere agreement, as was the case with the promise. Perhaps the clearest is the following, taken from his commentary on

pacto non oritur actio was transformed, since *nudo pacto* was no longer understood as that which lacked a stipulatory form, but that which lacked a cause.[9] This point of view was taken up by Grotius and Domat: the mere agreement of wills is binding as long as it is supported by a reasonable motive, which may even be the intention to donate.[10] The alliance between consent and cause had succeeded in defeating the need for form.

C. The Conflict between Causalism and Consensualism

The defeat of formalism eventually led to the confrontation between consensualism and causalism.[11] On the one hand, a series of authors emerged, such as Pufendorf, Thomasius and Wolff, who understood that, once the formalism of the Roman types of contract disappears, the demand for cause loses its meaning. Mere consensus will be obligatory, whatever its reason, and without the need for a cause to justify it.[12]

On the other hand, another group of authors emerged, headed by Connanus, who understood that mere consent is not binding unless it is reinforced by a cause, now understood as counter-performance. Certainly, Baldus de Ubaldis and his followers had taken for the enforceability of the promise in canon law the cause of the *stipulatio*, any reasonable motive, even the mere motivation of giving or favouring. But the Roman jurists also spoke of cause in relation to other transactions, the innominate contracts. These were agreements whereby the parties undertook to exchange goods or services, but which only became binding once one of the parties had fulfilled the agreement. This performance was also called cause, and it was therefore said that unnamed contracts only became binding once they had a cause.[13] Thus, in a more mercantilist society, these authors preferred to understand that the cause required for the promise to become obligatory was not that of the stipulation, but rather that of the innominate contracts,

Justinian's code: 'Sed contra opponitur, quod immo agitur ex nudo pacto ut extra de pactis cap 1 (X. 1,35,1) et sic videtur, quod ista lex corrigitur per ius canonicum. Solutio: non corrigitur haec lex, quia illud capitulum loquitur in nuditate respectu solennitatis verborum, non respectu causae. Unde omnia iura civilia, quae loquutur de contractibus innominatis, habent etiam locum de iure canonico. Unde contractus innominati etiam de iure canonico non pariunt actiones, nisi per implementum, ut numero extra, de electione, canon cum inter R seniorem [X. 1,6,16]' (Baldus de Ubaldis, in primum, secundum et tertium codicis librum, num 4 ad C. 2,4,28, in *Commentaria Omnia*, vol V (first published Venetiis, 1591; Goldbach, Keip Verlag, 2004) 124 r. As will be discussed later, the performance of one of the parties was considered the cause in these unnamed contracts, and therefore no cause existed until one party performed it.

[9] A Guzmán Brito, 'Causa del contrato y causa de la obligación en la dogmática de los juristas romanos, medievales y modernos y en la codificación europea y americana' (2001) 21 *Revista de Estudios Histórico-Jurídicos* 209, 306. See also Söllner (n 2) 263.

[10] H Grotius, *Inleiding tot de Hollandsche Rechts-geleertheyd*, III,51 (RW Lee (trans), *Introduction to the Jurisprudence of Holland*, vol I (first published Oxford, Oxford University Press, 1953; Aalen, 1977) 305ff). J Domat, *Les loix civiles dans leur ordre naturel*, Première partie, Livre premier, Titre I, s 1, 4–6 (Paris, 1745) 20.

[11] On that, see T Mayer-Maly, 'Der Konsens als Grundlage des Vertrages' in H Hübner (ed), *Festschrift für Erwin Seidl* (Cologne, Peter Hanstein Verlag, 1975) 124–25.

[12] On this line of thinking, see KP Nanz, *Die Entstehung des allgemeinen Vertragsbegriffs im 16. bis 18. Jahrhundert* (Munich, Schweitzer, 1985) 140ff.

[13] The fundamental text in this respect was one by Aristo and Ulpianus, D. 2,14,7,2–4. On that text, see Kaser (n 1) 526, fn 36; Zimmermann (n 2) 549–50; F Gallo, 'Ai primordi del passaggio della sinallagmaticità dal piano delle obbligazioni a quello delle prestazioni' in A Burdese (ed), *Le dottrine del contratto nella giurisprudenza romana* (Padua, Cedam, 2006) 159ff and 172ff; M Schermaier, 'Kausalität oder Finalität? Überlegungen zur causa in Ulpian D. 2,14,7' in T Finkenauer and B Sirks (eds), *Interpretationes Iuris Antiqui. Dankesgabe für Shigeo Nishimura* (Wiesbaden, Harrassowitz Verlag, 2018) 293ff.

and that only a counter-performance justified a promise.[14] The cause of the donation (*causa donationis*) would be too weak for that, so the Romans demanded a stipulation to strengthen it. A similar development took place in English common law, so that in that system too the idea became established that a promise not supported by a counter-performance did not produce an obligation.[15]

The doctrine supported by the authors who dispensed with the cause and defended the sufficiency of the exchange of consents to create the obligation was consolidated in the Central European Civil Codes, such as the Austrian Allgemeines Bürgerliches Gesetzbuch, the German bürgerliches Gesetzbuch (BGB) and the Swiss Code of Obligations, but also in the now repealed Portuguese Civil Code of 1965 and in the Dutch Civil Code of 1992. They do not mention cause as a requirement for the existence of a contract, and therefore seem to accept the obligatory nature of the donation and of the mere unilateral declaration intended to create an obligation.

Pothier instead followed the causalist doctrine. In his well-known Treatise on the Law of Obligations, he required the concurrence of a cause to give rise to the contract, he did not appear to include donation among these causes and he did not consider the mere unilateral will to be bound as a way of creating an obligation.[16] His point of view was followed by the Napoleonic Civil Code, and from there it was extended to other codes, such as the Italian Code of 1865 or the Spanish Code of 1889, which also require the concurrence of a cause for the contract to arise and seemed to reject the sufficiency of the *causa donationis* to create an obligation.[17] Certainly, there is a debate in these legal systems about the concept of cause, and cause is sometimes used as the common intention of the parties in entering into the contract; however, the precedents of the French Civil Code, and Article 1274 of the Spanish Civil Code itself, which reproduces these precedents almost verbatim, clearly indicate that the concept of cause corresponds primarily to that of counter-performance.[18] This point of view, albeit through a totally

[14] On this doctrinal current, see U Petronio, 'Sinallagma e analisi strutturale dei contratti all'origine del sistema contrattuale romano' in J Barton (ed), *Towards a General Law of Contract* (Berlin, Duncker & Humblot, 1990) 215.

[15] See B Häcker 'Causa und consideration – ein historisches Dialog' in Albers et al (n 7) 340; see also J Gordley, *Foundations of Private Law* (Oxford, Oxford University Press, 2007) 288; but see DJ Ibbetson, 'Consideration and the Theory of Contract in Sixteenth Century Common Law' in Barton (n 14) 67ff, who supports the idea that in 16th century consideration was already observed as a counter-performance (or antecedent duty owed by the promisor) which justified the obligation. See also ch 3 in this book, by DJ Ibbetson, 36–42.

[16] The issue, however, is controversial: in the list of causes, Pothier cites the cause of beneficence, but then does not cite donation among the contracts of beneficence. If one also takes into account that he maintains the real and non-consensual character for most of these charitable or gratuitous contracts, it would be surprising if he accepted its consensual character for the donation (purely lucrative, without any counter-performance). See Pothier, *Traité des obligations* (Paris, Debure, 1761) nos 10, 12 and 41.

[17] The authors of the French Civil Code, at Napoleon's proposal, expressly refused to classify donations as contracts, as the First Consul considered that only acts with reciprocal performances could be classified as such. As Fenet states, 'le Premier Consul dit que le contrat impose des charges mutuelles aux deux contratants; qu'ainsi cette expresión ne peut convenir a la donation', and his proposal was accepted by the Conseil d'Etat: PA Fenet, *Recueil Complet des Travaux Préparatoires du Code civil*, vol XII (Paris, 1827) 261, 263.

[18] In his presentation of the Draft Code to the legislature, Bigot-Préameneu stated that 'In n'y a point d'obligation sans cause: elle est dans l'intérêt réciproque des parties ou dans la bienfaisance de l'une d'elles' (there is no obligation without cause: it lies in the reciprocal interest of the parties or in the benefit of one of them): Fenet, *Recueil Complet*, vol XIII (Paris, 1827) 228. The 'cause de bienfaisance' is that relating to so-called 'contrats de bienfaisance' (Art 1105 of the original version of the Napoleonic Code: gratuitous contracts), which include mandate, loan, bailment and deposit, but not donation, which, as seen in the previous footnote, does not constitute a contract for the French Code.

different evolution, was also followed by English law, in which the idea was consolidated that mere consent was not enough to be bound, but that it required a consideration, understood as a counter-performance, even if merely nominal, that would justify the arising of the obligation.

Apparently, therefore, two contractual systems coexist in Europe, one which I have called *consensualist* and the other *causalist*, depending on whether they consider the will to be a sufficient means of creating obligations or require that it be supported by an adequate cause. If we consider that, in the reform of the French Civil Code of 2016, all mention of the cause has disappeared, and that this element really emerged as an instrument to overcome an already abandoned formalism, it could be thought that causalism's days are numbered and that the consent of the parties is now the only requirement to create an obligation. But this diagnosis is perhaps premature: even the countries that seem to have renounced the requirement of cause continue to take into account its strength and consistency when it comes to creating an obligation.[19]

II. The Lack of Cause or Consideration and the Rejection of the Purely Consensual Donation

A. Donation in Typically Causalist Systems: England and Spain

Having presented the contrast between causalist and consensualist systems, depending on whether or not a causal element (cause or consideration) is required for the agreement to be binding, it must be said that the two European legal systems that most clearly embody causalism today are those of England and Spain. It is true that the English concept of consideration and the Spanish concept of cause are not similar: the English term *consideration* refers to the counter-performance or counter-promise required for a contractual obligation to arise, whereas the continental institution of the *causa*, inherited in Spain, refers certainly also to that (cause in the objective sense), but at the same time, and without the need to take into account many nuances, to the common intention that leads the parties to enter into a contract (cause in the subjective sense).[20] However, despite these differences, both systems can be called causalist, or, if preferred, 'considerationist', since in both, for an obligation to arise by mere consent, a counter-performance or counter-promise is required.[21] If I am inclined not to include

[19] See ch 7 in this book, by Olivier Deshayes.

[20] The most common definition of consideration describes it as being either a detriment to the promisee (in that he gives value) or a benefit to the promisor (in that he receives value): see E McKendrick 'Contract: In General' in A Burrows (ed), *Principles of the English Law of Obligations* (Oxford, Oxford University Press, 2015) 1.33. A very classic definition given by *Currie v Misa* (1875) LR 10 Ex 153, 162: 'A valuable consideration, in the sense of the law, may consist either in some right, interest, profit, or benefit accruing to the one party, or some forbearance, detriment, loss, or responsibility, given, suffered, or undertaken by the other.' See also E Peel, *Treitel: The Law of Contract*, 15th edn (London, Sweet & Maxwell, 2020) para 3-004. On the concept of cause, and this objective and subjective sense, see for France, prior to the abolition of the case in 2016, J Carbonnier, *Droit civil – Les obligations*, 22nd edn (Paris, PUF, 2000) para 58; P Malaurie and L Aynès, *Droit des obligations*, 7th edn (Paris, LGDJ, 2015) para 621; for Spain, L Díez-Picazo and A Gullón, *Sistema de Derecho civil*, vol II-1, 10th edn (Madrid, Tecnos, 2012) 36.

[21] On the relationship between the doctrines of cause and consideration, see Zimmermann (n 2) 504–07.

the Italian or Belgian legal systems among the causalists for these purposes, in spite of their requirement for a cause, it is precisely because its function in these systems has more to do with the control of legality or reasonableness of the transaction than with the counter-performance that justifies the obligation.[22]

Having clarified the question of ascription, it is logical that those causalist systems refuse to attribute obligatory force to a mere consensual promise of donation: the lack of counter-performance must exclude its obligatory character. This is clearly the case in English law, which denies binding force to the promise of donation precisely because of its lack of consideration. It is obligatory only if it is done 'under seal' (in a deed).[23] Here, form replaces lack of consideration.

Spanish law also rejects that a donation agreement can be obligatory. This does not only depend on the fact that the Spanish Civil Code requires that the donation, if it is of immovable property, must be recorded in a public document, and if it is of movable property, it must be made in writing or with delivery of the thing (Articles 632 and 633 of the Spanish Civil Code). Rather, it is a consequence of the fact that the donation in the Spanish legal system is a dispositive transaction, by means of which ownership is instantly transferred, without giving rise in any case to an obligation to transfer in the future.[24] This has been repeatedly affirmed by the Spanish Supreme Court, which has denied effectiveness to obligatory documents of donation, even public documents.[25]

B. Donation in Consensualist Systems: Germany and France

If what I have called consensualism were coherent, it would have to accept the obligatory force of the donation, without demanding any additional requirement with respect to the rest of the contracts, given that the existence of cause or consideration, understood as counter-performance, does not change the nature of the transaction. What is surprising, however, is that the consensualist legal systems impose special formal requirements on it.

This is the case in German law, where its consensual system finds its Achilles heel in the donation. Here, consent is not sufficient; § 518 BGB states that a notarial deed is required. If this is missing, only the handing over, according to the second paragraph,

[22] See Arts 1343–45 of the Italian Civil Code and Arts 5.53–5.56 of the new Belgian Civil Code.

[23] J Cartwright, *Contract Law*, 3rd edn (Oxford, Hart Publishing, 2016) 132; McKendrick (n 20) 1.31.

[24] J Ataz, 'Sobre la obligatoriedad de las promesas gratuitas aceptadas' in J Ataz and CL García (eds), *Estudios sobre la modernización del Derecho de obligaciones y contatos* (Pamplona, Aranzadi, 2019) 84ff; JM Miquel 'Donaciones en convenio regulador' in P Abad (ed), *Derecho de familia – homenaje a Encarnación Roca Trias* (Madrid, Sepin, 2021) 320ff. However, it should not be forgotten that other authors are now in favour of admitting a donation of obligatory effects: P Castaños, *La donación obligacional* (Madrid, Reus, 2021); JL Arjona, 'El precontrato de donación: consideraciones sobre su posibilidad o imposibilidad en el Derecho civil español' (2022) 75 *Anuario de Derecho civil* 839. The last author recognised, however, that the common opinion in Spain is against the validity of the obligatory donation (915).

[25] Judgment of the Supreme Court of 10 May 2019 (no 265/2019) in a promise of donation in a public deed (later revoked). Also, among the most recent, see Supreme Court judgments of 22 June 1982 (no 303/1982), 24 January 2008 (no 8/2008) and 31 March 2011 (no 217/2011). All these decisions refer to a decision of 6 June 1908 (Jurisprudencia civil, 1908-2, no 84) which denied the effectiveness of a promise of donation. An exception appears to be the Supreme Court decision of 6 April 1979 (no 132/1979), which does accept a donation with binding effect; however, the judgment has not been reiterated.

can validate the transaction. In spite of the theoretical consensualism, where there is no sufficient cause, counter-performance, form must now come to the rescue of consent.

The development in France marks its own evolution from causalism to consensualism and, at the same time, it demonstrates that, despite this slippage, the concurrence of counter-performance determines the very value of consent. The French Civil Code, as much or more than the Spanish Civil Code, to which the former served as a model, contained sufficient elements to reject the possibility of a donation with obligatory effects, since it neither attributed a contractual nature to the donation nor admitted that it concerned future assets.[26] However, since the publication of the French Civil Code, French doctrine has preferred to reduce or reinterpret these legal data, admitting the contractual nature of the donation and minimising the importance of causality.[27] As a result, it was soon accepted that the donation could have binding effect, provided that it was recorded in a public document. The disappearance of the cause and the purely consensual characterisation of the contract brought about by the reform of the Code in 2016 has not altered this situation.[28] Italian law, whose conception of cause will be discussed later, also admit the obligatory effect of the donation, but also requires it to be recorded in a public deed.[29]

As can be seen, the three contractual systems I have introduced above – formal, consensual and causal – are not as distant from each other as might seem. Causalism should exclude obligatory donation, but at least in England, it relies on form to achieve obligatory force. Consensualism should protect it without any further requirements; but it is very likely that even in Germany the cause carries more weight than its doctrine is prepared to admit (after all, the cause is nothing more than the justification for the patrimonial detachment, always more reasonable as counter-performance than as liberal intention), and for this reason it also ends up resorting to the help of form, requiring its support when the contract implies an impoverishment without any counter-performance whatsoever. Only Spain, with its absolute rejection of obligatory donation, seems to have taken causalism on this point to its ultimate consequences.

III. Cause and Consideration as the Basis for the Distinction between Onerous and Gratuitous Contracts

Savigny, in a well-known text, declared that the distinction between onerous and gratuitous contracts does not refer to the legal side of the transaction, but only to its intended external purpose.[30] Certainly, that distinction being based only in the nature of the

[26] On the qualification of the donation as an act and not as a contract in Art 894 of the French Civil Code, see n 17. The prohibition of future assets is contained in Art 943.

[27] Thus, the prohibition of the donation of future assets was understood as a refusal of a donation whose effectiveness remains in the hands of the donor: C Demolombe, *Cours de Code Napoléon*, vol XX (Paris, Durand-Hachette, 1868) paras 373ff; M Planiol and G Ripert, *Traité pratique de Droit civil français* (Paris, LGDJ, 1957) paras 438.

[28] S Piédelièvre, *Succession et libéralites* (Paris, Larcier, 2014) para 508; F Terré, Y Lequette and S Gaudemet, *Les successions, les libéralités*, 5th edn (Paris, Dalloz, 2024) para 525.

[29] Arts 769 and 782 of the Codice civile.

[30] FC von Savigny, *Das obligationenrecht*, vol II (Berlin, Veit, 1853) § 52, 13.

transaction counter-performance (cause), it would have no transcendence in a non-causalist system. The point is that, in spite of this, the distinction between gratuitous and onerous acts still plays a role in Germany, and in any legal system: we can point out a number of consequences which, in one way or another, are related to the distinction between onerous and gratuitous contracts.[31]

1. First of all, as regards the capacity of the party performing the act, almost all legal systems require a higher capacity or a special authorisation to perform gratuitous acts. However, special capacity requirements are not required by law for onerous contracts.[32]
2. With regard to the interpretation of contracts, it is established that onerous contracts should be interpreted in the manner that more fairly reconciles the interest of the parties, while gratuitous contracts should be interpreted in favour of the lesser transfer of rights.[33]
3. Liability for legal defects and for material defects of the transferred thing occurs either only in onerous legal acts (which seems to me more appropriate) or also in gratuitous legal acts, such as donation, but then in a reduced form.[34]
4. Onerous acts enjoy a greater degree of firmness than gratuitous acts. Thus, the former, apart from special cases linked to the protection of the consumer or the weaker party, can generally be revoked only in case of mutual consent of the contracting parties. In the case of non-onerous transactions, on the other hand, such as in the case of donation, there are a large number of grounds for revocation.[35]

[31] On the distinction of gratuitous and onerous contracts in general, see JP Dawson, *Gifts and Promises: Continental and American Law Compared* (New Haven, Yale University Press, 1980); in relation to Spain, JM Prada, 'La onerosidad y gratuidad de los actos jurídicos' (1968) 16 *Anales de la Academia Matritense del Notariado* 255; in Germany, W Lorenz, 'Entgeltliche und unentgeltliche Geschäfte' in *Festschrift für Max Rheinstein II* (Tübingen, Mohr, 1969) 547–68; JD Harke, *Freigiebigkeit und Haftung* (Würzburg, Ergon, 2006).

[32] In Germany, for example, the BGB requires special authorisation for gifts of marital property (§ 1425), for donations made by the parents in representation of their child (§ 1641) and for donations or gratuitous dispositions by the guardian (§§ 1799 and 1854); and the executor is strictly limited in their ability to make gratuitous dispositions (§ 2205). According to French law, the legal representatives of a minor may not perform gratuitous acts (Arts 387-2 and 509 of the Code civil) and one spouse may not, without the consent of the other, dispose of marital community property gratuitously (Art 1422). In Spain, the guardian needs judicial authorisation to perform gratuitous acts (Art 287.3 of the Código civil), and gratuitous acts on marital property without the consent of both spouses are void (Art 1378).

[33] Thus, for Italian law, Art 1371 of the Codice civile, and for Spanish law, Art 1289 of the Código civil.

[34] The liability of the donor for legal or material defects of the thing is excluded, in general, in Spain (Art 638 of Código civil) and in France (according to Malaurie and Brenner, 'à la difference du vendeur, le donateur n'est pas tenu de garantir le donataire: c'est là une conséquence de la gratuité, si évidente, qu'aucun texte ne l'énonce': P Malaurie and C Brenner, *Droit des succesions et des libéralités* (Paris, LGDJ, 2020) para 355; Piédelièvre (n 28) para 520), whereas it is limited to cases where the donor knew about the defects and concealed them from the donee in Germany (§§ 523 and 524 BGB) and in Italy (Arts 797–98 of the Codice civile).

[35] Thus, in French law, although the reform of donations in 2007 has reduced the grounds for revocation, the Civil Code continues to allow revocation on account of the non-performance of the burdens under which it was made, on account of ingratitude, and, to a limited extent, on account of the occurrence of the birth of children (Arts 953ff of the Code civil); German, Italian and Spanish law also allow the revocation of donations in a number of cases (§§ 527, 528 and 530 BGB, Arts 800ff of the Codice civile, Arts 644ff of the Código civil respectively).

5. In insolvency proceedings, gratuitous acts or gratuitous benefits are much easier to challenge as they are considered directly detrimental to creditors, whereas onerous contracts require proof of detriment.[36]
6. The protection afforded to the person acquiring from a non-owner, based in the case of movable property on good faith, and in the case of immovable property on the protection offered by the land registry, extends more firmly to onerous acts than to those of a gratuitous nature.[37] Even in those legal systems where this is not directly the case, such as in Germany, enrichment actions of the person who lost the property have a wider effect on gratuitous acts than on onerous ones.[38]
7. In matters of inheritance, and for the purpose of determining the compulsory share in the case of forced heirs, donations and lucrative transactions are counted among the assets of the inheritance, whereas assets transferred by onerous contracts are not considered for this purpose.[39]
8. Finally, in matrimonial property regimes, assets acquired by the contracting parties by onerous contracts are not treated in the same way as assets received by way of donation. Generally speaking, the former are part of the matrimonial community, whereas the donated assets belong to the spouse to whom they have been donated.[40]

IV. Onerous, Gratuitous and Lucrative Acts and their Consensualisation

Up to now, I have preferred to speak of a distinction, which is very common in legal doctrine, between onerous and gratuitous acts, including the donation within the latter. But I recognise that, in relation to the cause, and as many other authors, typically Capitant, have defended, the distinction between acts must rather be threefold or tripartite, between onerous, gratuitous and lucrative acts.[41]

By onerous contracts, I mean those in which there is an interest on both sides, which is legally embodied in the existence of an exchange of various benefits. This is the case with purchase and sale, lease or exchange. In them, as Domat said, the cause of each obligation lies in the obligation of the other party.[42]

[36] See, eg Arts 238 and 423 of the British Insolvency Act 1986; § 134 of the German Insolvenz Ordnung; Arts L632-1 and L632-2 of the French Commercial Code; Art 2901 of the Codice civile; Arts 1291 and 1297 of the Código civil.

[37] This is the case in Spain for acquisitions resulting from the effect of the land registry (Art 34 of the Spanish Land Registry Act).

[38] Thus, in Germany, § 816 BGB states that 'If an unauthorised person disposes over an object and the disposition is effective in relation to the authorised person, then they are obliged to surrender to the authorised person the benefit obtained by the disposition. If the disposition is gratuitous, then the same duty applies to a person who as a result of the disposition directly gains a legal advantage.'

[39] See for France, Arts 913 and 919-1 of the Code civil; for Germany, § 2325 BGB; for Italy, Art 556 of the Codice civile; for Spain, Art 818 of the Código civil.

[40] Thus, Art 1405 of the Code civil; § 1374 BGB; Art 1346 of the Código civil; Art 179 of the Codice civile.

[41] H Capitant, *De la cause des obligations* (Paris, Dalloz, 1923) 6; for a historical perspective, see J Michel *Gratuité en droit roman* (Brussels, Université Libre de Bruxelles, 1962) 293, 300.

[42] J Domat, *Les loix civiles dans leur ordre naturel*, Part 1, Book 1, Title I, s 1, 5 (Paris, 1745) 20.

By gratuitous contracts, I mean those in which there is a benefit for one party, to whom a favour is done, but without detriment to the property of the other. This is the case with commodatum, gratuitous loan or mandate. In all of them, the party not interested in the contract favours the other, but without corresponding financial impoverishment. If their estate is deprived of an asset, as in the case of a loan of money, they are compensated by a credit that will be the object of future collection. Theoretically, there is no enrichment or impoverishment of either of the contracting parties, although it is true that one of them is favoured. As Domat said, these contracts are functionally bilateral, as the obligation of one party is anticipated in order to constitute the obligation of the other party. From a causal point of view, the performance of one party finds its cause in the promise of repayment made by the other party.

By lucrative acts, I mean those in which there is a single performance, typically a donation. In these cases, there is only an impoverishment of one party, parallel to the enrichment of the other. As there is no counter-performance, their cause is considered too weak to give rise to an obligation by itself, and requires a formal complement. They are acts much closer in nature to a legacy or inheritance than to a bilateral contract.

The different structures in relation to the cause of these three types of acts explains the different evolutions they have undergone in relation to the requirements for their conclusion. As seen above, there is a historical trend towards the consensualisation of contracts: but this tendency operates at different rates, depending on the counter-performance of each contract.

As is well known, Roman jurists accepted the consensual nature of only a limited number of contracts. Among them, most were onerous (sale, lease, society). Only the mandate, then always gratuitous, was included among the consensual contracts, and even that with certain limitations.[43] The other contracts were essentially real contracts, requiring for their conclusion the delivery or performance of what was promised. Donation was not even considered a contract.

During the modern age, an evolution took place which led to the acceptance of the consensual nature of all onerous contracts: the existence of a counter-performance in them led to the acceptance of the consensualisation of unnamed real contracts (of the type *do ut des, do ut facias, facio ut facias*). In these, the existence of the counter-performance restricted the risks of a hasty conclusion, and no special formal requirements were therefore required.[44] On the other hand, the category of named real contracts (gratuitous loan, loan for use, deposit) remained alien to consensualisation: in these transactions, one of the parties was doing a favour to the other, and although he did not suffer a definitive impoverishment (the favoured party had to return what he had received), it did not seem appropriate to impose performance against his will.[45]

[43] The withdrawal of the agent was always allowed under certain conditions: Paul. D. 17,1,22,11; Herm. D. 17,1, 25; Inst. 3,26,11.

[44] H Coing, *Europäisches Privatrecht*, vol I (Munich, Beck, 1985) 399ff.

[45] H Coing, *Europäisches Privatrecht*, vol II (Munich, Beck, 1989) 435; for the loan, see Zimmermann (n 2) 164.

Most European Civil Codes received this doctrine of the non-obligatory nature of gratuitous contracts prior to their performance by one of the parties.[46] However, it cannot be concealed that over the course of the last 100 years a doctrinal tendency towards consensualisation has been felt in almost all continental legal systems, and that the very concept of the real contract has fallen into crisis.[47]

English law, on the other hand, has remained on the fringes of this last movement and, at least where such contracts are gratuitous, it stands firm on their real character. In this way, and remaining faithful to its own history, English law has arrived at a fairly coherent contractual systemisation, based on consideration: onerous contracts are consensual and directly binding; gratuitous contracts keep their real character; while the donation, in which one party suffers a diminution of property, requires particular formal requirements.[48] The thought that any contractual liability must be based on a price or on reliance, but not on mere promise, and that no one can be obliged to a favour, underlies the whole system.[49]

V. The Dangerous Role of the Cause as a Control for the Reasonableness of the Contract

So far, I have spoken of cause and consideration as the counter-performance that justifies the enforceability of the promises that integrate the contract. As is known, there is another concept of cause, related not to the obligation, but to the whole agreement, the common purpose sought by the parties with the contract. This concept has more to do with the legality of the contract, and will therefore be dealt with in the following chapter. But there is still another concept of cause, very widespread in Italian doctrine, but also in Spain, which is closely related to the enforceability of contracts: cause will be the socio-economic function that the contract fulfils and that justifies its protection by the legal system. This definition of cause has its origins in Scialoja and Betti, and found particular acceptance in the Italian Civil Code of 1942.

According to this approach, the cause will serve to analyse the utility of the contract from the socio-economic point of view. To give some examples, the cause of a sale will be the transfer of goods in exchange for a sum of money, and that of a lease will be the delivery of goods in exchange for a rent. Named contracts are so because the legal

[46] This was the case in Germany in the original version of § 607 relating to simple loan, which is nowadays drafted according to the consensual principle. The real vision is still to be seen in §§ 598 and 688, which deal with the loan of use and the deposit. In France, the real character of the loan of use, the simple loan and the deposit can clearly be seen in Arts 1875, 1892 and 1915 of the Code civil. In Spain, the real character of these contracts is observed in Arts 1740, 1753 and 1758 of the Código civil. The same is true in Italy, in Arts 1766, 1803 and 1813 of the Codice civile.

[47] In general, see Zimmermann (n 2) 165; for Germany, HKK//Meyer-Pritzl, §§ 607–09, paras 19, 49–50; for Spain, L Díez-Picazo, *Fundamentos de Derecho civil patrimonial*, vol I (Pamplona, Civitas, 2007) 167; for France, and although the 2016 reform maintains the concept of a real contract in Art 1109 of the Code civil, see F Terré, P Simler, Y Lequette and F Chénedé, *Les obligations* (Paris, Dalloz, 2022) paras 211 and 213. Only Italy does not seem to question the real character of gratuitous contracts: A Trabucchi, *Instituzioni di Diritto civile* (Milan, Cedam, 2022) para 79.

[48] McKendrick (n 20) 1.32; Peel (n 20) 3-169 and 3-170.

[49] See PS Atiya, *The Rise and Fall of Freedom of Contract* (Oxford, Oxford University Press, 1979) 1, 689.

system has considered their cause to be useful and worthy of approval, and has therefore regulated them. Unnamed contracts do not enjoy this privilege, and it will therefore be necessary to examine in each case whether the objective purpose sought by them deserves the protection of the legal system.[50]

It cannot be denied that the explanation is clear, and this concept of cause can help to solve certain problems. For example, it has been widely used to justify the rejection of fiduciary transactions, relating to the transfer of property for security or administration purposes, which are always problematic: given that there are typical mandate or security contracts that fulfil the function of these fiduciary transfers without the risks they entail, there is no cause or socio-economic justification for their approval.[51]

But the problems with this explanation are wide-ranging. On the one hand, although the concept of cause as a socio-economic function may be useful, the truth is that it has nothing to do with the whole historical development of the institution.[52] Furthermore – and this is fundamental – this conception of cause entails a serious limitation of contractual freedom. If the cause is the function that the contract fulfils and whose recognition by the legal system gives it binding force, it will result in the parties having to justify its usefulness for each atypical contract. The control of contracts will no longer be concerned only with their legality, but also with their reasonableness. Judges and courts might not grant protection to a contract, not because it is illegal or immoral, but simply because it is, in their view, unnecessary or unreasonable, since there are other parallel means to achieve the same end. As can be understood, this would introduce a serious limitation to contractual freedom, since this, in my opinion, should be limited by the law, morality or the rights of third parties, but not by abstract criteria of the contract's reasonableness.[53]

[50] Accordingly, Art 1322, second paragraph of the Codice civile provides that 'the parties may conclude contracts that do not belong to the types having a particular discipline, provided that they are aimed at realising interests worthy of protection according to the legal system'.

[51] Both the Italian and Spanish doctrines approach the problem of these fiduciary transactions from the point of view of the cause, and treat the lack of cause as a socio-economic function. See R Sacco and G de Nova, *Il contratto*, vol I (Turin, Utet, 1993) 673–74; G Galicia Aizpurua, *Causa y garantía fiduciaria* (Valencia, Tirant, 2012) 127ff.

[52] See Sacco and de Nova (n 51) 641ff.

[53] See G Albers, 'Why Cause of Contract Again and How?' in Albers et al (n 7) 7; AM Garofalo and FP Patti, 'La causa tra fisiologia e patología del contratto' in Albers et al (n 7) 477–80. In this context, it cannot be overlooked that the Italian Civil Code of 1942 accepted such a concept of cause precisely because of the restrictive ideology of freedom that lays behind it. The following words of the then Minister of Justice are, by contrast, a clear exponent of the risk that such a conception of cause entails for contractual freedom: 'Non ostante gli equivoci e le critiche a cui il requisito della causa ha dato luogo, si è stimato necessario conservarlo e anzi conferirgli massima efficienza, non solo e non tanto in omaggio alla secolare tradizione del nostro diritto commune (che ha pure il suo peso) quanto, e sopratutto, perchè un codice fascista, ispirato alle esigene della solidarietà, non può ignorare la nozione della causa senza trascurare quello che deve essere il contenuto socialmente utile del contratto. Bisogna infatti tener fermo … che la causa richiesta dal diritto non è lo scopo soggiettivo, qualunque esso sia, perseguito dal contraente nel caso concreto … ma è la funzione economico-sociale che il diritto riconosce rilevante ai suoi fini e che sola giustifica la tutela dell'autonomia privata. Funzione pertanto che deve essere non soltanto conforme ai precetti di legge, all'ordine pubblico e al buon costume, ma anche, per i riflessi diffusi dall'art. 1322, secondo comma, rispondente alla necessità che il fine intrinseco del contratto sia socialmente apprezzabile e come tale meritevole della tutela giuridica': Relazione allá Maestá del Re imperatore del Minitro Guardisigilli (Grandi) presentata nell'udienza del 16 marzo 1942-XX per l'approvazione del Testo del 'Codice civile', no 613, in *Codice Civile, Testo e Relazione Ministeriale* (Rome, 1943) vol XXI, 132. As Gregor Albers says 'thus, causa was considered a control mechanism essential for a fascist code': Albers (ibidem) 8.

VI. The Contraposition between Causalism and Abstraction

So far, we have basically seen the dichotomy between causalism and consensualism, and I have tried to show how, despite the supposed consensualism of many legal systems, in all of them, in one way or another, the greater or lesser strength of the cause of the obligation plays a role in its enforceability. Thus, the weakness of the cause of the donation is manifested in the need for greater formal requirements for its conclusion (section II above) and the lesser firmness of gratuitous transactions in a range of consequences discussed above (section III). That lesser causal consistency of gratuitous transactions also determines in some systems, such as the English one – and the solution seems to me to be appropriate – that they do not reach the status of consensual acts, but only real acts (section IV).

Nonetheless, there is another dichotomy in relation to cause that is perhaps of greater practical significance: that which distinguishes between causal and abstract systems. The difference between these two concepts does not concern whether or not consent is sufficient to form the obligation, but the relationship between a unilateral promise and the act that explains it (acknowledgement of debt, intention to donate, reinforcement of an obligation, etc). The binding force of such a unilateral act depends on the causal or abstract structure of the system.

As can be understood, any legal system must provide for control in order to avoid those unilateral promises becoming binding in the absence of their cause. In the so-called causal systems, this control acts directly, so that a unilateral binding act will be ineffective if it is shown that its cause does not exist. This is the point of view of the systems that, for these purposes, I call causalist, such as the majority of European civil law.[54] On the other hand, in the so-called abstract systems, this control acts indirectly. A binding unilateral act, if it is indeed configured as abstract, will be immediately effective even if it has no cause, eg because it was issued in error. Abstraction will break the direct causal link between the binding act and its cause, so that the non-existence of the latter will not automatically render the former null and void, but only challengeable. Therefore, the distinction between causation and abstraction does not stem from the fact that some acts depend on a cause and others do not, as is sometimes said, but in the way in which they depend on that cause: directly or indirectly. The causal system controls the existence of cause ex ante, the abstract ex post.

The most historically successful and widely used example of abstract obligation as described is the Roman *stipulatio*, which has served as an example for all such agreements. It consisted of an oral and solemn question about a promise to give or to do something formulated by the stipulator to the promisor, to which the latter answered in the affirmative, respecting certain formal rules. The conclusion of the *stipulatio* was usually documented in an evidentiary instrument (*cautio*), and gave rise to an action

[54] On this structure, see B Rodríguez-Rosado, 'El reconocimiento de deuda y sus efectos' (2008) 20 *Revista de Derecho patrimonial* 103–8.

to enforce the performance of the promise.[55] The stipulation must have arisen as a wholly abstract act, ie one whose validity was independent of the cause for which it was granted (be it, for example, the existence of a previous debt, the will to donate or set up a dowry, or to give a sum on loan). However, the possibility of challenging it in case of non-existence of the cause, by means of an *exceptio doli*, was soon introduced.[56] In the classical period, this challenge to the lack of cause took two different routes. If the stipulation itself mentioned the cause for which the obligation was created (*stipulatio discreta*), the non-existence of the cause rendered the obligation directly ineffective. On the other hand, if the stipulation did not mention the cause of the obligation (*stipulatio indiscreta*) and this did not exist, the promisor had to invoke the *exceptio doli* to allege the lack of cause. Afterwards, and at least in the post-classical period, this diversity of the regime of contestation evolved into one of burden of proof: in the stipulation that did not mention the cause, it was the stipulator who, if the promisor denied its existence, had to prove it, whereas in the stipulation that mentioned the cause, it was the promisor who contested it who had to prove its non-existence.[57] Moreover, a specific remedy, the *querella non numeratae pecuniae*, was developed for the most serious case of lack of cause, that in which the promisor went ahead to promise the restitution of a sum of money on a loan that was not delivered. Justinian limited the interposition of this remedy, including when it was formulated by way of exception, to a period of two years, with the result that, once this period had elapsed, the promise was totally abstracted from its cause.[58]

The authors of the *ius commune* carried out a series of transformations on the *stipulatio*, leading to the loss of its abstract character. On the one hand, the oral *stipulatio* was confused with the document that contained it, the so-called *cautio*. But it turned out that the idea had spread that these documents were not binding if they did not express their cause. Moreover, the specific actions that had arisen in Roman law from the *stipulatio* had disappeared. Thus, the *cautio* and the *stipulatio* became evidentiary documents whose function was to reinforce an obligation that had already arisen.[59] It was only in commercial practice that certain types of formal documents (today known as negotiable instruments: cheque, promissory note, bill of exchange) emerged whose existence was abstract with regard to the debt that they documented.

This situation of the disappearance of abstract obligations in the civil sphere was consolidated in the following centuries. Any type of binding document was only valid

[55] There is some discussion of the action arising from the stipulation. It seems that initially there was an *actio ex stipulatu*, but that in classical times it was replaced by the *actio certi* and the *actio incerti*, depending on what was the object claimed: M Kaser, R Knütel and S Lohsse, *Römisches Privatrecht* (Munich, Beck, 2021) § 40,2.

[56] J de los Mozos, 'La carga de la prueba de la *causa stipulationis* y el concepto de causa' (2007–08) XX–XXI *SCDR* 303, 310. See also ch 1 in this book, by FJ Andrés, 6.

[57] See Kaser (n 1) 541–42; M Kaser, *Das römische Privatrecht*, vol II (Munich, Beck, 1975) 378–80; Zimmermann (n 2) 91–94, 550; A d'Ors, *Derecho privado romano* (Pamplona, Eunsa, 1996) §§ 430–32; HRP/Finkenauer, § 21, paras 17 and 83 in U Babusieux et al, *Handbuch des Römischen Privatrechts*, vol I (Tübingen, Mohr, 2023). Also ch 1 in this book, by FJ Andrés, 10–12.

[58] C. 4,30,14. See also the bibliography cited in the previous note.

[59] HKK/Thier, para 9. Among the oldest literature, see G Chevrier, *Essai sur l'histoire de la cause dans les obligations* (París, Sirey, 1929): on the approximation between *stipulatio* and document, 33–38; on Bartolo and Baldo and their insistence on the necessity of mentioning the cause in the document, 122–32.

insofar as the documented debt actually existed, unless it was accepted as a donation, when its requirements had been met. The French Civil Code originally included this doctrine in Article 1132, which contained a rebuttable presumption of the existence of cause.[60] And this seems to be the view shared by most European legal systems, including the English one.

In the nineteenth century, however, Germany began to develop a position in favour of the effectiveness of abstract unilateral declarations of obligation in civil law. In the context of the revival of the Roman system by the historical school and Savigny's position in favour of abstraction in general, Otto Bähr proposed the admission of unilateral declarations of obligation of an abstract nature, that is to say, independent of the existence and validity of the cause which led to their issue, and their purpose being the creation or recognition of an obligation.[61] According to his proposal, this would make such binding declarations firm, irrespective of the problems that might affect their cause: the non-existence or invalidity of the latter should only give rise to a personal action for unjust enrichment aimed at depriving it of binding force, but only ex post and with personal effectiveness. The proposal was favourably received in German legal science, so that it was included in the drafts of what was to become the German Civil Code, finding definitive acceptance in §§ 780 and 781 BGB.[62] The first recognises the binding force of the obligatory promise and the second of the acknowledgement of debt, both independently of the existence or not of the cause of their issuing, the lack of which would only give rise to an action for unjust enrichment, expressly provided for in § 812 II BGB.

However, the truth is that the strong abstract effect envisaged for unilateral promises and acknowledgements of debt in the German Civil Code was greatly tempered in the final regulation of these paragraphs. On the one hand, as is always the case, the abstraction was counterbalanced by greater formalism, and §§ 780 and 781 BGB demand a requirement of written form, which limits the supposed direct binding effect of the will promoted by Otto Bähr and the doctrine that took up his ideas. And in the specific case of the promise of donation, the BGB's drafting committee felt that, in order not to circumvent its formal requirements, it should also require the form of a notarial deed for the abstract promise that would include it, and this was laid down in § 518 BGB.[63] But if these rules were not in themselves restrictive of abstraction, others were included that clearly limit this effect. Thus, § 821 BGB establishes that prescription does not act against the obligee by an abstract promise who wishes to oppose by way of exception the non-existence of cause of that promise. And in addition to that, as § 404 establishes that in the case of an assignment the debtor may raise against the new creditor the defences that he already had against the old one, the result will be that the supposed personal effect of the defence of unjust enrichment in the case of lack of cause of an abstract obligation is greatly extended in practice. If we add to all this the fact that §§ 656 II and 762 II BGB establish the direct ineffectiveness of a promise or

[60] The article thus follows the French tradition prior to the Code, which had already accepted the value of documents evidencing or certifying a debt, even if they do not state the cause of it: ibid 231–37.

[61] O Bähr, *Die Annerkennung als Verplichtungsgrund* (Cassel, Verlag von Oswald Bertram, 1855) esp 151ff.

[62] HKK/Thier, §§ 780–82, paras 17ff.

[63] Grüneberg/H Sprau, BGB, § 780, para 6.

abstract acknowledgement of a debt resulting from a marriage intermediation contract or from illicit gambling, and that the majority of the doctrine considers that abstract promises or acknowledgements arising from immoral or illicit transactions are also null and void, it follows that in practice the supposed abstract effects of these promises or unilateral acknowledgements of obligation are greatly reduced, and it is understandable that the doctrine has said that their practical effectiveness goes little further than a reversal of the burden of proof.[64]

VII. Conclusions

The existence of a cause of the obligation or a consideration was introduced in the Middle Ages as a requirement that sought to ensure the existence of a free and conscious will to enter into a contract. In this sense, they were elements that guaranteed the existence of the will to be bound. Although cause was included in the French Civil Code and in others that followed it as a requirement of the contract, it can be said that it evolved from being a requirement to become an element that qualified or rated the will to be bound and the obligation itself arising from the contract. Thus, it came to be understood that the diversity of causes determined whether that will to be bound was sufficient on its own to give rise to the obligation and also delimited the force that the obligation had to have. So, all civil law systems, even those that make no mention of cause, appreciate the lesser consistency of the lucrative cause, and therefore demand special requirements of form for the will thus founded to give rise to an obligation. In the same way, if transactions with gratuitous cause enjoy less protection than onerous ones, this is due to the lesser consistency of the gratuitous cause compared to the onerous one. It can therefore be said, as Gregor Albers has stated, that in civil law systems today cause is no longer so much a requirement of the contract as an element that qualifies the obligation arising from it.

In common law legal systems, such as that of England, it can certainly be said that consideration is still a prerequisite for the creation of contractual obligations, since there the absence of consideration excludes the formation of the contract. Nevertheless, when things are looked at more closely, one can see that the practical function of consideration is not excessively different from that of cause. If in continental systems the weakness of the lucrative cause means that the will requires a complement of form, there it is directly stated that the obligation addressed to the donation must be constituted in a formal way, arriving at the same result. And the weakness of gratuitous transactions is manifested in the English system even more consistently than in the continental systems, reserving the real character for such contracts. As can be seen, although in different ways, all legal systems accept a diversity of effects between the

[64] For this weakening of abstraction, see G Albers, 'Das nicht so abstrakte Schuldversprechen' (2018) 73 *Juristenzeitung* 114ff. Underlining that the practical effect of abstract promises and recognitions is a reversal of the burden of proof, Grüneberg/Sprau, § 780, para 1; Jauernig/Stadler, §§ 780–81, para 3. For his part, Medicus said years ago that such abstract promises and acknowledgements of debt were relics of the past with little practical effect: currently, see D Medicus and S Lorenz, *Schuldrecht – Besonderer Teil* (Munich, Beck, 2018) § 52, para 9.

lucrative, gratuitous and onerous transactions, which has no other foundation than the doctrine of cause and consideration.

Certainly, the cause seems to have lost consistency in more recent Civil Codes. But this does not mean that the causal element of the obligation has lost its force: it is enough to think that these legal texts generally continue rejecting the binding force of the unilateral declaration to be bound precisely because there is no counter-performance to justify it.[65] It could be said that, as is often the case, the attempt to push cause and consideration out the door ends up leading to their entry through the window. It is perhaps the best example of what might be called the eternal return of legal institutions.[66]

[65] G Christandl, 'Commentary to 2:107' in N Jansen and R Zimmermann (eds), *Commentaries on European Contract Laws* (Oxford, Oxford University Press, 2018) 298.
[66] See T Mayer-Maly, 'Die Wiederkehr von Rechtsfiguren' (1971) 26 *Juristen Zeitung* 1.

12

Cause and Control of Legality and Morality of Contracts

JUAN PABLO MURGA FERNÁNDEZ

I. Introduction: The Complexity of the Subject Matter, the Freedom of Contracts as a Starting Point

This chapter deals with one of the most obscure aspects of contract law, which is the control of legality and morality of contracts. The subject of illegality and immorality is one of great complexity and its effects are by no means uniform.[1] The difficulty of the matter is shown by the difficulties presented when addressing the topic within the framework of the European principles: they entered the European principles at a comparatively later stage.[2]

The starting point would be the reference to an essential principal of contract law, the freedom of contract, developed during the nineteenth century. The economic reason why the law enshrines this principle and legitimises these relationships derived from the autonomy of the parties' will is to be found, above all, in its dynamic function. This function consists of making possible a constant renewal, of facilitating the circulation of goods, and a certain rotation in the use of services and resources as needs arise in social life and in economic traffic.[3] This is, however, a highly complex matter that touches on the very concept of contract and its configuration in the light of the

[1] J Beatson, A Burrows and J Cartwright, *Anson's Law of Contract*, 31st edn (Oxford, Oxford University Press, 2020) 405. On this subject, see in great detail under Spanish law P Saborido Sánchez, *La causa ilícita: delimitación y efectos* (Valencia, Tirant lo Blanch, 2005).

[2] S Meier, 'Illegality' in N Jansen and R Zimmermann (eds), *Commentaries on European Contract Laws* (Oxford, Oxford University Press, 2018) 1888–89; the author justifies this late inclusion regarding illegality in the European principles: 'The reason for the rather late inclusion of rules that belong to the core of the law of contract and are of considerable practical importance seems to be the inherent difficulty in drafting international rules on illegal contracts. First, there are considerable differences in the national laws, in particular between the civil and the common law, which have not yet been the object of thorough comparative research. Second, as long as the Principles are regarded as international rules to be applied against the background of different national legal systems, the problem arises as to which national or international legal and extra-legal standards are to be regarded as relevant. This has proven to be the most controversial question during the debates in the course of the drafting both of the PECL and the PICC.'

[3] E Vázquez de Castro, *Ilicitud contractual. Supuestos y efectos* (Valencia, Tirant Lo Blanch, 2003) 55.

times. Indeed, the evolution of contractual freedom is a history of constant tension between the individual freedom characteristic of the liberalism enshrined since the French Revolution and the limits to this freedom linked to state intervention.[4] It is also a central aspect for the comparison between the shaping of contract law in civil and common law legal systems.

Given the complexity of the subject matter, the detailed explanation of which is beyond the scope of this chapter, it is undeniable that this freedom to create contracts is not unlimited.[5] The legal system confers power for the creation of contracts and must control that this power is not used to contravene what the legal system has provided. By virtue of the principle of contractual freedom, every contract will enjoy the qualities granted by the legal system as long as it remains within the limits set by it. For instance, Article 1255 of the Spanish Código Civil establishes that 'The contracting parties may establish the agreements, terms and conditions they deem convenient, provided that they are not contrary to the law, morality or *ordre public*'. Article 1102 of the French Code civil affirms that

> [e]veryone is free to contract or not to contract, to choose the person with whom to contract, and to determine the content and form of the contract, within the limits imposed by legislation. Freedom of contract does not permit derogation from rules of public policy.

Article 1162 of the Code civil decrees that 'A contract cannot derogate from public policy either by its stipulations or by its purpose, whether or not this was known by the parties'. This is also the case of sections 134 and 138 of the German Bürgerliches Gesetzbuch (BGB): 'A legal transaction that violates a statutory prohibition is void, unless the statute leads to a different conclusion'; 'A legal transaction that offends common decency is void' (§ 138, first paragraph BGB).

Under English law, a clear differentiation exists between two categories of contract illegality: statutory illegality and common law illegality. Statutory illegality encompasses cases where a contract is explicitly or implicitly forbidden by specific legislation or statutory law. On the other hand, common law illegality pertains to situations where a contract is deemed illegal based on established legal principles, judicial precedents or public policy considerations, rather than specific statutes.[6]

[4] On this evolution, see the excellent synthetic exposition carried out by L Díez-Picazo, *Fundamentos de Derecho Civil Patrimonial*, vol I, 3rd edn (Cizur-Menor, Civitas, 2007) 143–57, and references therein. For example, echoing Friedmann's explanation, Díez-Picazo underlines how, before the First World War, the rule of absolute fidelity to the contract was strictly observed and absolute impossibility, material or legal, was the only way to free oneself from contractual obligations. The war, the German hyperinflation of 1922 and the Great Crash of 1929 opened up the first loopholes. It is characteristic and symptomatic that the French theory of unforeseeability, first developed in administrative contracts in the famous Bordeaux case, dates back to 1916. Unforeseeability in French law, frustration in English law, the *rebus sic stantibus* clause or the basis of the transaction opened the way so that, in the case of extraordinary and unforeseeable events that make contractual obligations excessively onerous, the courts could sometimes release the contracting parties from the excessively onerous contract, and in other cases, even proceed to a revision of the terms of the contract: idem 150. On this point, E Roppo, 'Il controllo sugli atti di autonomia privata' (1985) III *Rivista Critica del Diritto Privato* 485, indicates that 'The problem of the relationship between private autonomy and the legal system is essentially the problem of the controls that the legal system exercises over acts of private autonomy'.

[5] R Zimmermann, *The Law of Obligations. Roman Foundations of the Civilian Tradition* (Oxford, Oxford University Press, 1996) 706: 'In all modern legal systems the freedom of the parties to determine the content of their transaction is limited not only by statutory prohibitions but also by certain extra-legal standards.'

[6] Meier (n 2) 1888.

A first conclusion can be drawn: all legal systems regard illegality and immorality as unbreakable limits to contractual freedom.[7] They are therefore, as will be shown, two closely connected concepts[8] in which the greatest difficulty lies in determining their content and, in particular, their effects.

The structure to be followed in the comparative analysis of this complex subject that will be carried out in the following pages is as follows: firstly, a brief outline will be given of the historical background of the figure, particularly from the continental perspective, in Roman law and in *ius commune* (section II). Next, the meaning of the illegality and immorality of the contract will be determined (section III). Thirdly, the most significant methods by which the control of the legality and immorality of the contract is addressed will be studied (section IV). Finally, the effects that derive from the illegality or immorality of the contract will be determined (section V). In all cases, an attempt will be made to provide a comparative view, with reference to European principles on contract law. It should be stressed that in a volume such as the present one, which focuses on the cause, the section that is of greatest interest is the way in which the legal systems deal with the problem of the illegality or immorality of the contract (section IV). However, it should be added that the most complex and debated issue (also from a practical point of view) is undoubtedly the consequences of such illegality or immorality[9] (section V of this chapter). On this last point, the developments in English law since *Patel v Mirza*[10] are of the greatest interest as a source of inspiration for possible future developments in European legal systems.

II. Illegality and Immorality: A Brief Historical Background (Particularly, Roman Law and *Ius Commune*)

The historical development of the civilian approach to the legality of contracts reveals a complex and evolving path. In early Roman law, there was little consideration for imposing external restrictions on private legal agreements established through formal legal rituals. At this stage, the sole determinant of a contract's validity was adherence to the proper form.[11] At that time, the legislative power's scope concerning transactions was primarily limited to the imposition of penalties for disregarding prohibitions.

It was only during the later period of the Roman Republic that the notion emerged that statutes could explicitly nullify transactions that violated their provisions. Statutes

[7] H Kötz, *European Contract Law*, 2nd edn (Oxford, Oxford University Press, 2017) 109: 'However committed a legal system may be to the principle of freedom of contract, it is bound to deny enforcement to a contract which conflicts with the law or good morals or offends "public policy" or is "contraire aux bonnes moeurs ou à l'ordre public"'.

[8] B Häcker, 'The Impact of Illegality and Immorality on Contract and Restitution from a Civilian Angle' in S Green and A Bogg (eds), *Illegality after Patel v Mirza* (Oxford, Hart Publishing, 2018) 340.

[9] This is emphasised in Beatson et al (n 1) 405: 'A central problem has been a failure to recognize that, while there is an initial question as to what counts as illegality for these purposes (ie what types of conduct are covered by "illegality") the vast bulk of the law is concerned with the effect of illegality on a contract and on consequential restitution (ie the recovery of benefits conferred under the contract).'

[10] *Patel v Mirza* [2016] UKSC 42, [2017] AC 467.

[11] Zimmermann (n 5) 698.

undertaking this function became known as *leges perfectae*. This development led to a fundamental threefold classification of legislative enactments during the classical era of Roman law. A *lex perfecta* was a statute that declared contracts in violation of its terms to be invalid. A *lex minus quam perfecta* imposed no more than a public law penalty for such violations, whereas a *lex imperfecta* did not encompass any sanction at all.[12]

Up until around the middle of the second century BC, statutes falling under the category of *leges minus quam perfectae* were predominantly prevalent.[13] However, with the emergence and subsequent acceptance of the new legislative approach encapsulated in *leges perfectae*, this form of legislation swiftly became the preferred method for enforcing prohibitions. As the transition to the Empire was underway, accompanied by a notable increase in the level of state control and regulation, the stricter and more conclusive nature of *leges perfectae* gained prominence. Consequently, the vast majority of prohibitions were henceforth formulated in the form of *leges perfectae*.

In the year AD 439, Emperor Theodosius took an additional significant step in this context: he decreed that any acts, agreements or transactions that violated statutory prohibitions were to be considered null and void.[14] This new decree implied that these actions were deemed completely non-existent, regardless of whether the statute explicitly outlined such consequences or not. He therefore turned all significant statutes into *leges perfectae*.

This new approach taken by Theodosius in AD 439 was eventually incorporated into Emperor Justinian's comprehensive compilation of Roman law in the sixth century.[15] From there, it became an integral part of the evolving European *ius commune*. As a result, the inclusion of Theodosius's enactment in Justinian's compilation contributed to the dissemination and influence of this legal doctrine throughout European legal traditions.

For this reason, among civilian lawyers, there was a prevalent assumption that persisted until well into the nineteenth century. This assumption held that contracts affected by illegality were inherently and automatically void. The general belief was that unless the relevant statute explicitly dictated consequences that contradicted this automatic invalidity, such contracts would be rendered null and void. However, the extraordinary confusion surrounding the notions of invalidity and ineffectiveness of the contract at the time (which is still latent in many Civil Codes in force, as is the case of the Spanish one) made it very difficult to establish uniform and clear effects derived from the illegality of the contract.

The nineteenth century marked a significant turning point in legal thinking, bringing about greater conceptual clarity and introducing a more purpose-driven approach to the examination of illegality in contracts and legal transactions. Scholars began to acknowledge that the Theodosian decree, which had influenced legal thought for centuries, was, at most, a guideline for interpreting statutes. It was increasingly recognised that the determination of how contracts or other legal transactions were affected by

[12] On this classification, see ibid 697–701, and references therein.

[13] Zimmermann (n 5) 698 gives an important example of *leges minus quam perfectae* in the field of succession law: 'The *lex Furia testamentaria* (fixing the maximum amount of a legacy that a person was allowed to receive at one thousand asses).'

[14] Throughout the enactment of the so-called *lex non dubium* of 7 April 439.

[15] Codex 1,14,5.

illegality should be guided by the specific statute in question. The interpretation would depend on the wording and structure of the statute, its historical context and, most importantly, its underlying purpose or intent.

As the legal journey within the civilian tradition progressed, it culminated in a strong emphasis on teleology – a focus on understanding the purpose and objectives behind the law and how they should guide the assessment of illegality in contracts and legal transactions. This marked a departure from the earlier notion that illegality would automatically void contracts, shifting towards a more nuanced, context-dependent and purpose-driven approach to the issue.[16]

III. First Matter: What is the Meaning of Illegality and Immorality?

A. The Difficulty in Distinguishing Illegality from Immorality

In section I of this chapter, it was noted that different legal systems impose limits to freedom of contract that vary between the reference to the law itself, morality (*bonnes moeurs, buon costume* or *Gutte Sitten*) and public policy (*ordre public*).

In some cases, the reference to the law as an insuperable limit to contractual freedom is affirmed autonomously (this is what happens with section 134 BGB referring exclusively to the law, while section 138.1 refers to *Gutte Sitten*), and in others cases, it is affirmed jointly with the reference to morality or public order (this is the case of Article 1255 of the Código Civil, Article 1102 of the Code civil or Article 1322 of the Italian Codice Civile).[17] With the passing of time, moreover, it can be observed that the reference to morality has been embedded in the concept of public order (this is the case with the current Article 1102 of the Code civil, although Article 6 continues to refer to *bonnes moeurs* as a general limit to conventions between private individuals).

Traditionally, it seemed that the reference to the law was to written norms, while the notion of morality was identified with extra-legal norms. It is also added that the law in this sense is that which is of a mandatory nature, ie those norms which by definition have a legal consequence that prevails and is always imposed, regardless of the will of the recipients of the law.[18]

However, the fact that morality has been absorbed by the concept of public order, and given that the latter concept must be understood as the guiding principles of the

[16] Häcker (n 8) 341–43.

[17] This is also the case of § 879 of the Austrian Allgemeines Bürgerliches Gesetzbuch (ABGB); Art 20 of the Swiss Obligationenrecht (OR); Art 3:40 of the New Dutch Civil Code (Burgerlijk Wetboek or BW) of 1992.

[18] The issue of mandatory law, both domestic and foreign, has many variants arising from different legislative policies. In international contracts, in particular, it is a very complicated issue. These complications were seen in the Vienna Convention on Contracts for the International Sale of Goods. By the express exclusion of Art 4a of the Convention, without which it would have been rejected by the states, it is ensured that the mandatory rules of domestic law that make a contract illegal, whether directly affecting international trade or affecting domestic public policy, are safeguarded. Consequently, the validity of a contract of sale is thus subordinated to a number of provisions which are neither homogeneous nor equivalent from one country to another.

legal order enshrined in the respective constitutional texts, it can be concluded that the violation of a law can also entail the violation of public order. In other words, morality and public order need not necessarily be identified with an extra-legal norm.

This explains why the concepts 'illegal contract' and 'immoral contract' have come to be referred to by terms that may appear to be synonymous and are sometimes used as such.[19] Both terms have been used interchangeably to encompass a broader concept than the one to which they technically refer. That is to say, in their most generic sense, they may refer to those contracts that are rejected in whole or in part by any element of the legal system in general.[20]

Under English law, a contract that is not expressly prohibited by statute may still be deemed illegal at common law if enforcing it would go against public policy. Within this broader context of illegal contracts, there exists a specific sub-category that pertains to agreements contrary to good morals.[21]

With respect to the European principles, both the Principles of European Contract Law Project (PECL) and the Draft Common Frame of Reference (DCFR) distinguish between contracts contrary to the so-called 'fundamental principles'[22] and contracts infringing 'mandatory rules'.[23] It is surprising that the European principles avoid any reference to classical notions such as 'morality' or 'public order'. In the commentary by the drafter of this section of the European principles, the use of the terms 'mandatory rules' and 'fundamental principles' are justified on the grounds that they are

> intended to avoid the varying national concepts of immorality, illegality at common law, public policy, *ordre public* and *bonnes moeurs*, by invoking a necessarily broad idea of fundamental principles of law found across the European Union, including European Community law.[24]

As regards the legal bases from which these principles can be drawn, the following are indicated: the EC Treaty, eg in favour of free movement of goods, services and persons, protection of market competition; the European Convention on Human Rights, eg the prohibition of slavery and forced labour (Article 3) and rights to liberty (Article 5), respect for private and family life (Article 8), freedom of thought (Article 9), freedom of expression (Article 10) and freedom of association (Article 11), and the rights to marry (Article 12) and peaceful enjoyment of possessions (First Protocol, Article 1);

[19] The theoretical distinction between these two concepts can be made in the following way. (i) Illegal contract in the strict sense: this refers only to those contracts that are rejected as a whole or in part by positive law. In this conception, the only benchmark for the consideration of a contract as illegal would be the legal or normative limit. Illegality would require a clash or frontal contravention of the contract itself or its effectiveness with the legal provision. (ii) Immoral contract in the strict sense of the term: an immoral or illicit contract is any contract that is not specifically prohibited or censured by positive legal norms, but is vitiated because it goes against ethical norms, good customs or general principles of public order: Vázquez de Castro (n 3) 50. Häcker (n 8) 340 underlines that 'in the civilian tradition, illegality and immorality are closely connected concepts'. Hence, the practical difference between illegal and immoral contracts is extraordinarily complex.

[20] J Santos Briz, *Derecho Civil, Teoría y Práctica*, vol I (Madrid, Edersa, 1978) 610.

[21] Meier (n 2) 1892.

[22] PECL 15:101; DCFR II-7:301.

[23] PECL 15:102; DCFR II-7:302.

[24] H McQueen, 'Illegality and Immorality in Contracts: Towards European Principles' in AS Hartkamp, MW Hesselink, E Hondius, C Mak and E Du Perron (eds), *Towards a European Civil Code*, 4th edn (Alphen aan den Rijn, Kluwer Law International, 2010) 555ff.

and the European Union Charter on Fundamental Rights, which includes many of the rights already mentioned and adds such matters as respect for personal data (Article 8), freedom to choose an occupation and right to engage in work (Article 15), freedom to conduct a business (Article 16), the right to property (Article 17), equality between men and women (Article 23), children's rights (Article 24), rights of collective bargaining and action (Article 28), protection in the event of unjustified dismissal (Article 30) and a high level of consumer protection (Article 38).[25]

The first conclusion that can be drawn from this analysis is that the notion of extra-legal standards has diminished in importance due to the widespread incorporation of fundamental rules and values into legal norms. This transformation is particularly evident in the inclusion of human rights catalogues within constitutions. As a result, many principles and values once considered external to the legal system have now become integral parts of the law itself.[26] Hence, it may make more sense to address the problem in terms of a unitary notion, where the emphasis is placed on the type of norm that is infringed, the extent of the infringement and the contractual consequences that result from it.

B. Emblematic Cases of Illegality and Immorality

At this point, it is worth highlighting the cases that are traditionally included in the different legal systems in relation to those contracts that, without being expressly prohibited by a legal provision, are deemed invalid because they are considered illegal or immoral. In this sense, the most prominent examples tend to be those that are specifically contrary to morality or public order (regardless of whether or not these notions are enshrined in a correlative positive norm).

It is widely acknowledged that the content of concepts like *boni mores*, *ordre public* or 'public policy' can vary based on the specific society and time period.[27] However, despite these variations, the fundamental or core content of these concepts is remarkably similar across different European jurisdictions.[28] This is a necessarily casuistic matter, although doctrine and case law tend to try to systematise different categories of cases that are far from being exhaustive nor unchangeable.

The most characteristic cases generally accepted in European legal systems are listed very clearly by Meier:

1. Contracts aiming to commission or remunerate a criminal act or a civil delict.
2. Contracts that excessively limit an individual's personal or economic autonomy. For instance, contracts that restrict an individual's freedom to marry or divorce, or those that touch on a person's religious beliefs, are generally disapproved of in legal systems worldwide.

[25] ibid 555ff.
[26] A similar conclusion is observed by Meier (n 2) 1891.
[27] Kötz (n 7) 110 stresses the variability of cases that may be considered illegal, due to the passage of time and the jurisdiction concerned: 'Contracts which until quite recently were regarded as offensive may now be perfectly acceptable.'
[28] Meier (n 2) 1892.

3. In the economic realm, agreements like non-compete clauses, entered into by former employees, business partners or business sellers, may be deemed invalid if they are deemed excessive, considering factors like their scope, duration and corresponding obligations.
4. The same scrutiny applies to long-term contracts in which operators of establishments like petrol stations or inns agree to exclusively source their products from a specific company, such as an oil company or brewery. Contracts that harm the interests of third parties in the economic sphere, such as those jeopardising the rights of other creditors, also fall into this category.
5. Other types of contracts may be invalidated for unduly interfering with the administration of justice. These include contracts that exclude the jurisdiction of a court or agreements that involve the payment of fees to court witnesses. In principle, promises of contingency fees may also be subject to invalidation, although recent statutory changes have introduced exceptions to this prohibition in the last few decades.
6. Another classic scenario that is commonly included by different jurisdictions in the scope of contractual illegality is that of contracts qualified as sexually immoral. Contracts for leasing premises for the operation of a brothel and contracts associated with prostitution inherently contravene the *boni mores* – however, this is gradually losing prominence in some legal systems.
7. National laws also exhibit significant divergence concerning the evaluation of contracts within the domain of reproductive medicine. For instance, agreements related to sperm donations or surrogate motherhood are subject to widely varying legal assessments and treatments across different jurisdictions. The legal landscape in this area is notably complex and subject to ongoing discussions and adaptations in response to changing societal norms and ethical considerations.[29]

IV. What is the Mechanism to Address the Illegality and Immorality of the Contract?

This section is undoubtedly the most relevant in a volume such as this one, dedicated to the study of the cause. As will be seen, the cause (certainly in a specific meaning practically designed to tackle this problem) is one of the instruments used to face the issue

[29] ibid 1892–93. In English law, the set of cases that fall into the category of 'illegal contracts' are similar in many ways. Beatson et al (n 1) 407–09 clarify that 'while commentators and judges are fond of hypothetical examples where the relevant illegal conduct is the common law crime of murder – eg A contracts with B, a hitman, to murder C – most of the cases coming before the Courts on illegality in relation to contract have involved crimes that are statutory offences … although there have been some cases in the past that might be interpreted as supporting an approach that civil wrongs always count, the view taken by the Supreme Court in the leading case of *Les Laboratoires Servier v Apotex Inc*, was that, unless dishonesty is an essential element, torts and other civil wrongs do not constitute relevant illegal conduct. This may mean that this type of illegal conduct does not extend very far beyond crimes because it would appear that almost all torts that have dishonesty as an essential element also constitute crimes; and conduct that is contrary to public policy (for example, sexual immorality, interference with the administration of justice, the committing in a friendly foreign country of what is there a criminal act, the ousting of the jurisdiction of Courts, the exclusion of liability for a person's own fraudulent misrepresentation, and an unreasonable restraint of trade).'

of the illegality or immorality of contracts. In order to make a comparative analysis of this question, it is worth drawing a distinction between the answers offered in civil law systems and that followed in English law. Within the civil law systems, following here the systematisation proposed by Häcker,[30] a distinction shall be made between models of *direct invalidation* of the contract and cases of *indirect invalidation*.

A. The Treatment of Illegality and Immorality in Continental Systems: Direct and Indirect Invalidation Models

Starting with the systems of direct invalidation of the contract, Austria and Germany can be singled out as representative examples. There is a general provision stating that the contract is invalid for contravening (without going into detail on the specific element of the contract affected by illegality or immorality) a legal prohibition or morality. It thus refers to the contract as a whole. The literal wording of the provisions reflecting this overall approach to the illegality and immorality of the contract is set out thus:

> § 879(1) of the Austrian Civil ABGB of 1811 provides that: 'A contract which contravenes a statutory prohibition or good morals is void.'
>
> § 138(1) of the German Civil Code of 1896 (BGB) provides that: 'A legal transaction which contravenes good morals is void.' § 134 BGB, when addressing separately illegality, adds: 'A legal transaction which contravenes a statutory prohibition is void unless the statute provides otherwise.'

A second model in the continental sphere is the one that can be described as 'indirect' invalidation of the contract. Here, it is a matter of dealing with illegality by referring to a certain essential element of the contract. The most representative example was given in the former wording of the Code civil, where the questions of illegality and immorality were redirected to the object or the cause of the contract. To the extent that any of these essential elements were affected, the contract would have no legal effect, as it would not be concluded. In this sense, it is worth highlighting the text of the former Article 1108 of the Code civil, in which it was determined that the existence of an agreement with a certain and lawful object, based on an equally lawful cause, was essential for the validity of the contract. From this perspective, contracts considered illegal or immoral sometimes referred to the object and sometimes to the cause. Since the 2016 reform of the French law of obligations, the requirement of cause as an essential element of the contract has been abolished. The question of illegality and immorality (an expression replaced by the notion of public policy, although still generally present in the unmodified Article 6 as limits to party autonomy) is elucidated in the current Article 1162, which states that 'A contract cannot derogate from public policy either by its stipulations or by its purpose, whether or not this was known to the parties'.

The indirect invalidation of the contract on the grounds that some of its essential elements are affected by illegality or immorality is the approach still followed by Italy

[30] Häcker (n 8) 343ff.

and Spain (in this last case, however, with the nuances that will be highlighted, and which are not always sufficiently emphasised at a comparative level). In the case of Italy, this can be seen in Articles 1343–46 of the Codice Civile. In the case of Spain, the situation is very peculiar. Article 1261 of the Código Civil lists the essential requirements of the contract. Article 1271 refers to the object of the contract and its validity requirements. And Article 1275 refers to the conditions of validity of the cause.

> Article 1261 of the Código Civil: 'A contract does not exist unless the following requirements are met: 1.º Agreement of the contracting parties.
>
> 2.º Object which is certain and which is the subject matter of the contract.
>
> 3.º Cause of the obligation that is established'.
>
> Article 1271 of the Código Civil: 'All things that are not beyond the trade of men, even future things, can be the object of a contract.
>
> However, no other contracts can be made concerning a future inheritance than those whose object is to effect between living persons the division of an estate and other partitioning dispositions, in accordance with article 1056.
>
> All services which are not contrary to the law or to morality may also be the object of a contract'.
>
> Article 1275 of the Código Civil: 'Contracts without cause, or with unlawful cause, have no effect. A cause is unlawful when it is contrary to law or morality'.

As can be observed immediately, the question of illegality and immorality is dealt with in the final part of Article 1271 in relation to the object, as well as in the final part of Article 1275 in relation to the cause.

In general terms, the legality of the object refers to its suitability for legal transactions in accordance with the legal system in which the contract is made and is to be performed. A distinction is usually made of the thing that is the object of the contract, because its lawfulness is equivalent to its marketability or appropriability. This requirement should not be confused with the fact that certain things are of limited or restricted trade (weapons, narcotics, etc), because they are subject to criminal sanctions or administrative controls; in these cases, there can be no question that the illegal object and the contract concluded is valid in civil law (regardless of the corresponding criminal or administrative sanction). In the case of services, the requirement of legality consists of not being contrary to law or morality. Although the provision speaks only of services, seeming to restrict it only to those cases in which the object is a positive activity, it must also be extended to negative conduct (when there is an obligation or legal duty to act in a certain way, the commitment to abstain can be qualified as illegal). The classic examples of illegal services are often given as life-long leasing of services, marriage brokerage, sex procuring, etc.[31]

As far as cause is concerned, it should be noted that it is an ambiguous figure that plays multiple functions, hence the different notions of the cause.[32] In the case of

[31] MªC Gete-Alonso y Calera, 'Comentario al artículo 1271' in C Paz-Ares, L Díez-Picazo, R Bercovitz, P Salvador Coderch (eds), *Comentario del Código Civil*, vol II (Madrid, Ministerio de Justicia, 1991) 474.

[32] On the diversity of doctrines on the cause, see the clear exposition provided by B Rodríguez-Rosado, *Fiducia y pacto de retro en garantía* (Madrid, Marcial Pons, 1998) 59ff.

Spanish law, focusing on the illegality or immorality of the contract, recourse to cause is made through its so-called 'subjective' configuration: that is to say, cause understood as the common intention or motivation pursued by the parties when concluding the contract.[33] This is an attempt to deal with the problem raised by the contract with a lawful object in which the purpose pursued is contrary to the legal system. This means that a new concept of cause has to be coined, which has a bearing on the subjective purpose or motivation pursued by the parties to the contract. The classic example is that of a contract for the sale of a knife (a clearly lawful object) which is concluded for the purpose of murdering a third party.

The possible recognition of the unlawful motive or purpose as constituting the cause in Article 1275 of the Spanish Código Civil raises a twofold problem. On the one hand, to what extent does the illegal or unlawful purpose assume the status of a cause of action within the meaning of Article 1275? On the other hand, what is the degree of knowledge and cooperation of the other party that is necessary for the motive or purpose to become a cause?[34]

In addition to all this, it is worth adding a great particularity that has been noticed in relation to Spanish law: there is a provision with a general scope, the wording of which bears important similarities with § 134 BGB: Article 6, paragraph three of the Spanish Código Civil. The wording of this provision is as follows: 'Acts contrary to mandatory and prohibitory norms are fully void, unless a different effect is established therein for the case of contravention.' The wording of this rule is the result of an amendment made in 1974, which replaced the more generic former Article 4(1). As is the case in Germany, Article 6(3) is subject to important interpretative controversies, which will not be dealt with in detail here, as it is beyond the scope of this chapter. It is sufficient to point out the most noteworthy aspects on the basis of the abundant case law issued on the matter by the Spanish Supreme Court in recent decades. In the first place, a general sanction is provided for all types of acts (not only those of a contractual nature and, logically, also contracts themselves) carried out in breach of the legal rules: the radical nullity of such acts. It is a sanction, moreover, that is contemplated with a subsidiary character: it will only be applied when a different sanction is not provided for in the infringed norm itself. Likewise, the sanction refers to norms of a 'mandatory or prohibitive' nature. In the latter case, important clarifications have been introduced by Spanish doctrine and case law: the provision does not refer to non-mandatory provisions and the allusion to 'prohibitive' norms must be understood as referring to prohibitive norms of a mandatory nature. It would seem sufficient for the legislator to refer to the 'mandatory' norms, without further ado. However, it is specified that there must be a contradiction between

[33] On this point, see extensively ch 8 in this book, by Antonio Legerén-Molina, where it is emphasised that 'this notion is now linked to the subjective aims of the parties (*cf* SCJ 19-11-1974, ECLI:ES:TS:1974:2818). It is, therefore, not something objective and invariable. The intention, the purpose, the common motive is elevated – in the legal sense – to the cause of the contract, and impresses on the will "the [in this case] unlawful and reprehensible finalistic direction of the agreement' (SCJ 20-07-2006, ECLI:ES:TS:2006:4457). Although the particular motivations of each party, as long as they are lawful, are irrelevant from a legal point of view – unless they are elevated as to be a "specific cause" or are configured as a condition or mode – this is not the case when the common purpose is unlawful or immoral (*cf* SCJ 24-04-2013, ECLI:ES:TS:2013:2753). In these cases, contracts are relevant to the legal system'.

[34] JL Lacruz Berdejo, A Luna Serrano, J Delgado Echevarría and F Rivero Hernández, *Elementos de Derecho Civil*, vol II, 2nd edn (Barcelona, Librería Bosch, 1987) 186.

the legal act carried out and a mandatory norm, without a simple non-conformity being sufficient for this purpose. In this sense, the provision takes on its full meaning in relation to (mandatory) rules containing a prohibition. It is only such rules which in their own sense can be infringed by acts contrary to them and which can lead to the nullity of acts carried out contrary to the prohibition imposed.[35] In other words, only a norm which prohibits a conduct can be infringed by a positive act of contravention; a norm which 'prescribes' a conduct can be infringed not by acts, but by the omission of the obligatory conduct; however, the omission is not an act on which nullity can be predicated.[36]

As far as the practical application of Article 6.3 is concerned, the Spanish Supreme Court proclaims a 'flexible' application of the norm. It is not necessary for the validity of the act or contract to be imposed by the infringed norm, but it must be determined by way of interpretation as the most appropriate solution (ie when the 'lightness' of the case does not recommend nullity, or when there are no overriding reasons to deprive the validity of the transaction). The result of this doctrine has been, in practice, to disqualify the civil relevance of a large part of the sectorial law of an administrative nature, and to admit only on rare occasions that its infringement is relevant for the invalidity of the contract.[37]

Beyond these clarifications on the interpretation and application of Article 6.3 of the Código Civil, what should be emphasised is that the Spanish model is a hybrid one. The invalidity of the contract due to illegality and immorality can be tackled indirectly, by referring to essential elements of the contract (both the object and the cause understood in a subjective sense, as has been pointed out), but also directly, by means of a general provision that proclaims the invalidity of acts contrary to mandatory norms (provided that the norm itself does not contemplate a different sanction). In practice, these different ways of dealing with illegality and immorality create confusion, as it is difficult to know when to take action through the unlawfulness of the object or of the cause, or through the general clause of Article 6.3. In this sense, the words of Clavería are very illustrative: Clavería advises any lawyer who finds himself in the situation of making allegations to request the declaration of nullity of the contract in cases of illegality or immorality to jointly invoke Articles 1255, 1271, 1275 and 6.3 of the Código Civil.[38]

[35] MA Pérez Álvarez, 'Efectos de las normas jurídicas' in P de Pablo Contreras (ed), *Curso de Derecho Civil*, vol I, 7th edn (Madrid, Edisofer, 2022) 178–79.

[36] AF Carrasco Perera, 'Comentario al artículo 6.3' in R Bercovitz Rodríguez-Cano (ed), *Comentarios al Código Civil*, vol I (Valencia, Tirant lo Blanch, 2013) 154ff.

[37] ibid 154–56, and the appropriate case law references therein, which highlight cases in which nullity has been ruled out despite the fact that the action is clearly contrary to a mandatory provision: eg the sale or lease of subsidised housing; the lease of a lorry prohibited by sectorial regulation; the sale of goods at higher prices than those set by law; contracts that infringe the system of administrative ownership of pharmacies; the incorporation of companies whose purpose is to carry out lawful activities, but reserved to a profession by a corporate rule; contracts contrary to the regulations on administrative incompatibilities; or those businesses that incur a fiscal irregularity.

[38] LH Clavería Gosálbez, *La causa del contrato* (Zaragoza, Bolonia Publicaciones del Real Colegio de España, 1998) 115–16, 185. Similarly, MJ Marín López, 'Requisitos esenciales del contrato. Requisitos accidentals del contrato' in R Bercovitz Rodríguez-Cano (ed), *Tratado de Derecho de Contratos*, vol I, 2nd edn (Valencia, Tirant lo Blanch, 2013) stresses that 'It is often difficult to distinguish between the illegality of the cause and the illegality of the object. A contract with an unlawful object is always a contract with an unlawful cause (eg I am obliged to murder another in exchange for money). But not vice versa: it is possible that the object is lawful and the cause unlawful.'

From a practical point of view, however, the result achieved will be the same: nullity of the contract, that is to say, its invalidity or ineffectiveness (though with the important nuances that the case law makes according to the circumstances of the case – a casuistic and flexible component that is consubstantial to this matter, as will be seen in the study of the different legal models).

In the comparative context, the answers offered to the declaration of illegality or immorality of the contract (apart from the route of direct or indirect invalidation) are not precise, although they have the same common denominator: invalidity or ineffectiveness of the contract, qualified according to the specific circumstances (fundamentally, nature of the infringement, interests underlying the infringed rule, etc). This flexibility is sometimes of a case law nature (this is what happens in Austria or Spain) and is sometimes provided for in the articles of the respective Civil Code (such as Article 1179 of the Code civil or Article 3:40 of the New Dutch BW).[39]

B. The Treatment of Illegality and Immorality in English Law

English law, as already reiterated, traditionally distinguishes between two types of illegality: that arising from the breach of a statutory prohibition and that contrary to public policy (illegality at common law). Unlike in the continental models, it is not a matter of looking for an element of the contract from which to deduce the illegality of the contract, nor of proclaiming a general rule of invalidation of contracts contrary to the law, morality or public order. Rather, it consists in identifying a set of cases that clearly give rise to the qualification of the illegality of the contract, which may be given by a breach (express or implied) of a statutory provision or a breach of public policy – even if this is not expressly or implicitly sanctioned by a statutory provision.

The examples of illegal contracts at common law are very similar to those considered illegal due to immorality in civil law. For instance, the courts have established that certain contracts contravene public policy if their objects are immoral (like supporting prostitution), when they interfere with the administration of justice or when they attempt to circumvent the authority of the courts. In the commercial sphere, a significant principle is that a contractual term limiting a party's ability to pursue a trade or profession (referred to as a 'covenant in restraint of trade') is unenforceable unless it can be demonstrated to be reasonable, not only with respect to the parties involved, but also concerning the broader public interest. The implications of illegality and public policy on a contract's validity can vary, as is the case in the generality of European legal systems (as already stated). When illegality arises from a specific statutory provision, the statute may specify the consequences.[40] In other instances, the courts may categorise the contract as 'void' or 'unenforceable'. However, this voidability is not comparable to that arising from a mistake in the contract, in that it is possible for property to pass under an illegal contract, and therefore for the property rights of the transferee to be given legal effect.[41]

[39] Häcker (n 8) 348.

[40] In the same vein as § 134 BGB and Art 6.3 of the Código Civil.

[41] J Cartwright, *Contract Law. An Introduction to the English Law of Contract for the Civil Lawyer*, 4th edn (Oxford, Hart Publishing, 2023) 204.

C. The Treatment of the Illegality and Immorality of Contracts in the Principles of European Contract Law

The most representative sources of reference in this respect are the Principles of European Contract Law (published in three parts between 1995 and 2002) and the Draft Common Frame of Reference (2008–09). In particular, the focus will be exclusively on the DCFR, insofar as it is built on the basis of the PECL and given that in this area the provisions are practically identical between the two supranational instruments. Articles II. – 7:301 and II. – 7:302 DCFR provide as follows:

> Article II. – 7:301: 'Contracts infringing fundamental principles.
>
> A contract is void to the extent that: (a) it infringes a principle recognised as fundamental in the laws of the Member States of the European Union; and (b) nullity is required to give effect to that principle.'
>
> Article II. – 7:302: Contracts infringing mandatory rules.
>
> '(1) Where a contract is not void under the preceding article but infringes a mandatory rule of law, the effects of that infringement on the validity of the contract are the effects, if any, expressly prescribed by that mandatory rule.
>
> (2) Where the mandatory rule does not expressly prescribe the effects of an infringement on the validity of a contract, a court may: (a) declare the contract to be valid; (b) avoid the contract, with retrospective effect, in whole or in part; or (c) modify the contract or its effects.
>
> (3) A decision reached under paragraph (2) should be an appropriate and proportional response to the infringement, having regard to all relevant circumstances, including: (a) the purpose of the rule which has been infringed; (b) the category of persons for whose protection the rule exists; (c) any sanction that may be imposed under the rule infringed; (d) the seriousness of the infringement; (e) whether the infringement was intentional; and (f) the closeness of the relationship between the infringement and the contract.'

The effects linked to the declaration of illegality or immorality will not be analysed here, but rather the model adopted to deal with it according to the European principles. In this sense, it can be said that the system chosen is that of direct invalidity by means of general rules that distinguish: the infringement of fundamental principles on the one hand (this would include the classic cases of public policy, common law illegality, *ordre public, boni mores* or immorality); and the infringement of mandatory rules, in which case the preferential solution is the application of the legal consequence provided for in the infringed norm.[42]

D. Brief Considerations on the Mechanism Chosen to Deal with Illegality: Is this the Most Relevant Issue? The Futility of the Subjective Notion of Cause in this Context

Ultimately, what is decisive is not so much the mechanism used to tackle the illegality or immorality of the contract, but the effects that derive from such a qualification – effects

[42] This is clearly evocative of the wording of § 134 BGB or Art 6.3 of the Spanish Código Civil, although, as described in greater detail in the following section of this chapter, a list of different flexible solutions of

which, as will be seen below, are mediated by a set of classic rules from which the case law seems to try to escape in all cases in which the justice of the specific case requires it. English law seems to have taken a definitive step towards this flexible and multifactorial approach to the problem since the emblematic case of *Patel v Mirza* in 2016.[43]

On the other hand, the reference to the cause to address this problem brings more confusion than clear advantages. Indeed, it has led to the creation of a new notion of cause (subjective cause), which adds even more complexity and confusion to a sufficiently complex matter. It is not clear what practical consequence is obtained by redirecting the problem through this subjective notion of cause. In the case of Spanish law, for example, it would be sufficient to allude to the general limits of the freedom of contract in Article 1255, the lawfulness of the object in Article 1271, or the general formula of Article 6.3 of the Código Civil.

V. The *Quid Iuris* of the Issue: The Effects of the Declaration of Illegality or Immorality of the Contract, 'Restitution'

A. A Brief Historical Overview Explaining Certain Rules Still in Force and under Discussion

In classical Roman law, contracts were only legally binding if they fell within specific categories, such as stipulations or certain types of real or consensual contracts. When an agreement did not fit these categories, and one party had fulfilled their obligations without receiving the promised performance from the other party, they could seek recourse through a legal action known as *condictio* (specifically *condictio ob rem*, later referred to as *condictio causa data causa non secuta*) to recover what they had provided.

However, this remedy was not applicable in cases involving illegal agreements. There are two distinct scenarios to consider:

1. Illegality on the recipient's side: in situations where the recipient of the performance, say A, acted illegally, such as paying B to prevent B from committing a crime or to induce B to fulfil existing obligations. A was entitled to recover their performance through the *condictio ob turpem causam*, regardless of whether B had fulfilled their promise.
2. Mutual illegality: when both parties engaged acted illegally, for instance, A paying B to commit a crime or give a judgment in A's favour, A was prohibited from initiating a *condictio*, regardless of whether B had fulfilled their promise.

The Roman jurists recognised that in cases where only one party had fulfilled their obligations, denying the right to recovery could result in an unjust advantage for the other party. This principle was reflected in the maxim *in pari delicto* (or *in pari turpitudine*) *potior est conditio possidentis*, meaning that when both parties were involved in the illegality, the position of the possessor (the recipient of the performance) was stronger.

subsidiary application is added, which depart from the apparently rigid German and Spanish solutions, and come closer to the current English law configuration.

[43] See n 10 above.

Since there were arguments both for and against allowing recovery in these situations, the Roman legal tradition often opted to maintain the status quo.[44]

Both the *condictio ob turpem causam* and the exclusion of recovery in cases of illegality involving both parties were integrated into the *ius commune*. Hence, the *in pari delicto* rule, which barred recovery in the event of illegal contracts, continued to be a fundamental component of the *ius commune*. This rule was frequently grounded in the overarching principle, *nemo auditur turpitudinem suam allegans*, which signifies that no one would be heard by the court when they plead their own wrongdoing.[45]

B. *In Pari Tuirpitudine* as a General Feature of All European Legal Systems: 'Effects' and 'Defects'

The *in pari turpitudine* rule has endured in the majority of European legal systems. This is the case of § 1174 ABGB,[46] Article 2035 of the Codice Civile,[47] § 817 BGB[48] or Articles 1305 and 1305 of the Código Civil.[49]

The rationale behind this rule, which has faced considerable criticism in modern times, is rooted in common sense: (i) the law is not inclined to assist a party who has knowingly engaged in reprehensible behaviour that places them outside the boundaries of the legal order; (ii) the claimant should not be allowed to build their case on their own wrongdoing; (iii) upholding the dignity and integrity of the court is of paramount importance; and (iv) denying restitution can serve as a form of punishment for the parties involved and act as a deterrent against engaging in immoral and illegal activities.

However, it is essential to acknowledge that this rule also has significant drawbacks: (i) in cases where both parties have performed their respective obligations, the exclusion of restitution perpetuates the illegal circumstances without providing a remedy; and (ii) when only one party has fulfilled their obligations, the denial of recovery may result in an overly severe penalty relative to the degree of illegality, leaving the other party with an undeserved advantage.

There are cases that show the unjust result to which this rule can lead. In 2018, Belgian newspapers reported a case in which five Iranian refugees sued a trucker whom they had paid to illegally transport them from a Belgian city to England. The refugees paid the trucker €1400 each for the trip, which never materialised. According to the *in pari turpitudine* rule, they would not be able to claim restitution, regardless of the criminal consequences which human trafficking clearly had with respect to the trucker.[50]

[44] Zimmermann (n 5) 844ff.

[45] Meier (n 2) 1921–22.

[46] In the chapter on service contracts.

[47] In the chapter on unjust enrichment.

[48] The rule takes the form of a restriction of the *condictio ob turpem causam*; however, it is generally agreed that it applies to all claims in unjustified enrichment: Meier (n 2) 1923.

[49] In the chapter on void and avoided contracts.

[50] Case reported in J Delvoie and S Declercq, 'Restitution of Performance Under an Illegal Contract: A Belgian Perspective on Patel v Mirza' (2018) 2 *European Review of Private Law* 245; see also references therein.

Some of these criticisable aspects of the classical doctrine of *in pari turpitudine* are attempted to be overcome by the Spanish Código Civil, which on this point adds some quite genuine aspects that are rarely seen on a comparative level. As noted above, the Spanish Código Civil addresses this issue in Articles 1305 and 1306, which read as follows:

> Article 1305: 'When the nullity arises from the illegality of the cause or object of the contract, if the fact constitutes a crime or fault common to both contracting parties, they shall have no action against each other, and action shall be taken against them, and the things or price which were the subject matter of the contract shall be applied as provided for in the Criminal Code with respect to the effects or instruments of the crime or fault.
>
> This provision is applicable to the case in which there is only a crime or fault on the part of one of the contracting parties; but the one who is not guilty can claim what he has given, and is not bound to fulfil what he has promised'.
>
> Article 1306: 'If the fact in which the *ob turpem causam* consists does not constitute a crime or a fault, the following rules shall be observed:
>
> (1) Where the fault is on the part of both contracting parties, neither of them may repeat what they have given under the contract, nor claim performance of what the other has offered.
>
> (2) Where it is on the part of one contracting party only, he cannot repeat what he has given under the contract, nor can he claim performance of what he has been offered. The other, who is a stranger to the *ob turpem causam*, may claim what he has given, without the obligation to fulfil what he has offered'.

In short, what is essentially determined by these provisions is the following:

1. If both parties are culpable of the illegality of the contract, neither of them may obtain restitution of what they would have given by virtue of the contract.
2. If only one of the parties is culpable of the illegality of the contract, he will have no action to recover what he would have given; and the innocent party will have the right to obtain restitution.
3. In cases where the illegality of the contract is constitutive of a crime or civil wrong, the things or price of the contract shall also be subject to the application provided for in the Criminal Code[51] (namely, it will go the public coffers).[52]

With this last nuance, Spanish law avoids one of the criticisms of the *in pari turpitudine* doctrine: in the case where the illegality of the contract constitutes a crime involving both contracting parties, the exclusion of restitution will not perpetuate the illegal situation.

The practical application of this rule, however, shows that there are numerous exceptions that are introduced by the courts for reasons of justice. Two recent examples can be given from Spanish case law.

[51] Arts 127–29 of the Spanish Criminal Code.

[52] JR García Vicente, 'Comentario a los artículos 1305–1306' in Bercovitz Rodríguez-Cano, *Comentarios* (n 36) 9272–74.

(i) Sentence of the Spanish Supreme Court, 23 March 2021[53]

A company belonging to a drug dealer concludes a loan contract guaranteed with a mortgage to disguise the laundering of money obtained from drug trafficking. The company used for laundering is declared bankrupt and it is questioned whether the bank's loan can be a privileged loan because it is secured by a mortgage.

In the course of the proceedings, the borrower and also the bank's agents were criminally convicted (in the latter case, for imprudence). The nullity of the loan contract is invoked on the grounds of unlawfulness of the cause, but is the rule *in pari turpitudine* applicable?

The Supreme Court affirms that the unlawfulness of the contract cannot be assessed as there was no common purpose (or purpose intended by one party and consented to by the other) of committing a crime through the conclusion of the mortgage loan contract, since the bank's representatives were only convicted for imprudence (ie not for intentional criminality).

(ii) Sentence of the Spanish Supreme Court, 30 May 2016[54]

Two shareholders transfer their shares apparently to four other persons. This is a purely fictitious ownership, constituting a case of *fiducia cum amico*. The purchasers were obliged to follow the instructions of the apparent vendors with regard to the exercise of all rights derived from the titles. In return, they obliged themselves to pay to the trustees all expenses arising for them from the formal ownership. After a few years, they demanded the return of the shares. The fiduciary holders objected on the grounds that they had not been paid the agreed expenses.

The First Instance Court ordered the restitution of the shares. The Court of Appeal held that the contract had been entered into for the purpose of concealing the securities from the applicants' creditors, which rendered the contract unlawful. For this reason, it considers that nothing can be claimed from the defendants under the contract, in accordance with the provisions of Article 1306 of the Código Civil.

The Supreme Court reverses the appeal judgment: in a case such as the present case of *fiducia cum amico*, in the face of a claim for the shares and stocks that were the object of the *fiducia*, the fiduciaries cannot invoke the provision contained in Article 1306 of the Código Civil regarding the concurrence of a *causa torpe* to avoid compliance with the obligation to return the shares and stocks whose ownership was not actually transferred between the parties in a causal system of transfer of ownership such as ours.

In short, it can be observed that Spanish case law makes a flexible use (trying to find some subterfuge that is often quite artificial) of the *in pari turpitudine* rule, which it adapts to the circumstances of the case with great elasticity.

[53] ECLI:ES:TS:2021:1079.
[54] ECLI:ES:TS:2016:2564.

C. The Abandonment of the Doctrine of *In Pari Turpitudine*: English Law after *Patel v Mirza* and European Contract Law Principles

Throughout this chapter, it has been anticipated that the jurisprudential doctrine established in English law after *Patel v Mirza* marked a turning point in the treatment of the illegality of contracts. Indeed, the *in pari turpitudine* legal doctrine was traditionally adopted in England, as expressed by Lord Mansfield, who stated that 'no court will lend its aid to a man who founds his cause of action upon an immoral or an illegal act'.[55] Over time, however, various exceptions have eroded the effectiveness of this rule. With the groundbreaking decision in 2016, the English Supreme Court has seemed to virtually derogate the *in pari turpitudine* rule – in particular, in cases of common law illegality and with regard to the possible restitution of payments arising from an illegal contract. The classic Roman doctrine of *in pari turpitudine* has been definitively overturned and it favours the proclamation of possible restitution, taking into account a set of factors that must be weighed according to the specific circumstances of each case.

Without going into detail, it is worthwhile briefly reproducing the constituent facts that were presented in this emblematic case. One party (Patel) provided £620,000 to the other party (Mirza) with the intention of placing bets on a bank's share prices using insider information. Mirza anticipated that his contacts would notify him about a government announcement regarding the bank, which was crucial for the intended betting. However, the expected information did not materialise, and as a result, the planned bets were never placed. The party who was supposed to execute the bets did not return the money to Patel, who subsequently filed a legal claim to recover the funds. The opposing party argued that the claim should be dismissed due to the illegality of the arrangement.

In this leading case, the English Supreme Court has introduced a totally new perspective on illegality in common law, which has not only affected unjust enrichment, but has also had major implications for private law in general. The fundamental principle now is that the claimant's involvement in illegal activities, or the illegal actions of another person that can be attributed to the claimant, does not automatically prevent them from pursuing a civil claim. Instead, the key consideration is whether enforcing the claim would be detrimental to the integrity of the legal system. This determination is based on a set of factors outlined by the Supreme Court, including:

1. The underlying purpose of the breached prohibition and whether that purpose would be better served by denying the claim.
2. Any other relevant public policy considerations affected by the denial of the claim.
3. Whether denying the claim is a proportionate response to the illegality, recognising that criminal punishment falls within the purview of the criminal courts.

[55] *Holman v Johnson* (1775) 1 Cowp 341.

This new approach is designed to restrict the circumstances in which the defence of illegality can be successfully invoked.[56]

A similar pattern is provided by the DCFR. As already noted, a distinction is made between the infringement of so-called fundamental principles (where the notions of public policy, common law illegality, *ordre public*, *boni mores* or immorality would fit in) and the infringement of mandatory rules (which do not enshrine these fundamental principles). In the first case, the legal consequence is radical nullity. For the second, two possible answers are offered: firstly, recourse to the specific consequence which, if applicable, determines the mandatory rule infringed; otherwise, the court will have a list of possible answers, ranging from the affirmation of the validity of the contract to the declaration of its total or partial nullity, as well as its possible modification. Moreover, in order to adopt the above decision, the court must take into consideration a set of factors (in this, identification with the doctrine of the English Supreme Court in *Patel v Mirza* is evident). The factors are the following: (i) the purpose of the rule which has been infringed; (ii) the category of persons for whose protection the rule exists; (iii) any sanction that may be imposed under the rule infringed; (iv) the seriousness of the infringement; (v) whether the infringement was intentional; and (vi) the closeness of the relationship between the infringement and the contract.

With regard to the dispute on the restitutionary consequences of illegal contracts, Articles II. – 7:303 and II. – 7:304 DCFR, the former deals with the consequences arising from a contract which is void or is avoided in relation to the property rights conveyed by virtue of such an illegal contract. It makes a cross-reference to the provisions of the DCFR on transfer of property and unjust enrichment. For its part, Article II. – 7:304 discusses a noteworthy legal recourse where a party, whose contract is deemed void or is avoided due to illegality, is granted the right to seek damages from the other party involved.

Focusing on the reference to the provisions on unjust enrichment which are of interest to us here, the relevant provision is contained within Book VII of the DCFR, in the section that pertains to defences. It is entitled 'Illegality'. Article VII. – 6:103 DCFR reads as follows:

> Where a contract or other juridical act under which an enrichment is obtained is void or avoided because of an infringement of a fundamental principle (II. – 7:301 (Contracts infringing fundamental principles)) or mandatory rule of law, the enriched person is not liable to reverse the enrichment to the extent that the reversal would contravene the policy underlying the principle or rule.

This statement confirms the existence of an *ex turpi causa* defence in principle, while explicitly acknowledging that its boundaries or extent can be defined by policy considerations. This rule, together with the range of factors and the variety of solutions that the judge may adopt in cases of contract illegality, shows the extraordinary similarity already noted between the DCFR and the solution adopted by the English Supreme Court in *Patel v Mirza*.[57]

[56] Cartwright (n 41) 204.
[57] Häcker (n 8) 368–69.

VI. Some Final Concluding Remarks

The control of the legality and morality of contracts is an essential feature of any contractual system. It makes no difference whether the emphasis is placed on legality, the notion of morality, public policy, or the legal or extra-legal character that motivates the unlawfulness of the contract. It also makes no sense to look for a specific element of the contract to deal with this matter. As Lacruz Berdejo et al stated in this sense, it is irrelevant to identify clearly what the illicit element of the contract is; the important thing is to know whether or not the illegality is sufficient to invalidate it.[58] The key, therefore, is to determine whether or not the contract is contrary to the legal/moral rule, to clarify the scope and seriousness of the infringement (in view of the interests protected by the legal/moral norm affected) and to determine the specific consequence that corresponds to this analysis. For all these reasons, the position adopted by the English Supreme Court in the emblematic case of *Patel v Mirza* can be said to be much more reasonable, overcoming the rigidity of *the in pari turpitudine* rule, which may constitute an eventual effect of contractual illegality, but never an apparently immutable general rule that has to be excepted with artificial doctrinal and jurisprudential constructions.

Focusing on the role played by cause in this context, there is no advantage in resorting to a new notion of cause in subjective terms. This has only aggravated its already difficult understanding, which should therefore be limited to its original and objective notion, closely linked to English consideration.

[58] Lacruz Berdejo et al (n 34) 184–85.

13

Cause, Consideration and Frustration

ROCÍO CARO GÁNDARA

I. General Overview

The 'frustration' of contract is a concept created by the English doctrine, used in this chapter in a general sense, that means the effects of supervening changes in circumstances, unforeseen and unforeseeable at the time of the conclusion of the contract, which render its performance impossible, unattainable, absurd or excessively onerous, to the point of releasing the debtor from the original contractual obligations.

Three different groups of situations can be included in the broad concept of 'frustration' of contracts, as parts of the general doctrine: (i) when the performance becomes physically or legally impossible ('impossibility'); (ii) when the performance is still physically or legally possible but the underlying purpose of the contract is no longer attainable, and the performance becomes useless or valueless to its recipient ('frustration' *sensu stricto*); and (iii) when the performance, though physically and legally still possible, has become excessively onerous or burdensome ('impracticability', or 'excessive hardship'). The practical differences, in every case and country, are not always easy to ascertain. Only a certain group of cases of discharge of contracts by supervening events is clearly included in the first category ('impossibility'), but the last two subsets entail significant practical problems to be identified as 'frustration' *sensu lato*, because every legal system assigns them different scopes and consequences.[1]

This work aims to be a historical and comparative analysis, with references to English, Anglo-American, French, Spanish, German and Italian law, and special mentions to the statutory law, the leading cases law, the scholars' doctrine from those legal systems and, finally, some international uniform law texts.

II. Historical Survey

The 'frustration' of contract is a general and comprehensive concept that encompasses all different excuses for non-performance: circumstances and solutions that challenge

[1] A Karampatzos, 'Supervening Hardship and Subdivision of the General Frustration Rule: A Comparative Analysis with Reference to Anglo-American, German, French and Greek law' (2005) 2 *European Review of*

the general principle of *sanctity of contract* or *pacta sunt servanda*.[2] These circumstances have been handled by two doctrines drawn from two different sources. On the one hand, Roman law developed a doctrine of 'impossibility' to deal with impossible performances: the Roman maxim *impossibilium nulla obligatio est*, originally coined by the Roman Jurist Celsus, is contained in Justinian's Digest,[3] and it means that a legal obligation that is impossible to be performed must be excused. On the other hand, canon law developed the *clausula rebus sic stantibus* as a doctrine of changed circumstances to deal with unexpected events that make a performance of greater or lesser value than anticipated by the parties. The origin of *clausula rebus sic stantibus* dates back to a text by Cicero, quoted by Saint Augustine, which was later incorporated into canon law.[4]

In the medieval and early modern periods, jurists developed philosophical and moral explanations for these doctrines. Regarding the first problem, they said that nobody could be bound to do the impossible, but they could not explain why. On the second problem, they applied Aristotelian and Thomist ideas to contract law, to formulate the 'doctrine of *causa*'; at the same time, they developed a good explanation about the effect of unexpected circumstances, through the idea of the 'implied conditions' (in contracts), *rebus sic stantibus*. This was introduced in the fourteenth century in civil law by the commentator Bartolus of Saxoferrato and his pupil Baldus de Ubaldis. Later, the doctrine of *clausula rebus sic stantibus* was further developed and simplified by the natural lawyers, but in the nineteenth century it was forgotten, because of the rise of the paradigm of autonomy of will, and the expression of liberal economic logic in civil and common law.[5] Nevertheless, the twentieth century saw the collapse of that paradigm, through the failure of classical contract law.[6] As will be seen in the following pages, the prominence achieved in recent decades by the supervening change in circumstances of the contract has contributed decisively to that crisis.

III. Comparative Survey

A. Introduction

All legal systems which are analysed here have considered the problem of the effects on contracts of changes in circumstances brought about by supervening events, but they

Private Law 105, 106–07 and 147; AH Puelinckx, 'Frustration, Hardship, Force Majeure, Imprévision, Wegfall der Geschäftsgundlage, Unmöglishkeit, Changed Circumstances. A Comparative Study in English, French, German and Japanese Law' (1986) 3 *Journal of International Arbitration* 47, 66.

[2] Among others, see E Peel, *Frustration and Force Majeure*, 4th edn (London, Sweet & Maxwell, 2022) 1.

[3] D 50,17,185; R Zimmermann, *The Law of Obligations. Roman Foundations of the Civilian Tradition* (Oxford, Clarendon Press, 1996) 686.

[4] J Gordley, 'Impossibility and Changed and Unforeseen Circumstances' (2004) 3 *American Journal of Comparative Law* 513, 530; FJ Chamie, 'El principio general de *reductio ad aequitatem* por desequilibrio contractual' (2012) 1 *Revista de Derecho Privado* 219, 222 and 275; M de Cossio, *Frustraciones y desequilibrios contractuales* (Granada, Comares, 1994) 17.

[5] J Gordley, *The Philosophical Origins of Modern Contract Doctrine* (Oxford, Oxford University Press, 1991); Karampatzos (n 1) 108.

[6] PS Atiyah, *The Rise and Fall of Freedom of Contract* (Oxford, Clarendon Press, 2003); R Caro Gándara, 'The Relational Justice of Contract' in A Cosseddu (ed), *The Role of Fraternity in Law. A Comparative Legal*

have used different tools or devices, and with different intensities, to solve them. The law systems presented below are ordered from those systems defending the 'sanctity of contract' most faithfully to those that have more clearly mitigated its effects.

B. Common Law

(i) Anglo-European Common Law

Traditionally, common law has not recognised the effect of the supervening impossibility of performance or, at least, excessive hardship. The introduction of hardship clauses has always been considered a burden of the parties, especially in commercial contracts. Only when there are no explicit or implicit provisions in this sense, does the doctrine of frustration of contract operate, and then only in very strict circumstances.

The English common law doctrine of 'absolute contracts' is expressed in *Paradine v Jane* (1647),[7] which established absolute liability for contractual debts. The case law dates back to the time of the English Civil War, when the British Royalist forces took possession of land owned by the plaintiff, Paradine, which was under lease to the defendant, Jane. The Royalists held the land from 1643 up to 1646, when they finally relinquished it. Paradine brought suit against Jane for breach of contract. Jane pleaded that the realm had been invaded by an alien enemy, which was an event out of his control that deprived him of the profits of the land with which to pay the rent. The King's Bench stated that even in some previous cases it did not allow a lessor to proceed against a lessee in times of war, and Jane was still liable for the rent.

The doctrine of frustration was introduced in *Taylor v Caldwell* (1863),[8] when the plaintiff hired the defendant's music hall for concerts over four nights. Before the first event took place, the hall was accidentally destroyed by fire, and the plaintiff claimed damages for the loss suffered. The Queen's Bench decided that the defendants were not liable for damages, because the doctrine of the sanctity of contracts was applicable only to a positive and absolute promise, but not when the contract contained an 'implied condition' stating that 'the parties shall be excused in case, before breach, performance becomes impossible from the perishing of the thing without the fault of the contractor'.[9]

Though the doctrine of frustration was first related to cases where the physical subject matter of the contract had perished, the principle of *Taylor v Caldwell* was subsequently extended to other cases where the common venture envisaged by the parties was frustrated. Specifically, in some maritime cases, the ship owner was unable to provide the chartered ship at the right time and place because, without any fault on his side, the ship had been damaged or requisitioned, or the port nominated by the charterer was closed because of war. The first decision in this regard was

Approach (London, Routledge, 2021) 259, 279; R Caro Gándara, 'En la secular búsqueda europea de un paradigma de justicia contractual: el enfoque de justicia relacional' in S Sánchez Lorenzo (ed), *Derecho contractual comparado. Una perspectiva europea y transnacional* (Cizur Menor, Aranzadi, 2016) vol I, 55 and 118.

[7] EWCH KB J5 (1647).

[8] (1863) 3 *B & S* 826, 122 Eng Rep 309.

[9] ibid 833–34 and 839.

Jackson v Union Marine Insurance Co Ltd (1874).[10] Jackson, who owned a ship, entered into a charter party for the ship to go from Liverpool to Newport with a cargo of iron rails to be used for a new line in San Francisco. The ship ran aground on the first day of the journey, and it took six months to repair it. The jury held that the delay for repairs was so long as to bring the contract to an end in a commercial sense, and the court considered that the jury had been correct.

The doctrine finally appeared in legislation in the Sale of Goods Act 1893, section 7. And later, with the famous 'coronation cases', the cancellation of an expected event consolidated the doctrine of 'frustration of purposes'. In the most important of these cases, *Krell v Henry* (1903),[11] the plaintiff hired his balcony to the defendant to watch the coronation procession of King Edward VII, but the coronation was postponed because of the illness of the king, and the hirer refused to pay for the hire. In the written contract, the parties had not expressly referred to the purpose of the hiring, but the Court of Appeal regarded the attendant circumstances in order to discover 'the foundation of the contract': both parties considered the viewing of the procession as the sole purpose of the hiring.[12]

As a consequence of the First and Second World Wars, English courts have been applying the 'doctrine of frustration of contract' in cases of legal impossibility or supervening illegality (similar to frustration by subsequent change in the law) when the government forbids the performance of a contract due to war and other wartime restrictions.[13] In peace times, English courts also apply the doctrine of frustration of contracts where the change of circumstances so delays performance or alters its nature that the performance rendered thereafter would be something 'fundamentally or radically different' from what was envisaged by the parties at the time of the conclusion of the contract. Along this line, the closure of Suez Canal in November 1956 led English courts to declare in several cases that there was a frustration of contract because the alternative route was much longer and the freightage was far more expensive. In *Ocean Tramp Tankers Corp v V/O Sovfracht (The Eugenia)*,[14] the Court of Appeal held that a time charter party was not frustrated even though the route around the Cape of Good Hope was longer and more expensive, because it was not a 'fundamentally different' voyage: the cargo of metal goods would not be affected by the longer route and there was no special reason for an early arrival.[15] The 'radical difference test' had been established before by Lord Radcliffe in *Davis Contractors Ltd v Fareham Urban District Council* (1956)[16] as a general criterion of frustration, which excludes commercial hardship, when a contract becomes simply more difficult or expensive to perform.[17]

[10] (1874) LR 10 CP 125.

[11] [1903] 2 KB 740.

[12] EG McKendrick, 'Discharge by Frustration and Force Majeure Clauses' in HG Beale (gen ed), *Chitty on Contracts*, vol I, *General Principles*, 34th edn (London, Sweet & Maxwell, 2021) 1907ff, 1910; L Merret, 'Sale of Goods' in HG Beale (gen ed), *Chitty on Contracts*, vol II, *Specific Contracts*, 34th edn (London, Sweet & Maxwell, 2021) 1943ff, 1964.

[13] The outbreak of war renders illegal all relationship between British people and alien enemies; see McKendrick (n 12) 1924; E Peel, *Treitel: The Law of Contracts*, 13th edn (London, Sweet & Maxwell, 2011) 938.

[14] [1964] 2 QB 226.

[15] ibid 240.

[16] [1956] AC 696, 729.

[17] N Andrews, 'Categories of Frustration' in N Andrews, A Tettenborn and G Virgo, *Contractual Duties: Performance, Breach, Termination and Remedies*, 3rd edn (London, Sweet & Maxwell, 2020) 381.

J Lauritzen AS v Wijssmuller BV (The Super Servant Two)[18] set out five propositions, which describe: (i) how the doctrine of frustration of contract operates 'to mitigate the rigour of the common law's insistence on literal performance of absolute promises … to give effect to the demands of justice, to achieve a just and reasonable result, to do what is reasonable and fair, as an expedient to escape from injustice where such would result from enforcement of a contract in its literal terms after a significant change in circumstances'; (ii) it 'discharge(s) the parties from further liability'; (iii) 'automatically'; (iv) 'it should not be due to the act or election of the party seeking to rely on it'; and (v) the event must occur 'without blame or fault of the side of the party seeking to rely on it'.[19]

The first position brings us the not at all peaceful question of the juristic basis of the frustration doctrine. There are different interpretations about what the judge must do ('construction of the contract') – but not always why – when applying the 'frustration of contract doctrine'.[20] Some consider that, under this doctrine, the judge must ask what type of agreement reasonable parties would have reached if, at the time of the conclusion of the contract, they had foreseen the subsequent events and made some provisions for them; others consider that courts give the parties the fair and reasonable solution that the changed circumstances demand on the basis of justice.[21] Perhaps there is no great difference between these two views. As Lord Radcliffe said in *Davis Contractors v Fareham*: 'the spokesman of the fair and reasonable man, who represents after all no more than the anthropomorphic conception of justice, is and must be the court itself'.[22]

In recent decades, there has been a tendency to move to a multifactorial test or approach, which takes into account all the circumstances of the case[23] and renders a fundamental role to proper risk allocation, that is, whether those events that change the circumstances must be considered risks that a reasonable businessman would put on the contractor seeking to avoid the contract. In this sense, *Edwinton Commercial v Tsavliris Russ*[24] confirms the exceptional nature of frustration: the charter was not frustrated as the contractual risk of the delay was on the charterers, the detention of the vessel was foreseeable and the purpose for which the vessel was chartered had been performed.[25]

More recently, Marcus Smith J held in *Canary Wharf (BP4) t1 Ltd v European Medicines Agency* that

> when one seeks to describe what a party promised, one does not recite the individual tests and conditions, but has regard to something much more elemental, that cannot necessarily be

[18] [1990] 1 Lloyd's Rep 1.

[19] ibid 8.

[20] Peel, *Frustration and Force Majeure* (n 2) 602 and 612.

[21] Rijs LJ in *Edwinton Commercial Corp v Tsavliris Russ Ltd ('The Sea Angel')* [2007] EWCA Civil 547 held that 'the dictates of justice' is 'the ultima ratio of the doctrine'.

[22] Above n 16, 728.

[23] As Lord Reid and Lord Radcliffe held in ibid 720 and 729: 'The terms which are in the contract read in the light of the nature of the contract, and of the relevant surrounding circumstances when the contract was made.'

[24] Above n 21.

[25] Peel, *Frustration and Force Majeure* (n 2) 64; Andrews (n 17) 384 and 389; N Andrews, *Contract Law in Practise* (Oxford, Oxford University Press, 2021) 570.

> captured in the precise terms used by the parties in their contract, but which requires reference to what I will term the parties' 'common purpose'.[26]

In these words, continental scholars have seen a link between the *cause* in continental law, especially the Italian *causa concreta*, and the 'common purpose' of the parties in English law, in a functional sense and beyond of its dogmatic roots, in order to propose common solutions to supervening events in European contract law.[27]

Regarding the effects of frustration in common law, it brings the contract to an end forthwith and automatically. It totally discharges both parties from their further contractual duties even if the performance of only one of them is affected by the supervening event, and the courts do not have any power to adjust or modify the terms of the contract to the new circumstances. If the circumstances fulfil the requirements, the contract is totally discharged, but if they do not satisfy them, the contract remains totally in force (an 'all or nothing' situation).[28] The power to modify a contract by the court has only been recognised in special legislations (ie during the two world wars and the COVID-19 pandemic).[29]

(ii) Anglo-American Common Law

In the USA, there are different groups of cases according to whether the change of circumstances renders the performance impossible (impossibility), much more difficult (impracticability) or worthless or pointless (frustration *sensu stricto*). The first group of cases includes situations in which performance is rendered absolutely impossible for the debtor, and the second one, those in which the change of circumstances has rendered performance for the debtor much more onerous or costly. In this sense, § 261 of the Restatement (Second) of Contracts (1981) declares that the debtor is free from his obligation if, after the formation of the contract, his performance is made impracticable by no fault of his own, due to the occurrence of an event the non-occurrence of which was a basic assumption of the contract. § 2-615 of the Uniform Commercial Code (UCC) (for sales contracts) declares that a delay in the delivery or the non-delivery of goods does not constitute a breach of contract if performance as agreed has been made impracticable by the occurrence of a contingency, the non-occurrence of which was a basic assumption on which the contract was made. Some authors consider these provisions to be *empty formulas* without effective content, but the study of cases allows the time when the debtor will be released by a change of circumstances to be deduced: the mere fact that something has become more expensive does not itself make it a case of impracticability, because each party must bear some risks.[30]

The 'doctrine of frustration' (*sensu stricto*) has been limited to cases of extreme hardship, that is, to cases where the promised performance can be rendered but, because of

[26] [2019] EWHC 335 § 29.
[27] F Mezzanotte, 'Lo scopo contrattuale nella doctrine of frustration' in G Albers, FP Patti, D Perrouin-Verbe (eds), *Causa contractus* (Tübingen, Mohr Siebeck, 2022) 675, 701.
[28] *National Carriers Ltd v Panalpina (Northern) Ltd* [1981] AC 675, 700 and 707.
[29] Peel, *Frustration and Force Majeure* (n 2) 551; Peel, *Treitel: The Law of Contracts* (n 13) 968 and 986.
[30] K Zweigert and H Kötz, *An Introduction to Comparative Law* (Oxford, Claredon Press, 1998) 532.

unforeseen circumstances, it has become very largely futile or pointless. This doctrine has been included in the Restatement (Second) of Contracts (1981), § 265.[31]

The 'failure of consideration' has been used in the USA as a theory to explain why the doctrine of frustration discharges both parties of the contract: the defendant is discharged by supervening impossibility, but the plaintiff by 'failure of consideration', as adopted in the Restatement (Second) of Contracts (1981), § 237: 'it is a condition of each party's remaining duty to render performances under an exchange of promises that there be no uncured material failure by the other party to render any such performance at an earlier time'.[32] In § 2-615 UCC (for sales contracts), the buyer may be discharged, even though its own duty to pay is not impracticable, because the seller's duty to deliver is discharged by impracticability.[33] This conception of frustration has been refused in English law.[34]

Regardless of what goes on in English courts, American rules of law recognise the power of the courts to adapt or alter the contract in cases of supervening events. In *Aluminum Corp of America v Essex Group Inc (the ALCOA case)*,[35] the contract provided that Essex had to deliver aluminium to ALCOA to smelt it. Because it was a long-term contract, it contained a flexible pricing formula, allowing ALCOA to increase its prices, but it was not sufficient when the 1973 energy crisis exploded. It was held that ALCOA was entitled to relief on the ground of impracticability and the court substituted a new formula for the flexible one.[36] In cases of temporary impossibility, the duty to perform may be merely suspended when performance is 'materially more burdensome' than that originally undertaken (Restatement (Second) of Contracts, § 269).[37]

The adaptation or alteration of a contract by supervening events is contained in § 2-613(b) UCC: it provides that where goods identified at the time of contracting suffer partial casualty, the buyer may take the remaining available quantity 'with due allowance from the contract price'. § 2-615(b) applies the principle of pro rata allocation where a supervening event affects only a part of the seller's capacity to perform; in such cases, the buyer has the right to modify the contract.[38] Comment 6 to § 2-615 UCC provides for 'adjustment' where 'neither sense nor justice is served by either answer when the issue is posed in flat terms of excuse or no excuse'. In similar terms, § 272(2) of the Restatement (Second) of Contracts provides in more general terms that where total discharge 'will not avoid injustice, the court may grant such relief as justice requires'.[39]

C. France

The 1804 French Civil Code (CC, Code civil) only regulated the effects of supervening events that produced absolute impossibility through the concepts of *cas fortuit*, *force*

[31] EA Farnsworth, *Contracts*, vol II, 4th edn (New York, Aspen, 2004) 724; NR Weiskopf, 'Frustration of Contractual Purpose. Doctrine or Myth?' (1996) 70 *St John's Law Review* 239, 271.
[32] Weiskopf (n 31) 251 and 268.
[33] ibid 255 and 268.
[34] Peel, *Frustration and Force Majeure* (n 2) 56–57.
[35] 499 F Supp 53 (1980).
[36] Peel, *Frustration and Force Majeure* (n 2) 549.
[37] ibid 546.
[38] UCC, s 2-616(1)(b).
[39] Peel, *Frustration and Force Majeure* (n 2) 550; Weiskopf (n 31) 260.

majeure (Article 1148) and the loss of the thing owed (Article 1302), according to the text in force from 17 February 1804 to 1 October 2016.[40]

The scope of 'impossibility' of performance has been extremely narrow because the 'sanctity of contract' did not allow the judicial intervention (*intangibilité du contrat pour le judge*). Such rigid interpretation of Article 1134, paragraph 1 CC 1804 (*les conventions légalment formées tiennent lieu de loi à ceux qui les ont faites*)[41] stemmed from a reaction against the excess of judicial intervention on the 'Ancien Régime'.[42] The French milestone case is *Canal de Craponne*.[43] In 1567, Adam de Craponne constructed a canal in Pélissanne and undertook to maintain it against a payment fixed in the contract for irrigating the fields of the farmers. Centuries later, the sum had become derisory and completely disproportionate to the cost of maintaining the canal. Alan Craponne's heirs sued for an increase and the lower court granted it, but the farmers sought a revision. The Civil Chamber of the Cour de cassation, in a judgment rendered on 6 March 1876, notwithstanding the fact that the obligations were disproportionate due to inflation, held that unexpected circumstances would not impact on the contract, on the basis of Article 1134 CC (1804), because the judge should not have the power to change the terms of the contract as ascertained by the parties on their private autonomy. This doctrine remained in force, but it has been criticised since the first decades of the twentieth century by the movement named *solidarisme contractuelle*.[44]

After the First World War, the inflexibility of the courts forced the legal scholars to seek a way in which the change of circumstances renders the debtor released from his obligation under the comprehensive term of *imprévision*. Some of them tried to extend the concept of *force majeure*, others sought to apply Article 1134.3 CC to say that contracts ought to be performed in good faith (*de bone foi*), while still others tried to use the intention of the parties as a ground for adapting a contract to a change of circumstances. Sometimes, *clausula rebus sic stantibus* was considered as an unwritten principle of law, and the absence of the balance between the performance of the parties was interpreted as a problem of a partial lack of *causa* or an anomaly of *causa* in an objective sense (objective cause or cause of the obligation, that is, in synallagmatic contracts, the performance of the other party, close to the concept of 'consideration').[45]

Some of these solutions have been welcomed by lower courts, but the Cour de cassation quashed them on the grounds of the very strict conditions of *force majeure*, because they were not cases of absolute impossibility of performance. Nevertheless, the Conseil d'État, the highest administrative court, in the case *Gaz de Bordeaux* (1916),[46]

[40] Ordonnance nº 2016–131 du 10 février 2016 portant réforme du droit des contrats, du régime général et de la prevue des obligations.

[41] Currently Art 1103 of the Code civil.

[42] Karampatzos (n 1) 137; D Perrouin-Verbe, 'L'évènement imprevu et le bouleversement de l'equilibre contractuel en droit français' in Albers et al (n 27) 553 and 555.

[43] Cas Civ 6 March 1876; H Capitant, F Terré, Y Lequette and F Chénedé, *Les grands arrest de la jurisprudence civile* (Paris, Dallloz, 2015) no 165, 172.

[44] See R Demogue, *Traité des obligations en général*, vol VI (Paris, Rousseau, 1931) 9; Caro Gándara, 'En la secular búsqueda' (n 6) 90.

[45] Perrouin-Verbe (n 42) 553 and 561.

[46] CE, 30 March 1916, S 1916.3.17.

elaborated a theory of unforeseeable difficulties where the economic balance of the contract was disturbed to fix a compensation on the grounds of public interest in the continuance of contracts which are essential to conduct public life in an orderly fashion. The general lighting company of Bordeaux sought to make the city of Bordeaux bear the additional cost the company incurred due to the very sharp increase in the price of coal, which had multiplied fivefold between the signing of the lighting concession and the year 1916. The Conseil d'État ruled that, in principle, the concession contract definitively regulates the obligations of the concessionaire and the grantor, and that the variation in the price of materials due to economic circumstances is a market hazard that the concessionaire must assume; however, when the economy of the contract is upset due to events that the parties could not foresee (in this case, the First World War), the concessionaire cannot be required to ensure the operation of the service under the conditions originally taken. Therefore, the company was required to provide the service, but was entitled to be compensated for the financial consequences of the situation which exceeded the normal economic risk. This doctrine has been extended in the field of administrative contracts under three conditions: (i) the event must be unforeseeable; (ii) it must radically change the balance of the contract's economy; and (iii) the difficulty must not result from the fault or negligence of the party invoking the doctrine.[47]

After the First and Second World Wars, several statutes came into force which enabled the courts to rescind or suspend certain types of contracts that had been concluded before the outbreak of the wars. However, these statutes were considered only exceptions to the general rule or principle of adherence to the original contract.[48]

French businessmen had reacted to the restrictive attitude of the Cour de cassation by expressing different types of clauses of hardship in their contracts, making an express allocation of risks, especially in international contracts, or submitting to arbitration and giving power to the arbitrator to adapt the contract to altered circumstances according to good faith.[49]

The reform of the French Civil Code, which came into force on 1 October 2016, totally eliminated the concept of cause from the Code civil[50] – ie it is no longer an essential element of the contract (see Article 1128 CC) – and introduced the *théorie de l'imprévision*, distinguishing excessive hardship (Article 1195) from impossibility (Articles 1351 and 1351-1, *l'impossibilité d'exécute*). Article 1351 CC states that the impossibility to execute the performance releases the debtor entirely when its results come from a definitive case of *force majeure*, unless he has accepted to assume the risk or he is in default. And Article 1351-1 says that when the impossibility of performing results from the loss of the thing owed, the defaulting debtor is released if it is proven that the loss would also have occurred even if the execution had taken place.

[47] H Lesguillons, 'Frustration, Force majeure, Imprévision, Wegfall der Geschäftsgrundläge' (1979) 5 *Droit et Pratique du Commerce International* 507, 525 and 528.

[48] Karampatzos (n 1) 138.

[49] ibid 139; P Stoffel-Munck, 'l'imprévision et la réforme des effets du contrat' (April 2016) *Revue des contrats* 30, 31.

[50] But not its functions, included in a number of particular solutions; see Perrouin-Verbe (n 42) 554 and 570; T Genicon, 'L'avenir de la cause en droit français des contrats' in Albers et al (n 27) 715 and 731.

The conditions of application of Article 1195 are very strict: (i) an unforeseeable change of circumstances at the conclusion of the contract; (ii) the excessive hardship of the execution; and (iii) the event cannot be a normal risk that the debtor must assume.[51] Once the conditions are met, Article 1195.2 sets forth the effects. It gives the judge a wide power to review the contract or to terminate it[52] only in default of a renegotiation agreement between the parties or, secondarily, in default of an agreement to terminate the contract or to submit it to the courts.[53] The provision is supplementary and the parties can waive the judicial review of the contract. This subsidiary nature leads some authors to maintain that this judicial intervention is more theoretical than real, because the parties, in many cases, will be very interested in introducing clauses of hardship in their contracts.[54]

Article 1195 CC is influenced by Article 1:110 of the Draft Common Frame of Reference (DCFR), Article 6:111 of the Principles of European Contract Law (PECL) and Articles 6.2.2 and 6.2.3 of the Unidroit Principles of International Commercial Contracts (PICC).[55] French scholars hold that it expresses a new, more flexible conception of the binding force of the contract and must be completed with the new Article 1104 CC,[56] but that depends on its interpretation by French courts.[57]

D. Spain

(i) Supervening Impossibility

When an obligation to deliver is impossible in a supervening way without fault of the obligor or without the obligor being in default, the consequence contained in Article 1182 of the Spanish Civil Code (SCC, Código civil) is the extinction of the obligation. Article 1184 SCC states that the debtor will also be released from the obligation to perform when the performance is legally or physically impossible. Both provisions are expressions of the principle contained in Article 1156 SCC, which regulates, as a cause for the extinction of obligations, the impossibility of providing with the expression 'loss of the thing due'. This expression must be interpreted in a broad sense, as destruction or disappearance. In the same way, Article 1122 SCC says that the thing is lost when it perishes, goes out of business or disappears so that its existence is unknown or it cannot be recovered – that is to say, when the obligation cannot be performed or be replaced by a different one.[58] The impossibility must be physical or legal, objective,

[51] O Deshayes, T Genicon and I-M Laithier, *Réforme du droit des contrats, du régime général et de la preuve des obligations* (Paris, Lexis-Nexis, 2018) 390, 404.

[52] ibid 414, 418.

[53] Stoffel-Munck (n 49) 34.

[54] Deshayes et al (n 51) 415, 419–20; Stoffel-Munck (n 49) 33; P Simler, *Commentaire de la réforme du droit des contrats et des obligations* (Paris, LexisNexis, 2016) 33–34.

[55] See section IV below.

[56] 'Les contrats doivent être négociés, formés et exécutés de bonne foi. Cette disposition est d'ordre public.'

[57] Albers et al (n 27) 553, 567–68; B Ancel, B Fauvarque-Cosson and J Gest, *Aux sources de la réforme du droit des contrats* (Paris, Dalloz, 2017) 174–81.

[58] MJ Marín López, 'Comentarios a los artículos 1182 y 1184 del Código civil' in R Bercovitz Rodríguez-Cano (ed), *Comentarios al Código civil*, vol VI (Valencia, Tirant lo Blanch, 2013) 8731; JL Lacruz Berdejo,

absolute, durable, unforeseeable and not chargeable to the debtor.[59] To declare that impossibility, it is necessary to analyse the content of the obligation as determined by the parties in the contract, taking into account the circumstances of the case. The Spanish Tribunal Supremo has established in numerous judgments that the impossibility must be definitive to expunge the obligation and it must be subject to restrictive interpretation.[60] However, in some cases, it has not been easy to separate impossibility from excessive hardship.

*(ii) Excessive Hardship (*Excesiva Onerosidad *or* Dificultad Extraordinaria*)*

There are cases in which the performance continues to be possible but has become burdensome, implying an alteration of the contractual balance in the long term or the delayed execution of the contract. To give a fair answer to these situations, which are not regulated by the SCC, Spanish case law applies the *clausula rebus sic stantibus*, grounding it, mostly, in the principles of good faith (Article 1258 and the general clause of Article 7 SCC)[61] and equity (the general clause of Article 3.2 SCC).[62] But the application of the *rebus sic stantibus* doctrine has not been uniform, and the *clausula* has also been grounded in the supervening anomaly of the concrete *causa*, in the sense that the function of the contract disappears, totally or partially, when the contractual balance between the performances of a synallagmatic contract is broken.[63] These arguments have mostly been held in cases of economic impracticability, especially during periods of economic crisis, when the Spanish Tribunal Supremo has made the application requirements of the *clausula* more flexible,[64] under the influence of the international uniform law texts and the doctrine of scholars.[65] *Cláusula rebus sic stantibus* has also been applied based on the doctrine of the disappearance of the contractual basis.[66] Sometimes it has also been

Elementos de Derecho civil, vol II. 1 (Madrid, Dykinson, 2011) 189; M Castilla Barea, *La imposibilidad de cumplir los contratos* (Madrid, Dykinson, 2001) passim.

[59] STS 22.04. 2014 (RJ 2014/2345); STS 30.04.202 (RJ 2002/4041) and jurisprudence cited there.

[60] See the jurisprudence cited in A Legerén Molina, 'La equiparación de la dificultad extraordinaria de cumplimiento a la imposibilidad sobrevenida de la prestación. Análisis crítico' (2024) III *Anuario de Derecho Civil* 1085, 1096–1102 and 1150.

[61] MP García Rubio, 'Comentario del artículo 1258 SCC' in A Domínguez Luelmo (ed), *Comentarios al Código civil* (Valladolid, Lex nova, 2010) 1385.

[62] STS 05.10.1989 (RJ 1989/6888). JM Miquel González, 'Cláusulas generales y desarrollo judicial del Derecho' (1997) 1 *Anuario de la Facultad de Derecho de la Universidad Autónoma de Madrid* 297; S Sánchez Lorenzo, 'La frustración del contrato' in Sánchez Lorenzo, *Derecho contractual comparado* (n 6) vol II, 739.

[63] F de Castro y Bravo, *El negocio jurídico. Tratado práctico y crítico de Derecho civil* (Madrid, Instituto Nacional de Estudios Jurídicos, 1967) 29; L Díez-Picazo, 'La cláusula rebus sic stantibus' in *Ensayos Jurídicos (1953–2011)*, vol 2 (Cizur Menor, Aranzadi, 2011) 2274–85.

[64] STS 30.06.2014, 333/2014 (RJ 2014/3526); STS 15.10.2014, 591/2014 (RJ 2014/6129), containing a revision of contracts by the court.

[65] Pointed out by MA Parra Lucán, 'Riesgo imprevisible y modificación de los contratos' [October 2015] *Revista CEFLegal*, no 177, 14, giving special reference to the influence, in this jurisprudence, of FJ Orduña Moreno and LM Martínez Velencoso, *La moderna configuración de la cláusula rebus sic stantibus. Tratamiento doctrinal y jurisprudencial de la figura* (Madrid, Civitas, 2013) passim.

[66] L Díez-Picazo, *Fundamentos de Derecho civil patrimonial. II. Las relaciones obligatorias* (Madrid, Civitas, 2008) 1065–71, embracing the doctrine created by Oertmann and developed by Larenz; analysing resolutions of the Spanish Tribunal Supremo applying this doctrine, see M García Caracuel, *La alteración sobrevenida de las circunstancias contractuales* (Madrid, Dykinson, 2014) 265–67.

considered in cases of unjust enrichment or enrichment without any cause.[67] It is necessary to take into account that, in Spanish law, at present, cause is an essential element of the obligations of the contract (Article 1261 SCC), whose absence – of existence, veracity and legality – is sanctioned with nullity of contract (Articles 1275 and 1276 SCC).[68] Nonetheless, this situation can change, as a 'Propuesta de modernización del Código civil en materia de obligaciones y contratos' ('Proposal of modernisation of the Civil Code in obligations and contract matters') was elaborated by a group of board members of the First Section of the Comisión General de Codificación (General Commission of Codification) and presented in July 2023 as a revision of the 'Anteproyecto' of 2009, which eliminates the *causa* as an essential element of the contract (Article 1218.2 of this Draft).[69]

Following a settled jurisprudence, a certain degree of alteration is required to understand that the contractual balance is broken or profoundly altered, so that a distortion of the contract has occurred. The requirements to apply the *clausula* are very strict: the Spanish Tribunal Supremo refers to extraordinary supervening events, unforeseen, unforeseeable and unchargeable to the parties of the contract, that suppose an exorbitant alteration of the economy of a long-term contract. The effect of application of the *clausula* is the termination of the contract if its revision is not possible, by the application of the principle of conservation of contracts,[70] and because the purpose of the clause is to compensate the imbalance of performances.[71] This is also the solution in international uniform contract law texts[72] and the Proposals of Reform of Código civil: Article 1213 of 'Propuesta de Anteproyecto de Ley de modernización del Código civil en materia de obligaciones y contratos', elaborated by the First Section of the Comisión General de Codificación in January 2009;[73] Article 526-5 of 'Propuesta de Código civil', elaborated by the Asociación de Profesores de Derecho civil in 2018;[74] and Article 1238.2 of 'Propuesta de modernización del Código civil en materia de obligaciones y contratos' ('Proposal of modernisation of the Civil Code in obligations and contract matters'), elaborated by the First Section of the Comisión General de Codificación and presented in July 2023.[75] This last text reinforces the obligation of renegotiation between the parties to adapt the contract or terminate it, as an expression of the general principle of good faith.

[67] STS 15.10.2014 (2014/6129); FJ Orduña Moreno and L Martínez Velencoso, *La moderna configuración de la cláusula rebus sic stantibus. Desarrollo de la nueva doctrina jurisprudencial aplicable al Derecho comparado* (Cizur Menor, Aranzadi, 2017) 204.

[68] See ch 8 in this book, by Antonio Legerén-Molina.

[69] www.mjusticia.gob.es/es/ElMinisterio/GabineteComunicacion/Documents/Propuesta%20de%20modernizaci%C3%B3n%20del%20C%C3%B3digo%20Civil%20en%20materia%20de%20obligaciones%20y%20contratos.pdf.

[70] Lacruz Berdejo (n 58) 509; LM Martínez Velencoso, *La alteración sobrevenida de las circunstancias. Un análisis jurisprudencial* (Madrid, Thomson Civitas, 2003) 363–72.

[71] Legerén Molina, 'La equiparación' (n 60) 34–35; García Caracuel (n 66) 328–41.

[72] See below, section IV.

[73] www.mjusticia.gob.es/es/AreaTematica/ActividadLegislativa/Documents/1292430960594-Propuesta_para_la_modernizacion_del_Derecho_de_obligaciones_y_contratos._Ano_2009.pdf.

[74] Asociación de Profesores de Derecho civil (Madrid, Tecnos, 2018).

[75] www.mjusticia.gob.es/es/ElMinisterio/GabineteComunicacion/Documents/Propuesta%20de%20modernizaci%C3%B3n%20del%20C%C3%B3digo%20Civil%20en%20materia%20de%20obligaciones%20y%20contratos.pdf.

Authors and jurisprudence have tried to mark the differences between supervening impossibility and excessive hardship, but it has not been an easy task.[76] Jurisprudence has pointed out that it is necessary to consider each individual case and its circumstances,[77] but, in this task, the Tribunal Supremo has sometimes concluded that when excessive hardship truly has an extraordinary nature, it can be equated to impossibility.[78] In those cases, the Tribunal Supremo uses terms such as 'exorbitant performance' and 'absolutely disproportionate sacrifices'.[79] Contrary to this generic statement, it has been considered that the terms are qualitatively different, because in situations of extraordinary change of circumstances, which makes the performance very or extremely onerous, or alter the contractual balance, the performance is still realisable, so they are not cases of impossibility – not even economic impossibility – but cases of supervening change of circumstances, and the remedy must be the application of *clausula rebus sic stantibus* and not the resolution of the contract. In this process, the normal *alea* of the contract is used as a determining criterion of ascertainment. This situation took place during the lockdown due to the COVID-19 pandemic, when it became necessary to review the rental price of the closed stores and shops.[80]

E. Germany

The doctrine of impossibility passed from the *ius commune* to the German Pandectists and then to the Bürgerliches Gesetzbuch (BGB, German Civil Code), and came into force in 1900. Nevertheless, the German scholars of the Gemeines Recht rejected the doctrine of the *clausula rebus sic stantibus* because of its vagueness, which is contrary to legal certainty, and because of the rejection of the natural law codes by the Historic School of Law. However, in the middle of the nineteenth century, Windscheid introduced the 'doctrine of the contractual assumption' (*Lehre von der Voraussetzung*) to give effect to supervening events. It was based on the idea that declarations of intentions are usually submitted to suppositions that could be affected by circumstances existing at the time of the conclusion of the contract and by supervening events. However, the doctrine of 'assumption' did not enter the BGB, because the drafter considered that the subjectivism of this doctrine would endanger the security of transactions, obscuring the distinction between conditions and motives.[81]

Soon, German legal writers gave the courts a general theory about altered circumstances. The most important one was Oertmann's 'doctrine of collapse of the foundation of the transaction' (*Lehre vom Wegfall der Geschäftsgrundlage*).[82] According to Oertmann, the foundation or basis of the transaction is the common assumption of

[76] Legerén Molina, 'La equiparación' (n 60) 1116–22.
[77] STS 05.05.1986 (RJ 1986/2339).
[78] STS 05.06.2014 (RJ 2014/3390); in cases of economic impossibility: STS 20.04.1994 [RJ 1994/3216], which, for the Tribunal Supremo, allows the resolution of the contract on the grounds of frustration of the purpose of the contract, and not the application of the *clausula rebus sic stantibus*.
[79] STS 06.05.1994 (RJ 1994/3888).
[80] Legerén Molina, 'La equiparación' (n 60) 1137–43.
[81] Zweigert and Kötz (n 30) 519; G Albers, 'Der Einfluss unerwarteter Ereignisse auf den Vertrag nach deutschem Recht' in Albers et al (n 27) 573, 575–82.
[82] P Oertmann, *Die Geschäftsgrundlage. Ein neuer Rechtsbegriff* (Leipzig, Erlangen, 1921).

the contracting parties regarding the current, future or continued existence of certain circumstances that can be expressed or not in a contract, and without which they would not have entered into the contract.[83] Like Windscheid's theory, Oertmann's was criticised because it was a psychological theory too. The latter differs from the other because the assumption must either be shared by both parties or, at least, manifested by one and accepted by the other at the conclusion of the contract, and not only by the party trying to be released from the contract.[84] Larenz, who developed this theory, distinguished a subjective and an objective base of the legal transaction (*Geschäftsgrundlage*). According to the distinction, the former includes a group of cases when both parties have an incorrect assumption about the circumstances of the contract and the latter includes another group of cases where a change of circumstances seriously impacts the economy or the purpose of the contract.[85]

German cases on the effect of altered circumstances are related to the effects of the two world wars in a country that was totally destroyed. German scholars declared performance impossible in the sense of § 275 BGB (*Ausschluss der Leistungsplicht*), even when it was only a case of 'economic impossibility' (*wirtschaftliche Unmöglichkeit*). So, they extended the traditional notion of impossibility to cases where the performance became an 'unconscionable' burden on the debtor. And the test of 'unconscionability of performance' (*Unzumutbarkeit der Leistung*) was strictly linked to the standard of good faith as imposed by § 242 BGB.[86]

In this sense, they have distinguished two lines of cases. In the first, one group in which the Reichsgericht[87] declared economic impossibility when a delay caused by war, revolutions or transport problems made the performance totally different in substance ot what was promised at the moment of the perfection of the contract. In the second series of decisions, the Reichsgericht released the vendor on the basis of economic impossibility when his performance was 'unconscionable' (*unzumutbar*), ie the vendor argued defence of ruination (*Einrede der Existenzvernichtung*) because of inflationary prices.[88]

In peace times, German courts have extended the doctrine of the collapse of the basis of the transaction to other cases, where more ordinary events (eg temporary export or import prohibitions) altered circumstances, but the Bundesgerichtshof,[89] despite invoking the 'doctrine of collapse of the foundation of the transaction', has used another formula to restrict the application of Oertmann's theory only in extraordinary cases of 'excessive supervening hardship' (*übermässige Leistungserschwerung*): 'only when this is indispensable in order to avoid an intolerable result incompatible with law and justice', in accordance with the standard of good faith (*Treu und Glauben*) of § 242 BGB.[90]

[83] ibid 37.

[84] Zweigert and Kötz (n 30) 522; Albers (n 81) 610–15.

[85] K Larenz, *Geschfätsgrundlage und Vertragserfüllung* (Munich, Beck, 1951) 15; Albers (n 81) 616–17.

[86] A Karampartzos, 'Supervening Hardship …' 122; R Zimmermann, *The New German Law of Obligations. Historical and Comparative Perspectives* (Oxford, Oxford University Press, 2005) 43–49.

[87] The highest Civil Court in Germany until 1945.

[88] K Zweigert and Kötz (n 30) 520.

[89] The highest German civil Court after 1945.

[90] Zweigert and Kötz (n 30) 535. However, some authors argue that in order to apply this doctrine of excessive supervening hardship, it is only necessary that there be no fault (or guarantee) of the debtor: see Albers (n 81) 602–03 and scholars cited in its note 140.

The vagueness of this formula confers a discretionary power on the courts that must be specified, taking into account the circumstances of each individual case. Its lack of predictability has been criticised as it endangers the security of transactions. Nonetheless, nowadays German case law and literature tend to consider the proper risk allocation between the contracting parties, namely a risk distribution which corresponds to the type of contract in question (*vertragstypsche Risikoverleitung*).[91]

Legal remedies of German case law include, first of all, the adjustment of the contract. The release of the contract has a subsidiary character, and it is used only in extraordinary circumstances (*ultima ratio*), when the continuation of the contract is unconscionable. Usually, discharge is not automatic, but depends on the right of rescission of the disadvantaged contracting party.[92]

On the occasion of a fundamental reform of the law of obligations of the BGB, which came into force on 1 January 2002, the 'doctrine of the collapse of the foundation of the transaction' was introduced into § 313 BGB (*Störung der Geschäftsgrundlage*). The provision is strictly regulated to allow contractual adjustment or discharge only in extraordinary cases and under narrow conditions that recall the previously reviewed case law. So, the essential factors of this statutory reform of 2002 are the 'unconscionability' (*unzumutbarkeik*) of the adherence to the unchanged contract, taking into account the risk allocation in the particular type of contract and the subsidiary character of the right to rescission or termination of the contract, as the *ultima ratio* when there is no room for adjustment.[93]

F. Italy

(i) Supervening Impossibility

Article 1463 (total impossibility) of the Codice civile (Italian Civil Code, ICC) enables the debtor, in synallagmatic contracts, to become free from his performance, and he may not demand his counter-performance in case of 'supervening impossibility' but must return what he has already received. Related to this, Article 1256 ICC states that obligations are extinguished when the performance becomes impossible for reasons not chargeable to the debtor. The resolution of the contract is automatic, so the debtor does not have to request it. In case of partial impossibility, the other party may demand a proportional reduction of his performance or the rescission of the contract when he does not have a relevant interest in the partial performance (Article 1464 ICC).[94]

The provision has been interpreted in two different ways. The first way, which is strictly objective, requires for its application an absolutely unsurmountable and

[91] Zweigert and Kötz (n 30) 535; Karampatzos (n 1) 185.

[92] Karampatzos (n 1) 125 and 127; T Rüfner, 'Art 6:111: Change of Circumstances' in N Jansen and R Zimmermann, *Commentaries on European Contract Laws* (Oxford, Oxford University Press, 2018) 899, 906; Zweigert and Kötz (n 30) 536.

[93] Karampatzos (n 1) 131 and 134; A Stadler, '§ 313' in R Stürner (ed), *Jauernig Komentar zum BGB*, 18th edn (Munich, CH Beck, 2021) 16–18; T Finkenauer, '§ 313' in *Municher Kommentar zum BGB*, vol 3, *Schuldrecht*, 9th edn (Munich, CH Beck, 2022) 82.

[94] F Galgano, *Trattato di Diritto Civile*, vol 2, *Le obbligazioni in generale. Il contratto in generale. I singoli contratti* (Padova, Cedam, 2015) 573ff; V Roppo, *Il contratto* (Milano, Giuffrè, 2011) 935–42.

objective supervening event, where the diligence of the debtor is not taken into account. The second one elaborates a notion of relatively impossibility, under the influence of German doctrine, where the 'limit of the sacrifice' determines the unenforceability of the performance of the debtor according to the general clause of fairness (*correttezza*) and good faith of Articles 1175 and 1375 ICC.[95]

Italian scholars have often highlighted the link between 'supervening impossibility' and cause, especially 'concrete cause', understood as the contractual purposes of the parties. It has been considered that the resolution of the contract by supervening impossibility is an expression of the functional synallagma, or principle of interdependence of the performances during the execution of the contract, which means the fundamental importance of the performance becoming impossible for the economy of that specific contract.[96]

This theory has had an important impact in the Corte di cassazione, which has declared the extinction of the contract by functional defect of the cause or because of the impossible realisation of the *causa negoziale concreta* in a functional sense (the specific interest that the parties pursue with the contract, taking into account all the circumstances of the case)[97] though not necessary of the performance. In some of these cases the Corte di cassazione speaks about *inutilizzabilità* of the performance where the supervening impossibility lies with the creditor, who can no longer receive it. Some authors have criticised this jurisprudence, considering that they are cases of unenforceability of the performance by application of the general clause of good faith (Article 1375 ICC).[98]

*(ii) Excessive Hardship (*Eccessiva Onerosità*)*

According to Article 1467 ICC, a long-term contract may be rescinded by the courts if the performance of a party becomes 'excessively burdensome' as a result of extraordinary and unforeseeable events. This is a general principle that has two exceptions: (i) the contract will not be rescinded if the subsequent difficulty falls within the normal risks of the contract (*nell'alea normale del contratto*); and (ii) the other party can avoid rescission of the contract by offering to alter its terms in an equitable way (*reductio ad aequitatem*). This situation allows the revision of the contract by the courts. Legal scholars in these cases appeal to the obligation of renegotiating the contract according to integrative equity (Article 1374 ICC) and good faith in the execution of the contract (Article 1375 ICC).[99] In the case of a unilateral contract, the obligor may not demand the rescission of the contract, but only a reduction of his performance or a change in the type of execution, *reductio ad aequitatem* (Article 1468 ICC). Random contracts are excluded (Article 1469 ICC).

[95] O Clarizia, *Sopravvenienze non patrimoniali e inesigibilità nelle obbligazioni* (Naples, Edizioni Scientifiche Italiane, 2003).

[96] CM Bianca, 'Causa concreta del contratto e diritto effettivo' [2014] *Rivista di Diritto Civile* 251, 256; CM Bianca, *Diritto civile. 5. La responsabilità* (Milano, Giuffrè Francis Lefèbvre, 2021) 385–86; R Rolli, *Causa in astratto e causa in concreto* (Padova, Cedam, 2008) 69–75.

[97] Rolli (n 96) 75–77.

[98] FP Patti, 'Sopravvenienze e causa concreta nel diritto italiano' in Albers et al (n 27) 637 and 645–48.

[99] E Gabrielli, *Studi sulle tutele contrattuali* (Padova, Cedam, 2017) 12.

Article 1467 ICC has been interpreted by Italian scholars and jurisprudence in very different ways. Sometimes it has been considered that it affects the object of the contract. Some jurisprudence has pointed out that it is a problem of the contractual assumptions of the parties. Indeed, for a time it was defended as the legal regulation of *presuposizione*, under the influence of Windscheid's theory.[100] But the principal Italian doctrinal stream has indicated that it is a problem of the supervening defect of the cause that prevents the subsistence of the contract.[101] The relationship between *eccessiva onerosità sopravenuta* and cause of the contract dates back to the explanatory Report of the Minister of Justice, Dino Grandi, to Codice civile 1942, which introduced to Italian law of contract the discipline of excessive supervening hardship with references to contractual balance.[102]

Cause in Codice civile 1942 is considered as a requisite for the validity of the contract (Article 1325), but has been used by different case laws to express the influence of supervening events on the contractual balance. In this sense, some jurisprudence has used *causa concreta* – or reason that concretely justifies the particular contract – to determine if the contract can still apply the interest of the parties in cases of functional defect of *causa*.[103]

This role of *causa concreta* has been questioned in different ways by authors and jurisprudence, especially with reference to its superfluous nature.[104] For instance, cause as the justification for a patrimonial attribution and the functional defect of it are taken into consideration to explain the obligation to renegotiate.[105] But is it really necessary? In fact, the remedies to supervening hardship have changed from the resolution of the contract to a duty of renegotiating based on integrative equity and good faith between the parties (Articles 1175, 1374 and 1375 ICC)[106] because they are remedies more adapted to current business, characterised as long-term relations or relational contracts.[107]

This is a common trend that is also understood by French and German law[108] and some uniform contract law texts that also include a more general duty of cooperation and loyalty between the parties.[109] The use of general clauses,[110] such as equity and

[100] Chamie (n 4) 254; Patti (n 98) 657–64.

[101] Rolli (n 96) 54–58, 67–68; Patti (n 98) 651.

[102] R Caro Gándara, 'El modelo contractual italiano' in Sánchez Lorenzo, *Derecho contractual comparado* (n 6) vol I, 327–29.

[103] E Gabrielli, 'L'eccessiva onerosità sopravenuta' in M Bessone, *Tratatto di diritto privato*, vol XIII (Turin, UTET, 2011) 339, 367–70; Rolli (n 96) 78–80.

[104] Patti (n 98) 649–64.

[105] Rolli (n 96) 80.

[106] T Mauceri, 'Sopravvenienze perturbative e rinegoziazione del contratto' [1997] *Europa e diritto privato* 1095; CM Bianca, 'La nozione di buona fede quale regola di comportamento contrattuale' (1983) I *Rivista di diritto civile* 205; Patti (n 98) 666–68.

[107] S Landini, 'Vincolabilità dell'accordo e clausole di rinegoziazione. L'importanza della resilienza delle relazioni contrattuali' (2016) 1 *Contrato e impresa* 179; S Trubiani, 'La rinegoziazione contrattuale tra onere ed obbligo per le parti' (2012) 6 *Obligazioni e contratti* 447; F Gambino, 'Rischio e parità di posizioni nei rimedi correttivi degli scambi di mercato' (2010) 1 *Rivista di diritto civile* 1041; F Macario, 'Rischio contrattuale e rapporti di durata nel nuovo diritto dei contratti: dalla presupposizione all'obbligo di rinegoziare' (2002) 1 *Rivista di diritto civile* 10063; G Sicchiero, 'Buona fede e rischio contrattuale' (2006) 4–5 *Contratti e impresa* 919.

[108] See sections III.C and III.E above, respectively.

[109] See section IV below; Chamie (n 4) 254.

[110] Cause has also been considered a general clause.

good faith, consequently implies assigning judges a discretionary decision-making power to adapt the content of the contract, bearing in mind all the circumstances of the case, through what has been described by the Corte di cassazione as *governo giudiziario della discrezionalità contrattuale*.[111] These considerations were taken into account in the Proposal to reform the Civil Code presented to the Italian Senate on 19 March 2019, which delegates to the government the right to modify the Codice civile. The text of the delegation refers in Article 1.i) to the right of the parties of a contract that becomes excessively burdensome, due to exceptional and unforeseeable circumstances, to renegotiate in good faith, or, if there is no agreement, to ask the judge to adapt the contractual conditions in order to restore the balance between the performances of the parties.[112]

IV. International Uniform Contract Law Texts

The Vienna Convention on Contracts for the International Sale of Goods (VC) does not contain a specific regime for supervening change of circumstances nor for excessive hardship, but Article 79 regulates excuses for non-performance that are cases of disclaimer of the VC's strict system of liability.[113] Scholars do not agree about its scope of application: from more restrictive interpretations, which only include cases close to impossibility, to more extensive ones, which also encompass economic impossibility, impracticability and excessive hardship. In this sense, the PICC have been considered as general principles of international commercial trade, to integrate the gaps of the VC by application of Article 7.2 PICC.[114]

PICC, PECL, DCFR and the Common European Sales Law (CESL) start from the *pacta sunt servanda* principle (PICC 6.2.1, PECL 6:111(1), DCFR III.-1:110(1), CESL 89(1)), then make exceptions to it in cases that are very similar to each other, but with some small differences. They envisage a change of circumstances that occur after the conclusion of the contract and render the performance excessively onerous (PECL 6:111, CESL 89) or so onerous that it would be manifestly unjust to hold the debtor to the obligation (DCFR III.-1:110), or supposes a fundamental alteration of the contractual equilibrium (PICC 6.2.2). In all of them, the onerousness may be caused either by an increase in the cost of performance or by a devaluation of the counter-performance, with the same formula as Article 1195 of the French Code civil and Article 1467 of the Italian Codice civile. The effects are also very similar in all of them: the parties may reach an agreement or, if they do not succeed, the court has the power to adapt or rescind the contract (PICC 6.2.3, PELC 6:111(3), DCFR III.-1:110(3) (d), CESL 89(2)). The requirements are very similar: the change in circumstances could not reasonably have been taken into account at the time of the conclusion of the contract

[111] Caro Gándara, 'El modelo contractual italiano' (n 102) 331.

[112] F Macario, 'Dalla risoluzione all'adeguamento del contratto – Appunti sul progetto di riforma del codice civile in tema di sopravvenienze' (2020) V *Il Foro italiano* 102; F Gambino, 'Il rinegoziare delle parti e i poteri del giudice' [2019] *Jus civile* 397; P Sirena, 'Eccessiva onerosità sopravvenuta e rinegoziazione del contratto: verso una riforma del codice civile?' [2020] *Jus* 14.

[113] AM Garro and AL Zuppi, *Compraventa internacional de mercaderías* (Buenos Aires, Abeledo Perrot, 2012) 331.

[114] Peel, *Frustration and Force Majeure* (n 2) 553–55; García Caracuel (n 66) 433–35.

by the disadvantaged party (PICC 6.2.2(b), PECL 6:111(2)(b), DCFR III.-1:110(3)(b), CESL 89(3)(b)); the events are beyond his control (PICC 6.2.2(c)); and the risk was not assumed by him in the contract (PICC 6.2.2(d), PECL 6:111(2)(c), DCFR III.-1:110(3)(c), CESL 89(3)(c)).[115]

V. Conclusions

Formula pacta sunt servanda and *clausula rebus sic stantibus* are two specific rules to express two general and fundamental different principles: security and stability in transactions that, as has traditionally been held, demand the inviolability of the contractual agreements ('sanctity of contract'), on the one hand, and equitable contractual justice, which advises the termination or revision of the contract, on the other. The greater influence of one or the other determines the nature and the effects of supervening events in all of the countries and texts analysed.

The practical results are difficult to compare because of their different historical-political and social-economic circumstances. Nevertheless, we can highlight some general trends. (i) During the last century, law systems have evolved from narrow and subjective solutions to more extensive and objective ones. (ii) The facts of the specific cases and the allocation of risks are increasingly relevant in all of the countries analysed. (iii) In most of them, except Italy and Spain, the question is not usually linked to the theory of cause. (iv) International uniform law texts have an important influence on statutory national reforms and the orientations of new case law.

[115] Rüfner (n 92) 899–911; García Caracuel (n 66) 435–42.

14

Causa, Consideration and Unjust(ified) Enrichment

BIRKE HÄCKER

I. Introduction

Let me start with a confession. The topic the conference organisers and editors of this collection have asked me to explore from a comparative perspective, '*Causa*, Consideration, and Unjust(ified) Enrichment', is both extremely exciting and tremendously daunting. It is exciting because it brings together, in a triangular fashion, themes and topics I have been thinking about for a long time. However, it is also daunting because there are so many different aspects and facets to each of the three elements in the title, all mind-bogglingly complicated in their own right in just one jurisdiction alone, that tackling the whole trio within the confines of a single comparative chapter feels like a near-impossible task.

I take this task to be centred on the interrelationship between, on the one hand, the notions and doctrines of *causa* and/or consideration and, on the other hand, the law of unjust or unjustified enrichment in the broadest possible sense. With this handle in mind, the question is: what causes the difficulty? It is essentially rooted in three main factors. These are worth highlighting up front – not so much as an exculpatory defence for the analytical complexity (or indeed shortcomings) of what follows, but because certain patterns flowing from them will keep coming to the surface and will ultimately determine the shape of the present inquiry.

The first factor is the lack of stable terminology. Notions such as *causa*, 'cause' or 'consideration' are ambiguous. Not only are they not readily 'translatable' from one legal system to the other, but they are context-dependent even within a given legal system, such that they can take on different meanings depending on where exactly and how exactly they are used. Moreover, what counts as an 'unjust' or 'unjustified' enrichment also differs significantly between systems, as already indicated by the divergence in terminology. My own attempt to grapple with the issues will be confined to the three jurisdictions I know best, English, German and French law, but I am hoping that one or the other observation may also be of interest in other systems.

The second problem is that two of the three jurisdictions considered here have undergone or are undergoing big changes with respect to our three focal points. The 2016 reforms of the French law of obligations famously suppressed the concept of *la cause* as a requirement for the validity of contracts and made certain adjustments to what might be described, in a broad sense, as the French law of unjustified enrichment.[1] In England, the orthodox doctrine of consideration has been significantly loosened over the past decades,[2] and it only narrowly escaped further erosion in the last big Supreme Court decision concerning variation of contracts.[3] Moreover, the English law of restitution for unjust enrichment appears to be in a permanent state of flux, regarding both its core structure and its proper remit. It is, in fact, quite hard to know what exactly the legal position and basic framework *is* with respect to restitution for unjust enrichment – as opposed to what participants in the debate suggest it *should* be. Since this is not the place to rehearse any of these debates in detail, even a basic depiction of English law inevitably entails a personal judgement call and a degree of (over)simplification.

Thirdly and finally, several different layers of the analysis need to be kept neatly apart and yet brought together later on for the sake of seeing the larger picture. On the transactional side, which is the usual point of departure for discussions of *causa* and consideration, we can distinguish (theoretically at least) between the 'obligational' level of contracting and the stage at which proprietary consequences or other shifts of wealth eventuate. The latter may be called the 'dispositive' level or the 'transfer' or 'performance' level. The way in which the obligational and dispositive levels interact varies between jurisdictions, and as a result the significance and function of the law of unjust(ified) enrichment also varies. Moreover, all three jurisdictions recognise a part of the law of unjust(ified) enrichment which is not, or not directly, transfer- or performance-related. Although the history, nature and content of that part also differs substantially, we may ask what it tells us about a given system's notion of *causa* or legal basis.

In the following, I will try to do two things. First, I will disentangle as briefly as reasonably possible different contexts and senses in which the terminology of *causa*[4] and 'consideration' is – or was – used at different levels within the three legal systems (section II). Then I will point to a number of tricky questions pertaining to the relationship between these notions and the law of unjust(ified) enrichment (section III). My aim is to explain, against the backdrop of the preceding comparison, how and why those questions arise, and what their implications might be. It is not to provide definitive answers or to argue strongly in favour of any particular view. If some of the questions and potential implications seem 'odd' to readers or take them outside their well-settled national doctrinal comfort zones, then that is just the kind of intellectual stimulus and healthy disruption that a comparative perspective brings to the table.

II. Different Notions of *Causa* and Consideration

The core meaning of the Latin term *causa* is 'reason' or 'cause', in the sense of something giving rise to something else. The former is thus at least a part of the 'causal'

[1] See Arts 1128, 1302 et seq and 1303 et seq CC (new 2016 version).

[2] Through doctrines such as that of promissory estoppel and the recognition in principle that a 'practical benefit' can constitute valuable consideration (see the text to and following nn 27–28 below).

[3] *Rock Advertising Ltd v MWB Business Exchange Centres Ltd* [2018] UKSC 24, [2019] AC 119.

[4] Or terms generally treated as synonyms, such as 'cause', 'legal basis', etc.

chain leading to the latter. As is well known, however, the concept of 'causation' is not entirely straightforward, either in the physical world or in the legal sphere.[5] In the present context, these difficulties are exacerbated by the fact that there is no visible causal link between a particular transaction or enrichment we are analysing and its supposed *causa*. The link, if it exists, is a purely normative one. It tells us what accounts for and/or justifies the particular transaction or enrichment as a matter of law. The closest we get to a real-world fact is that the causal link or justification we are looking for may occasionally be mediated through a person's mind, in the sense that we can ask what drove the person to transact. At other times, however, subjective motivations are irrelevant or simply absent.

A. *Causa* and Consideration at the Obligational Level

(i) The Causa *Concept at the Obligational Level*

The *causa* concept at the 'obligational' level of contracting is by far the most venerable of the notions we are looking at. Its evolution from its Roman terminological foundations via the theoretical elaboration during the medieval and early modern periods right down to modern civilian doctrine and numerous codifications is well documented in the literature, including the present collection and other seminal conference volumes.[6] In essence, the *causa* concept here explains – or was and is used to explain – *why*, following an agreement or undertaking, a particular person (the debtor) owes another person (the creditor) a particular obligation. As part of the movement that shaped the original Roman law of various contracts into a general civilian theory of contract, the *causa contractus* came to be rationalised as the purpose that stood behind and was pursued through a particular agreement. The central case was the reciprocal contract, with an exchange of promises and ultimately performances, the idea being that each party undertakes an obligation *in order to* secure the other party's counter-promise or counter-performance (ie *acquirendi causa*).[7] In such a scenario, each promise constitutes the *causa obligationis* of the other. Typically, this is expressed in Latin phrases such as *do ut des* and *facio ut facias*.

One might ask why the parties' agreement should not in and of itself be sufficient to justify the enforcement of the promises contained therein; in other words, why should a designated *causa contractus* be required at all? This objection was indeed raised in due course against the *causa* doctrine of the *ius commune* – but an outright revolution could not happen until the will theory of contracting had highlighted the parties' *consensus* as the key element upon which their mutual obligations rested. Once *consensus* had taken centre stage, the prominence of *causa* began to wane. Debates starting in the late eighteenth and continuing throughout the nineteenth century, coupled with Carl Friedrich von

[5] See eg the classic monograph by HLA Hart and AM Honoré, *Causation in the Law* (Oxford, Clarendon Press, 1960), 2nd edn (Oxford, Clarendon Press, 1985).

[6] See esp the historical contributions in Part I (chs 1–5) as well as the 'national reports' in Part II (chs 6–10) of this book; see also the contributions in G Albers, FP Patti and D Perrouin-Verbe (eds), *Causa Contractus* (Tübingen, Mohr Siebeck, 2022).

[7] To the extent that gratuitous (liberal) promises were deemed enforceable, their justification was that they had been made *donandi causa*.

Savigny's generalisation of 'contract' far beyond the realm of obligations,[8] led to the *causa* requirement of contractual validity being deliberately left out of the German *Bürgerliches Gesetzbuch* (BGB, the German Civil Code) and a number of other modern codifications. In its stead, the parties' free volition became the focal point of attention. What was needed to generate an enforceable contractual obligation was not merely that there should be some outward manifestation of accord or some formal undertaking (as, for example, in the Roman *stipulatio*), but that this outward manifestation should actually be underpinned by the full and free consent of the parties involved. Only then could their private autonomy function as the source and basis of the legal relationship being created or changed.

It would be wrong to conclude, however, that obligatory contracts are therefore 'abstract' rather than 'causal' under the BGB and in other modern systems which have dispensed with the contractual doctrine of *causa*. The fact that *causa* no longer features as an express validity requirement does not mean that obligatory contracts regularly do without it. It is widely recognised in German law that most obligatory contracts are *by their very nature* causal. All the nineteenth-century debates achieved – and sought to achieve – is that the BGB lists amongst the special contracts one type of obligatory agreement which is truly 'abstract' in nature and can therefore be validly concluded even in the absence of an agreed purpose. This is the so-called 'abstract obligatory promise (or contract)' in §§ 780 et seq BGB.[9] What, then, about the other, more conventional types of contract, such as sale? In what sense are they 'causal' despite the BGB's silence on the matter? The best answer is that they inextricably carry their *causa* within themselves, such that the contract and its *causa* always stand and fall together. To make this statement more concrete by reference to an example: if two parties freely agree on the core elements of a sale, namely the thing to be sold and the price to be paid for it (*essentialia negotii*), then the *causa contractus* is necessarily present. It forms part of the very definition of a sale.[10] If, on the other hand, the parties are at cross-purposes (eg one intending to sell, the other to hire) or their volition is impaired by some relevant defect of consent, the entire agreement is undermined, with the result that a potential problem with the underlying *causa* does not surface.

Being almost a century older than the BGB, the French Code civil (CC, French Civil Code) originally went down a different route – and with it numerous codifications modelled upon it. Article 1108 CC, as enacted in 1804 and in force until just a few years ago, listed the existence of a 'lawful cause' (*cause licite*) as an essential validity requirement of every contract. In its absence, the contract was *nul* ('null') and could

[8] FC von Savigny, *System des heutigen Römischen Rechts*, vol 3 (Berlin, Veit, 1840) 309: 'Vertrag ist die Vereinigung Mehrerer zu einer übereinstimmenden Willenserklärung, wodurch ihre Rechtsverhältnisse bestimmt werden' (roughly to be translated as: 'A contract is where several persons unite to bring about a coinciding declaration of intention, whereby their legal relationships are determined'). This wide definition of 'contract', which interestingly appears to be inspired by Digest 2.14.1.1, allowed Savigny to include within the category not merely obligatory agreements, as conventionally done, but also 'real agreements' (concerning the transfer of property or other assignable rights: see the text to nn 34–36 below) and even arrangements outside the private law sphere, such as treaties in constitutional and public international law.

[9] This does not mean that the obligation based on the promise or contract is unimpeachable where there is in fact no valid *causa* underlying it – that inquiry is, however, relegated to the law of unjustified enrichment: see section II.B(ii) below.

[10] See eg W Flume, *Allgemeiner Teil des Bürgerlichen Rechts*, vol 2, 4th edn (Berlin, Springer, 1992) 170.

be declared to be such in an *action en nullité*. Obligations without a *cause*, or based on a 'false cause'[11] or an illicit *cause*, were decreed to have no effect.[12] Over the following two centuries, *la cause* turned out to be a highly complex, but also extremely malleable (and for this reason very useful) concept, which generated a substantial amount of case law and much discussion. It performed a range of different functions, from linking performance and counter-performance in synallagmatic (ie reciprocal) contracts and explaining their interdependence, to invalidating contracts entered into in order to pursue an unlawful purpose, and it was occasionally even employed to monitor the economic viability of certain business ventures or to control and strike out unfair contract terms.[13] Many fine-grained attempts at categorisation ensued.

For our purposes, it is worth noting that what emerged from the French debates were two main approaches to determining *la cause* of a contractual obligation or indeed of the contract itself (another slight ambiguity here). One way of looking at the matter was objective and essentially 'typified': for instance, to stay with the above example, the seller of goods typically contracts in order to receive payment, while the buyer typically contracts in order to obtain the goods themselves. *La cause* was thus frequently determined objectively by reference to the content of the contract. In gratuitous contracts such as gifts, however, the matter is already more difficult: the donor's 'liberal intent' (*intention libérale*) was said to be the relevant *cause* here. It is easy to imagine that, depending on how far the law was willing to dig down into a donor's mind, we can either end up with a fairly bland typified notion of 'liberal intent' or one which very concretely latches onto the individual donor's specific motives for making the gift (and potentially rendering the gift *nul* in the case of a causative motivational mistake). There is a whole spectrum between objectivity and subjectivity. A more subjective approach to *la cause* was at any rate an obvious analytical alternative to the purely objective determination. Clearly at the subjective end of the spectrum lay the French inquiry into *la cause* when it came to unlawful purposes. If the driving force in entering a contract was some illegal motive or one offending public policy and the standard of good morals, the most reliable way of invalidating the agreement (which may look perfectly innocuous from the outside) was an extreme 'subjectivisation' of *la cause*.[14]

The 2016 reform of the French law of obligations eventually suppressed the doctrine of *la cause*, so that *la cause* today no longer features in the list of validity requirements.[15] Yet this does not mean that French law now adopts a wholly 'abstract' notion of obligatory transactions. Just as under the German BGB, obligations remain 'causal' by their very nature. What the suppression of *la cause* instead entails is an increased focus on the quality of consent and the introduction into the French Civil Code of a number of specific provisions picking up various functions previously performed by *la cause*.

[11] The term 'false cause' had nothing to do with any misdescription or pretence, but simply denoted the absence of a valid *cause* from the debtor's point of view.

[12] Art 1131 CC (old).

[13] See, respectively, Cass civ 1re, 3 July 1996, D 1997.500 note Reigné (*Point Club Vidéo*), Com 22 October 1996, D 1997.121 note Sériaux (*Chronopost*).

[14] See Art 1133 CC (old). There was, of course, also a question whether or not such an 'illicit' motive needed to be shared by, or at least known to, both parties. The Court of Cassation ultimately thought not: Cass civ 1re, 7 October 1998, D 1998.563, concl Sainte-Rose.

[15] Art 1128 CC (new).

For instance, there is a new ground of 'nullity' for defective consent for *liberalités* (~ gifts) induced by the motivational mistake of the giver.[16] In reciprocal contracts, the synallagmatic connection and interdependence between the parties' primary duties of performance is now spelt out explicitly,[17] and a minimum reciprocity requirement at the inception of 'onerous' contracts is ensured by them being declared *nul* where a promised counter-performance is 'illusory or derisory'.[18] The control of unfair terms (especially exemption clauses) formerly achieved by the courts through the doctrine of *la cause* is today delegated to a special provision effectively casting the leading case into statutory form.[19]

The upshot is that *la doctrine de la cause* is indeed 'suppressed' rather than abolished in French law. Its distilled core now lies in the typical purposes pursued by various kinds of contracts, whether these be of an 'onerous' or a 'liberal' nature. Similarly to the position that has prevailed in German law since 1900, the attention formerly paid to *causa* at the obligational level will likely become submerged as the debate shifts almost entirely to whether the parties have given their full and free consent to the contract. This requires close scrutiny of the contract formation stage, especially regarding relevant defects of consent (and the concomitant grounds of avoidance or 'annulment'), and a careful monitoring of the line between agreements intended to be legally binding and mere social arrangements (ie the line reflected by the presence or absence of an intention to create legal relations).

(ii) The Doctrine of Consideration at the Obligational Level

The English doctrine of consideration, though chronologically younger than the civilian concept of *causa*, has a history that is no less varied or complex. This is not the place to explore its genesis[20] or whether and to what extent it may have been influenced by the Roman-canonical notion of *causa*.[21] We can simply note that:

> In formal terms, it is difficult to talk of any doctrine of 'consideration' before about 1560. While it seems clear that lawyers before this time had the idea that there was some additional factor that was needed to make promises binding, there was no consistent way of describing it. The sources reveal a variety of terms: consideration, *causa*, recompense, *quid pro quo*. As the action of assumpsit became established, consideration emerged as the term that described the necessary feature.[22]

[16] Art 1135(2) CC (new).

[17] Arts 1219–20 CC (new) codifying the defence of non-performance.

[18] Art 1169 CC (new) acting as a qualification to the general principle in Art 1168 CC (new).

[19] Art 1170 CC (new) replicating the *Chronopost* decision (see n 13).

[20] See ch 3 in this book, by David J Ibbetson.

[21] In the past, it has variously been suggested that 'consideration' in English law evolved as a self-standing concept, but not in isolation from notions already in existence (such as *causa*): SFC Milsom, *Historical Foundations of the Common Law*, 2nd edn (London, Butterworths, 1981) 357–58; JH Baker, 'Origins of the "Doctrine" of Consideration, 1535–1585' in MS Arnold et al (eds), *On The Laws and Customs of England: Essays in Honor of Samuel E Thorne* (Chapel Hill, University of North Carolina Press, 1981) 336, 341: 'It is … impossible to assert that the nascent phrase represented precisely the notion of *quid pro quo* or *causa*. There is a very strong case, on the other hand, for saying that it actually combined both notions.'

[22] D Ibbetson, *A Historical Introduction to the Law of Obligations* (Oxford, Oxford University Press, 1999) 142.

Over the next couple of hundred years, lawyers grappled more or less overtly with what exactly it was that made parol promises (ie those not encapsulated in a deed) binding. Reciprocity was clearly the central case, but the question arose whether having a reasonable motive for promising something or being under a pre-existing 'moral obligation' to do so could also count as consideration. During the eighteenth century, Lord Mansfield made several attempts to establish the sufficiency of a promisor's serious intent (of which he thought consideration to be no more than strong evidence).[23] The rise of the will theory might have supported such a development and set English law on a more civilian path, yet in 1840 a lid was finally put on the matter by the (re)affirmation in *Eastwood v Kenyon* that consideration was not only an indispensable ingredient, but also that nothing short of providing some *fresh* value would satisfy the requirement.[24]

This is how English law arrived at the classic modern definition in *Currie v Misa*: 'A valuable consideration, in the sense of the law, may consist either in some right, interest, profit, or benefit accruing to the one party, or some forbearance, detriment, loss, or responsibility, given, suffered or undertaken by the other.'[25] The contractual doctrine of consideration is therefore by-and-large objectively orientated. A tinge of subjectivity comes into play only when determining whether the promisor really wanted and requested something (eg a forbearance on the part of the promisee), such that the parties' undertakings are in fact reciprocal. It is, incidentally, in this form that the English doctrine began to have reverse repercussions on the civilian notion of *causa* in some parts of the world where the colonial legal legacy had placed the two in close proximity.[26]

The further travails of consideration are well known and will not be rehearsed here. Suffice it to say that the doctrine has come under pressure from various sides, but has not (yet?) succumbed. On the one hand, the rise and ever-broadening recognition of 'practical benefit' as valuable consideration[27] has made the concept more flexible, yet also denuded it of its economic core. The evolution of the doctrine of promissory estoppel,[28] on the other hand, means that the role of consideration is nowadays often confined to that of a 'sword'. So long as the recipient of a promise has detrimentally relied upon it, the estoppel defence provides a 'shield' against claims by the other party that are incompatible with the assurance. This is, of course, not the same as allowing estoppel to replace consideration outright. Nonetheless, in combination with the 'practical benefit' doctrine the modern position does not seem far off Lord Mansfield's idea that any seriously intended promise ought to be prima facie binding.

[23] See esp *Pillans v van Mierop* (1765) 3 Burr 1663, 97 Eng Rep 1035; *Atkins v Hill* (1775) 1 Cowp 284, 98 Eng Rep 1088; *Hawkes v Saunders* (1782) 1 Cowp 289, 98 Eng Rep 1091.

[24] *Eastwood v Kenyon* (1840) 11 Ad & El 438, 113 Eng Rep 482. See already the earlier case of *Rann v Hughes* (1778) 4 Brown PC 27, 2 Eng Rep 18; 7 Term Rep 350 (note) 101 Eng Rep 1014 (note).

[25] *Currie v Misa* (1875) LR 10 Ex 153, 162. See already the remarkably similar statements in *Stone v Withipole* (1589) and *Slade v Morley* (1602), as cited in J Baker, *Baker and Milsom: Sources of English Legal History. Private Law to 1750*, 2nd edn (Oxford, Oxford University Press 2010) 533, 534 and 460, 468, respectively.

[26] For an overview of the 'historical dialogue' between the two concepts, see B Häcker, 'Causa und consideration. Ein historischer Dialog' in Albers et al (n 6) 323, here esp 348–53.

[27] The leading case is the Court of Appeal decision in *Williams v Roffey Bros & Nicholls (Contractors) Ltd* [1991] 1 QB 1.

[28] The foundational case here is *Central London Property Trust Ltd v High Trees House Ltd* [1947] KB 130.

In practice, a serious commitment is arguably already all that is required for the variation of contracts (as opposed to their creation).[29] Much more doubtful is whether English law would ever be willing to give up consideration at the inception of a contract. It is in my view likely to continue insisting on parol promises being part of a 'bargain' when first undertaken – whether in the sense of genuine arm's length reciprocity or merely in the nominal or 'formal' sense exposed by Oliver Wendell Holmes.[30] Even if there is a certain parallel here with the civilian notion of *causa*,[31] it would be rash to conclude that the English doctrine of consideration is inevitably destined for the same fate as the French *doctrine de la cause*. While consent (which is purely objective in the case of English law) will no doubt stay centre stage and henceforth attract more and more of the limelight in all systems, the bargain theory seems too firmly engrained in the common law tradition to be overthrown by a will-theory-based side wind.[32]

B. *Causa* and Consideration at the Dispositive (~ Transfer or Performance) Level

When we shift our focus from the 'obligational' to what I have called the 'dispositive' level, involving the execution of actual transfers rather than executory contracts and promises, we once again encounter the concepts of *causa* and consideration, yet confusingly with different meanings, connotations and functions. Some differences are slight, others fundamental. A further difficulty is attributable to the fact that the *causa* for a transfer is often not directly visible. Depending on the kind of transfer system a jurisdiction operates, the notion of *causa* shifts its shape and can only really be viewed through the lens of the law of unjust(ified) enrichment.

(i) 'Causal' and 'Abstract' Transfer Systems

It is well known that there are two types of transfer systems as far as the relationship between a disposition and the 'cause' behind it is concerned (using 'cause' in the literal and broad sense here to avoid grappling with its technical meaning just yet). The transfer either requires some reason, purpose or underlying obligation to be legally effective, or it does not. If the existence of a 'cause' is a condition of validity, then we are dealing with a 'causal' transfer system. If not, then the transfer system is 'abstract'.

[29] Indeed, US law formalises this position in § 2-209(1) of the Uniform Commercial Code.

[30] OW Holmes Jr, *The Common Law* (London, Macmillan & Co, 1881) 273: 'In one sense, everything is form which the law requires in order to make a promise binding over and above the mere expression of the promisor's will. Consideration is a form as much as a seal.'

[31] WW Buckland and AD McNair, *Roman Law and Common Law: A Comparison in Outline* (Cambridge, Cambridge University Press, 1936) 177: 'Our doctrine of consideration has become so artificial in modern times that it is not now possible to speak of it as *quid pro quo*. It has thus been said [by Oliver Wendell Holmes: see n 30] that it is essentially a "form" in the sense that it is an element additional to consent, necessary to make the agreement binding … Indeed it is not easy to see much difference between "form" in Mr Justice Holmes' sense and the notion of *causa*.'

[32] With terminological acknowledgement of what Denning LJ said in *Combe v Come* [1951] 2 KB 215, 220.

While 'abstract' dispositive transactions have been around for a long time,[33] they were not fully theorised or conceived as a distinct category until well into the nineteenth century. Just as Savigny's very broad notion of 'contract' had paved the way for the inclusion in the German BGB of 'abstract obligatory promises',[34] so it had an even profounder impact on the way German law conceptualises dispositive transactions and particularly so-called 'real agreements'. These are seen as strictly separate transactions from the underlying obligatory contract (if any).[35] They are not merely *exceptionally* 'abstract', like the 'abstract obligatory promise', but *routinely* so.[36] The 'principle of abstraction' has become a hallmark of the German BGB. It pervades the entire dispositive level, from property transfers to the assignment of claims, and it even extends, for instance, to grants of legal authority in the agency context. It is for this reason that looking at transfers in isolation cannot really tell us much about the meaning of *causa* at the dispositive level.

It is fair to say that, outside Germany, the 'principle of abstraction' has fascinated more lawyers than it has persuaded to follow suit. Many, if not most, continental systems continue to adhere to the idea that, in principle, transfers of property or other dispositions need to be supported by a *iusta causa* in order to be fully effective. One reason why a transfer system might be 'causal' is that it does not formally distinguish between the 'obligatory' and 'dispositive' transactions. While the different levels may well be acknowledged as such in theory, it is simply not possible to accommodate abstraction without also committing to a principle of separation.[37] French law is such a causal transfer system. It understands property transfers envisaged by an obligatory contract (such as sale) as being effected by that very *same* contract, whether instantaneously or subject to some delay (eg in the case of a reservation of title clause).[38]

Rather bizarrely from a comparative point of view, it is very hard to pin down English law when it comes to categorising transfer systems as 'causal' or 'abstract'. There are clearly some pockets of abstraction, particularly in the realm of immovables, and it is almost[39] beyond dispute that causality prevails in the sale of goods. That said, there are also large areas where we simply cannot be certain which model English law follows. Elsewhere, I have described the resulting patchwork either charitably as a 'weird-and-wonderful

[33] There is little doubt that, in Roman law, conveyances by *in iure cessio* and (in classical times at least) by *mancipatio* were 'abstract'. Some controversy surrounds the *traditio*. However, I do not intend to enter a historical debate here on the (supposed) requirement of *iusta causa traditionis*.

[34] See n 8 above and the text thereto, as well as the text to n 9.

[35] This is the so-called 'principle of separation' (*Trennungsprinzip*).

[36] In a sense, however, 'abstraction' is merely a default rule for dispositive transactions in German law (albeit a strong and sticky default). Parties are free to make the dispositive transaction 'causal' by expressly including within it a condition to the effect that the disposition shall only be valid if it is supported by an underlying obligation or *causa*.

[37] Note that the reverse is not true (not even indicatively). Austrian and Spanish law, for instance operate a principle of separation, yet are both firmly committed to a 'causal' transfer system. The transactional separateness of contract and conveyance can be inferred from the fact that a *traditio* is required to effect the transfer.

[38] That the acquisition of ownership could be down to the *effect* of an obligation has always been clearly spelt out in Art 711 CC and is now reconfirmed under the heading 'effet translatif [du contrat]' in Art 1196 CC (new). Note, however, that the 2016 reform of the French law of obligations actually brought about a slight shift in the way this property transfer is conceptualised: G Helleringer, 'The Proprietary Effects of Contracts' in J Cartwright and S Whittaker (eds), *The Code Napoléon Rewritten: French Contract Law after the 2016 Reforms* (Oxford, Hart Publishing, 2017) 207, 208–11.

[39] Critical: W Swadling, 'Rescission, Property, and the Common Law' (2005) 121 *LQR* 123.

mixture of both' or less charitably as a plain 'muddle'.[40] Most scholars and practitioners today appear impliedly to assume that transfers by delivery (such as gifts by hand or cash payments of money) as well as by deed, where the obligatory contract is not used as a vehicle of conveyance, follow an abstract transfer model.[41] This is relevant here because *if and where* the concept of *causa* (or a *causa*-equivalent) at the dispositive level is indeed best viewed through the lens of the law of unjust(ified) enrichment broadly conceived, it is helpful to bear one in mind when discussing or assessing the other against the background of the relevant transfer system. We will see later on, however, that traditional English law poses additional challenges in this regard.[42]

(ii) Causa *Through the Lens of the German Law of Unjustified 'Performances'*

Let us then begin by first looking at *causa* through the lens of the German law of unjustified enrichment, or more specifically through the lens of the German law of unjustified 'performances'. The use of the term 'performance' (*Leistung*) indicates that we are concerned with claims for the recovery of benefits 'deliberately and purposively' bestowed by a claimant upon a defendant and increasing the defendant's wealth.[43] Under the so-called Wilburg/von Caemmerer dichotomy,[44] these claims are grouped together in the category of *Leistungskondiktion*. They are the *condictio indebiti*,[45] the *condictio ob causam finitam*,[46] the *condictio ob rem* (or *condictio causa data causa non secuta*)[47] and the *condictio ob turpem vel inustam causam*.[48] It will be recalled that the gist of the German principle of abstraction is that, provided all the relevant conditions of validity are met, dispositions are valid whether or not they are supported by an underlying *causa*. Where the latter is lacking or frustrated, it falls to the law of unjustified enrichment to correct the resulting (often proprietary) misallocation of assets and rights through providing a personal claim to have the disposition reversed. This is the realm of the *Leistungskondiktion*.

The above list, in combination with what was said about the principle of abstraction, already reveals a potential tension between two different meanings of *causa*: one objective, the other more subjective. Most German lawyers consider the *condictio indebiti* to be the central case of a *Leistungskondiktion* and regard the relevant *causa* as the obligation in pursuance of which a performance was rendered (but which turns out not to exist). This amounts to an objective understanding of *causa* or 'legal basis'

[40] B Häcker, 'Contract and Conveyance: The Further Repercussions of Different Transfer Systems' in J Cartwright and AM López y López (eds), *Property and Contract: Comparative Reflections on English and Spanish Law* (Oxford, Hart Publishing, 2021) 89, 132 and 98 respectively.

[41] See the short overview ibid 98–101; see also the more detailed treatment in E Bant and M Harding (eds), *Exploring Private Law* (Cambridge, Cambridge University Press, 2010) 200, esp 205–09.

[42] See section II.B(iv) below.

[43] German lawyers define *Leistung* as 'bewusste und zweckgerichtete Mehrung fremden Vermögens'.

[44] Foundational: W Wilburg, *Die Lehre von der ungerechtfertigten Bereicherung* (Graz, Leuschner & Lubensky, 1934); E von Caemmerer, 'Bereicherung und unerlaubte Handlung' in H Dölle, M Rheinstein and K Zweigert (eds), *Festschrift für Ernst Rabel*, vol 1 (Tübingen, Mohr Siebeck, 1954) 333.

[45] § 812(1), 1st sentence, alt 1 BGB.

[46] § 812(1), 2nd sentence, alt 1 BGB.

[47] § 812(1), 2nd sentence, alt 2 BGB.

[48] § 817, 1st sentence BGB.

(*Rechtsgrund*). On this understanding, the legal basis for a performance is the contractual or other (eg statutory) obligation which the performance discharges. In the case of the *condictio ob causam finitam*, the legal basis initially exists, but later falls away with prospective effect (eg where a gift is revoked after being made).

Yet there is another approach towards *causa*, which is actually the more venerable. According to this (subjective rather than objective) understanding, *causa* refers to the purpose pursued by rendering performance. The *Leistungskondiktion* is warranted where the envisaged purpose of performance fails to be achieved. In the case of the *condictio indebiti*, for instance, the purpose of performance is to discharge a debt – the transferor is acting *causa solvendi*. If that debt does not exist, the purpose necessarily fails and the performance can be recovered through a claim in unjustified enrichment.

In the case of the *condictio indebiti*, the objective and subjective approaches are two sides of the same coin and it hardly matters which we adopt. However, other performance-based claims rely on the more subjective understanding of *causa*. The other name of the *condictio ob rem*, applicable outside the contractual context, describes this idea very precisely: a *condictio* lies where something is given for a purpose which fails to be achieved (literally: *causa data causa non secuta*). In order to prevent the transferor's mere unspoken motives generating a claim, the purpose has to be one that is either agreed between the parties or is at least known and accepted by the recipient of the performance. The *condictio ob turpem vel inustam causam* also brings the purpose-orientation of the *causa* concept to the fore: it applies where 'the *purpose of a performance was so defined* that the recipient has, by his acceptance of it, violated a statutory prohibition or good morals' (emphasis added).[49]

(iii) Causa *Through the Lens of the French Law of Restitution Following 'Nullity' and 'Undue Payment'*

A number of aspects immediately strike foreign lawyers about the French law governing this area. One is that the law called 'unjustified enrichment', now codified under that heading (*l'enrichissement injustifié*)[50] but until 2016 based on case law and known as *enrichissement sans cause*,[51] scarcely comes into play in the legal analysis of the scenarios we are looking at here.[52] Instead, and this is the second striking aspect, the relevant cases typically fall to be dealt with under one of two distinct regimes: the contractual action for 'nullity'[53] and the rules on 'undue payment'.

[49] Note the important qualification in § 817, 2nd sentence BGB, according to which the claim is usually barred if the claimant who has rendered performance 'is guilty of the same contravention' (of the statutory prohibition or the standard of good morals).

[50] Art 1303 et seq CC (new).

[51] It appears that the rebranding was connected with the suppression of the (contractual) *doctrine de la cause* in the 2016 reforms, although the notion of *la cause* in the enrichment context actually differed from that in the contractual context and although no substantive change in the law was intended: E Descheemaeker, 'The New French Law of Unjustified Enrichment' (2017) 25 *Restitution Law Review* 77, 79.

[52] There is, admittedly, a residual role of the general enrichment action in cases resembling the *condictio causa data causa non secuta* and dealing with transfers made for an extra-contractual purpose that fails to be realised.

[53] Historically, looking back at its Roman origins, the action for nullity appears to have evolved from the praetorian doctrine of *restitutio in integrum* rather than from the *condictiones* known to the *ius civile*.

Where, under the pre-2016 version of the French Civil Code, a party wanted to assert that a contract lacked a *cause licite*, or where before and since the reform some other ground of nullity is made out, the appropriate course of conduct was and remains to bring an 'action for nullity' before a competent court.[54] In the wake of this action, any benefits conferred in pursuance of the contract that is declared *nul* have to be returned to the party from whom they originated. Remarkably, until 2016, this was not expressly spelt out anywhere in the Code; rather, it was simply regarded as a necessary consequence of the 'annihilation' of the contract (*l'anéantissement du contrat*) and was therefore seen as part-and-parcel of contract law rather than as having anything to do with 'undue payments' or the like.[55] Since the 2016 reforms, the relevant rules have been contained in a new set of provisions headed *les restitutions*,[56] to which the provisions on nullity now refer.[57] For our purposes, the important takeaway message is that, as far as the consequences of nullity go, there is an immediate and direct link in French law between the reasons for the invalidity of the contract (including formerly the absence of a *lawful cause*) and the restitutionary response flowing from that nullity. In other words, French law does *not* interpose a new, second layer at which the *causa* concept becomes relevant afresh to the reversal of the disposition.

By contrast, where a transfer is made in pursuance of a merely *supposed* obligation (contractual, statutory or otherwise) which later turns out not to exist, the transferor's claim to restitution is based on the rules governing 'undue payment' (*le paiement de l'indu*, previously described as *la répétition de l'indu*).[58] The word *paiement* here refers to any performance by the claimant[59] and not merely the payment of money, as the English translation might perhaps suggest. Although the term 'cause' is not used, there is a close relationship between the recovery of 'undue payments' reflecting the Roman *condictio indebiti* and the immediately ensuing (now newly inserted) section concerning unjustified enrichments.[60] The former is, in a sense, *lex specialis* vis-à-vis the latter. In providing that restitution must be made where something is received 'without being due' (*sans être dû*), the French Civil Code appears to adopt an objective view of what it is that justifies the recovery – namely, the absence of the supposed obligation. This resembles the German objective understanding of *causa* at the dispositive level. However, the more subjective view is also reflected in the text, albeit more faintly. By explaining that every payment 'presupposes a debt' (*suppose une dette*), the Code impliedly acknowledges the

[54] Where the complaint was that, despite the claimant's own performance under a reciprocal contract, the other party had failed to render the promised counter-performance, the action brought for this particular 'failure of *cause*' was often an *action en résolution* (thus approved by the Court of Cassation) rather than the *action en nullité*.

[55] See eg Cass civ 1re, 24 September 2002, no 00-21.278, Bull civ I, no 218, 168, emphasising the distinction between restitution consequent on the annulment of a contract, where the regime is 'subject to the rules of nullity', and the recovery of what are now called 'undue payments' ('les restitutions consécutives à une annulation ne relèvent pas de la répétition de l'indu mais seulement des règles de la nullité'). Historically, the French action for nullity appears indeed to have grown up from the praetorian doctrine of *restitutio in integrum* rather than from the *condictiones* known to the Roman *ius civile*.

[56] Arts 1352 et seq CC (new).

[57] Art 1178(3) CC (new) concerning *la nullité*. Similar references are contained in other provisions of the Code (see n 113 below).

[58] Arts 1302 et seq CC (new); Arts 1376 et seq CC (old).

[59] Including, since 2016, also services rendered to the defendant.

[60] Arts 1303 et seq CC (new), on which see the text to nn 87–89 below.

importance of the purpose for which a performance is rendered, namely that a *paiement* is by its very nature rendered *solvendi causa*.[61] One could argue that this failure to achieve the intended purpose is the real reason why the payment can be recovered if it turns out not to have been due.

Prior to the 2016 reform, the restitutionary regimes consequent on the nullity of contracts and undue payments were thought of as strictly separate,[62] but since then both have been taking the reader to the same new, unified provisions on *les restitutions*.[63] In that sense, the connection between the two scenarios is now more visible than it used to be. Yet this does not mean, on the other hand, that when we look at *les restitutions* we see a unified French notion of *causa* staring back at us. At the dispositive level, the *causa* concept in French law was and remains context-specific and to some extent hidden somewhere amongst the elements of any given cause of action.

(iv) From 'Failure of Consideration' to 'Absence/Failure of Basis' in the English Law of Unjust Enrichment

In English law, the notion of *consideration* – and, as we shall see, to some extent even an equivalent to the notion of *causa* – also plays a role at the dispositive level when analysed through the lens of the law of unjust enrichment. However, it takes on a different meaning from 'doctrine of consideration' at the obligational level outlined above.[64] To get to grips with its meaning, it is important to bear in mind a key structural difference between the English law of *unjust* enrichment as conventionally understood and the civilian idea of a (more or less unified)[65] law of *unjustified* enrichment. While the latter focuses on the absence of a *causa* or legal basis capable of providing a justification for the defendant's enrichment,[66] the former looks to identify so-called 'unjust factors' as positive reasons for the restitutionary claim. Typical unjust factors are mistake, undue pressure (especially duress) and, crucially here, 'failure of consideration'. Although unjust enrichment as a field in its own right is barely half a century old,[67] the underlying approach appears to be reflected as long ago as in the seminal eighteenth-century case of *Moses v Macferlan*,[68] where Lord Mansfield stated in respect of the performance-based so-called action for money had and received:

> [I]t lies for money paid by mistake; or upon a consideration which happens to fail; or for money got through imposition, (express, or implied;) or extortion; or oppression; or an

[61] *cf* Descheemaeker (n 51) 84, who explains that this to some extent makes up for the fact that a requirement formerly read into the restitutionary claim, namely that the claimant should have made a mistake (*erreur*) when rendering payment, has been jettisoned by the 2016 reform for straightforward cases of the *condictio indebiti*.

[62] See eg the quote in n 55 above.

[63] See the references in nn 56–58 above.

[64] *cf* above, section II.A(ii).

[65] But see discussion in section III.C below.

[66] Or, more specifically in the present performance context, for the claimant's performance to the defendant.

[67] Its establishment in England owes much to the seminal textbook by R Goff and GH Jones, *The Law of Restitution* (London, Sweet & Maxwell, 1966); the final judicial recognition came (only) with the House of Lords decision in *Lipkin Gorman (a firm) v Karpnale Ltd* [1991] 2 AC 548.

[68] *Moses v Macferlan* (1760) 2 Burr 1005, 97 Eng Rep 676.

> undue advantage taken of the plaintiff's situation, contrary to laws made for the protection of persons under those circumstances.[69]

In speaking of a 'consideration which happens to fail', Lord Mansfield did not mean the kind of consideration that makes a promise enforceable in the contractual context, since that is typically a counter-promise. By contrast, the unjust factor called 'failure of consideration' refers to the actual performance of the counter-promise,[70] or indeed, outside the contractual context, to the achievement of the extra-contractual purpose that the claimant pursued in rendering performance to the defendant. There is a distinct similarity here with the civilian *condictio causa data causa non secuta*, and it has been argued that this is in fact exactly what Lord Mansfield had in mind.[71] If so, then *consideration* and *causa* may be counterparts as much at the dispositive level as they are at the obligational level. And there is in fact another, connected similarity. The shift in the meaning of 'consideration' between the obligational and the dispositive level was actually mirrored in French law prior to the 2016 reforms: for while the *cause* of one party's contractual obligation could be seen as lying in the other's counter-promise, when the complaint was that the contractual *cause* had subsequently failed for want of reciprocation, what was meant by *la cause* was the counter-performance rather than the counter-promise.[72]

It will be evident from the above list of 'unjust factors' that they are by-and-large[73] orientated towards the 'vitiated' or 'qualified' consent of the claimant enricher, so that they have 'subjective' undertones. Mistake is an instance of consent 'vitiated' from the outset, while failure of consideration is based on 'qualified' consent where the condition of the defendant keeping the enrichment subsequently fails. In the unjust factor world, the objective presence or absence of a 'legal basis' for the enrichment is only of indirect relevance: it acts as a defence, so that even if otherwise all the essential elements of a claim have been made out (eg in a mistaken payment case), the claim will nonetheless falter if the defendant was legally entitled to the enrichment (eg under a valid contract).[74]

[69] ibid 1012 and 680–81, respectively.

[70] As Viscount Simon LC explained in *Fibrosa Spolka Akcyjna v Fairbairn Lawson Combe Barbour Ltd* [1943] AC 32, 48: 'in the law relating to the formation of contract, the promise to do a thing may often be the consideration, but when one is considering the law of failure of consideration and of the quasicontractual right to recover money on that ground, it is, generally speaking, not the promise which is referred to as the consideration, but the performance of the promise. The money was paid to secure performance and, if performance fails the inducement which brought about the payment is not fulfilled. If this were not so, there could never be any recovery of money, for failure of consideration, by the payer of the money in return for a promise of future performance, yet there are endless examples which show that money can be recovered, as for a complete failure of consideration, in cases where the promise was given but could not be fulfilled'.

[71] See P Birks, 'English Law and Roman Learning in Moses v Macferlan' (1984) 37 *Current Legal Problems* 1, 18.

[72] This similarity is highlighted by B Nicholas, *The French Law of Contract*, 2nd edn (Oxford, Clarendon Press, 1992) 122.

[73] This is otherwise for the so-called 'policy unjust factor' recognised in the overpaid tax case of *Woolwich Equitable Building Society v IRC* [1993] AC 70.

[74] I have in the past described this as an 'indirect accommodation' of the 'absence of basis' approach: B Häcker, 'Unjust Factors versus Absence of Juristic Reason (*Causa*)' in E Bant, K Barker and S Degeling (eds), *Research Handbook on Restitution and Unjust Enrichment* (Cheltenham, Edward Elgar, 2020) 290, 301–02.

Yet the traditional 'unjust factor' approach to restitution for unjust enrichment has come under pressure over the past two to three decades. Although English courts have repeatedly reaffirmed the orthodoxy,[75] some key academics began to call for a reorientation of the subject around a civilian-style 'absence of basis' notion, whether in the form of a realignment *in toto*, as most prominently argued by the late Peter Birks shortly before his death,[76] or at least in respect of certain performance-based claims, as recently proposed by Robert Stevens.[77] It is not possible to resolve or even outline the whole debate here,[78] but it is worth noting in the present context that 'failure of consideration' as a concept played a crucial role in sparking it.

The development was occasioned by a spate of cases concerning highly speculative interest-swap arrangements which many local authorities had entered, despite it being outwith their competence, rendering the relevant contracts void.[79] Courts nonetheless had difficulty ordering restitution. The recognised unjust factors often did not quite fit the bill. In this situation, some decisions started to invoke the 'absence of consideration' as a reason for restitution, thereby indicating that a payment had been made in purported performance of an invalid contract.[80] As one judge put it, 'it is the very fact that the contract is ultra vires which constitutes the total failure of consideration justifying the remedy of money had and received or restitution for unjust enrichment'.[81] This involved a shift of meaning from what is traditionally understood by 'failure of consideration', but it opened the door to focusing more directly on whether or not a performance was actually owed by the claimant to the defendant. 'Failure of consideration' thus became 'absence of consideration', and 'failure' or 'absence of consideration' in due course turned into 'failure' or 'absence of basis'.[82] Peter Birks concluded:

> The swaps cases show that the invalidity of a contract is in itself the reason why there has to be restitution of enrichments transferred under it. The invalidity means that those enrichments have no explanatory basis. They are transferred *sine causa*. After the swaps cases English law is bound to use this civilian method of answering the third question [ie when an enrichment is to be considered 'unjust'].[83]

[75] Recently and perhaps most emphatically in *Swynson v Lowick Rose LLP* [2017] UKSC 32, [2018] AC 313, [32] (Lord Sumption); *Samsoondar v Capital Insurance Co Ltd* [2020] UKPC 33, [2021] 2 All ER 1105, [21] (Lord Burrows).

[76] P Birks, *Unjust Enrichment* (Oxford, Oxford University Press, 2003) and 2nd edn (Oxford, Oxford University Press, 2005).

[77] R Stevens, *The Laws of Restitution* (Oxford, Oxford University Press, 2023) esp Part II (chs 3–6) headed 'Unjustified Performance'.

[78] For an overview with further references, see Häcker, 'Unjust Factors' (n 74) 303–12.

[79] *Hazell v Hammersmith and Fulham London Borough Council* [1992] 2 AC 1.

[80] See esp *Westdeutsche Landesbank Girozentrale v Islington London Borough Council; Kleinwort Benson Ltd v Sandwell Borough Council* [1994] 4 All ER 890, 924 (Hobhouse J); *Guinness Mahon & Co Ltd v Kensington and Chelsea Royal London Borough Council* [1999] QB 215, 227–28, 230 and 236 (Morritt and Walker LJJ).

[81] *Guinness Mahon* (n 80) 227.

[82] More recent cases appear to prefer the language of 'failure of basis' over 'absence of basis'.

[83] Birks, *Unjust Enrichment*, 2nd edn (n 76) 113. Birks also repeatedly warned against the dangers of 'corrupting' of the word 'consideration' by varied usage: ibid 110 and 129–60.

C. *Causa* in the Law of Unjust(ified) Enrichment Outside the 'Performance' Context

We have seen that, in the performance context, the notion of *causa* (and to some extent also that of consideration) has the potential to take on different shades of meaning at the dispositive level. The objective appearance of *causa* in the context of 'causal' or 'abstract' property transfer systems thus becomes markedly more nuanced when one considers it through the lens of the law governing 'undue payments', or in other systems, unjust or unjustified enrichments, especially through the lens of the equivalents to the *condictio indebiti* and the *condictio ob rem (condictio causa data causa non secuta)*. An element of subjective purpose here begins to compete with a purely objective understanding.

As might well be expected, this is different when one turns to 'non-performance cases' as these would be described in the Wilburg/von Caemmerer taxonomy,[84] namely cases where the defendant's enrichment does not result from some 'deliberate and purposive' transfer or other wealth-increasing act on the part of the claimant. In German law, this is the realm of the so-called *Eingriffskondiktion* (concerning enrichment by infringement of another's rights), the *Verwendungskondiktion* (concerning improvements made to another's property, typically land) and the *Rückgriffskondiktion* (concerning the payment of another's debt in the absence of other recourse mechanisms). What always matters is whether the defendant was objectively *entitled* to the enrichment, whether by dint of statute, by contract or otherwise.[85]

In French law, non-performance cases are mostly captured by the (subsidiary) general action for unjustified enrichment.[86] Modelled on the Roman *actio de in rem verso*, judicially recognised in the famous *Boudier* case[87] and finally put on a statutory footing by the 2016 reforms,[88] the relevant provision now states that 'an enrichment is unjustified where it stems neither from the fulfilment of an obligation by the person impoverished nor from his intention to confer a gratuitous benefit'.[89] Although the latter indicates that the justification for retaining an enrichment (formerly known as its *cause*) may be subjectively motivated, on closer inspection the 'intention to confer a gratuitous benefit' actually takes us straight into the performance context.[90] In genuine non-performance cases, we are of necessity thrown back onto an objective legal reason for the resulting shift in wealth. To the extent that non-performance scenarios are

[84] See n 44 above and the text thereto.

[85] For further discussion, see section III.E below.

[86] But see the caveat in n 90 below. It is also worth noting in this context that typical 'infringement' cases will often already be caught by the delictual general clause in Art 1240 CC (new), with its wide notion of 'fault'. This allows the French law of extra-contractual liability to do a part of the work which under the German BGB is relegated to the *Eingriffskonditkion*.

[87] Cass req, 15 June 1892, DP 1892.1.596, S 1893.1.281 (*Patureau-Miran v Boudier*).

[88] Arts 1303 et seq CC (new).

[89] Art 1303-1 CC (new) in the 'official' translation by J Cartwright, B Fauvarque-Cosson and S Whittaker.

[90] Since the performance/non-performance distinction drawn in Germany is alien to French doctrine, it cannot be neatly mapped onto the French provisions. Just as some 'non-performance' cases may be regarded as falling under the provisions governing *les restitutions* (see n 91 immediately below and the text thereto), so some 'performance' cases appear to feature within the general enrichment action now codified in Arts 1303 et seq CC (new).

exceptionally governed by the 'undue payment' provisions rather than the subsidiary regime for 'unjustified enrichments', as arguably where someone discharges another's debt and seeks recovery from the true debtor,[91] all that counts is which of the two parties ultimately has to bear the financial burden. Again, this is a purely objective question.

Under English law, too, if non-performance cases can teach us anything at all,[92] it is that the normative basis of such claims is determined objectively rather than subjectively. Mistaken improvements of another's property believed to be the improver's own may yield a claim or at least a possessory lien[93] based on unjust enrichment quite irrespective of the improver's inadvertence.[94] Subrogation similarly depends on the legal system ultimately requiring the defendant to shoulder the debt which the claimant ended up discharging. And infringement cases akin to the German *Eingriffskondiktion*, sometimes controversially explained by reference to a supposed unjust factor called 'ignorance' or 'powerlessness',[95] invariably assume that the defendant was not entitled (at common law, by statute or otherwise) to arrogate to him- or herself the proceeds from the exploitation of the claimant's right.

In summary, where an enrichment not brought about by the claimant's performance has to be surrendered, any conceivable legal basis or *causa* capable of providing the defendant with a defence against the claim necessarily corresponds to some objective (normative) justification or legal entitlement. The remainder of this chapter will focus primarily on performance cases, and will then revert to the broader law of unjust(ified) enrichment only in the last subsection.

III. Tricky Questions Concerning Unjust(ified) Enrichment and *Causa*/Consideration

A whole series of interesting – yet tricky – questions arise when one considers, in the light of the foregoing, the relationship between the notions of *causa* and/or consideration on the one hand, and the law of unjust(ified) enrichment on the other. As previously mentioned, the aim here is to flag and contextualise them so as to bring them to the reader's attention rather than necessarily arguing for any particular answer.

[91] See Art 1302-2 CC (new). It is not entirely clear how this new provision, especially its para (*alinéa*) 2, is to be interpreted or classified: O Deshayes, T Genicon and YM Laithier, *Réforme du droit des contrats du régime général et de la preuve des obligations. Commentaire article par article*, 2nd edn (Paris, LexisNexis, 2018) 623–24.

[92] But see the paragraph following n 148 below.

[93] Note that, under German law, the claimant will not be able to invoke the *Verwendungskondiktion* (and thus have no free-standing claim in unjustified enrichment, but at most a lien-like right of retention) where the parties' relationship is governed by the special rules pertaining between the owner of an object and its illegitimate possession (§§ 987 et seq BGB).

[94] See *Greenwood v Bennett* [1973] QB 195; Torts (Interference with Goods) Act 1977, s 6. Mistaken improvement cases such as *Greenwood* are fiendishly complicated under English law, not least on account of the doctrine of relativity of title. For a critical discussion, see Stevens (n 77) ch 14, esp 267–68.

[95] See eg A Burrows, *The Law of Restitution*, 3rd edn (Oxford, Oxford University Press, 2011) ch 16, esp 403–06.

A. Can Unjust Enrichment Tell Us Anything about the Doctrine of Consideration?

A puzzle which besets the English (contractual) doctrine of consideration to this day is whether a lack of consideration merely means that the affected promise is unenforceable or whether the absence of consideration undermines the entire contract, rendering it invalid. Remarkably, the question itself is rarely asked. We can only infer its existence from the fact that consideration is sometimes portrayed as a validity requirement of a contract under English law and at other times viewed through the party-specific lens of enforceability. Indeed, occasionally the two perspectives are merged, as when common lawyers speak of contracts being 'void and unenforceable' for want of consideration.[96]

Underlying the puzzle are two connected phenomena. Firstly, there is already an ambiguity in the very notion of 'contract'. While some authors describe a contract as 'a *promise or set of promises* which the law will enforce', others define it as 'an *agreement* giving rise to obligations'.[97] This uneasy hovering between a unilateral and a bilateral conception of contract is explained by the fact that English law never quite emancipated itself from the procedural focus on the specific forms of action, even after a coherent theory of contract law was developed during the nineteenth century. Secondly, we know from French law that it is possible to draw a distinction between the *cause* of an obligation under a contract (*la cause de l'obligation*) and the *cause* of the contract itself (*la cause du contrat*).[98] Yet no parallel distinction is made in English law, at least not expressly. The most we can say is that the consideration for each promise or performance is the counter-promise or counter-performance, and that, taken together, these provide the essential reciprocity which informs the common law notion of contract and which constitutes the contractual 'consideration' in an overarching sense.

Civilian lawyers, of course, separate sharply between contracts and obligations which are 'void' or 'invalid' and those which are merely 'unenforceable'. The litmus test lies in the law of unjustified enrichment. While 'void' or 'invalid' contracts and obligations cannot justify the defendant keeping an enrichment received from the claimant, an 'unenforceable' claim that is nevertheless fulfilled can. The latter functions as a legal basis and is commonly known as a 'natural obligation'.[99] To frame the matter subjectively, if a claimant performs to the defendant *solvendi causa* and the envisaged obligation exists, then that purpose is achieved even if the defendant could not actively have enforced the claimant's performance.

[96] See eg *Gaisberg v Storr* [1950] 1 KB 107, 114–15 (Asquith LJ).

[97] On these 'competing definitions', see S Whittaker in H Beale (ed), *Chitty on Contracts*, 35th edn (London, Sweet & Maxwell, 2024) vol 1, [1-031]–[1-033], with further references.

[98] See eg Cass civ 1re, 12 July 1989, no 88-11.443, Bull civ I, no 293, 194: 'si la cause de l'obligation de l'acheteur réside bien dans le transfert de propriété et dans la livraison de la chose vendue, en revanche la cause du contrat de vente consiste dans le mobile déterminant, c'est-à-dire celui en l'absence duquel l'acquéreur ne se serait pas engagé.' On the various different 'constructions of *causa*' mode generally, see G Albers, 'History of a Notion' in Albers et al (n 6) 19, 33–36.

[99] See eg the French Art 1302(2) CC (new): 'Restitution is not allowed as regards natural obligations which have been voluntarily discharged.'

One might thus assume that the above-mentioned puzzle surrounding consideration could be resolved quite easily: by asking whether a performance rendered in fulfilment of a promise not supported by consideration can be recovered. Yet since, on the established orthodox understanding, the English law of unjust enrichment revolves around 'unjust factors' rather than a lack of legal basis, this is not as straightforward as may first appear. We have seen that legal bases *are* relevant in the English law of unjust enrichment, but instead of their absence founding a restitutionary claim, their presence may act as a defence. The first question is therefore always whether or not the claimant's consent in rendering performance to the defendant was 'vitiated' by some recognised form of mistake or pressure. Only then can we inquire into the existence and/or validity of a contractual or other legal basis capable of justifying the enrichment.

As far as the unjust factor 'mistake' is concerned, an additional difficulty derives from the fact that, until just a few decades ago, it was thought that only liability mistakes counted, and only if they were mistakes of fact rather than law.[100] This means that it is hard to find a test case in which a promise not supported by consideration was fulfilled by the promisor under the impression of an *operative* mistake, where recovery then actually turned on the legal status of the promise (namely, whether or not it could function as a defence). A typical and plausible mistake might be one concerning the validity/enforceability of the promise or contract, but that, of course, is precisely the kind of mistake long ruled out by the 'mistake of law' bar. If the performing party was not mistaken, ie if they performed knowing that they were not required to, then no claim arises whichever approach to unjust enrichment one takes: either for want of an unjust factor or because such a fully voluntary enrichment is treated as a 'gift' and therefore constitutes a legal basis in its own right.[101] In the alternative to mistake, if the performance has been rendered as the result of some improper pressure, notably duress, then an operative unjust factor is easily found. However, the pressure brought to bear on the claimant would then also allow him or her to rescind (for duress) any potential underlying contract;[102] or the law might indeed not recognise the 'performance' as referable to the original promise at all. Both scenarios would tell us nothing about the legal status of a promise or contract lacking consideration.

The upshot is that – contrary to what one might expect – the English law of unjust enrichment, as it stands, cannot help us determine whether such promises or contracts are 'invalid', 'void' or merely 'unenforceable'. Though it would nowadays not be impossible to construct a case where the distinction matters, none has as yet emerged organically from decisions of the past. In this sense, it is at least not evident that the law of unjust enrichment exercises any ex post control with respect to the contractual doctrine of consideration. Were the question ever to arise in practice, the law of unjust enrichment may well choose not to interfere, ie not to reverse the performance in question. If so, we would at any rate know that promises which are accepted, but not supported by consideration, are in fact akin to unenforceable 'natural obligations'.

[100] These (supposed) restrictions were jettisoned in *Barclays Bank Ltd v WJ Simms Son & Cooke (Southern) Ltd* [1980] QB 677 and *Kleinwort Benson Ltd v Lincoln City Council* [1999] 2 AC 349, respectively.

[101] Birks, *Unjust Enrichment*, 2nd edn (n 76) 142, 148–52. German lawyers will at this point immediately think of the defence in § 814 BGB.

[102] Assuming (for the sake of the envisaged testing) that a lack of consideration renders contractual promises unenforceable rather than void.

B. What are the Functions of Unjust(ified) Enrichment in Causal Transfer Systems?

It is widely recognised that, in abstract transfer systems, there is a direct link between the law of unjust(ified) enrichment and property law – in that the law of unjust(ified) enrichment here 'counterbalances' the effects of the principle of abstraction. It plays an essential role in monitoring the presence or absence of a *causa* for a given transfer (or other performance) where the existence of a valid *causa* is not a prerequisite for the validity of the disposition itself. In abstract systems, the 'control' of *causa* is thus 'postponed' and takes place ex post, rather than ex ante as in causal systems; this generates what might be called a 'strong' law of unjust(ified) enrichment.[103] As Barry Nicholas once observed:

> [T]he more readily a system gives abstract effect to a conveyance or other transaction (ie allows it to be effective although its accompanying cause is vitiated by mistake or other defect), the more prominent will be the need for a remedy in terms of unjust enrichment.[104]

Indeed, there are good reasons for thinking that the German law of unjustified enrichment is, in doctrinal terms, among the most developed in the world precisely because of the attention it commands in 'making up' for the consequences of abstraction by means of the *Leistungskondiktion*.

Yet while it is undoubtedly true that the law of unjust(ified) enrichment therefore carries less weight in causal transfer systems, this does not necessarily mean that it is irrelevant or, by comparison with German law, any less useful. For Austrian law, which operates a causal *traditio* system based (similarly to Spanish property law)[105] on separation *without* abstraction, Karl Spielbüchler has explained that performance-based enrichment claims simply take on a different *function* in an environment where the absence of a *causa* prevents the passing of property or other valid transfers from occurring.[106]

Considering the same issue in the context of French law, which also operates a causal system,[107] the difficulty arises that the law of 'unjustified enrichment' properly so called (*l'enrichissement injustifié*) has little to say about situations where a purported transfer or other performance lacks a valid legal *cause*. Instead, as we have seen, the relevant cases are mostly governed by the rules on *les restitutions* following 'undue payment' or the judicial 'annulment' of a contract.[108] For present purposes, it is therefore these two we must scrutinise (their role and function) with respect to the French property

[103] See ch 9 in this book, by Gregor Albers; ch 11, by Bruno Rodríguez-Rosado.

[104] B Nicholas, 'Unjustified Enrichment in the Civil Law and Louisiana Law, Part 1' (1962) 36 *Tulane Law Review* 605, 608.

[105] See eg AM López y López, 'Contract and the Transfer of Ownership in Spanish and Latin American Law' in Cartwright and López y López (n 40) 19, esp 21–24.

[106] K Spielbüchler, 'Die Leistungskondiktion im System der kausalen Übereignung' [2001] *Juristische Blätter* 38. Spielbüchler goes on to argue that the Austrian law of unjustified enrichment ought therefore to take less (blind) inspiration from the German debate and to make certain choices differently and independently.

[107] See the text to n 38 above. Note that, unlike Austrian or Spanish law, French law does not require a *traditio* for property to pass.

[108] See section II.B(iii) above, esp the text to and following n 53.

transfer system, and not the new, subsidiary regime of *l'enrichissement injustifié*. An example may illustrate the problem.

Assume that a claimant, erroneously believing herself to have concluded a valid contract of sale with the defendant, hands over to the defendant the object of the supposed sale. Given the causal nature of the French transfer system, one would think that no property could pass in such a case,[109] and that the claimant could recover possession of the object by the defendant by means of an ordinary *vindicatio*.[110] If so, then the question arises whether and how such a *vindicatio* (an action *in rem*) competes with a claim to the recovery of the claimant's 'undue payment' to the defendant (asserted by an action *in personam*), the preconditions of which would also appear to be met. A similar question could be asked in a situation where the contract of sale is initially valid but is subsequently avoided, eg on account of an operative mistake, or prior to the 2016 reform for lack of a *cause licite*. What, then, is the relationship between a court order for restitution and a hypothetically competing *vindicatio*? As far as can be established, French law does not have any settled answers.[111]

Whereas Austrian lawyers live with the concurrence of *vindicatio* and *condictio* (in this case, a *condictio possessionis* to reclaim the possession bestowed on the defendant by the claimant's performance) and only consider curtailing the former where it risks conflicting with the latter, various accounts are conceivable for the French system. It may be that the *action en revendication* and an action for 'undue payment' are available in parallel. Alternatively, the latter may take precedence over the former as the more specific regime (thereby enlarging its practical significance); or maybe *la restitution* is simply the form that a *revendication* takes in all 'undue payment' and annulment cases.[112] Indeed, it has been suggested that the new provisions on *les restitution* in Articles 1352 et seq CC might in future come to be regarded as generally applicable to the *action en revendication*, just as they are applicable in all 'undue payment' and various failed contract scenarios,[113] regardless of the fact that the legislator did not originally envisage putting them to this purpose.[114]

Regardless of what the most compelling account may be, it is clear that in French law, too, the provisions doing the work of the *condictio indebiti* and the *condictio sine causa*, though largely outside the passage called *l'enrichissement injustifié*, are by no means obsolete merely because French law operates a causal transfer system. If anything, they take on a different role where there is a potential concurrence with the *vindicatio*. In addition, there will be many cases where no *action en renvendication* is available – whether because the claim concerns money or other fungibles which cannot

[109] Interestingly (and rather bizarrely if one takes the causal principle seriously), this is not beyond doubt: Descheemaeker (n 51) 82.

[110] The *action en revendication* is not expressly spelt out by the French Civil Code, but is said to be implied in it.

[111] The question is either not seen or largely ignored by French scholarship. For a notable exception, see C Simler, 'L'action en revendication et le régime des restitutions issu de l'ordonnance du 10 février 2016' [2018] *Recueil Dalloz* 1923.

[112] See Häcker, 'Contract and Conveyance' (n 40) 121.

[113] Beside the references to Arts 1352–1352-9 CC in Art 1302-3(1) CC (*paiement de l'indu*) and Art 1178(3) CC (*nullité du contrat*), there are also similar references in Art 1187(2) CC (*caducité du contrat*) and Art 1229(4) CC (*résolution du contrat*).

[114] Suggestion discussed by Simler (n 111).

be 'vindicated' on the French understanding,[115] because the object to be vindicated has been lost or destroyed, because the claimant's performance consisted in a service rendered rather than a property transfer[116] or because the disposition in favour of the defendant was (exceptionally) 'abstract' after all.[117] All of this demonstrates that the French regime governing the reversal of 'unjustified' transfers should not be rashly discounted and deserves much more attention than it traditionally commands.[118]

To summarise and sharpen the point: in a causal transfer system, the main function of the law of unjust(ified) enrichment in performance cases is not to 'counterbalance' the strength of property law; rather, its function should be to fine-tune as best as possible the process of reversing a given performance (or unwinding mutual performances) between the parties. This is something the regime of the *vindicatio*, which typically has to cater for the involuntary loss of possession, is ill-equipped to do.

C. (When) Does a Lack of *Causa* Mean that Property Does Not 'Really' Pass?

This third question is connected with the second, but in a sense it approaches the matter from the reverse angle, as will become obvious in a moment. Its inspiration and starting point is the so-called 'proprietary theory' of unjust enrichment first formulated by the Australian scholar Samuel Stoljar.

Stoljar argued 'the only way of *completely* transferring money (or, for that matter, any other thing) is by way of a transaction', with 'transaction' being defined as 'a transfer or payment that is truly consensual as well as intended to be final and irrevocable'.[119] He went on to reason that where a transfer is beset by an unjust factor such as mistake, 'The obvious corollary is that not only can [the claimant-transferor P] recover his money where no such transaction takes place, *but that this right of recovery derives from his own right of property*' (emphasis added).[120] Therefore, in Stoljar's view,

> the recovery of anything, whether money or land or chattels, rests on the claimant (P) being able to show that what he seeks to recover in fact 'belongs' to him, having a better 'title' to it than the person (D) from whom recovery is sought.[121]

[115] This is so irrespective of whether the notes and coins or other generic items can still be identified in the defendant's possession.

[116] The 2016 reform of the French Civil Code brought services cases within the remit of the action for 'undue payment'.

[117] Contrary to first appearances, so-called *billets non causés* are not an example of abstraction in French law because in such cases the existence of a valid cause was always (rebuttably) presumed: *cf* Art 1132 CC (1804). However, it is widely thought that negotiable instruments (*titres négotiables*) are truly abstract (*actes abstraits*) because they are 'detached' from their cause and valid solely by virtue of being signed: see F Terré, P Simler, Y Lequette and F Chénedé, *Droit civil: Les obligations*, 12th edn (Paris, Dalloz, 2019) 1718 (para 1648).

[118] A notable recent contribution to the French scholarly debate has been made by V Pinel le Dret, 'Essai sur les quasi-contrats en droit privé français: Analyse historique et comparative avec égards aux droits allemand et anglais' (doctoral thesis, Université Paris I Panthéon-Sorbonne, 2023).

[119] S Stoljar, *The Law of Quasi-Contract* (Sydney, Law Book Co, 1964) 6.

[120] ibid.

[121] S Stoljar, 'Unjust Enrichment and Unjust Sacrifice' (1987) 50 *MLR* 603, 603.

While this may look like the description of a causal transfer system in an unjust factor world, it would be wrong to think that Stoljar and his modern-day disciples[122] are necessarily seeking to deny that legal title actually passes in such cases. It is widely assumed (and in essence not disputed, at least by today's followers of Stoljar) that although English law operates a causal consensual transfer system similar to the French when it comes to the sale of goods, conveyances effected by delivery or deed are typically abstract.[123] In fact, this is precisely what lies at the heart of the modern 'proprietary theory' of unjust enrichment. One could summarise the view by saying that, although title (ie property) *technically* passes in a mistaken transfer case, it does not *really* pass in the way it should, namely, in Stoljar's words, 'completely'; normatively, the mistaken transferor remains 'entitled', and the claim in unjust enrichment reflects that proprietary remnant.[124] Put differently, the defendant's liability to make restitution is seen as a function of the claimant's continued 'interest' in the asset.

Thus expressed, there is more of a similarity with the role of unjustified enrichment in German law than in French law – except that the 'proprietary theory' regards the duty to make restitution as a reflection of an 'imperfect' transfer, while the BGB (as conventionally understood) uses and indeed needs personal restitution as a counter-balancing mechanism precisely because a transfer voluntarily executed is 'perfect' regardless of its underlying *causa*. Yet how significant is this remaining difference on closer inspection? The question is not one that can be fully resolved here, but it is worth raising expressly, for it can tell us a great deal about the role of unjust(ified) enrichment in an abstract transfer system and can indeed potentially qualify the much-criticised rigidity of abstraction itself.

If, for a moment, one lets go of the idea that a legal system's choice on the allocation of property rights – especially the decision on whether or not a valid conveyance requires the support of a valid *causa* – comes first and logically precedes the role it ascribes to the law of unjust(ified) enrichment, then it becomes obvious that both aspects need to be viewed together. If and where a claim in unjust(ified) enrichment springs up the moment a mistaken transfer is effected, the transferee's receipt is never an unencumbered one, but is burdened from the outset by the duty to make restitution to the transferor. Many common lawyers (even those who reject Stoljar's view) recognise this by treating the transferee as a constructive trustee of the asset/right received and by acknowledging that the transferor obtains or 'retains'[125] an equitable interest in it. Although the theory of so-called 'proprietary restitution'[126] was born in a very different cradle from Stoljar's 'proprietary theory', the net result on both understandings is that the legal system maintains or (re)establishes an *in rem* connection between the claimant transferor and the right or asset conveyed away.

[122] Such as P Jaffey, 'Two Theories of Unjust Enrichment' in J Neyers, M Mclnnes and S Pitel (eds), *Understanding Unjust Enrichment* (Oxford, Hart Publishing, 2004) 147; C Webb, *Reason and Restitution: A Theory of Unjust Enrichment* (Oxford, Oxford University Press, 2016).

[123] See the text to n 41 above.

[124] See Webb (n 122) chs 3–4, esp 73 et seq.

[125] The language of 'retaining' was famously used by Goulding J in *Chase Manhattan Bank NA v Israel-British Bank (London) Ltd* [1981] Ch 105.

[126] On 'proprietary restitution' generally, see the overview by T Liau and R Leow, 'Proprietary Restitution' in Bant et al (n 74) 476.

In Germany's abstract transfer system, this connection is purely personal in doctrinal terms, given that all claims in unjustified enrichment (*condictiones*) are inherently *in personam*. The personal nature of the claim is also why the BGB legislator ultimately rejected the suggestion that there ought to be a special priority for enrichment claimants in the enrichment debtor's insolvency where the asset to be returned is still identifiable amongst the bankrupt's assets.[127] However, a less teleologically minded approach would be willing to concede – following Savigny – that the *condictio* might actually be viewed as a special mechanism that allows abstract conveyances to be 'rescinded as invalid' for lack of a *causa*.[128] This would open the door to a new understanding, according to which the transferor's restitutionary right to recover a specific asset is 'not merely some [ordinary] claim with relative effect',[129] but rather signals normatively that, *inter partes* at least, the economic allocation of the asset to the transferor continues as before. The *Leistungskondiktion* can thus be understood as a kind of substitute *vindicatio* in an otherwise abstract property law system,[130] and reservations about affording the claimant priority in the defendant's insolvency appear less well founded.

D. Are Rights to Rescind Themselves Generated by Unjust(ified) Enrichment?

This fourth question is perhaps even more 'disconcerting' than the previous one, in that it will fundamentally challenge the imagination of lawyers accustomed to thinking in a particular way about the law of unjust(ified) enrichment, namely as encompassing 'claims' that reverse performances or enrichments otherwise obtained at the claimant's expense. That unjustified enrichment as a legal event should be capable of generating proprietary interests as well as purely personal rights[131] is already hard to fathom for someone trained in the civilian tradition. But that rights to avoid a transaction for particular defects of consent (at least where rescission functions as a self-help remedy rather than relying on a court order) might also be based on unjustified enrichment will no doubt push credulity. Yet there is a serious debate about just this question in English law,[132] which – as I hope to show – would be very useful for civilians to understand and engage with.

[127] A Achilles, H Gebhard and P Spahn (eds), *Protokolle der Kommission für die zweite Lesung des Entwurfs des Bürgerlichen Gesetzbuchs*, vol 2 (Guttentag, Berlin, 1898) 721–24.

[128] In this vein, see eg HH Jakobs, 'Gibt es den dinglichen Vertrag' (2002) 119 *Zeitschrift der Savigny-Stiftung für Rechtsgeschichte. Romanistische Abteilung* 269, esp 300–04, 319 and 323–24, drawing on Savigny (n 8) 358–63. See also B Häcker, *Consequences of Impaired Consent Transfers* (Tübingen, Mohr Siebeck, 2009/ Oxford, Hart Publishing, 2013) 207–08.

[129] Jakobs (n 128) 322, fn 138: 'nicht irgendeine nur relativ wirkende Forderung'.

[130] In Germany, the 'substitutive' function of the *condicatio* (so-called *Vindikationsersatzfunktion*) is more commonly discussed in connection with § 951 BGB, a provision granting restitution following the loss of property as a result of accession, specification, etc.

[131] On so-called 'proprietary restitution', see n 126 and the text thereto.

[132] For a short overview with further references, see Häcker, 'Contract and Conveyance' (n 40) 122; Häcker, *Consequences of Impaired Consent Transfers* (n 128) 106–09 and 171.

In order to do so, the first thing civilians, and German lawyers in particular,[133] must abandon is their very narrow conception of 'unjustified enrichment' as being essentially the rules contained in §§ 812–822 BGB. Instead, they would need to embrace a much wider understanding, one that encompasses not merely the miscellany of various other enrichment-type personal claims scattered throughout the BGB,[134] but one that gets right to the heart of the matter by asking what, deep down, justifies a particular right or power which the legal system bestows upon individuals.[135] That would still leave most civilians objecting that since the rescission of a contract is a *precondition* for a remedy in unjustified enrichment, the right to rescind as such cannot logically itself be generated by the event of 'unjustified enrichment'. Indeed, this objection is expressly or impliedly also raised in the common law debate.[136]

However, bearing in mind that, in analysing transactions, the core focus has long shifted from their *causa* to the quality of the parties' consent in entering them,[137] and further bearing in mind that under the old French system the lack of obligational *cause* used to be asserted by a judicial action for nullity in much the same way as a defect of consent is asserted,[138] it becomes possible to understand that the right to rescind is itself a legal power to secure restitution where otherwise the opponent would be unjust(ifiab)ly enriched by the mere fact that the transaction happened. It makes no difference to this analysis whether the transaction in question was of a personal or a proprietary nature, or both. In all cases, the other party has obtained something through the transaction (namely, a right *in personam* and/or a right *in rem*) which they ought not to have obtained, but which the legal system nonetheless treats as a given unless and until the transaction is set aside. Even though a contract should, under the will theory of contracting, theoretically be null and void where it is beset by a relevant defect of consent, this is not how legal systems adhering to the will theory choose to handle the situation. Instead of automatic invalidity, they have opted for an avoidance model,[139] and this model logically entails that the asserted defect of consent or other deficiency besetting the transaction is seen as a ground for restitution.[140]

[133] I will not venture to say much about the French law of *l'enrichissement injustifié* since this notion is very specific and does not really correspond to what is meant here by 'unjustified enrichment': *cf* the text accompanying nn 107–08 above.

[134] Especially provisions like § 951 BGB or § 684 BGB, which expressly refer to §§ 812 et seq.

[135] In the common law world, the strongest proponent of such an approach was the late Peter Birks.

[136] G Virgo, *The Principles of the Law of Restitution*, 4th edn (Oxford, Oxford University Press, 2024) 24–27, for instance, speaks (only) of the 'restitutionary consequences' of rescission, while the underlying justification and process of rescission itself is seen as being exclusively a matter of contract law.

[137] See the paragraph above containing n 8, as well as that containing nn 15–19 and the immediately following paragraph at the very end of section II.A(i) above.

[138] See the text preceding and accompanying nn 11–12 above, as well as the text accompanying n 54. Interestingly, although an absence of *cause* was originally understood as a ground of 'absolute nullity' (meaning that anybody could claim annulment of the contract), French courts later qualified this position and treated many cases as leading only to 'relative nullity' (meaning that, as with defects of consent, the action could only be brought by the other party).

[139] Further details and references regarding German law can be found in Häcker, *Consequences of Impaired Consent Transfers* (n 128) 172–73.

[140] See already the explanation given by L Jacobi, 'Die fehlerhaften Rechtsgeschäfte: Ein Beitrag zur Begriffslehre des deutschen bürgerlichen Rechts' (1896) 86 *Archiv für die civilistische Praxis* 51, 76: 'so ist damit anerkannt, daß dieses Moment nicht einen Thatbestandsmangel darstellt, sondern nur als außerhalb des Thatbestandes liegender Restitutionsgrund (*ex aequitate*) in Betracht kommt'.

Why might it be helpful to look at the matter in this way? I have suggested elsewhere that, as far as German law is concerned, it potentially paves the way for a new understanding of § 122 BGB.[141] Headed 'Rescinding Party's Liability to Compensate', § 122 BGB provides:

> (1) If a declaration of intention … has been avoided on the basis of §§ 119, 120, then, if the declaration was one addressed to another party, the person making it must compensate the other … for any loss suffered as a result of relying on the validity of the declaration, but not beyond the amount of the interest which the other … has in the validity of the declaration.
>
> (2) The liability to compensate does not arise if the party suffering the loss knew of the … ground for avoidance or would have known of it but for his negligence (ought to have known).

Effectively, therefore, anyone rescinding a contract for some problem arising within their own sphere (whether on account of a unilateral mistake or on account of a problem in the transmission of their declaration) is obliged under German law to compensate the other party's reliance interest, unless the other party was aware of the problem or ought to have been so aware. Over the years, the provision has been explained and justified in various ways, be it as a version of the doctrine of *culpa in contrahendo* or an instance of a non-fault-based liability for inducing detrimental reliance.[142] Yet against the backdrop of what was said above, it may actually be better understood as a special version of the disenrichment defence (otherwise associated with § 818(3) BGB).[143]

The idea is that an innocent 'enrichee' who has obtained the benefit of some right as a result of the transaction now to be set aside should not be left out-of-pocket by the restitutionary response. In the ordinary law of unjustified enrichment, this is achieved by reducing the enrichor's personal claim accordingly and/or by ordering counter-restitution. Within the framework of the law of rescission, the same result can be achieved either by making a successful rescission conditional upon restoring the other party's pre-contract position[144] or by requiring the rescinding party to compensate the other's reliance interest subsequent to rescission. German law has gone down the latter path. It is submitted that this account of § 122 BGB – as a corollary of rights to rescind being generated by the other party's unjustified enrichment – has the advantage of elucidating the liability as being quite naturally strict.

E. *Causa*, Legal Basis and the (Dis?)Unity of the Law of Unjust(ified) Enrichment

In this final section of the chapter, we need to shift focus from 'performance' cases to the broader law of unjust(ified) enrichment. It has been questioned for some time how far

[141] Häcker, *Consequences of Impaired Consent Transfers* (n 128) 174.

[142] For an overview, see M Schmoeckel, J Rückert and R Zimmermann (eds), *Historisch-kritischer Kommentar zum BGB*, vol 1 (Tübingen, Mohr Siebeck, 2003) §§ 116–124, paras [92]–[103] (MJ Schermaier).

[143] If so, then it is worth noting that while, in the ordinary law of unjustified enrichment, only defendants who positively knew of the lack of *causa*, or whose receipt contravened a statutory prohibition or offended good morals, are disqualified from invoking disenrichment (see §§ 818(4) 819 BGB), § 122(2) BGB extends the disqualification to people who were merely negligent in not realising that a problem existed.

[144] In English law, this is the realm of the so-called '*restitutio in integrum* bar' to rescission.

down the (at least superficial) 'unity' of the field actually reaches. For civilian systems, and German law in particular, Nils Jansen has argued that although 'it would be wrong to infer that the Pandectists went "wrong" when establishing the idea of unjustified enrichment as a separate part of the law', nonetheless nowadays 'the idea of a unified law of enrichment has broken into parts'.[145] In a similar vein, Robert Stevens recently launched a forceful attack on the subject as built up in the common law world over the course of the twentieth century:

> [T]here is no unified area of law called 'restitution' or 'unjust enrichment'. There are instead … seven or eight different kinds of private law claim, none of which has anything important in common one with another, that have been grouped together by commentators … 'Restitution' or 'unjust enrichment' should cease to be discussed as unified areas of law.[146]

The purpose here is not to weigh in on this debate, but merely to point out that the many variations in the meaning of *causa* or legal basis (or indeed 'consideration' in the old terminology of the common law), whose absence or failure is said to lie at the heart of the broader law of unjust(ified) enrichment, may well be counted as another string in the bow of these critics.

We have seen at various points throughout this chapter that, viewed through the lens of unjust(ified) enrichment and depending on the circumstances of the particular case, *causa* or legal basis can either be equated with some normative allocation decision defined 'objectively' by the law or can be a 'subjective' purpose defined by the parties themselves. In transfer or 'performance' cases, it is often possible to run both analyses in parallel (eg a payment made *solvendi causa* has a legal basis in the subjective sense if the purpose of discharging a debt is achieved, and it has a legal basis in the objective sense if the debt to be discharged existed),[147] but in non-performance cases *causa* cannot be purpose-orientated and is inevitably something else, something that has to be determined by objective normative standards.[148]

Yet just as there are a whole series of different situations whose (sole) commonality is that the enrichment to be surrendered was not purposefully bestowed on the defendant and thus not brought about by the claimant's 'performance', so there are also a whole series of different ways in which *causa* becomes relevant – or not. In infringement cases, for instance, the focus lies not so much on *justifying* a shift of wealth as on *identifying* to whom the legal system allocates a particular benefit in the first place.[149] In subrogation-type cases of financial recourse, the question is who ultimately ought to bear a particular liability in economic terms; and in cases where the defendant has expended money on the claimant's asset (without thereby rendering a performance to the claimant), *if* a self-standing claim in unjust enrichment is warranted at all,[150] then providing a secondary

[145] N Jansen, 'Farewell to Unjustified Enrichment?' (2016) 20 *Edinburgh Law Review* 123, 147. But *cf* the response by P Letelier, 'Another Civilian View of Unjust Enrichment's Structural Debate' (2020) 79 *CLJ* 527. See also ch 15 in this book, by Nils Jansen.

[146] Stevens (n 77) 3.

[147] See section II.B above, especially II.B(ii).

[148] See section II.C above.

[149] For German law, see Jansen, 'Farewell to Unjustified Enrichment?' (n 145) 143 and the references therein.

[150] In many situations, the most the claimant will have is a right to retain possession of the improved asset until the defendant reimburses (a part of) the expenditure: *cf* the comments and references in nn 93–94 above.

explanation for why the enrichment lacked a legal basis seems largely superfluous. It is in any event clear that the absence of some objectively defined *causa* is at most a very tenuous link tying non-performance cases together, and it arguably even highlights the deep-seated disunity of the (supposed) field.

IV. Conclusion

This observation concludes the survey of the relationship between *causa*, consideration and the law of unjust(ified) enrichment. Its main findings can be summarised thus: the concept of *causa* and consideration can be found at both the obligational and the dispositive levels. It takes on various nuances of meanings, even within the context of just one level. The law of unjust(ified) enrichment is typically understood as a 'link' between the two levels. In some systems, it counterbalances a principle of abstraction by providing an ex post facto control of *causa* where it is possible to bestow rights on another, particularly by transfer, without a valid legal basis for doing so. Where a transfer is 'causal' from the outset, by contrast, the function of unjust(ified) enrichment shifts to fine-tuning the unwinding of such transactions. The relationship between the *condictio* and the *vindicatio* then needs to be worked out. Suggestions that, even in abstract systems, a lack of *causa* may mean that property does not 'really' pass *inter partes*, or the idea that rights to rescind obligatory contracts for defects of consent may themselves be enrichment-based, will no doubt surprise many readers. But the beauty of comparative law is that it allows us to think outside of our accustomed national doctrinal boxes, and the more this process generates new perspectives on the relationship between *causa*, consideration and the law of unjust(ified) enrichment, so much the better.

Conclusions

15

Farewell to *Causa*?

Lessons from European History

NILS JANSEN

I. Comparative Law, Legal History and Legal Doctrine

For centuries, the learned lawyers of Europe were taught in universities to treat *causa* as a core concept of private law. The *ius commune* doctrines on *causa* featured prominently not only in the law of contracts, but also in property law and in the law of unjustified enrichment. Jurists relied on this concept to determine whether a contractual agreement was legally binding, whether a contract was void on grounds of illegality or immorality, or whether it had to be readjusted because a party's reasonable expectations had been disappointed.[1] *Causa* helped to interpret contractual agreements, and it was used to decide whether a transfer of property was effective or whether a shift of property should be reversed. More fundamentally, *causa* was the doctrinal tool for reflecting on and redefining the social functions and the morality of contract law. Much of what is discussed today under the heading of 'theory of contract' was once part of the doctrines of *causa*. In the common law, a similar picture emerges with the notion of *consideration*, which was employed in very similar contexts and hence was meant to perform very similar functions.

Despite this glorious past and despite their unquestioned role in the law of unjustified enrichment (see section VI below), *causa* and *consideration* seem to have fallen into disgrace as elements of the doctrinal language of contract law in more recent times. As Gregor Albers and Wojciech Dajczak observe,[2] the concept of *causa* had been in decline on the continent since the days of natural law and the late German *usus modernus*; it therefore did not find its way into the contract law provisions of the German or Polish Civil Codes. In the same vein, David Ibbetson and John Cartwright observe that

[1] G Albers, 'History of a Notion' in G Albers, FP Patti and D Perrouin-Verbe (eds), *Causa contractus* (Tübingen, Mohr Siebeck, 2022) 19–36; G Albers, 'Why Cause of Contract Again, and How?' idem 1–16; G Christandl in N Jansen and R Zimmermann (eds), *Commentaries on European Contract Laws* (Oxford, Oxford University Press, 2018) Art 2:101(1), n 19; A Thier, § 311 I, nn 15ff in J Rückert, M Schmoeckel and R Zimmermann (eds), *Historisch-kritischer Kommentar zum BGB*, vol 2, *Schuldrecht Allgemeiner Teil* (Tübingen, Mohr Siebeck, 2007).

[2] Chapter 9 in this book, by Gregor Albers; chapter 5, by Wojciech Dajczak.

consideration is still theoretically important, as there will be no contract in English law unless there is good consideration. Yet, the practical significance of this requirement had always been limited, and it has been marginalised in the course of the last decades.[3]

It was in view of these developments that, in the twentieth century, prominent comparative lawyers criticised the two doctrines – *causa/cause* and *consideration* – as dysfunctional and overly complex.[4] As a consequence, neither concept made it into the various 'non-legislative codifications',[5] viz restatements of European and transnational contract law.[6] Indeed, *la cause* did not even find a place in more recent continental codifications, such as the Dutch Burgerlijk Wetboek, and it was even abolished by the French legislature in 2016.[7] Given the historical significance of the French Code civil as a model for many other codifications, on the one hand, and the prominent role that the concept of *la cause* had played in French doctrine until 2016, on the other, this was a highly symbolic act. European private lawyers seemed to be listening to the death knell of a millennia-old core element of private law.

In recent years, however, comparative lawyers and legal historians have begun to reflect again upon these developments and to question whether it was really wise to abolish *la cause* so suddenly.[8] Some of the contributors to this volume add to such scepticism as well.[9] Albers, for instance, argues that German law, despite doing away with *causa* as an element of contract law doctrine, has always taken a causal approach; similarly, Bruno Rodríguez-Rosado and Birke Häcker show that *causa* still plays an important role in many European legal systems in which it has formally been abolished.[10] According to Häcker, a comparison of *causa* and *consideration* generates 'new perspectives', in particular as far as the law of unjustified enrichment is concerned, and Albers even argues that German law today 'suffers from' the eighteenth and nineteenth centuries' 'attempts to suppress *causa*'. It is therefore remarkable that not all legal systems once modelled upon the French Code civil have followed the French example. In Belgium, for instance, the law of obligations was reformed in 2022/23 without abolishing the notion of *la cause* (see Articles 5.27 and 5.53–5.56 of the Belgian Code civil); likewise, the requirement of a legitimate *causa* has survived in Articles 8(2), 39, 70(d) and 85 of the Principles of Latin American Contract Law.[11] A number of contributors

[3] Chapter 3 in this book, by David J Ibbetson; chapter 6, by John Cartwright.

[4] K Zweigert and H Kötz, *An Introduction to Comparative Law*, 3rd edn (trans T Weir, Oxford, Oxford University Press, 1998) 381, 390ff; R Zimmermann, *The Law of Obligations. Roman Foundations of the Civilian Tradition* (Cape Town, Juta, 1990/Oxford, Oxford University Press, 1996) 504ff, 549ff, 553ff and 556f.

[5] N Jansen, *The Making of Legal Authority: Non-legislative Codifications in Historical and Comparative Perspective* (Oxford, Oxford University Press, 2010); *cf* also R Zimmermann, '"Wissenschaftliches Recht" am Beispiel (vor allem) des europäischen Vertragsrechts' in C Bumke and A Röthel (eds), *Privates Recht* (Tübingen, Mohr Siebeck, 2012) 21–48.

[6] On which see N Jansen and R Zimmermann, 'European Contract Laws. Foundations, Commentaries, Synthesis' in Jansen and Zimmermann, *Commentaries* (n 1) 1–18.

[7] Christandl (n 1) Art 2:101(1), n 17.

[8] See Albers et al (n 1).

[9] See, in particular, Dajczak (n 2) 88: '*causa* is dead, long live cause'.

[10] Chapter 11 in this book, by Bruno Rodríguez-Rosado; chapter 14, by Birke Häcker.

[11] For the principles, see R Momberg and S Vogenauer, 'The Principles of Latin American Contract Law: Text, Translation and Introduction' (2018) 23 *Uniform Law Review* 144. *Causa* is regarded as a requirement for the conclusion of the contract (Art 8 PLACL); it needs to be legitimate (Art 39(2)); and it is relevant also in the contexts of interpretation of contract (Art 70) and frustration (Art 85).

to this volume, even if not singing such countermelodies loudly, look sceptically upon the surprisingly fast European developments in recent decades. They invite the reader to rethink and reassess the notion of *causa*, on the one hand,[12] and its apparent abolishment, on the other.[13]

For many legal scholars, it seems to be natural to pursue such fundamental doctrinal reflection in the form of historical comparative law. This method is more than the combination of two disciplines; it is based on the conviction that legal phenomena can often only be properly understood by crossing historical and comparative perspectives. The reconstruction of historical lines of development gains in sharpness from a comparative perspective; conversely, comparative findings can often only be explained by genetic connections which become visible only from a historical point of view.[14] Thus, Albers reminds his readers that the German idea of an abstract contract (§§ 780, 781 of the German Civil Code) was designed in response to the 'irritating encounter with the French Code'; and while abstraction seemed to make legal relationships independent of the motives of the parties, it was recognised as a general principle that abstract rights can be reclaimed if there is no sufficient *causa*. Clearly, such observations shed new light and help one to better understand both French and German law. Nevertheless, it is not always obvious how different approaches and methods, such as history and comparison, can contribute to a common perspective. Historical research often does not speak to the comparatist, and there is important comparative research without any historical dimension. But this is not a theoretical question to be discussed in the abstract. Scientific methods are practical tools for research. They are meant to help answer specific questions. As everywhere in academia, the proof of the pudding is in the eating in the science of law as well. Hence, it needs to be asked, for instance, why it could be helpful for a modern comparative lawyer to understand what Aristo meant when he spoke of *causa* in the context of innominate real contracts,[15] or how discussions in the *ius commune* contributed to the present ambiguity of *la cause*.[16]

If the question is thus posed in this more specific and practical way, the answer must relate to the European perspective on legal doctrine: this volume brings together legal historians and comparative lawyers in their role as European private lawyers. There is thus a common perspective for all the contributions, which is defined by the horizon of European private law. All contributions to this volume understand European private law as a common tradition of doctrinal legal thinking with quite deep historical roots.[17] Primarily, therefore, they do not aim to contribute to narrowly disciplinary discussions concerning, for example, the exact meaning of a specific text by Aristo;[18] hence,

[12] For Spanish law, see chapter 8 in this book, by Antonio Legerén-Molina; more generally, see Rodríguez-Rosado (n 10).

[13] See chapter 7 in this book, by Olivier Deshayes.

[14] N Jansen and S Meier (eds), *Iurium itinera. Historical Comparative Law and Comparative Legal History* (Tübingen, Mohr Siebeck, 2022).

[15] Chapter 1 in this book, by Francisco J Andrés Santos.

[16] Häcker (n 10).

[17] On this notion of a European *acquis commun* of private law, see Jansen and Zimmermann, 'European Contract Laws' (n 6) nn 12ff.

[18] T dalla Massara, 'Die *causa* des Vertrages im Denken des Aristo: zu den Ursprüngen einer Idee' in Albers et al (n 1) 37–66, with further references on the author's previous work.

Francisco Andrés Santos, in his essay on 'Cause in ancient Roman law of contract', is convincingly brief on the issue.[19] The focus of this book is on European private law; its purpose is to deepen our understanding of European legal thinking and of national doctrines in their relation to the European perspective. Thus, while Häcker describes and compares the ambiguities of *la cause* and *consideration* in contemporary European legal systems, Andrés Santos explains the general and highly ambiguous meaning of *causa* in Latin in general, and in Roman law in particular.

Andrés Santos's chapter is of particular importance for the present volume as it makes clear that the complexity of *la cause* has not been the result of over-juridification in recent centuries. The notion of *causa* has never inspired a layman's imagination; yet even the Roman jurists did not assign a specific doctrinal meaning or function to this concept. Like many modern jurists, they used it topically, as an argument, in quite different contexts, such as transfers and pledges of property, unjustified enrichment, contract interpretation or validity of and exceptions to stipulations – here, Andrés Santos explains very clearly how the originally abstract *stipulatio* was later assimilated to causal contracts. From a doctrinal European perspective, the decisive point is thus the extremely thin empirical content of the Roman *causa*, which made it an example of the typically non-doctrinal Roman *Juristenrecht*. It would have been surprising if later jurists had been able to build coherent doctrinal theories on those quite divergent Roman sources. Thus, Andrés Santos's insights into ancient Roman law are obviously of the highest importance for any jurist, who wishes to understand properly the inextricable history of *causa* in the *ius commune* and, ultimately, in modern European legal systems. Indeed, many problems became apparent as early as with the complex debates on *causa* among the Italian glossators, and Bartolus, Baldus and Aquinas, on the one hand, and on the quite divergent rules on abstract *instrumenta* in Aragonese law, on the other.[20]

II. Legal Doctrine

This is an academic book on legal doctrine. Its contributors speak as legal scholars, not as practical lawyers, judges or officials in the government. Their task is not to make the law, to propose new rules or to decide cases. Rather, it is to rethink, keep in good shape and improve the law's language and its doctrinal structure.[21] Doctrinal legal scholarship therefore focuses on doctrinal models, ie on the conceptual and systemic tools for legal thinking. With such models, scholars construct concepts, doctrines and other intellectual tools as instruments to be used in legal practice.[22] Usually, such models combine a

[19] Andrés Santos (n 15) last page.

[20] Chapter 2 in this book, by João de Oliveira Geraldes; see also Zimmermann, *Obligations* (n 4) 549ff; M Schermaier, 'Die Rolle der *causa* bei der Überwindung des Typenzwangs durch die mittelalterlichen Juristen' in Albers et al (n 1) 97–152.

[21] N Jansen, 'The Point of View of Doctrinal Legal Science' in T Kuntz and PB Miller (eds), *Methodology in Private Law Theory: Between New Private Law and Rechtsdogmatik* (Oxford, Oxford University Press, 2024) 179–204.

[22] *cf* H Kantorowicz and EW Patterson, 'Legal Science – A Summary of Its Methodology' (1928) 28 *Columbia Law Review* 679, 682ff; Kantorowicz, 'Staatsauffassungen. Eine Skizze' (1925) 1 *Jahrbuch für*

functional analysis of institutes, doctrines and concepts with the design, viz construction, of alternative concepts and other tools. Of course, doctrinal scholarship of this sort may – and shall! – generate new insights; it may help one to better understand difficult legal problems; and academics are, of course, called upon to criticise inherited legal propositions and suggest alternative ways forward. But it is important to understand that the focus of this book is on the doctrinal structures, ie on the law's language, rather than on its normative substance.

Legal doctrine, it has often been said, is a complex matter.[23] Different jurists, and jurists in different legal systems, not only employ quite different doctrinal models, but even work on the basis of quite different conceptions of legal doctrine. Thus, in many legal systems, doctrine is treated as a practical tool for teaching and applying the law (practical doctrine). Alternatively, it may be regarded as an instrument to reflect and better understand the normative foundations of legal systems (philosophical doctrine). While the basic question of *causa* and *consideration* in terms of practical doctrine would be '*when* is a contract binding?', philosophical doctrine would rather ask '*why* is a contract binding?'. Practical doctrine should be smart, ie parsimonious, elegant, and easily comprehensible and applicable. Hence, practical doctrine must not be too complex; its 'proof' is plausibility and simplicity. Philosophical doctrine, in contrast, should be stimulating; it may be comprehensive and provide the jurist with deep legal insights. Its proof lies in its explanatory power. It is no surprise that philosophical doctrine has often been quite complex. Nevertheless, Rudolf von Jhering argued, convincingly, that good legal theory was always simple and clear. Its ideal was to reduce the complexity of the law to 'simple propositions'.[24] Good explanations are brief and easy to understand.

It is important to see that in both forms, legal doctrine – like every theory – is an instrument. Its justification lies in its ability to help European jurists describe and analyse their legal systems. As in any science, the task of scholars is therefore to rethink and criticise inherited concepts and doctrinal models, to improve existing doctrine and to propose better alternatives. The function of legal science can therefore never be simply to preserve inherited doctrines; even if legal certainty and reliability are important legal virtues, traditions of doctrinal thinking have no value in themselves. Of course, jurists may develop a strong intellectual affection for their doctrinal inheritance; their thinking

Soziologie 101, 102f: rational sciences concerned with the scientific construction of objective meaning (mathematics, doctrinal sciences). Later, in particular, see H Heller, *Staatslehre in der Bearbeitung von Gerhart Niemeyer*, 6th edn (Tübingen, VA, 1983) 54ff and 60ff. Today, C Schönberger, *Der 'German Approach'. Die deutsche Staatsrechtslehre im Wissenschaftsvergleich* (Tübingen, Mohr Siebeck, 2015) 50f: development of models, function types and typologies, informed by comparative experience.

[23] N Jansen, 'Rechtsdogmatik im Zivilrecht' in *Enzyklopädie zur Rechtsphilosophie* (2011) www.enzyklopaedie-rechtsphilosophie.net.

[24] The classic authority is R von Jhering, *Der Geist des römischen Rechts auf den verschiedenen Stufen seiner Entwicklung*, vol I, 2nd edn (Leipzig, Breitkopf und Härtel, 1866) 65; R von Jhering, *Der Geist des römischen Rechts auf den verschiedenen Stufen seiner Entwicklung*, vol II, 2nd edn (Leipzig, Breitkopf und Härtel, 1869) 343, 354: legal scholarship as the attempt to reduce the complexity of the law and to reformulate the complex substance of a multitude of legal provisions in a 'simple proposition (einfacher Satz)'; *cf* also R von Jhering, 'Culpa in contrahendo oder Schadensersatz bei nichtigen oder nicht zur Perfection gelangten Verträgen' (1861) 4 *Jherings Jahrbücher* 1, 32; R von Jhering, *Das Schuldmoment im Römischen Privatrecht* (Gießen, 1867) 40: 'einfacher Satz'. For a detailed analysis, see N Jansen and M Reimann, 'Begriff und Zweck in der Jurisprudenz – Ein Geburtstagsblatt für Rudolf von Jhering' (2018) 26 *Zeitschrift für Europäisches Privatrecht* 91, 101ff.

is usually path-dependent, as they have to use the law as it stands with its existing legal tools when addressing new issues. Nevertheless, it would be a mistake for European jurists to see their task as merely reflecting upon, or 'thinking together', national legal traditions which have followed different paths since the eighteenth century. There is no value in such adherence to a common past; legal scholars are not the curators of museums for doctrine. Rather, European jurists should understand that the Europeanisation of legal thinking creates the opportunity to rethink and revise the European heritage as a whole. From such a perspective, the different national and historical solutions are models for the future development of European law. The common perspective makes it possible to evaluate different approaches, and to understand their merits and deficits. And in view of this, it even becomes possible to reformulate, or perhaps cut off, those doctrines that do not serve their functions well anymore, and to think about alternative models where the inherited doctrinal language no longer fits its purpose.[25]

III. *Causa, La Cause* and *Consideration*

The distinction between practical and philosophical approaches to legal doctrine helps one to better understand the contributions to this volume and to relate them to one another. Thus, while Andrés Santos shows that *causa* in Roman law was a practical tool used by the jurists to describe the functioning of innominate real contracts and thus to determine when a *conventio* gave rise to binding obligations,[26] *la cause* was later turned into a means to reflect the foundations of contract law (see section IV). Similarly, Cartwright shows that the main role of *consideration* in present common law is to define contracts as bargains, which are binding not because of the parties' consensus, but rather because of their mutual legitimate expectations.[27] Thus, even if the concept of *la cause*, and perhaps also the notion of *consideration*, are unnecessary as legislative tools, the idea of a contract's *causa* might still have something to say to the European contract lawyer in terms of philosophical doctrine.

It has probably not been a coincidence that the genuinely European history of *causa* began in the twelfth century with the rise of *causa* as a *causa finalis* in its Aristotelian sense, and gained momentum one century later with the contribution of Aquinas.[28] Now, Aquinas's theory of *causa* was part of his great project of reconciling philosophy, theology and law. He did not intend to change the law; rather, he sought to make sense of the relevant theological and legal authorities. In a similar way, the medieval jurists, from the glossators to Bartolus and Baldus, tried to make sense of the recently recovered Roman sources; and to do so, they simply assumed that *causa* had a clearly delineated doctrinal function which they sought to reconstruct. Indeed, it probably never occurred to them that they were neither continuing the pragmatic discussions of the Roman

[25] For more detail, see Jansen, 'Point of View of Legal Science' (n 21); Jansen, 'Rechtsdogmatik, Rechtswissenschaft und juristische Praxis. Zum gesellschaftlichen Ort und wissenschaftlichen Selbstverständnis universitärer Rechtsdogmatik' (2018) 143 *Archiv des öffentlichen Rechts* 623.
[26] Ulpian, D 2,14,7,2 and 4; see Andrés Santos (n 15).
[27] Cartwright (n 3).
[28] de Oliveira Geraldes (n 20).

jurists nor thinking and arguing like their Roman predecessors. The texts of the Digest and the Codex had originally been written as legal opinions or instructions, ie as contributions to ongoing legal debates. In medieval times, they were read as if they were acts of legislation. Thus, they were transformed into legal authorities which accordingly had to be interpreted in an exegetical, scholastic fashion. Later, jurists in many legal systems would think along similar lines. To medieval jurists, it was obvious that *causa* – a concept that in some texts in the Digest explains the binding effect of innominate real contracts and was used in a similar way also in the context of *stipulationes* – related to the very nature of contracts and was the foundation of their binding nature.[29] Those jurists did not realise that Roman lawyers had never regarded the many different types of contractual obligation as a unified whole, that they had no set of general requirements for the conclusion of a contract and that they had never thought about a consensual or real contract's *causa*. With their assumption that every promise was made for a purpose, viz for a *causa finalis*, the medieval jurists thus marginalised the *stipulatio*, which had once been an abstract unilateral promise. The touchstone was the *stipulationes sine causa*, ie stipulations made in writing without any indication for which purpose they had been made. Under Roman law, such *stipulationes* were valid unless the defendant raised a defence arguing that there had been fraud on the claimant's side. Now such stipulations were held void, which in effect meant that the *stipulatio* had been transformed into a causal contract. Probably without being aware of it, the medieval jurists fundamentally reshaped the legal system they had inherited.

It was a paradoxical consequence of this rise of *causa* in medieval law that European jurists began to understand the necessity and the existence of truly abstract promises, most importantly in contexts where third-party interests were concerned. Early and still important examples were letters of credit and bills of exchange. It was probably with such needs of merchants in mind that medieval Aragonese legislators, as João de Oliveira Geraldes reminds the readers of this volume,[30] explicitly provided for the validity of *instrumenta*, ie of abstract promises documented in writing. True, the Aragonese jurists instantly began to debate whether this really meant that obligations could be fully abstract; moreover, they had to ask whether there was any legal remedy, if such an *instrumentum* had been erected without good *causa*. Yet, legislators have rarely been impressed by philosophical doctrines, and the focus of such legislation was obviously on legal rules, viz on practical doctrine, rather than on philosophical or legal explanation. Thus, while it is certainly true, as many contributions to this volume emphasise,[31] that contractual promises usually have a *causa*, practical-minded men in medieval times began to see that there were contexts, such as financial markets, where a debtor could not be allowed to raise the defence of a lack of *causa*. Where obligations are transformed into tradable assets, their nature needs to be determined by the legitimate expectations of market participants, rather than by the logic of synallagmatic fairness. European legislators have always been aware of practical needs of this sort.

[29] For what follows, see also Zimmermann, *Obligations* (n 4) 549ff, with further references on the sources and modern literature.
[30] de Oliveira Geraldes (n 20) 8ff.
[31] Albers, 'Why Cause' (n 1) 12; Albers, 'History' (n 1) 25; Rodríguez-Rosado (n 10); Häcker (n 10).

The idea of *causa* should not only be juxtaposed with abstract conceptions of contracts, however. The discussions in late medieval and early modern law about *pacta nuda* and the binding effect of *consensus* (agreements) may likewise be seen as the flip side of the rise of *causa*.[32] Indeed, if the essence of a contract was the parties' mutual promises given for a good *causa*, it was difficult to understand why agreements should *not* be binding if there was good consideration (*causa*). As we have seen, by the thirteenth century it was commonly assumed that *stipulationes* and real contracts were legally effective because of the underlying *causa*, rather than because of their particular form or because of a specific *res* (the giving of a thing). The idea that agreements (*pacta*) needed to be 'vested' with some further element in order to become effective therefore no longer appeared plausible. Why was it not sufficient to 'vest' a promise with a good *causa*? When Baldus explained the canon law principle *pacta sunt servanda*[33] with the doctrine of *causa* – according to Baldus, every *pactum* based on a good *causa* was binding in law[34] – this doctrine seemed an evident expression of natural justice. No wonder that later medieval and early modern jurists began to regard the additional *vestita* required by the Roman authorities as exceptional particularities which had to be interpreted narrowly. The consensus theory of contracts and the idea of *pacta sunt servanda* were perhaps less an expression of a more liberal conception of private law or of an idea of contract as promise[35] than an indirect consequence of the rise of *causa*. In any event, in order to understand the history of European contract law, the rise of consensus theories must be analysed in its relation to both (abstract) formalism and the rise of *causa*.[36]

IV. The Idea of Contract

In contract law theory, *causa* is the explanation of a contractual promise. The idea that a good *causa* should be required for a contract to become binding thus rests on the intuition that if a promise has been made without any such *causa*, or without a good *causa*, then there is no plausible explanation for this promise. Obviously, something has gone wrong with such a promise, and lawyers will have to think about a remedy. All this is undeniably true; yet, it does not follow that *causa* or a comparable concept should be regarded as a legal requirement for a contract's validity.

If you ask a lawyer for an explanation of a specific contractual agreement, you may get many, quite different, answers.[37] The explanation of a contract may relate to

[32] Zimmermann, *Obligations* (n 4) 252f.

[33] Huguccio, Summa decretorum, ad *Causa* 12,2,66; reproduced in P Landau, 'Pacta sunt servanda. Zu den kanonistischen Grundlagen der Privatautonomie' in P Landau, *Europäische Rechtsgeschichte und kanonisches Recht im Mittelalter* (Badenweiler, Bachmann, 2013) 766ff.

[34] Baldus de Ubaldis, *Commentaria omnia*, vol 5 (Venice 1599, reprinted 2004) C 3,36,15, n 3: 'iure canonico oritur actio ex nudo pacto, dummodo habeat causam'; A. Söllner, 'Die causa im Kondiktionen- und Vertragsrecht des Mittelalters bei den Glossatoren, Kommentatoren und Kanonisten' (1960) 77 *Zeitschrift für Rechtsgeschichte (romanistische Abteilung)* 182, 247ff.

[35] C Fried, *Contract as Promise: A Theory of Contractual Obligation* (Cambridge, MA, Harvard University Press, 1981). The idea is, of course, much older.

[36] Rodríguez-Rosado (n 10) 185ff, 191ff.

[37] *cf* chapter 4 in this book, by David Deroussin; chapter 10, by Francesco Paolo Patti; Rodríguez-Rosado (n 10).

the whole agreement or to the individual promises. It may refer directly to the other party's counter-performance, to an expected performance or to the promise of counter-performance. Alternatively, it may refer, more indirectly, to the parties' subjective motives – to the purpose for which they wish to acquire the object of their contract – or to liberality or generosity in the case of a gift. Indeed, the explanation may even refer to the interests of society in the conclusion and performance of agreements. A contract's *causa* may thus be some object received (*causa directa*) or the party's motive (*causa finalis*); it may be its specific content (*causa in concreto*) or the content that contracts of that kind have by definition (*causa in astratto*). It is this multiplicity of possible explanations for contracts and thus the ambiguity of *causa* that has always made it difficult for jurists to assign a clearly fixed legal meaning to the concept. In his article on the codification and interpretation of *la cause*, viz *causa* in France, Italy and Spain during the nineteenth century, David Deroussin shows how European jurists experimented, and struggled, with all these explanations – indeed, conceptions of *causa* varied not only between, but also within legal systems, as different notions of *causa* were associated with different types of (onerous, viz gratuitous) contracts and with different kinds of juridical problems.[38]

Now, as has been seen above, theories of *causa* have always been expressions of specific ideas of freedom and of more or less material conceptions of contract law. In this sense, such theories have indeed been 'revealing of a specific notion of contract and will'.[39] For a long time, the supporters of causal theories of contract law have been more interested in the fairness or social utility of contracts than in the autonomous contracting of citizens. Thus, today, Albers argues in a quite paternalistic fashion that 'private law is less about … the parties' will than about … the purposes they pursue through their will'.[40] It is probably no coincidence that the cradle of the modern French notion of *la cause* as an instrument of judicial control stood in the house of a French Jansenist (Jean Domat),[41] ie in an intellectual context in which the idea of a free human will was viewed with scepticism.[42] For Domat, what made a unilateral contract binding was not simply the donor's abstract will to give (*libéralité*), but 'un motif raisonnable & juste',[43] just as the cause in a mutual contract was the other party's counter-performance. Clearly, such considerations were not to be found in the natural law theories of contemporary Jesuit theologians such as Molina or Lessius. These Jesuits proceeded from a significantly more positive vision of humanity and human will; for them, the free will and the consent of the parties to a contract was a sufficient basis for their mutual obligations.[44] Thus, Lessius made it quite clear that any free promise was binding before God, and he

[38] Deroussin (n 37).

[39] Deroussin (n 37) Conclusion.

[40] Albers (n 2) Conclusion.

[41] J Domat, *Les loix civiles dans leur ordre naturel* (Paris, Desaint, 1777) 1,1,5: 'l'obligation seroit nulle si dans la verité elle étoit sans cause'. See Deroussin (n 37).

[42] On the impact of Jansenism on Domat's *loix civiles*, see I Birocchi, 'Les loix civiles dans leur ordre naturel' in S Dauchy et al (eds), *The Formation and Transmission of Western Legal Culture. 150 Books that Made the Law in the Age of Printing* (Berlin, Springer, 2016) 230; D Gilles, 'Jean Domat (1625–1696)' in O Descamps and R Domingo (eds), *Great Christian Jurists in French History* (Cambridge, Cambridge University Press, 2019) 211, 217ff.

[43] Domat (n 41) 1,1,1,6.

[44] W Decock, *Theologians and Contract Law. The Moral Transformation of the Ius Commune (ca 1500–1650)* (Leiden, Brill, 2013).

justified the canon law's requirement of a *causa* with the argument that canon lawyers simply suspected fraud or mistake where no *causa* had been expressed.[45]

In the twentieth century, it was probably again no coincidence that the notion of *causa* has particularly fascinated Fascist legal theorists such as the leading Italian scholar Emilio Betti, and was thus incorporated, in its new Fascist version, into the provisions of the Codice civile (1942).[46] With his analysis of the recent Italian history of *causa*, Francesco Patti makes it very clear that this doctrine, which medieval jurists had originally developed to protect the autonomy of promisors, was transformed into 'an instrument to control the contractual autonomy of the parties'.[47] Contracts were no longer enforced because this was what the parties wanted or had agreed upon, but rather because, in the eyes of a Fascist judge, their agreement was 'worthy of legal protection' (Article 1322(2) of the Codice civile).[48] Even if, during the last decades, legal theory has again transformed such provisions into a means to protect the fairness of contracts, the Fascist experience still leaves a stale aftertaste.

In the light of such observations, it has been quite plausible for French jurists to argue that the doctrine of *la cause* gave expression to a conception of contract according to which 'the individual will', even if in consensus with another party's will, 'is not in itself normative',[49] and hence to assume that abolishing *la cause* was an expression of, or would ultimately lead to, a more liberal conception of contract law.[50] Nevertheless, as a matter of historical fact, this assumption was wrong. During the second half of the twentieth century, European contract law was substantially materialised in many respects, with material conceptions of contractual freedom and contractual equality replacing previously formal ones.[51] Judicial control of unfair contract terms stems from this period; most provisions of consumer law are mandatory; and doctrines such as frustration of contract and change of circumstances have been acknowledged in all European legal systems. Information duties have become pervasive, the principle of equal treatment is today a matter of course and consumer rights of withdrawal complement the inherited rules on defects of consent. Yet, this century was also the period in which *la cause* has come into increasingly rapid decline.

It has probably been a consequence of these seemingly paradoxical developments that, today, the connection between particular conceptions of *causa* and specific rules seems to exist more in the philosophical minds of jurists than in actual law.[52] Common law jurists emphasise that judges only exceptionally find a contract void for lack of *consideration*;[53] according to Ibbetson, it is no more than 'an empty shell of

[45] L Lessius, *De iustitia et iure*, vol III (Paris, 1618; ed and trans N Jansen, K Wille and K Liebrand, Stuttgart, frommann-holzboog, 2025) 2,17,4 (n 23).

[46] Albers, 'Why Cause' (n 1) 8.

[47] Patti (n 37) in particular 166–68, 173f.

[48] 'Le parti possono anche concludere contratti che non appartengano ai tipi aventi una disciplina particolare, purché siano diretti a realizzare interessi meritevoli di tutela secondo l'ordinamento giuridico.'

[49] Deroussin (n 37) Conclusion.

[50] See Albers, 'Why Cause' (n 1) 4f.

[51] C-W Canaris, 'Wandlungen des Schuldvertragsrechts – Tendenzen zu seiner "Materialisierung"' (2000) 200 *Archiv für die civilistische Praxis* 273.

[52] Albers, 'Why Cause' (n 1) 6ff; *cf* Dajczak (n 2).

[53] Ibbetson (n 3); Cartwright (n 3).

its former self'.[54] Judges are obviously much more concerned with giving effect to the will of the parties or with protecting the parties' reasonable reliance than with finding a bargain. Theories of *causa* and *consideration* have certainly been, and may still be, expressions of a particular conception of contract law, but today, the law's substance has largely become emancipated from philosophical doctrines of this sort. Indeed, when *causa* was abolished in Germany during the eighteenth and nineteenth centuries, this was meant and perceived as an aspect of a political liberalisation of private law. Quite a different understanding prevailed with the reform of the French law of obligations in 2016. Now, it was clear that French contract law would not become more 'liberal', or otherwise be changed, by dispensing with the notion of *la cause*; rather, this aspect of the reform was merely a legislative technicality, viz a doctrinal revision. Indeed, as Oliver Deshayes shows in great detail, the dismissal of *la cause* from the Code civil did not imply any change in the law's substance; rather, the most important previous judgements of the Cour de cassation on the meaning and significance of *la cause* have been restated in the code's new provisions.[55] It has been a consequence of this depoliticisation of *la cause* that the notion of *causa* has lost much of its former explanatory power in contract law. Having *la cause* or not having it hardly seems to make any difference.

V. The Functions of *Causa*

Given the concepts' original ambiguity, it is not surprising that in its long history the concept of *causa*, viz *la cause*, has been assigned a very wide range of quite different functions – with quite different interpretations of the concept's meaning in those different contexts. *Causa* has never been merely a touchstone to ensure the seriousness of the parties' contractual intentions. When the French legislator split up the previous functions of *la cause* in 2016, these functions were assigned to specific provisions on, inter alia, motivational mistakes of donors, the synallagmatic relation of duties in reciprocal contracts, the control of unfair terms (exemption clauses), the illegality of contracts and simulated transactions. Moreover, *la cause* and *causa* were also criteria for classifying types of contracts, for the interpretation of contracts and for the frustration of contracts and supervening impossibility. This is obviously too much and too diverse to be covered by a single legal concept; yet, the state of doctrine in other causal legal systems, such as those of Spain or Italy, is no less complex.[56] Nearly all contributors to this volume, including those who feel some sympathy for this old notion, are quite critical of the state of the current doctrine.[57] There is less agreement, however, as to which functions should ideally be discussed as the 'true' issues of *causa*. Indeed, the functions assigned to the concept vary significantly from one legal system to another. Problems that are addressed as a matter of *causa* in one legal system may be discussed totally independently of the

[54] Ibbetson (n 3) 46.
[55] Deshayes (n 13).
[56] Patti (n 37); Rodríguez-Rosado (n 10).
[57] See Legerén-Molina (n 12); chapter 13 in this book, by Rocío Caro Gándara.

concept in another legal system, even if *causa* is still a requirement of contract law. Today, these differences are probably too great to be bridged by one unified notion of *cause*; in fact, the disagreement between different contributions to this book about the 'true' meaning and functions of this concept are proof of the fact that it can no longer serve as a basis for a common language.

One example is excessive hardship (frustration or economic impossibility). This category has been treated as an issue of a more 'concrete' *causa* in Italy and Spain, although it had normally not become relevant, in this context, in French law.[58] In France, however, subsequent impossibility, which is often difficult to distinguish from hardship, has nevertheless been treated as an aspect of *la cause*.[59] It does not seem that either the Italian, Spanish or the French approach has significantly contributed to a higher predictability of the law or to a greater subtlety or fairness of its solutions. Rather, it has become difficult to disentangle the different rules on supervening impossibility, excessive hardship and *causa*. While Rodríguez-Rosado and Caro Gándara therefore criticise the use of *causa* in such contexts,[60] the 'advantage' of *la cause*, according to Deroussin, is its ability to 'explain … the rule according to which the subsequent impossibility of occupying the house rented releases the lessee from the payment of the rent'.[61] Another example is defects of consent, for which *causa* likewise became relevant in many legal systems, as it was assumed that a contract might be void if it was based on a false *cause*. Yet, it is not clear why such issues should not be addressed directly. Indeed, as far as the common law is concerned, it can be observed that the doctrine of *consideration* is losing its relevance while the rise of doctrines such as duress and economic duress makes it possible for judges to focus more directly, and in a more nuanced way, on the consent of the parties.[62] If clarity, predictability and simplicity are virtues of legal doctrine, such developments are probably a step forward.

From early on, the issues of illegality and immorality of contracts have been discussed in many legal systems as questions of *causa*. Under such an approach, a contract is void if either its object or its *causa* was illegal viz immoral.[63] Thus, where one party has bought some neutral object, such as a kitchen knife, for some illegal purpose, legal scholars have asked whether *la cause* is related to the parties' individual obligations or to the contract as a whole, whether it was 'really' objective or subjective, whether personal motive was sufficient to count as the relevant cause or whether some understanding between the parties as to the buyer's motive was necessary. Now, some of these questions really need to be answered. In fact, every legal system has to decide whether the illegal or immoral motives of one or both parties may invalidate a contractual agreement. But it is difficult to see any advantage in addressing such questions on the basis of purely conceptual considerations; and, as Juan Pablo Murga argues in his contribution to this volume,[64] it is highly doubtful whether the rather complex metaphysics of *la cause* has ever made it easier for judges and other practical lawyers to administer contract law in

[58] Caro Gándara (n 57) 232–235, 237–240; *cf* also Legerén-Molina (n 12).
[59] Deshayes (n 13) 107–109.
[60] Rodríguez-Rosado (n 10) 198f; Caro Gándara (n 57).
[61] Deroussin (n 37) 66ff.
[62] Cartwright (n 3); see also Häcker (n 10) 245–248.
[63] Chapter 12 in this book, by Juan Pablo Murga Fernández.
[64] 214f, 221.

a coherent way. In the end, there is no difference between saying, for instance, that a contract without a lawful *causa* is void and saying that an illegal contract is void.[65]

VI. Contract Law and Unjustified Enrichment

In many legal systems today, *causa* is of greater significance in the law of unjustified enrichment than in contract law. A claim for enrichment exists where one party has been enriched at another party's expense without any legal justification or legal basis (*causa*) for this shift of wealth. In particular, a performance, ie the attempt to discharge an obligation that has been made without a legal ground (*causa*), can be recovered.

Some jurists believe that where *causa* has been dismissed in the law of contracts, it will necessarily come back through the law of unjustified enrichment. In particular, it has been argued that the law of unjustified enrichment needs to provide a remedy where the purpose of a contractual transaction fails. Hence, according to authors such as Albers, the law of enrichment 'must explain *why* a buyer's obligation to pay the agreed contract price does not unjustifiably enrich the seller'.[66] But such suggestions are, with all due respect, misleading. In cases of defects of consent, change of circumstances or other grounds for invalidity, it is for contract law to decide whether the parties are bound to their contracts. The law of unjustified enrichment has to reflect, and give effect to, those decisions.[67] It therefore grants a claim where a transfer has been made on the basis of an invalid obligation, or where, for some other reason, it failed to discharge the obligation in question. If, however, the transfer was made on a valid obligation under to the relevant provisions of contract law and has effectively discharged that obligation, it would simply be absurd if the transfer could be reversed on the basis of unjustified enrichment. The concept of a legal obligation's bindingness, or legal validity, elegantly connects the law of contract with the law of unjustified enrichment without in any sense shifting the analysis of the *causa contractus* from contract law to unjustified enrichment.

VII. Conclusion

The idea of a contract's *causa* has always been an academic concept – and at times a powerful instrument in the hands of imaginative judges.[68] For many centuries, *causa* has thus helped European jurists to make sense of, and further develop, their laws of contract. The supporters of *causa* remember the great doctrinal achievements that have been made with this tool. Yet, the same authors admit that the concept has rarely made

[65] Zimmermann, *Obligations* (n 4) 553.
[66] Albers (n 2) 156.
[67] N Jansen, 'Doctrinal Design in Unjust Enrichment. On the Relation of Claims for Restitution and General Private Law' in S Peari and W Swain (eds), *Rethinking Unjust Enrichment* (Oxford, Oxford University Press, 2023) 237–49.
[68] *cf* Patti (n 37) III.

life easier for practical lawyers. Their defence of the doctrine is based on its former explanatory power and sometimes also on its alleged beauty.[69]

Now, in order to overcome the infelicitous present state of the doctrines of *causa*, these authors usually suggest simplifying them and, in particular, cutting out functions that do not 'really' pertain to the concept.[70] Yet, it is doubtful whether, after centuries of complex debates, doctrinal simplification can still be a convincing strategy. The problem is not that such simplification is impossible as a matter of doctrinal logic. The problem is rather the paradox of doctrinal writing. Today's legal literature is the breeding ground for tomorrow's new ideas and for future literature, and it seems that the more of such literature there is, the more fertile it becomes. In any event, more articles and books will unavoidably generate even greater complexity in the future. Where a legal problem is complex, every further academic contribution, even if it aims at simplifying existing doctrine, further complicates the issue. Legal theory cannot, therefore, cut down the complexity of *causa*. Indeed, this volume is proof of that observation. Although several of its contributors obviously regret the decline of *causa* and still believe in its explanatory potential, none of them suggest, or even claim to know of, a workable conception or definition of *causa* and its 'true' functions. Even the supporters of *causa* thus seem to share the feeling that it is over.

In the end, even conservative jurists may agree that the French decision to accord with the international trend of 'suppressing' *la cause* and thus to dispense with the notion, as far as the legislation on contracts is concerned, was a convincing step towards reasonable modernisation. The reason for such a conclusion is not, however, that contracts do not 'have' a *causa*, or that all problems will vanish if *causa* is dismissed. Gratuity, to give an example, will remain a difficult issue: it would be absurd to deny the differences between gratuitous and reciprocal promises, viz agreements,[71] and indeed the distinction is not always obvious.[72] But the concept of *causa* is simply neither necessary nor helpful in addressing such issues. Likewise, there can be no doubt that the purposes and motives of the parties to a contract may be, and occasionally are, legally relevant. But again, contract law may provide better tools, such as change of circumstances or illegality *tout court*, to address such questions. In short: the international and French approach was convincing because the European doctrines of *causa* have become too complex and because their diminishing explanatory power could no longer justify such an intellectual effort. The notion should not be revived in the classroom and academic textbooks or otherwise kept alive. Rather, it may be time to finally say farewell.

[69] Häcker (n 10).
[70] See Deroussin (n 37) 66ff; Legerén-Molina (n 12); Rodríguez-Rosado (n 10).
[71] Rodríguez-Rosado (n 10) 189ff.
[72] Albers (n 2) 157.

INDEX

www.ingramcontent.com/pod-product-compliance
Ingram Content Group UK Ltd.
Pitfield, Milton Keynes, MK11 3LW, UK
UKHW020845290926
15470UKWH00004B/1560

9 781509 971398